ROCKY MOUNTAIN NATIONAL PARK:

THE CLIMBER'S GUIDE

High Peaks

Bernard Gillett

Earthbound Sports, Inc.
Chapel Hill, NC

ROCKY MOUNTAIN NATIONAL PARK:
THE CLIMBER'S GUIDE
High Peaks

Printed in the United States of America

ISBN: 0-9643698-5-0

Published by
Earthbound Sports, Inc.
PO Box 3312
Chapel Hill, NC 27515
www.earthboundsports.com

Cover photo credits
Front : The beautiful, yet seldom visited Palisades on Longs Peak. Photo: Bernard Gillett
Back (left): Climbers on *Yellow Wall* (the Diamond) with Chasm View Wall in the background. Photo: John Gillett
Back(right): Bernard Gillett on the first ascent of *Olympic Games*. Photo: John Gillett

For my wife Sally, and our children Katie, Claire, and Mary

ACKNOWLEDGMENTS

I would like to thank the following people for dedicating time, talent, and information to this project.

Pat Adams, William Alexander, Doug Allcock, Roger and Bill Briggs, Andy Brown, Doug Byerly, Mike and Tommy Caldwell, Chip and Monika Chace, Michael Covington, Jim Detterline, Topher Donahue, Andy Donson, Eric Doub, Randy Farris, Mom and Dad Gillett, Robert and John Gillett, Sally Gillett, Stephan Greenway, Rick Guerrieri, Richard Harrison, Chris and Jerry Hill, Ellen Huber, Hal Huntsman, Kurt Johnson, Brandon Latham, Craig Luebben, Sean McMahan, Steve Muller, Terry Murphy, Don Otten, Tom Pomtier, Alvino Pon, Matt and Shawn Preston, Kath Pyke, Jeff Rickerl, Dean Rhode, Mark Ronca, Gary Ryan, Mike Schlauch, Dave Sheldon, Greg Sievers, Lawrence Stuemke, Pete Takeda, Rick Thompson, Clay Wadman, Kris Walker, Ed Webster, Kris and Randy Whorton, and anyone I may have overlooked.

This work is built on the efforts of earlier writers; it was through their guides that I came to know and love the climbs of the High Peaks. Thanks to Paul and Norman Nesbit, Walter Fricke, Richard DuMais, Chip Salaun and Scott Kimball. Information for a handful of other routes was borrowed from authors Cameron Burns, Peter Hubble, Jack Roberts, and Richard Rossiter.

A special thanks goes out to Ray Northcutt, Steve Komito, Mike Donahue, Billy Westbay, Douglas Snively, Harry Kent, Mike Caldwell, and Roger Briggs. My original intention was to include a short biography for each of these people as a tribute to both their influence on the Estes Park climbing scene, and their influence on my own climbing career. However, by the end of this project, the book had grown so large that much of what I had written needed to be excised. Information from the interviews I conducted with each climber still appears in the history section (found in *Estes Valley Park* volume), and I am grateful to them for sharing their old photographs and stories.

TABLE of CONTENTS

INTRODUCTION

Rocky Mountain National Park (RMNP) is situated just beyond the city limits of Estes Park, Colorado. Blessed with an abundance of high mountain walls and sub-alpine crags, this area is among the finest places to climb in the United States. When visiting Estes Park, one can enjoy short and fierce bolt routes, long arduous free climbs, big aid walls, classic bouldering, and alpine ice climbs. The 300,000 acres of scenic wilderness that RMNP provides is reason enough to visit — millions enjoy its magical beauty each year.

This book, *The High Peaks*, describes over 350 routes on the high peaks and alpine walls east of the Continental Divide in RMNP. With dozens of incredible mountain walls to choose from, RMNP boasts some of the finest alpine climbing in the United States. The famous Diamond on the East Face of Longs Peak attracts climbers worldwide, and numerous walls on the surrounding peaks all hold some notoriety within the United States climbing community. Majestic routes in every grade, from long free climbs to necky aid lines, provide climbing experiences of a lifetime for rock enthusiasts of all abilities.

Though trail information and trail maps are included, the newcomer to the area will benefit from a topographic map of the park. Be aware that the detailed route descriptions used in the sub-alpine areas are difficult to duplicate for the large faces found in the mountains. A good sense of route finding is essential when climbing these big walls.

Rocky Mountain National Park: The Climber's Guide, Estes Park Valley, is a companion guide that describes over 900 routes in the sub-alpine terrain surrounding Estes Park, including several important areas outside of the Park.

A chapter on ice climbing at the end of this guide describes over 120 routes of interest to the winter visitor.

ACCOMMODATIONS, FOOD, AND SUPPLIES

Estes Park is a booming tourist town in the summer that provides all the normal amenities associated with a small city. There's a Safeway grocery store, a health food market, numerous restaurants and fast food joints, and a couple coffee/bakery shops. Hotels, motels, and quaint cabins line most of the main traffic arteries — contact the Estes Park Chamber of Commerce for more information (970-586-4431, 500 Big Thompson Avenue, Estes Park, CO 80517).

Estes Park's nightlife is low key, with only a few bars, a microbrewery, and one movie theater (two in the summer). The finest entertainment is found at Lumpy Ridge, where howling packs of coyotes provide western music under starlit skies.

CAMPGROUNDS

Several of the campgrounds listed below are located close to various climbing areas described in the companion guide, *Rocky Mountain National Park: The Climber's Guide, Estes Park Valley*.

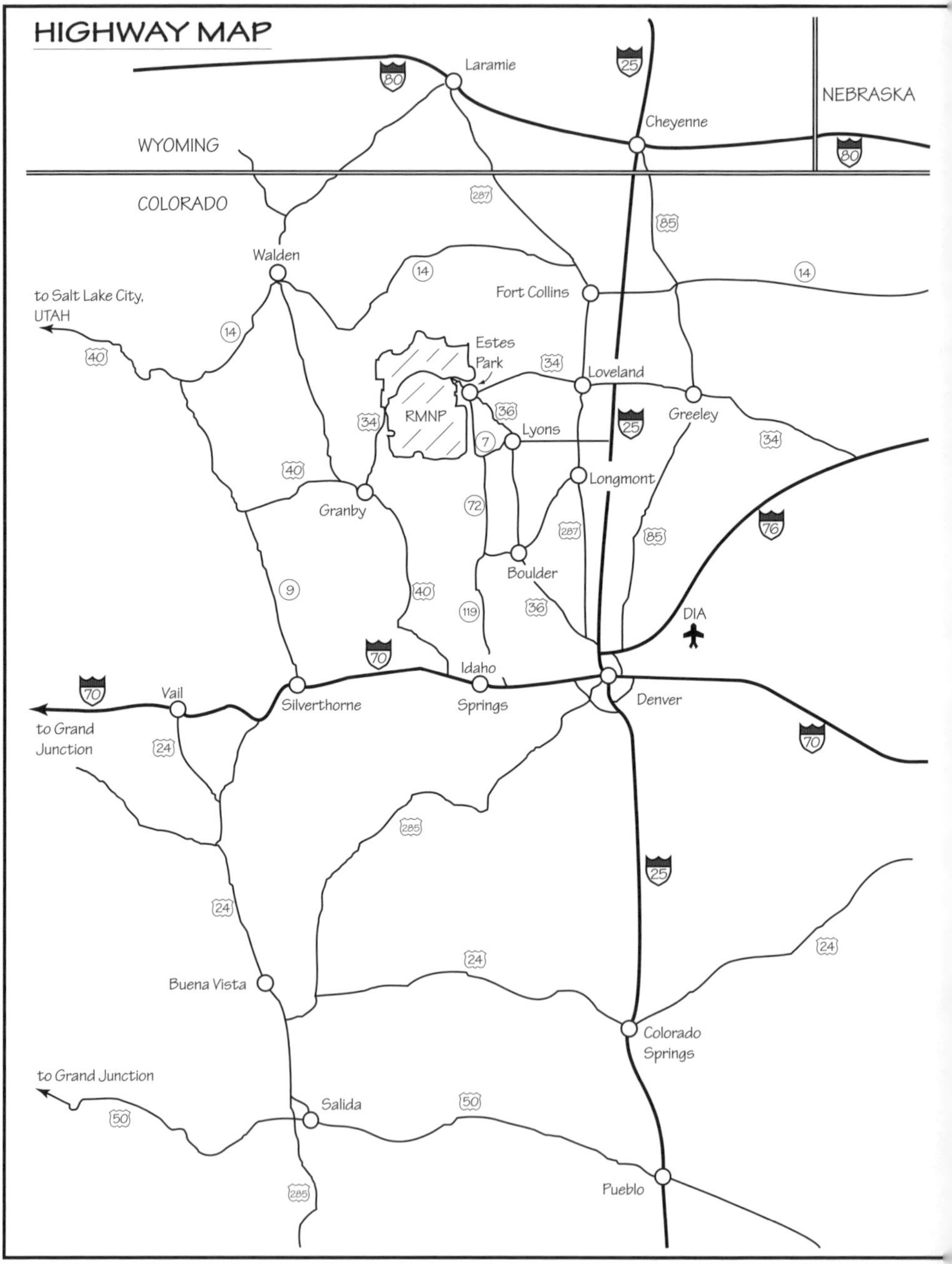
HIGHWAY MAP
Laramie
80
25
NEBRASKA
Cheyenne
WYOMING
80
COLORADO
287
85
Walden
14
14
Fort Collins
to Salt Lake City, UTAH
14
40
Estes Park
34
Loveland
RMNP
36
Greeley
34
7
Lyons
25
34
40
Longmont
Granby
72
76
287
85
Boulder
9
40
119
36
DIA
70
Idaho Springs
70
Vail
Silverthorne
Denver
to Grand Junction
24
70
285
25
24
24
24
Buena Vista
Colorado Springs
to Grand Junction
50
Salida
50
285
Pueblo

RMNP Campgrounds: It is difficult to find a campsite in RMNP on summer weekends despite numerous campgrounds in the area. There are four Park Service drive-in campgrounds of interest to climbers: **Glacier Basin**, **Moraine Park**, **Aspen Glen**, and **Longs Peak**. A fifth campground, **Timber Creek**, is of little use to most climbers as it is located on the west side of the Park, two hours from the climbs in this guide. These campgrounds are often full — reservations placed well in advance will assure you a site. Call 970-586-1206 (the public information office at RMNP) or make reservations through MIStix (800-365-2267). In addition to the difficulty in securing a site, one must work with the park regulation which allows only seven nights in the campgrounds during the summer months (only three at Longs Peak). Those planning an extended stay are encouraged to use one of many commercial campgrounds in the area, or try the primitive camping in Roosevelt National Forest.

Private Campgrounds: The nicest commercial campground for climbers is probably the **Estes Park Campground** (970-586-4188), located at the end of Spur 66. The climbs at Cottontail Crag are a ten-minute walk from the campground. Other commercial campgrounds include **Marys Lake Campground** (970-586-4411), located at the junction of Marys Lake Road and Peak View Drive. Bouldering is available along the shores of Marys Lake, and the bolted climbs of Prospect Mountain are one mile away. **National Park Resort Campground** (970-586-4563, 3501 Fall River Road, i.e. Highway 34) is found just before the Fall River entrance to RMNP and directly beneath MacGregor Slab. **Park Place Camping Resort** (970-586-4230) is on Highway 36 five miles east of Estes Park, and **Paradise RV and Travel Park** (970-586-5513) is at 1836 Highway 66. Showers are available at **Happy Camper Laundry and Showers**, 857 Moraine Avenue (Highway 36, the road leading to the Bear Lake entrance of RMNP).

National Forest Campgrounds: Farther afield is **Olive Ridge Campground** in Roosevelt National Forest, 13 miles from Estes Park on Highway 7, and not too distant from the Ironclads and the Longs Peak trailhead. Call 970-586-3440 (the Estes Park Ranger Station for Roosevelt National Forest) for information about Olive Ridge and other camping possibilities within the National Forest. Free (though primitive) sites are located near the Monastery and the Ironclads, as well as a few secluded spots in the Estes Park valley.

CLIMBING SHOPS

The best climbing store in town is the **Estes Park Mountain Shop** (formerly Wilderness Sports), located on the east end of town (358 E. Elkhorn, next to Ed's Cantina, a popular restaurant with heaping plates of good food). While other stores in town stock climbing gear, none has the selection found at the Mountain Shop. Estes Park's only climbing gym is located at the back of the store; it's small, but it beats climbing in the rain. **Komito Boots** (970-586-5391, next to the Post Office) has served Estes Park for almost thirty years as the local resole and boot repair shop.

CLIMBING SCHOOLS

The **Colorado Mountain School** (970-586-5758, across from Fun City on Moraine Avenue) is an accredited member of the American Mountain Guides Association and offers a full scope of climbing instruction and guiding. The school holds the concession to guiding in the Park, and this is the only (legal) company offering guided climbs in RMNP. They also rent mountaineering and camping equipment for a reasonable fee. The **Kent Mountain Adventure Center** (Harry Kent, 970-586-5990) specializes in courses built around rock climbing for kids (ages 9 -17).

CLIMBING SEASON, WEATHER

The rock climbing season in the high peaks generally extends from June through August, although some days in May and September may afford good climbing, particularly on the south-facing walls. Daytime temperatures at higher altitudes rarely reach above 65 degrees. However, the south-facing walls can offer comfortable conditions during the prime season. Nights are usually cool, and it is not uncommon for temperatures to drop below freezing in the mountains – pack extra clothing.

Though Colorado has a reputation for plenty of sunshine, the biggest hindrance to summer time climbing is poor weather. Powerful thunderstorms form over the Continental Divide like clockwork, usually arriving in the afternoon. These storms typically last for an hour or less, after which the sun returns, but they can be nasty and dangerous. A rain parka is recommended for even the sunniest mornings, as Estes Park weather changes rapidly. Snowstorms in the summer (at high altitude) are always a possibility.

Special consideration must be given to thunderstorms when venturing into the mountains. The Colorado Mountain Club (in a study completed with the National Weather Service) asserts that lightning strikes in the United States take more lives each year than tornadoes, hurricanes, or flash floods. Colorado receives more than its fair share of deaths caused by lightning due to the violent storms that so often sweep across the mountains. Be prepared to retreat or change plans during periods of inclement weather.

The winter weather is wildly variable, with balmy days of sunshine interspersed among temperatures that average 35 to 45 degrees in Estes Park, and of course a few desperately frigid days. The temperature usually plummets overnight, especially so when no cloud cover exists. Obviously it is colder at the higher elevations. High winds are also a problem (especially in the winter); they make climbing in marginal weather unbearable.

TOPO KEY

The chart below is useful in deciphering the topos. Due to space constraints, the 5th class prefix of a route's difficulty may be omitted. Keep in mind that while I have attempted to represent the features of a cliff as accurately as possible, errors, omissions of landmarks, and misinterpretations by the reader may occur.

ROUTE DESCRIPTIONS

Routes are described from one side of the cliff to the other. Often it is necessary to become familiar with an entire section of a cliff to discern the whereabouts of a particular route, as cross-references to other routes are frequently used. Several routes may be left out on the photographs to avoid a confusing array of lines. On the other hand, the topos (when provided) generally delineate every route.

Ice climbs are collected in a single chapter at the end of the guide even though ice and rock climbs often coexist on the same wall in the mountains. A dual labeling system is employed to avoid conflicting route designations: all of the rock climbs are numbered, while the ice climbs are prefixed with a capital letter (i.e. "B-4") that goes with each of the trailheads used to access the routes. Ice climbs are listed and shown on the photos and topos in the rock climbing section of the book, but they are not described until the final chapter.

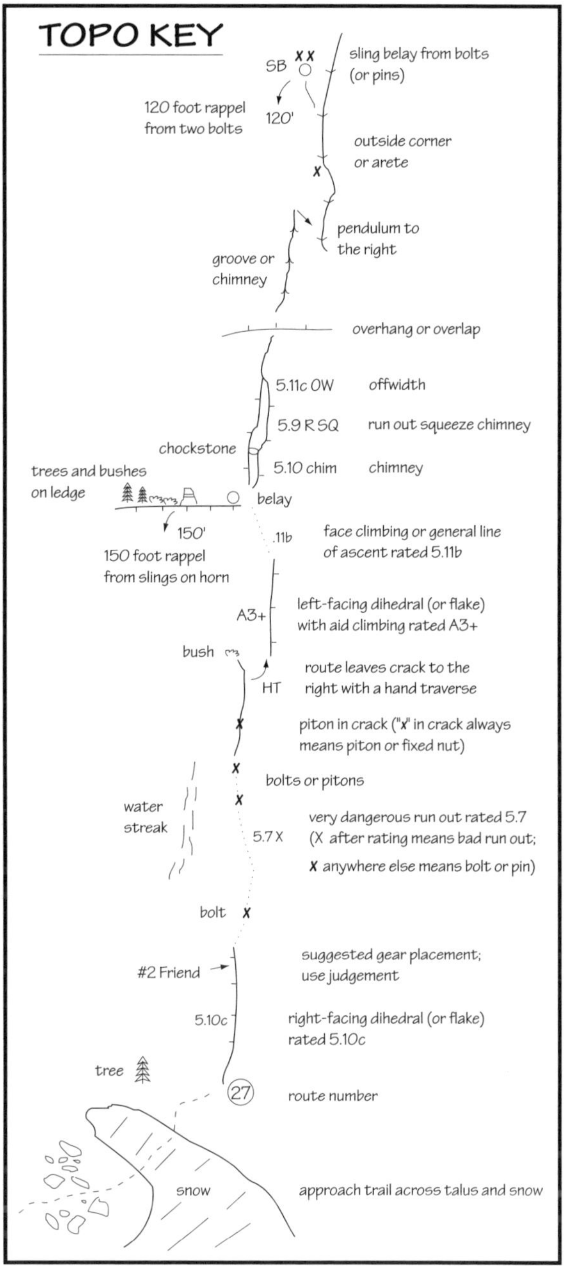

When using the words "left" and "right," it is assumed that the reader is facing the cliff, or facing down on the descent. Compass directions are used occasionally — keep in mind that these are not exact readings from a compass, but rather a general indication of bearing.

In describing each route, I have tried to provide the information needed to locate the line of ascent. It is impossible, however, to report on every aspect of a climb. If you can't figure out where a particular route goes, consider a retreat rather than brashly forging into the unknown. I would like to apologize in advance for any mistakes or mis-information that lead you to a bad experience.

Realize, too, that this book is built on the work of previous authors. The older books were written before topos were in vogue, and a wide variety of precision was employed in the route descriptions. For example, Walter Fricke's 1971 guide described the crux of **Stettner's Ledges** on Longs Peak as such: "One scheme to get started is to jam the finger tips of the left hand in a right-leaning crack on the 'ladder' wall, place the left foot on some minute nubbin, then sneak the right limbs into the small corner on the right." This is only one of several sentences written to describe forty feet of climbing. On the other hand, the entire passage for a five-pitch route on Pilot Mountain reads, "This route ascends knobby rock directly up the face to the summit knob." It is easy to pare down unnecessary verbiage when using older guides as a reference — "Climb out the right side of the alcove" adequately describes the crux on **Stettner's**. It is difficult, however, to build up spare descriptions to older climbs unless I personally repeat the route, or contact someone who has. Since I can't hope to climb even the majority of the routes included in this guide, vague accounts are used when needed (this is usually apparent when it occurs).

CORRECTIONS/NEW ROUTE INFO

Please send corrections, comments and new route information to the author at 1419 Paramount Pl, Longmont, CO 80501 or visit: www.earthboundsports.com.

EQUIPMENT

The typical crack climb in the mountains requires a full and varied rack. The following gear is recommended for most free climbs:

A few RPs or HBs

One to two sets of wired stoppers

Three or four Hexes (#5 – #8) or Tricams

One set of camming units from 0.5 to 3 inches (#0.5 – #3.5 Friend)

Quick draws and full-length runners

Extra carabiners

165 foot rope (some routes require a 200 foot rope)

Additions to (or omissions from) this recommended rack are usually included with the route descriptions, especially if the climb in question requires special gear. Often the description itself implies certain gear should be carried — it is not a good idea to climb "a long hand crack" armed with only one #3 Friend. Most parties carry extra gear for routes in the high peaks. A few rappel slings, gear you are willing to part with for long retreats, and even a light set of etriers provide insurance on the less traveled lines. Rack suggestions for aid climbs are not always included, though many of the aid routes at Lumpy Ridge and in the mountains can (and should) be done hammerless.

The last few years have seen an increase in the popularity of 55 meter and even 60 meter (185' and 200') ropes. Their use saves time and makes for a quicker retreat if established rappel routes are not used. The route descriptions in this book assume that a standard 50 meter (165') rope is employed unless otherwise noted.

RATINGS

Free Climbing: The Yosemite Decimal System is used for all rock climbs in this guide. Subdivisions within each numerical grade are indicated with a plus (+) or minus (-) for those climbs under 5.10, and with the letters a, b, c, and d for ratings of 5.10 and above. The overall grade assigned to a climb is a reflection of the hardest move encountered, unless a lengthy succession of difficult moves warrants a higher grade. Rating the difficulty of a climb is a subjective endeavor. Disagreements on ratings may arise due to the varying abilities of the climbers who rate them and obvious factors such as height. The following table gives a general translation of the Yosemite Decimal System for the uninitiated.

3rd class:	Easy, unroped scrambling
4th class:	More difficult scrambling (a rope may be prudent)
5.0 – 5.2:	Very easy roped climbing (5th class)
5.3 – 5.5:	Easy
5.6 – 5.7:	Moderate
5.8 – 5.9:	Difficult
5.10 – 5.11:	Very Difficult
5.12 – 5.13:	Extreme
5.14:	Currently the hardest free climbs in the world

Aid Climbing: Aid routes are given the usual A1 through A5 ratings. Advanced techniques have not evolved in RMNP to the extent found in Yosemite Valley, due largely to the fact that the emphasis has been toward free climbing since the 1970s. A discrepancy may be found between the newer ratings in Yosemite and the traditional ratings used in this guide. Still, routes rated A3 or harder can be dangerous.

NCCS Grades: The NCCS grades of I through VI are applied only to the bigger walls in the mountains. These grades reflect the overall length of a climb, or the normal time required to complete a route. Grade I routes are only a pitch or two, Grade II routes take about two to four hours; Grade III routes, a half day; Grade IV, a full day; Grade V, more than a day; and Grade VI routes are multi-day climbs. Again, these grades are only a general indication of the time required for a competent party to ascend a route, and they do not take into account the approach and descent times.

Protection Ratings: The availability of protection on a route is included after the difficulty grade. An **R** rating means the route in question will have run out sections (or dubious protection), where a fall could produce a bad injury or even death. An **X** rating indicates a very dangerous lead, where a fall at the wrong place will likely result in serious injury or death. Climbs receiving no protection ratings are generally regarded as safe for competent leaders, but most injuries occur on those climbs that are "well-protected," due to mistakes made by the leader or just bad luck. Run out sections that are relatively easy compared to the overall grade of the climb are not always noted. It is stressed here that the protection rating for a climb reflects only the prevailing opinions of the climbing community at the time this guide was published. Furthermore, the protection status of a route may change over time as fixed gear becomes unreliable, changes in the rock occur, and attitudes concerning what constitutes a safe route evolve. The latter point is important to keep in mind — it wasn't so long ago (before bolted routes became ubiquitous) that 20 foot run outs were just part of the game.

Quality Ratings: The final assessment of a climb used in this guide is a quality rating. A climb with no stars is poor to mediocre in quality (though some may find these routes enjoyable), or perhaps just obscure. This is particularly true of routes in the mountains that don't receive a great deal of traffic — they may offer great climbing, but not many people are aware of it. One star indicates a worthwhile route, two stars are given to exceptional climbs, while the three star rating is reserved for the finest routes in the area. The aid climbs and ice climbs in this book are not given quality ratings.

(?) Symbol: This book uses the (?) symbol in some cases where descriptions, ratings, first ascent credits, or other information is uncertain or highly suspect. Many routes, particularly in the high peaks region, are obscure, have had only one or two ascents, and were poorly described by the first ascent parties and subsequent guidebook editors. Some routes appear in older guidebooks, but have descriptions that are hard to follow.

Ice and Alpine Ratings: Please see page 229 in the ice climbing section.

REGULATIONS

The majority of the routes described in this guide lie within the borders of Rocky Mountain National Park. It is the reader's responsibility to become familiar with the regulations governing RMNP; a few of the more pertinent regulations are outlined below.

1. The use of motorized drills in RMNP is prohibited. Placing bolts by hand is allowed (as of 2000), but fixed protection should be kept to a minimum.

2. Removing vegetation, disturbing wildlife, destruction of the environment and littering are all punishable by fines. This includes the removal of plants and bushes from cracks, heavy-handed cleaning of routes, etc.
3. Dogs are not allowed on the trails, and must be leashed in parking areas at all times.
4. Bivouac permits are required for all overnight stays in the backcountry and cost $15. These can be obtained at the Backcountry Office next to the Visitor Center on Highway 36 (970-586-1242). A separate set of bivouac regulations is issued with the permit. There is no need to register for any climb in RMNP, but a sign out sheet is provided at Longs Peak. It is a good idea to inform someone of your plans before embarking on a long climb.

SAFETY CONCERNS

Climbing is an inherently dangerous sport and accidents will occur. RMNP has a well-trained rescue team available throughout the year. Contact a ranger in case of emergency (970-586-1399, or dial 911).

Fixed Gear: Realize that the fixed protection found on many of the older routes is deteriorating. The more recent bolted routes are probably in good shape as they use deep, three-eighths inch bolts, but you should never trust your life to one piece of gear. Consider my own experiences over the past two decades: I removed a quarter inch bolt on the Book with a few sharp tugs on a quickdraw; a three-eighths inch bolt on the Pear bolt popped out as I rappelled off a route (it was drilled only one inch deep). I've removed numerous pitons with my fingers on the Diamond and elsewhere, including Lumpy Ridge; and I rested on a Notchtop piton only to have it pull out. The dark, thin hangers found on many quarter-inch bolts in the area (Leeper hangers) have been recalled as they develop dangerous fractures and can break with body weight, and the aluminum hangers (known as "Gerry death hangers" by some) seen now and again tend to lever a bolt out of its hole when a downward force is applied to it. These days, quarter-inch bolts are widely regarded as death traps regardless of the hanger used — it's likely they've been in the rock for more than 15 years.

The problem is not limited to pitons and bolts — one summer I happened upon a #1 Friend on **D-7** that was fixed for life; the next summer I came back and removed it with ease. For many years climbers rappelled from runners wrapped around a flake on top of **Living Dead's** first pitch; the flake broke off (or perhaps was removed intentionally) in 1995 or 1996.

The point, of course, is that you should NEVER trust fixed gear, especially old fixed gear. Cracks change size, pitons and bolts shift and rust, rock fall might smash bolt hangers and cut rappel slings, and rappels from flakes or blocks may fail completely. Just before I leaned on that piton on Notchtop, I backed it up with a TCU. What could have been an ankle breaking long fall turned out to be no big deal. Back up fixed gear whenever possible.

Water: The water quality in RMNP has deteriorated over the last two decades, to the point where it is not safe to drink out of streams and lakes without first treating the water. In the past, one could drink out of just about any water source with no ill effects, but giardia bacteria are quite prevalent throughout the Park at the present time. Diarrhea is the most common symptom of giardiasis; medical treatment is necessary for severe cases. Water fountains are located at many of the trailheads used by climbers; however, these fountains are turned off in the winter.

Fauna: Wood ticks are present in the lower elevations in the spring and summer. These critters can pass on Rocky Mountain Spotted Fever and other diseases, so a thorough body inspection is recommended after every trip outdoors.

Marmots can be a nuisance to climbers who travel in the high country. All food, even in wrappers, is fair game as far as these rodents are concerned. They will chew through backpacks and bags to get at food left at the base. They also enjoy nibbling on salty (sweaty) leather boots. Bring a Tupperware container to store food at bivies, and bury leather boots under heavy rocks.

Sun: Climbers not used to the intense sunlight at elevation will be surprised at how quickly skin burns, especially in the high peaks and when traveling over snow — carry and use heavy-duty sunscreen to avoid painful blistering.

ENVIRONMENTAL CONCERNS AND ACCESS

The most important concern facing climbers today is access, or more accurately, issues that affect access. Climbers must act in a responsible manner in order to maintain climbing privileges on public grounds. Contributing money to The Access Fund, a non-profit organization devoted to preserving and attaining access to climbing areas, is an excellent way to show support and dedication to the environmentally sound ideas being promoted by this group. Please read and follow the Access Fund guidelines printed in this book, and be especially careful to use established trails to the cliffs. A bulletin board at the west end of the Twin Owls parking lot alerts climbers to cliff closures for nesting raptors and possible trail changes, and smaller signs are posted during nesting season at the other trailheads in the area. All climbers should avoid damaging flowers and lichens growing on cliffs.

LOCAL ETHICS

Estes Park is a bastion of traditional ethics. However, as in most areas around the U.S., bolted routes have been established at several crags (remember that motorized drilling is **not allowed** within the borders of RMNP). Prevailing opinion seems to be moving toward an acceptance of these routes provided they are worth climbing in the first place, though there are still those who decry the use of any bolts (especially in the higher peaks). Arguments concerning bolts placed on rappel or on the lead are not pertinent to the bigger picture; the real concern is the permanent addition of a bolt, not the method in which it is installed. In his 1986 guide to Estes Park climbing, Scott Kimball wisely predicted that "the era of the bolt route is upon us; it is inevitable — all the crack lines are exhausted." Indeed, in the fourteen years that have followed, more than 200 pitches in the Estes Park area have been bolted (probably more than 2,000 bolts).

It's my guess that this trend will continue for as long as it is allowed; climbers may lose the option to use bolts if the decision to place them is not carefully considered. Please make an honest assessment of a route's quality before scarring the rock forever. Avoid the temptation to bolt every climbable span of rock, especially near trails that non-climbers frequent. **Do not place bolts where good, removable protection can be used** — this kind of "convenience bolting" destroys the community's image as a group who generally takes care of the wilderness. Practices such as chipping holds, drilling pockets, reinforcing bad rock with epoxy, and adding bolts to existing lines are not acceptable. Take care of our limited resources.

On fixed gear: Please leave it alone when it is obvious that it has been left behind in a temporary situation — climbers often leave a few pieces of gear and even quick draws when working on a difficult route, or when establishing new routes. Don't steal fixed pins and bolt hangers from free climbs. These are often the only means of protection, and their removal creates a dangerous situation when people have come to rely on said gear. Abandoned gear (e.g. nuts or cams that are difficult to extract, or gear left on a retreat) has always been fair game in the climbing community, but taking anything beyond that is theft.

BOULDERING

A detailed listing of bouldering areas can be found in the companion guide, *Rocky Mountain National Park: The Climber's Guide, Estes Park Valley.*

HISTORY

A detailed history of climbing in and around RMNP can be found in the companion guide, *Rocky Mountain National Park, The Climbers Guide, Estes Park Valley.*

ORGANIZATION OF HIGH PEAKS GUIDE

This guide is organized primarily by trailhead access. Directions to individual mountains and climbs begin with travel directions to various trailheads including:

Wild Basin – pages 12-13

Longs Peak – page 28

Glacier Gorge – pages 93-94

Loch Vale – pages 147-148

Bear Lake – pages 93-94

Moraine Park – page 210

Mummy Range - page 220

Ice and alpine climbs are described in a separate section beginning on page 228.

LONGS PEAK and WILD BASIN TRAILHEADS

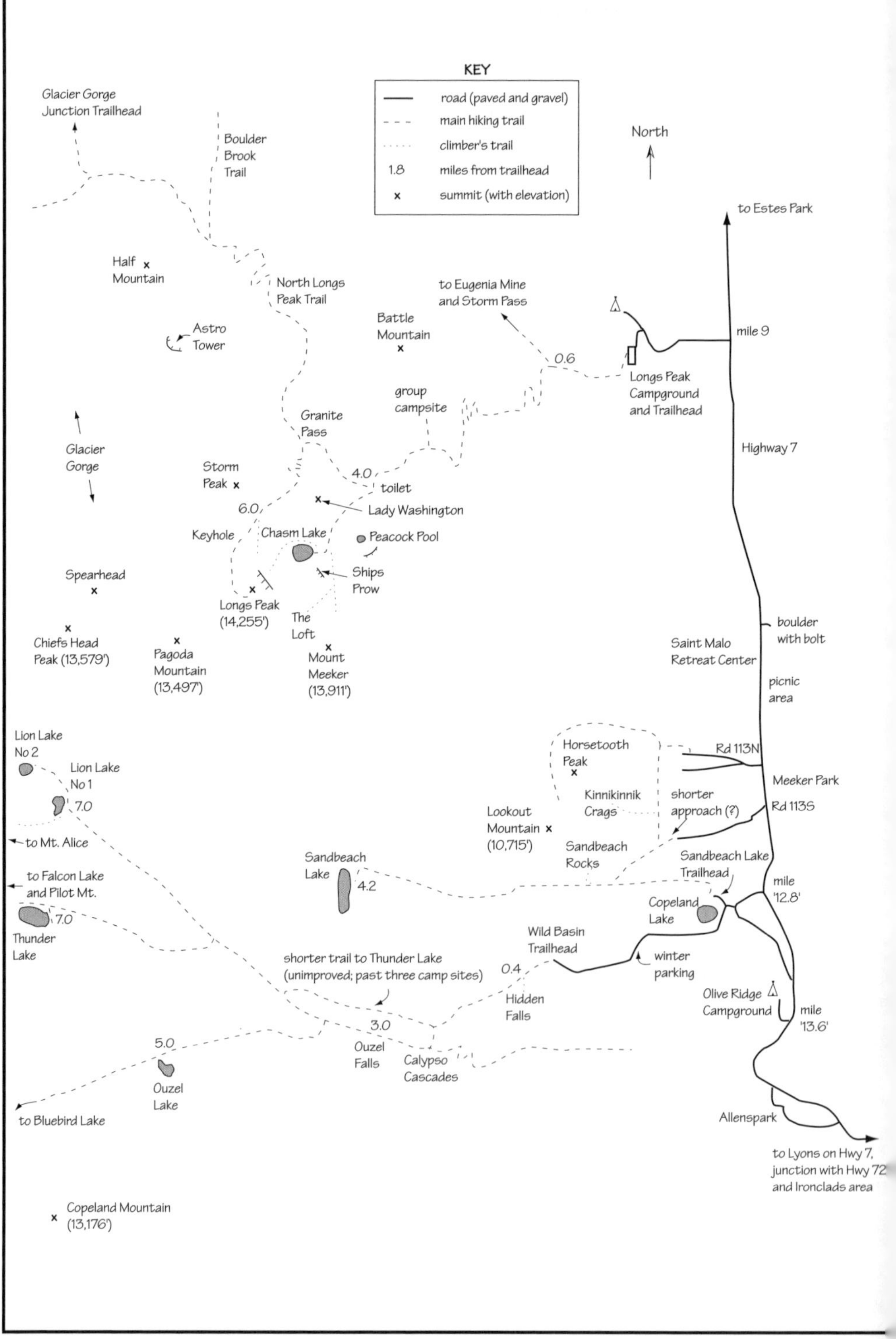
KEY
road (paved and gravel)
main hiking trail
climber's trail
1.8 miles from trailhead
summit (with elevation)
North
Glacier Gorge Junction Trailhead
Boulder Brook Trail
to Estes Park
Half Mountain
North Longs Peak Trail
to Eugenia Mine and Storm Pass
Battle Mountain
Astro Tower
mile 9
0.6
Longs Peak Campground and Trailhead
group campsite
Granite Pass
Glacier Gorge
Highway 7
Storm Peak
4.0
toilet
6.0
Lady Washington
Keyhole
Chasm Lake
Peacock Pool
Ships Prow
Spearhead
Longs Peak (14,255')
The Loft
Chiefs Head Peak (13,579')
Pagoda Mountain (13,497')
Mount Meeker (13,911')
boulder with bolt
Saint Malo Retreat Center
picnic area
Lion Lake No 2
Lion Lake No 1
7.0
Horsetooth Peak
Rd 113N
Meeker Park
Kinnikinnik Crags
shorter approach (?)
Rd 113S
Lookout Mountain (10,715')
to Mt. Alice
Sandbeach Rocks
Sandbeach Lake
4.2
Sandbeach Lake Trailhead
to Falcon Lake and Pilot Mt.
mile '12.8'
Copeland Lake
7.0
Thunder Lake
Wild Basin Trailhead
shorter trail to Thunder Lake (unimproved; past three camp sites)
0.4
winter parking
Hidden Falls
Olive Ridge Campground
mile '13.6'
3.0
5.0
Ouzel Falls
Calypso Cascades
Ouzel Lake
to Bluebird Lake
Allenspark
to Lyons on Hwy 7, junction with Hwy 72 and Ironclads area
Copeland Mountain (13,176')

WILD BASIN

Wild Basin is the circular valley in the southeast corner of Rocky Mountain National Park enclosed by high mountains on all sides, save for the narrow valve cut by North St. Vrain Creek to the east. This is beautiful hiking country, with long trails to alpine lakes, and several good ridge and peak scrambles. The climbing, however, is remote and mostly unattractive. The large east face of Mount Alice is certainly the most sought after objective in the area, but even it is seldom visited. The other climbs in Wild Basin are rather broken, and haven't seen more than a handful of ascents (if even that many); information regarding the particulars of these routes is scarce. Those who seek a wilderness climbing experience will find just that in Wild Basin, and the descriptions below won't spoil anything.

Travel Directions: Drive south on Highway 7 to the Wild Basin entrance of RMNP (about 13 miles south of Estes Park). A new entrance booth has been erected here; be prepared to pay a fee, or bring a Golden Eagle Pass. There are several trailheads on the road leading into the Wild Basin ranger station; they are described with the climbs.

COPELAND MOUNTAIN

A whale of a mountain, Copeland (13,176') sits on the southern rim of Wild Basin, south of Ouzel and Bluebird Lakes.

Approach: Hike to Pear Reservoir from either of two trailheads near the end of the road (use the Wild Basin trailhead, or a smaller lot about 0.3 mile before the road's end). There is only one technical route known to have been completed on the peak.

1 Southeast Face II 5.4
Walk to the south side of the east cirque of Copeland from Pear Reservoir (listed as Pear Lake on some maps) and follow a 4th class ramp that climbs up and right to the middle of the obvious wall. Several easy 5th class leads go straight up to the top of the wall, and from here, the summit of Copeland is a modest scramble to the west. Descend the east ridge (on the north side of the east cirque) to return to Pear Reservoir, or walk down the northeast ridge to Ouzel Lake for a traverse of the peak.

ISOLATION PEAK and EAGLES BEAK

Rugged Isolation Peak (13,118') is the furthest west of the peaks surrounding Wild Basin. It sits squarely on the Continental Divide, and the **North Ridge** route follows the divide to the summit. The spur extending east from the divide (near Frigid and Eagle Lakes) is Eagles Beak. The first three routes are on Isolation Peak; the last on Eagles Beak.

An odd landmark can be found near the shores of Eagle Lake. Look for a mineshaft a few yards down from the lake's outlet. The shaft was dynamited not for minerals, but water — though it was never completed, it was designed to drain Eagle Lake for communities on the eastern plains. There are several such lakes in RMNP bearing the scars of earlier days (Bluebird Lake, Sandbeach Lake, Pear Reservoir and Lawn Lake, to name a few). Many were artificially dammed to store water for later use, though most of the dams have since been destroyed. A big flood spurred on the removal of these dams in 1982, when the earthen berm holding back Lawn Lake failed — the entire lake drained in a few hours. Six people were killed, property damage in Estes Park was extensive, and a deep valley was created on lower Roaring Fork. Ironically, another lake was formed (Alluvial Lake) when the debris pouring out of Roaring Fork blocked up Fall River in Horseshoe Park.

1 North Ridge II 5.2 ★

Hike to Thunder Lake from the Wild Basin ranger station (about 7 miles) and continue past Lake of Many Winds to Boulder Grand Pass. The ridge extending south from the pass to the summit of Isolation Peak is almost two miles long, but the technical difficulties are confined to the middle third. Walk south from the pass across the western slopes of Tanima Peak until a gendarme on the ridge (The Cleaver) blocks the way. Scramble along the east side of The Cleaver, then south along the divide to a cliff band facing northeast. Pass this on the west (5.2), then stay on the narrow ridge to the last easy half mile leading to the summit. The best descent (2nd class) goes east from the summit toward Mahana Peak, then south past Isolation Lake to Pipit Lake. Go east from Pipit Lake to Bluebird Lake, but stay about 200 feet above its north shore until an easy path can be followed to the east side of the lake. Cross the outlet (which used to entail an exciting catwalk along an old cement dam) to the terminus of the Bluebird Lake trail and take that back to the trailhead (6+ miles).

A-5 North Face II AI 3

This alpine route ascends the north side of Isolation Peak, joining **North Ridge** near its top. See the ice climbing section.

2 West Ridge 4th class ★

From Fifth Lake (see description of the previous route in the ice climbing section, page 232), hike southwest to a saddle on the west ridge (at about 11,900'), and follow the ridge for a mile to the top. Descend as described in **North Ridge**.

3 East Face — Center Route II 5.8

This route climbs the buttress on the northeast side of Eagles Beak. Much effort is required to reach the buttress, as it is a fair distance from any decent trail. One method of approach goes past Bluebird, Pipit and Isolation Lakes to the saddle between Isolation and Mahana Peaks. Descend north from the saddle toward Eagles Beak and the buttress. Another leaves the Thunder Lake trail a short distance before the lake (0.7 mile), descends to North St. Vrain Creek, then bushwhacks up to Box and Eagle Lakes below Eagles Beak. This is shorter, but more overgrown. Once at the base of the face, locate a long right-facing dihedral in the center of the wall, and climb to a belay at its top. Climb a chimney on the right side of the flatiron above, belay, then follow more moderate cracks to the top. Descend southwest (2nd class).

PILOT MOUNTAIN

Pilot Mountain is similar to Eagles Beak in that it is the high point of a spur extending east from the Continental Divide — it is north of Falcon Lake, but south of Mount Alice. Two routes climb the broken, south-facing wall of the peak. The east-facing wall south of here, visible from Thunder Lake and leading directly to the divide, is apparently unclimbed.

Approach: Hike past the northern shore of Thunder Lake to Falcon Lake (about 8 miles from the Wild Basin ranger station).

1 Schist Wall II 5.7
Travel north from the west end of Falcon Lake to a point directly below the summit knob of Pilot Mountain, and climb straight up for five pitches with good belay stances. There are two choices for the descent from the summit. 1. Scramble west (4th class) along the spur to the divide, then go south to Boulder Grand Pass and drop past Lake of Many Winds to Falcon Lake or Thunder Lake. 2. Go west on the summit ridge to a saddle (4th class), then drop down the northern side of the mountain. If a return to Falcon Lake is desired, hike south (through trees) between Fan Falls and Thunder Falls, then contour west to Falcon Lake when the opportunity presents itself. This is off-trail hiking; it may be better to go all the way to Thunder Lake (instead of contouring west) to the path on its north shore. Hike out past Lion Lake No 1 to bypass Falcon Lake. FA: Paul Mayrose and Norman Harthill, 1966.

2 Granite Wall III 5.6
Go northwest from Falcon Lake to the far left side of Pilot Mountain's south face. Ascend the wall in eight pitches, with short crux headwalls and broken rock in between. The route ends on the divide; descend to Boulder Grand Pass, then into Wild Basin. FA: Mayrose and Harthill, 1966.

MOUNT ALICE

The east face of Mount Alice is one of the big walls in the park, 1,000 feet or more. It is quite visible from the plains, especially from points north and east of Boulder. Its north ridge (**Hourglass Ridge**) provides a peak scramble of classic proportions, one of the best in RMNP. On the other hand, in the opinion of one person who has done several routes on the east face, the rock climbs are somewhat lacking in quality. The lines are discontinuous, the entire upper headwall is mossy, teaming with plant life, and home to many birds, and free climbing generally requires extensive gardening with serious environmental impact.

The left side of the east face is divided by deep gully systems separating a few pillars and buttresses, and is generally unappealing. **Central Ramp** takes the obvious, tilted plane of rock in the middle of the wall, and the main east face lies to its right. Most of the routes are accessed with the long, grassy ledge system (some 4th class) that angles across the main face to the base of **Central Ramp**, though the snow chute to the left may be easier for the first three routes.

Approach: Begin at the Wild Basin ranger station and hike toward Thunder Lake, but take the right (signed) branch to Lion Lakes after five miles. Leave the trail at

Lion Lake No 1 and pick a line through scrubby trees that give way to alpine meadows and the base of the east face. This is an eight mile hike. Most parties prefer to bivy.

Descent: Descend the south ridge from the summit until it is obvious to turn east into the cirque between Alice and Pilot Mountain. This leads easily back to the base of the east face. One can also reverse **Hourglass Ridge**, but this takes much longer.

1 Central Pillar IV 5.9 A3

A long and narrow buttress left of **Central Ramp** tops out at a spire that is plainly visible from some vantage points. Arrive at the base of the buttress by climbing up the snow chute, then take an obvious line of thin cracks up the spire. Escape from the spire's summit with a 5.8 ridge to the top. A free route is rumored to exist on this part of the peak (5.11+, FA by Henry Lester and partner?); it may be a free version of **Central Pillar**.

2 Central Crack III 5.6 A1

Ascend the snow chute at the base of the wall, then scramble up the gully left of **Central Ramp** for 300 feet to the middle of three crack systems. Follow the general line of the crack for several pitches, one of which passes through a pegmatite band, and belay at a small stance beneath a large overhang midway up the wall. A short pitch avoids the overhang on the right via dirty slabs, then aids along a seam (KBs) back left and regains the crack system (crux). Three or four more pitches (with some rotten rock) continue up this to the top of the face, and these are followed with a thin ridge to the summit of the mountain. FA: Jim Walker, Clint Brooks, Dave Fedson and Charlie Ehlert, 1958.

3 Central Ramp III 5.8 ★★

This is one of the better lines on the mountain, climbing the tilted plane of rock just left of the main east face. Begin from the upper left side of the access ledge. 1. Climb an easy chimney on the left to reach the ramp, 5.5. 2 and 3. Two pitches of good crack climbing take a direct line up the ramp. 4. Continue to an area of ledges above the ramp, and belay on the highest ledge at the base of a left-facing dihedral capped with a roof. 5. The original route goes up the dihedral to the roof (5.7), aids around its right side (A2) and up a slot (A1) to a belay, then climbs a chimney behind the left side of a huge block to scrambling ground. Most parties do one of three free variations to avoid the roof. FA: Bob Culp and Larry Dalke, 1966. **Variation 1**: Climb the crack just left of the overhang, unpleasant 5.10. **Variation 2**: Start from the left end of the ledges atop pitch 4, and climb several short dihedrals to a left-leaning hand crack (5.8). Two more pitches of easier climbing go to the top of the buttress. **Variation 3**: Again, beginning from the ledges on top of the 4th pitch, traverse left on a dark band for 80 feet to an arete, then climb a short dihedral to a good ledge. Face climb to a chimney and follow that to moderate terrain.

4 Left Side IV 5.10a ★★

This is also a good route, climbing one of the nicer sections of rock the east face has to offer. Start below and left of the first continuous feature right of **Central Ramp**, a set of right-facing flakes which is furthest left of several such flakes. 1. Undercling into the leftmost flake and follow it for a pitch to a stance on the left, 5.9+. 2. Continue straight up flakes to a belay below a short slot, 5.9. 3. Climb through the slot (5.8) and follow a ramp/dihedral to a long, rising ledge system that spans much of the face. One can escape left on this ledge, around the corner to **Central Ramp**. To continue up, walk up the ledge 30 feet to a prominent right-facing dihedral. 4. Climb the dihedral for a full pitch, 5.10a. 5. At this point the dihedral tilts left, forming an exit ramp from the east face. Follow this ramp (5.10a, passing an overhang on the left, difficult protection) and turn the corner onto **Central Ramp** (now follow that route). **Variation 1:** At the end of pitch 3 (before moving right 30 feet), there is a right-facing dihedral leading off of the rising ledge system. Start at a crack 25 feet left of this and climb it to a belay stance at a jog. Continue up to a headwall (the dihedral converges with the crack at this point) and aid to the exit ramp (A1). **Variation 2:** The location of this variation is not certain, but it appears to take a dangerous seam about ten feet left of the second pitch (5.10 X). Upon reaching the rising ledge system, it moves left and climbs up very near to the arete separating the main face from **Central Ramp** (and utilizes and old bolt around the corner for pro). Above the bolt, it climbs seams and corners (one fixed nut) on the right, 5.9 R, then finally goes left and joins **Central Ramp**. FA of second variation: Jeff Rickerl and Rick Guerrieri (?), 1994.

5 Culp-Turner V- 5.11d ★

This old aid route (V 5.9 A3) features nice climbing on the first and sixth pitches; the rest of the route is said to be fair to marginal. Begin as with the previous route, and traverse broken ground to a stance beneath the next set of dihedrals to the right. A direct start over small overhangs can be followed as well (5.8 X). 1. Climb the right dihedral until it is possible to step into the left one, 5.11a. Follow that to a good ledge. 2. Move up and right past 5.8 flakes, then back left to an optional belay stance beneath a direct crack line. Continue up to a belay below a small roof. 3. Go straight up the crack to the rising ledge (**Left Side** is directly above), and then move right 50 feet to the base of triple right-facing flakes. 4. Climb along the right side of these flakes and belay when they end, 5.10c. 5. Step left to a grassy crack which is climbed to a stance below a wide crack capped with an overhang, 5.10d (short pitch). 6. Struggle up the wide crack (5.11d, or even 5.12a), turn the roof, and enter a perfect, golden corner. Jam this to a stance on the left, 5.11b. 7. Climb up to and through a wide roof (two fixed pins, 5.10d R, total munge) and take the crack above it until it is possible to escape left to **Central Ramp**. Join that route near its upper ledges. FA: Bob Culp and Jack Turner, 1972. FFA: Greg Davis and Kevin Cooney, early 1990s?

6 Jabberwock V 5.10 A4

The initial pitches of this route are unclear — the DuMais guide shows the route several corners right of **Culp-Turner** and left of the lightning-bolt roof of the next line, but one climber I spoke with feels quite certain that **Jabberwock** does not climb these. Start in a pair of right-leaning flakes just right of **Culp-Turner**, and climb the left one. The second pitch climbs to the right side of several small ledges, and the third angles up right to bigger ledges (bivy spot on lowest ledge) below a large arch/overhang. Nail through the overhang and follow an obvious crack up to the big ledge system (bivy); belay below a left-facing (and leaning) dihedral 30 feet right of **Culp-Turner**'s triple flakes. Follow the dihedral to a ledge on the right (possible bivy) and belay. Move left into a light-colored dihedral (just right of **Culp-Turner**'s sixth pitch) and nail it through the left side of an overhang, then work up right to a corner leading to a belay beneath a small overhang. Pass the overhang with a wide, 5.10 crack, and then tension right to a good ledge in a large dihedral. The final pitch climbs the dihedral through a 5.9 overhang, and goes to the ridge. Rack from RURPs to four inches, plus a few hooks. FA: Keith Lober and Joe Hladick, 1979.

7 Through the Looking Glass V- 5.11a A3

This circuitous route winds up the wall right of **Jabberwock**. Scramble up to a stance left of a block, which is below an obvious, lightning-bolt roof leaning right (50 feet above the access ledge). 1. Climb the leaning crack/corner that parallels the roof on the left, 5.10d R. Belay at a light band of rock. 2. Continue in the same line (5.11a) to a fork, and stay left, nailing up expanding flakes (A3). 3. Go to a quarter-inch bolt, face climb to the overlap above it (5.11a), then follow the overlap down and right for 30 feet. Sporty 5.10 face leads to a left-facing flake, and a double bolt belay. One can continue up and left to a stance beneath triple corners. 4. Step right from the high belay and follow a mossy, right-facing corner (the right-hand of three, 5.10) to a good ledge; belay at a block with slings. 5. Take a 5.9 crack off the left end of the ledge to a ramp, and follow that to the right side of **Jabberwock**'s arch/overhang. Move left, then aid through the roof at a bolt. Climb a crack leaning left (5.10a) to the rising ledge system (and the fourth belay) on **Jabberwock**. 6. Climb **Jabberwock**'s fifth pitch, a leaning dihedral, and belay on ledges to the right. At this point it may be best to finish on that route. 7. Make a long diagonal traverse up right on easy, but blocky rock — this pitch roughly parallels the obvious diagonal fault 70 feet below. 8. Climb straight up (5.10 A2) to the left end of a long overlap. 9. Follow the overlap up right, pendulum out of its right side, then go up (A2+) to another arching overhang. Nail that, and pendulum again to reach a ledge that leads off the face to the right. FA: Bruce Miller and Clay Wadman, 1994. **Variation:** A three pitch variant climbs the lightning-bolt roof (5.10a, A3+). Begin from the right side of the block, go up right past two fixed pins, then back left on a ramp to the bottom of the roof (5.10a). Follow the lightning bolt to its end, and go straight up past three bolts to a belay. Move right along an overhang, aid up past a bolt and drilled hook, and join the original third pitch at the sporty 5.10 face section. FA: Wadman (solo), 1994.

8 Good Vibrations V 5.9 A3

Begin a short way up the access ramp and climb up and right on broken rock for a pitch, 5.6. Aim for a V-shaped notch in a band of overhangs (the lower of two), and aid through it on the third pitch. Move up left to avoid the second roof band, reaching a prominent, right-slanting crack system. Follow this system for several pitches, then go straight up to a big, grassy ledge. This route, **Beyer's Solo**, and **Right Side** all merge here, and all finish by moving up and left to the final headwall above the ledge system; climb a deep chimney on the left to the top (5.7). FA: Harry Kent and Mike Neri, 1976.

9 Beyer's Solo IV+ 5.9 X A2

This dirty route has been seconded at 5.10+, but never led free. It starts about 100 feet right of the access ledge, and begins with 4th class scrambling; go to the highest of several belay stances. Climb up and left past blocky overhangs to the base of a vague, left-facing corner system, 5.9 X super choss. It is also possible to reach this from the left with some aid near the end of a long, rising traverse. Aid straight up (A2 or 5.10d TR) and belay 15 feet right of a down-pointing tooth in an overhang. Pass the roof and ascend a steep crack to a broken area; move up left to the left side of a huge orange block and belay. Climb the block (5.9), then go up through several gray corners (5.9 R) to a belay. At this point one can head up and left on a ramp for a pitch to join **Good Vibrations**, or up right to join **Right Side**. Both routes come together at the grassy ledge system, and finish with the chimney described in **Good Vibrations**. FA: Jim Beyer, 1978.

10 Right Side IV 5.7 A1

This route takes the big left-facing corner formed by a huge and rotten pillar at the right margin of the wall for three pitches (5.7 A1), then follows the narrow ridge slanting up and left for three more pitches (5.7) to the base of a chimney at the final headwall. Climb the chimney (5.7) on the last pitch. FA: Jeff Sherman and Greg Davis, 1974.

11 Hourglass Ridge 3rd class ★★★
The rocky north ridge of Alice constricts to a thin neck of stone above the Alice — Chiefs Head saddle before it widens again as it ascends to the summit. It is this exposed and exciting constriction that gives the route its name and flavor. Hike to the saddle by way of Lion Lakes and Snowbank Lake, turn south and take the mile-long ridge to the top (9 miles from the trailhead). Round the day out with a descent to Boulder Grand Pass (1.2 miles south), then turn east and hike down to Thunder Lake.

The west face of Mount Alice has a circuitous old route called **Roundabout** (5.6, not described in this guide) and a deep gully system, which is listed in the ice climbing section.

LONGS PEAK

The following climb is the only route on Longs Peak normally approached from Wild Basin; the rest are described following Mount Meeker.

1 Keplinger's Couloir 3rd class ★
Start at the Sandbeach Lake trailhead (this is located immediately east of Copeland Lake on the road leading into Wild Basin) and hike 4.2 miles to Sandbeach Lake along a well maintained trail. Strike out northwest, staying right of Mount Orton, and intersect Hunters Creek. Follow the creek until reaching a small pond (at 12,000' and a half-mile below Keplinger Lake), and then go north up a long couloir (the rightmost of several), gaining 2000 feet of elevation. The couloir ends at a headwall just left of the Notch on Longs Peak. Skirt the headwall on the left and cross slabs to the base of the Homestretch, the final test on the normal hiking route (see **The Keyhole** in the Longs Peak section, page 89). An ice axe is recommended for most of the year. FA: This was the line taken by the first recorded ascent of Longs Peak, on August 23rd, 1868*. The seven member party was led by Major John Wesley Powell, a veteran who lost his arm in the Civil War, and included L. W. Keplinger (a college student who had scouted the route as far as the Notch on Aug. 22nd, and was first to reach the summit the next day), William N. Byers (founder and editor of the *Rocky Mountain News*, a Denver based paper which survives today), W. H. Powell (a relative of Major Powell?), Samuel Gorman, Ned E. Farrell, and John C. Sumner. It is possible that members of the Arapaho tribe climbed Longs Peak from the south prior to 1868. In 1914, the Colorado Mountain Club sponsored a fact finding mission involving two Arapahos who had summered in Estes Park when they were young. The group toured much of RMNP in order to discover the Arapaho (and other) names given to the surrounding peaks. The two Arapaho men related stories that indicate the summit of Longs Peak was used to trap eagles. *In his 1963 book *Recollections of a Rocky Mountain Ranger*, Jack C. Moomaw (a long-time ranger in RMNP) puts the date of ascent at 1864. This is probably a misprint or mistake, as every other source I've come across uses 1868.

LONGS PEAK TRAILHEAD

Longs Peak and Mount Meeker, the two highest summits in the area, have been the focal point of alpine climbing in RMNP for more than a century. Both peaks are accessed from the Longs Peak trailhead off of Highway 7, about nine miles south of Estes Park. The Longs Peak Campground is also located here, a first-come, first-served, tents-only camping area with a three-day limit.

MOUNT MEEKER

Mount Meeker is the double-topped mountain southeast of Longs Peak. A narrow ridge called the Knife Edge connects the summits. The west summit is the higher of the two, and at 13,911 feet, it is the second highest peak in RMNP. All of the climbing takes place on the north face, which overlooks the Chasm Lake meadows. Climbers pausing to survey the wall can't help but notice the Flying Buttress, a graceful arete arcing toward the summit. Left of this is a similar (though not as dramatic) formation, the East Arete, and bending further left is a concave wall which diminishes in size as it reaches the Iron Gates — these are a pair of towers bordering the base of a talus gully leading to the east ridge of the peak. Because the wall faces north, snow and ice persist in several gullies near Flying Buttress, providing classic mixed climbing nearly year round.

Approach: The approach from the Longs Peak trailhead is straightforward: hike toward Chasm Lake, but leave the trail just before the lake at a lush meadow and patrol cabin. Pass beneath Ships Prow, then up to the foot of the wall. Directions to the trailhead and more detailed information concerning the trail system can be found under Longs Peak (see page 28).

Descent: From the summit, it is best to descend to the Loft (the wide, flat saddle between Meeker and Longs), and then go down the Ramp (see **The Loft** in the ice climbing section, page 234). This route can be previewed from below before embarking on a climb. For all of the climbs up to and including **East Arete**, the Knife Edge must be traversed (exciting 3rd class) if the summit is the goal. For those not continuing to the top, it is easiest to descend east to the first major break on the ridge. Turn left (north) and descend a loose talus gully between the Iron Gates to gentler slopes, which meet the Chasm Lake meadows.

Routes are described left to right along the north face, from the Iron Gates area to the Flying Buttress.

1 Sunshine Column II 5.9 ★

The name of this route is a bit misleading unless it is climbed in the afternoon — the wall here faces northwest, and is in the shade most of the day. There is a beautiful column on the east-facing wall around the corner, but it's not part of this climb. Hike to the right side of the western Iron Gate where a talus tongue reaches up into a small bowl and locate two right-facing flakes a bit left of center. Climb either of these flakes (5.6 on the left, 5.5 on the right) to a long ledge at 100 feet,

MOUNT MEEKER
The Loft
Glacier Ridge
B-8
The Ramp
Ships Prow
B-7
B-6
11
9
B-5
6
5
3
1
2
Iron Gates
12

MOUNT MEEKER - Left Side

1. Sunshine Column II 5.9 ★
2. Main Vein III 5.11c ★

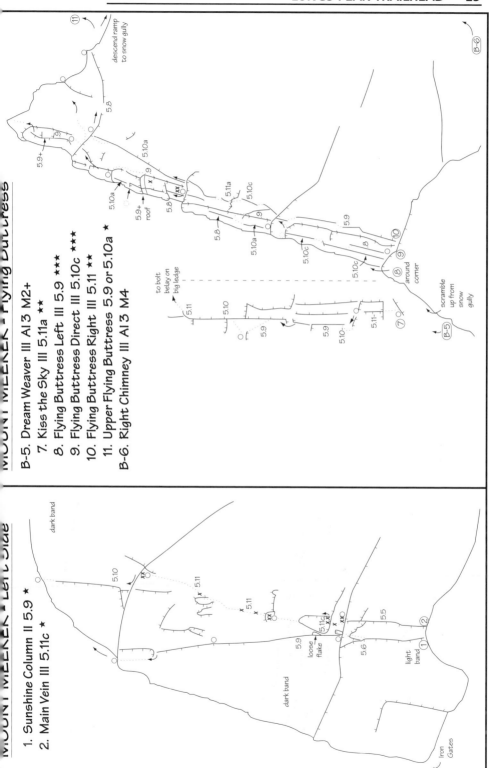

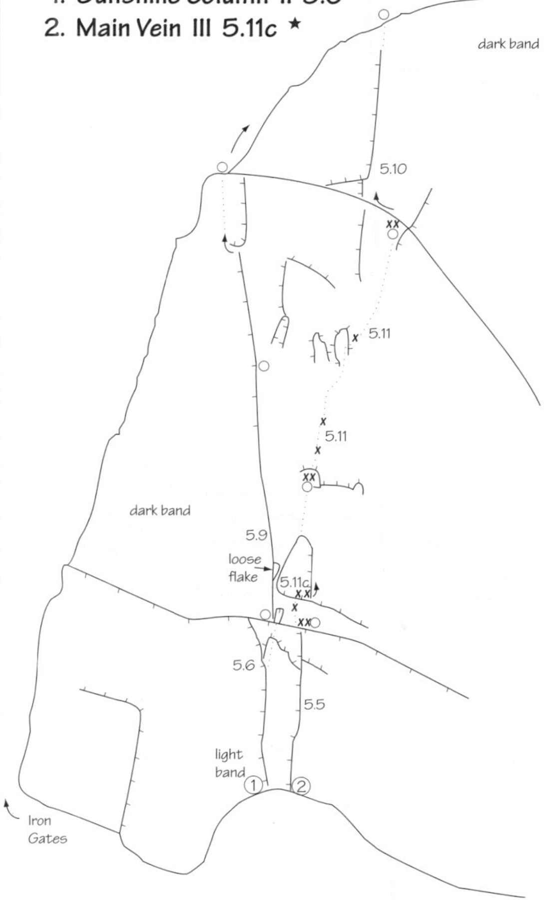

MOUNT MEEKER - Flying Buttress

B-5. Dream Weaver III AI 3 M2+
7. Kiss the Sky III 5.11a ★★
8. Flying Buttress Left III 5.9 ★★★
9. Flying Buttress Direct III 5.10c ★★★
10. Flying Buttress Right III 5.11 ★★
11. Upper Flying Buttress 5.9 or 5.10a ★
B-6. Right Chimney III AI 3 M4

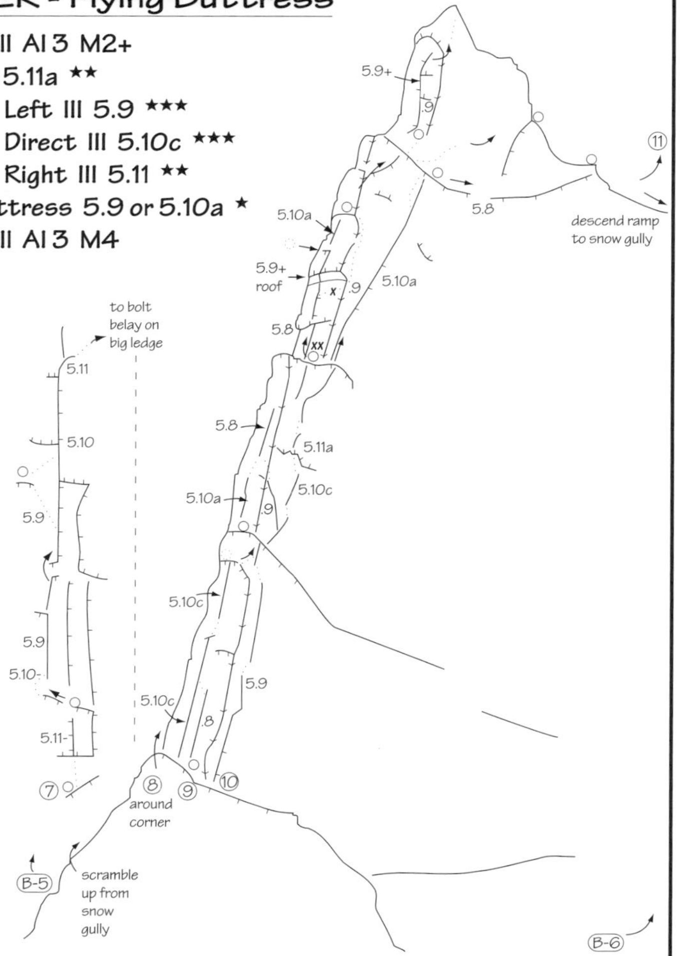

and move left to a belay piton; this is below a precarious flake 15 feet above. Climb to the top of the pillar, master a short crux in a dark band of rock, and then follow a large crack that angles left for a full pitch. Continue the crack to an overhang, turn it on the left, and then move up to a shelf on the prow of the buttress and belay. An easy pitch up and right ends on the east ridge of the mountain. Descend via the Iron Gates — there is a small ledge system connecting the talus tongue at the beginning of the route with the Iron Gates gully that is useful for retrieving gear left at the base. FA: Chip Salaun and Bill Alexander, 1974.

2 Main Vein III 5.11c ★

This route parallels **Sunshine Column on** the right, taking a direct line up the steep face. 1. Begin as with **Sunshine Column** and go up the right flake to a double bolt belay at the long ledge. 2. Climb to an overhang, then pull through to the right (crux) — a few bolts help to identify the line. Once over the roof, follow a difficult thin seam that opens up to a nice hand crack. Belay a short distance above at a bolted stance just left of a thin, long overhang, and on top of the dark band of rock cutting across the middle of the wall. 3. Climb straight up past two bolts (5.11), then angle right through the right side of an arch formed by a flake (bolt). Continue up to a bolted belay at a rising horizontal slash. 4. Move left on the slash to an obvious right-facing corner, and stem the corner to the top of the wall, 5.10. FA: Morris Hershoff, Forrest Noble, and Steve McCorkel, 1994. Another nearby line was begun in 1994 by the same team; by this writing it may have been finished. It features a very difficult bolted seam (5.12), and is projected to include a 5.12 pitch at the top of the wall.

3 Concave III 5.7 A3

Locate an indentation (usually snow-filled) in the wall about 100 feet right of **Main Vein**. A left-facing dihedral (leaning right) begins from the right side of the indentation. 1. Follow the dihedral to a big shelf, then move left (poor pro) to a good ledge, 5.7. 2. Mixed free and aid on expanding flakes leads up and a bit right for 90 feet to a stance beneath a short headwall. 3. Stretch left to begin aiding in a short, right-leaning crack (A3), then go straight up to a sling belay after a half pitch. 4. Begin with a few aid moves, then follow left-facing corners (5.7) to a small ledge. Zigzag to a big ledge near the top, then scramble to the east ridge. FA: Layton Kor and Larry Dalke, 1967.

4 Cobra II 5.7 A1

This route climbs a curving flake seen in the wide white band in the middle of the wall, between **Concave** and **Swayback**. Little else is known, except that a bit of aid was employed to begin the last pitch. FA: Layton Kor (solo), early 1960s.

5 Swayback II 5.7 ★

Swayback takes an arching line up the left side of the East Arete, where that formation meets the main wall. Start with a long, easy pitch (4th class ledges) to a huge boulder. Climb up and right for 50 feet, step left over a bulge, then straight up to a big belay flake. Cross a smooth slab up right and lieback a long flake to a small stance at its top, 5.7. Two pitches (straight up, then right) lead to the saddle behind the East Arete; follow that route. It is also possible to rappel from the saddle in a direct line to the ground (still on the left side), but this route is seldom climbed, and the rappel stations are likely very old (or not there at all). FA: Pat Ament and Fred Pfahler, 1964.

6 East Arete III 5.8 ★

This route climbs the outer edge of the East Arete. Begin from the snow gully on the left side of Flying Buttress, and follow a very easy ramp left to gain the arete. Climb this for a few pitches to its top, then traverse to the saddle behind it. Two more pitches trending a bit right go to the top of the face. FA: Becker, Gorman and Gustafson, 1955.

B-5 Dream Weaver III AI 3- M2+

This is the long and classic gully immediately left of Flying Buttress — see the ice climbing section.

7 Kiss the Sky III 5.11 ★★

This is a three-pitch variation to **Flying Buttress** that climbs the southeast-facing wall above **Dream Weaver**. The route begins down and left from the beginning of **Flying Buttress Direct**, below a thin, right-facing corner originating at an overhang. 1. Climb up to and through the roof and corner (5.11a), then belay beneath a left-facing dihedral (80 feet). 2. Traverse left under a crack, come at it from the left (5.10a), and follow it past a few ledges to a left-facing dihedral. Move up the dihedral, but then traverse up and left a fair amount to a belay at 200 feet. 3. Traverse back right to the line of the dihedral and climb it through the right end of an overhang (5.10). Stem the dihedral through another overhang (5.10+), subdue a 5.11 finger crack, then traverse up and right to the good ledge with bolts at the top of **Flying Buttress**' second pitch, 100 feet (all of the routes on the buttress belay here). 4. Climb the third pitch on **Flying Buttress Direct**, pulling through the 5.9+ roof and stepping left to a 5.10a seam. 5 and 6. Continue up **Flying Buttress Direct**. Rack up to a #4 Camalot and bring 200' ropes. FA: Doug Byerly and Sari Niccols, 1998.

Good rock and remarkable position make **Flying Buttress** one of the best routes that RMNP has to offer. Many variations have been completed over the years, to the point where it is easiest to describe three different climbs. Begin up the snow gully left of the buttress until it is possible to traverse up and right on a ramp system (easy scrambling for the most part; rope up if in doubt). Follow this to a narrow and smooth face at the base of the prow. One can also reach this point more directly with broken rock right of the snow gully (mostly easy with some 5.6).

The first ascent of the buttress was made in 1963 by John Reppy, Frank Carey, and Vert Arsegl, with short stretches of aid (5.8 A1). A photo in Fricke's guide indicates that they continued to the summit along the upper buttress. A free ascent in 1981 by M. Klecker, J. Orey and Bill Alexander stayed on the face of the prow for most of the way, though this probably wasn't the first free ascent of the buttress, and others have added pitches in the last two decades. The descriptions below do not reflect the original lines taken by these parties, and all end at the top of the fin forming the Flying Buttress. Most parties descend from here, traversing for several hundred feet right along the ridge connecting the buttress to the main face, then down a ledge and ramp system that leads into the snow gully on the right side of the buttress. Glissade down that to complete the descent. Or, follow **Upper Flying Buttress** to the top of the peak, and descend into the Loft.

8 Flying Buttress Left III 5.9 ★★★

Start on the east side of the prow at the base of a dihedral, just around the corner from the smooth face. 1. Climb the dihedral followed by a chimney on the right, then move up right to a stance on the prow, 5.8. Belay here, or climb around right and up to the next ledge at 165 feet (better). 2. Step back onto the east face and follow another dihedral, move left to a short corner, and regain the prow at a good ledge with bolts on the right, 5.9. Join the direct route from here, ending on the right-hand line to keep the grade at 5.9.

9 Flying Buttress Direct III 5.10c ★★★

This route strives to stay on the narrow face of the prow the entire way, with the crux coming on the first steep pitch (bring several small wires). 1. Climb a thin crack in the middle of the smooth face (5.10c), or the hand crack on the right (5.8), and continue up a thin seam to a stance (crux). Move right, then up for 15 feet to the next ledge. 2. Work straight up the face of the prow with thin cracks (5.10a), then jam an easier hand crack near the right edge. Step right onto the west side to finish the pitch, and belay at a good ledge with bolts. 3. Move up left and climb to a left-facing corner that ends at an intimidating roof, 5.8. Jam through the roof at a fist crack, 5.9+, step left to a thin seam, and take that (5.10a) to a stance on the right. One can also move right beneath the roof passing a bolt, and climb along its right edge (5.9, fixed pins) to the same stance. 4. Climb around to the right and follow a series of flakes and corners on the west side, never straying too far from the prow, and move back left to a belay on the right side of the final rib. **5.** Follow a steep, right-facing dihedral splitting the rib, then move right and up to the top of the buttress, exposed 5.9+, some fixed gear. **Variation:** It is also possible to belay short of the final rib, and begin a rising traverse right until the ridge connecting the buttress to the main wall is reached.

10 Flying Buttress Right III 5.11a ★★

This route stays right of the prow for its entire length, encountering leaning, steep, and sometimes awkward cracks. Start a few feet right of the prow. 1. Follow cracks near the prow for a long pitch to the "next ledge" mentioned in the previous two routes, 165 feet, 5.9. 2. Work right with leaning cracks and grooves to a roof pierced by two cracks, 5.10c, then pull through the roof (crux) and continue to the good ledge with two bolts. 3. Another long pitch climbs a shallow, left-facing dihedral/crack to some old slings (awkward 5.10a), then steps left and up to a ledge. 4 and 5. These two pitches traverse up and right, connecting short ramps and ledges with face climbing (5.8), and ending at the base of **Upper Flying Buttress**. FA: The second pitch, at least, seems to have been climbed first by Morris Hershoff and George Bell, 1993. Richard and Joyce Rossiter climbed the third pitch in 1984.

11 Upper Flying Buttress 5.9 or 5.10a ★

This is a good excuse for more climbing and a chance to bag the second highest summit in RMNP. Scramble up to the base of a steep, left-facing dihedral just left of a menacing offwidth and set a belay. Climb the dihedral (5.10a) and move right to a stance beneath a smaller left-facing corner. Climb this to a ledge (5.8 or 9) and belay. 4th class terrain gains the summit after several hundred feet. FA: Tom Sciolino and Richard Rossiter, 1980. **Variation:** Another line on the upper buttress begins down and right of the offwidth. Piece together disjunct cracks for 90 feet to a belay beneath a little roof (5.9). Move right around a corner to avoid the roof, and back left along a 5.7 crack. Head up left to join the 4th class terrain described above. FA: Jeff Lowe and Teri Ebel, 1990s.

B-6 Right Chimney III AI 3 M4

The gully immediately right of **Flying Buttress** — see ice climbing section.

B-7 Dark Star III AI 4+ M4

See the ice climbing section.

B-8 The Loft (or The Apron) WI 3

See the ice climbing section.

12 Peacock Wall II 5.9 A3+

Peacock Wall ascends the short cliff between Peacock Pool and the north face of Meeker. Approach from the patrol cabin, and start in the middle of the wall at a smooth slab with a single thin crack. Traverse into the crack from the left, and climb it to a stance beneath a short, thin dihedral (5.9). Follow the dihedral to the lower right side of a very apparent ramp, and ascend the ramp left for 40 feet to a belay. The short second pitch nails a bottoming crack (A3+, RURPs) to the next ramp (also obvious) and belays left of a black streak. Climb rotten rock left of the streak to a big, rotten flake, go up its left side, and finish with a loose and blocky 5.8+ slot. FA: Cub Shaefer and Pat Ament, 1965.

13 Santayana Slabs I 5.7

This route ascends the slabs on the southeast side of Mount Lady Washington, just above the trail to Chasm Lake, and roughly across the valley from **Peacock Wall**. The exact location is not known. FA: Mike Tobias, Mark Janson, and Diane Rheinert, 1970.

LONGS PEAK

Among climbers, Longs Peak is by far the most famous mountain in Colorado. Three great faces converge together in a huge cirque on the precipitous east side of the mountain, forming an awesome climbing arena. The world renowned Diamond in the center of the East Face is one of the finest alpine walls anywhere, housing many of the best routes in RMNP. The Lower East Face encompasses as much granite as the Diamond, although sporting it in a different style. On the right side of the cirque lies Chasm View Wall, a delightful cliff in its own right.

While these three walls are the focal point for climbing on Longs Peak, they only begin to tell the story of the great monarch of the northern Colorado Rockies — adventure resides on all facets of the mountain. The southeast ridge holds a splendid, though seldom traveled route with several interesting variations, while the walls on either side of this ridge provide great alpine climbing and high mountain cragging. The North Face, so prominent from the (now removed) shelter cabin in the Boulder Field, was the staging ground for countless guided ascents in the early years on the peak, and the sweeping slabs of the West Face would be teeming with climbers were it not for the grueling approach. So compelling is Longs that there are numerous alpinists who have climbed its walls again and again, racking up an incredible number of ascents. Shep Husted and Enos Mills, both guides from the early part of the 20th century, amassed 350 and 297 ascents, respectively. (My parents have a manuscript written by William Ramaley — *Trails and Trailbuilders of the Rocky Mountain National Park* — which claims Husted climbed Longs 938 times). Otto Van Allman, a guide who worked on the mountain in the 1950s, summitted 225 times, 109 of which were via the East Face. More recently, Roger Briggs of Boulder has climbed the Diamond 84 times to date, including a trip in which he biked from Boulder, ran up to the East Face, and free soloed **Casual Route** on the Diamond, all in 5 hours and 45 minutes. These love affairs with Longs Peak speak volumes — there are very few mountains that can claim such a devoted following.

Travel Directions: The approach to all of the climbs (save **Keplinger's Couloir**, which is described in the Wild Basin section — see page 20) begins from the Longs Peak ranger station and trailhead. Drive south from Estes Park on Highway 7 and turn right immediately after mile marker 9. A one mile paved road leads to the trailhead. The parking lot is often full by 5:00 a.m. during summer weekends, and even in winter it is a busy place. Overflow parking is permitted on parts of the access road.

Approach: A single trail leaves the parking lot, though it branches in various points along its trip to the summit. Stay left at the first two trail junctions which come at 0.6 mile and 2.7 miles — the lower right branch goes to Eugenia Mine and Storm Pass, while the upper right branch goes to the Battle Mountain campsite and through Jim's Grove (this is the old trail up to the Boulderfield). The next junction comes at 4.0 miles, and is located at the far west end of Mills Moraine. Go left toward Chasm Lake for all of the climbs on the east side of the mountain. The Palisades (a series of cliffs between the Loft and the Notch on the Wild Basin side) are also best approach from this trail. The right path at the Mills Moraine junction is the standard route (the **Keyhole Route**), and all climbs on the north and west faces are accessed from here. Note that one more trail meets the standard route at Granite Pass (5.0 miles from the trailhead). This is the North Longs Peak trail, which originates in Glacier Gorge. Stay left at this junction to continue up Longs Peak.

Descent: There are a number of options for descending from the summit — three major choices are listed here. For lines that do not reach the summit, information is given with the route descriptions.

The most common descent for technical climbers reverses **The Cables** — scramble down the north face to the top of the Cables and rappel (see **B-20** in the ice climbing section under Longs Peak, page 239). The best line of descent is not always apparent; it is suggested that climbers become familiar with the north face (and the entire mountain, as Longs is rather complex) before trying it in the dark. Once the top of the Cables is reached, rappel from huge eye bolts (two single-rope or one double-rope rappel) and scramble to Chasm View. From here it is an easy walk down to the hiking trail in the Boulderfield, or along the ridge to the Camel gully (see below).

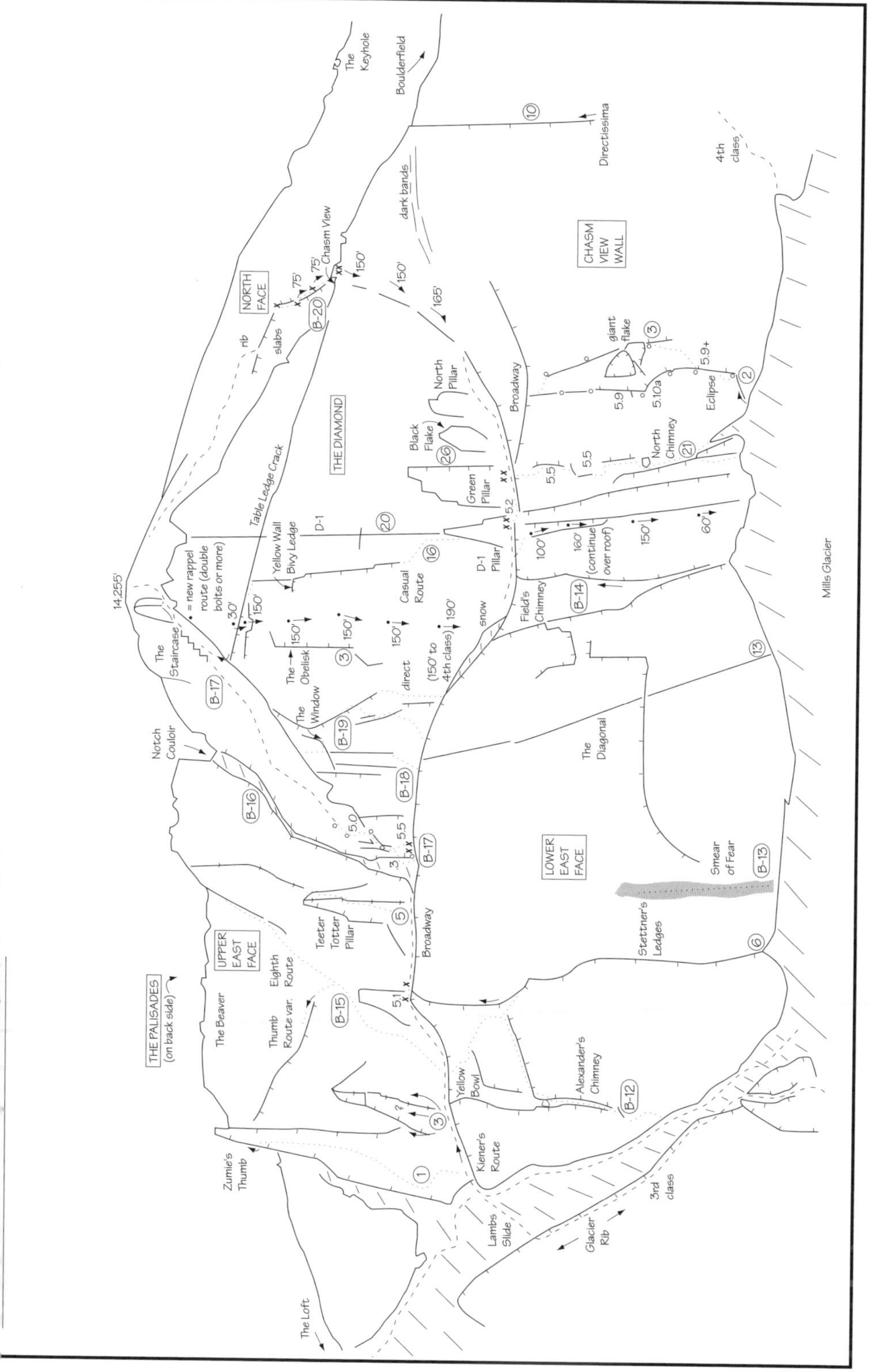
The Keyhole
Boulderfield
Directissima
4th class
dark bands
Chasm View
NORTH FACE
CHASM VIEW WALL
rib
slabs
giant flake
North Pillar
Broadway
THE DIAMOND
Black Flake
Eclipse
North Chimney
Table Ledge Crack
Green Pillar
D-1
Yellow Wall Bivy Ledge
D-1 Pillar
Casual Route
14,255'
= new rappel route (double bolts or more)
(continue over roof)
Field's Chimney
snow
The Staircase
The Obelisk
direct
(150' to 4th class)
Mills Glacier
The Window
The Diagonal
Notch Couloir
LOWER EAST FACE
Smear of Fear
Teeter Totter Pillar
Broadway
Stettner's Ledges
UPPER EAST FACE
Eighth Route
THE PALISADES (on back side)
The Beaver
Thumb Route var.
Yellow Bowl
Alexander's Chimney
Zumie's Thumb
Kiener's Route
Lambs Slide
Glacier Rib
3rd class
The Loft

Alternatively, one can descend from the summit by reversing the **Keyhole Route** (the main hiking trail, see page 89). This is difficult in the dark as well, especially for the uninitiated, and the portion of the route between the Boulderfield and the top remains icy and technical in early summer.

To return to the Chasm Lake cirque from the Boulderfield, follow the Camel gully. It begins near the low point of the ridge between Chasm View and Mount Lady Washington at a rock that looks like a camel. Head left down the narrowing talus slope south of the Camel formation to a snow-filled gully, then go right down the gully to the base of Mills Glacier.

A final option, seldom used though quite pleasant and fast, reverses **Clark's Arrow**; this is the first route listed below. It is not a good choice for those wishing to return to bivy sites above Chasm Lake because it joins the hiking trail below the lake. In winter, before the heavy snows of March, it is often the safest way off the summit.

Named Features: A great number of features on Longs Peak are named, some officially recognized by the U.S. Board on Geographic Names, and others known only by climbers and hikers. To facilitate an easier reading of the route descriptions, these features are briefly described below in a counter-clockwise manner around the peak. Those making a first acquaintance with Longs may be daunted by the extensive nomenclature, yet these names are part of her beauty and grandeur. A note on the names: many of them seem to have apostrophes missing — Lambs Slide, for example, rather than Lamb's Slide, and Longs Peak. This is due to the U.S. Board's preference for simple nomenclature. Climbers, however, haven't followed this lead, and thus names such as **Stettner's Ledges** and **Kiener's** prevail.

THE EAST FACE. The standard trail to the summit of Longs Peak reaches a major junction at the west end of **Mills Moraine**, 4 miles from the trailhead and directly beneath the bulk of Mount Lady Washington. The left branch leads to Chasm Lake, and most of the following features can be located while hiking to the lake. The flat and expansive saddle between Mount Meeker and Longs Peak is the **Loft**. Beneath this (on the east side) is a snow gully called the **Apron**, which constricts at a headwall, and then fans out above — (see **The Loft** in the ice climbing section). The **Ramp** is a rock shelf that bypasses the **Apron** on the left. **Glacier Ridge** (not to be confused with **Glacier Rib** — see below) is the spur originating from the **Loft** that forms the southern border of the Chasm Lake cirque. This ridge comes to an abrupt end at **Ships Prow**, the 400 foot cliff soaring above a patrol cabin below Chasm Lake. The **Beaver** is the portion of the southeast ridge extending from the **Loft** toward the summit of Longs; it is interrupted by the **Notch** (a wholly obvious feature). **Zumie's Thumb** is the pinnacle at the tail end of the **Beaver**. **Lambs Slide**, an icy chute, rises from the left edge of **Mills Glacier** (which is at the base of the East Face), and extends all the way to the **Loft**; the minor lip of rock which constrains its ice is **Glacier Rib**. The East Face rises above **Mills Glacier**, broken only by a long ledge system known as **Broadway**. The Lower East Face sits below **Broadway**, while the vertical facet of the **Diamond** is above. Right of these is the south-facing **Chasm View Wall**. **Chasm View** itself is the small notch at upper left that overlooks the **Diamond** from a vantage point at the base of the North Face. The **Camel** is a small rock formation near the low point of the ridge extending from **Chasm View** to Mount Lady Washington; it marks the top of the **Camel** descent gully, which in turn spills onto the northern arm of **Mills Glacier**. Got all that?

THE NORTH FACE. The right branch of the trail junction mentioned above continues around Lady Washington, goes through Granite Pass, and leads into the **Boulderfield**, an aptly named 300 acres of jumbled rocks that continues to shift and flow at a rapid rate (per geological time). A few backcountry camping sites are located here, along with a solar outhouse. The North Face sweeps up from the **Boulderfield**; the **Camel**, **Chasm View**, and the upper portion of the **Diamond** are visible from here (on the left). The **Keyhole** is the evident opening in the ridge between Longs and Storm Peak, the latter of which is the small knoll on the right. The snowfield left of the **Keyhole** is the **Dove**, and above its right (north) arm is a small notch called the **False Keyhole**.

THE WEST AND SOUTH FACES. The standard trail passes through the **Keyhole** and winds beneath the west and south faces on its way to the summit. It first crosses the **Ledges** (a narrow shelf system overlooking Glacier Gorge), and then ascends the **Trough** (a long talus gully falling all the way into Glacier Gorge) to reach the southwest ridge of the peak. This ridge leads to Pagoda Mountain, is peppered with gendarmes, and is called the **Keyboard of the Winds**. Back at the top of the **Trough**, the trail turns left onto the **Narrows** (another slender shelf), and finally reaches an area of slabs that lead to the summit. These slabs are the **Homestretch**, and they are perched at the top of **Keplinger's Couloir** on the west side of the **Notch**. Extending right from the **Notch** toward the **Loft** (on the west face of the **Beaver**) is a series of cliffs and towers known as the **Palisades**.

Route Descriptions: The routes below are described in a counter-clockwise manner, mostly following the pattern established by the nomenclature given above; that is, beginning with a few mountaineering summit routes up the southeast ridge (the Beaver) and the climbs on its back side (the Palisades), then dropping down to Ships Prow, and then into the great East Face cirque. The routes on the North Face are described next, followed by the West Face slabs.

Use Caution: Climbing on Longs Peak is a serious endeavor due to the involved routes, high altitude and fickle mountain weather. Forty to fifty deaths (several of them experienced climbers) have occurred on Longs Peak; this fact alone should convince people to take extra precautions when attempting the peak. Bring plenty of food, water and clothing, and treat the mountain with respect.

Southeast Ridge

This first group of climbs begins with an ascent of the Ramp to reach the Loft, though one could also gain this point with **Flying Dutchman** or **Lambs Slide** (see ice climbing section).

Approach: Hike toward Chasm Lake but stop just short at the patrol cabin below it — about 4.5 miles. Leave the main trail and follow a footpath along a stream and around the left side of Ships Prow, then onto a long snow/talus gully that leads directly to the Loft. A steep headwall about 400 feet below the Loft forces one left onto an obvious ramp (the Ramp); the headwall — the Apron — can be climbed directly via an ice pitch, steep snow, or wet fifth class rock depending on season, but the Ramp is preferred. Traverse left on the Ramp for about 200 feet, then turn uphill and follow a snow rib (or easy rock in mid summer, 3rd class). Above the rib, the angle eases and 300 feet of talus reaches the Loft.

1 Clark's Arrow 3rd class *

This is an old passage that links the Loft to the Homestretch, and thus the summit. It is the easiest route up Longs Peak after the **Keyhole Route**, and the shortest of the hiking options. After reaching the Loft, cross to its northwest edge (losing a bit of elevation near the end) and seek out a short cleft which drops down fifty feet to a shelf above Keplinger's Couloir (3rd class). The top of the cleft may be marked with a cairn, and there is at least one other passage nearby which also works. Once on the shelf, traverse north on a path that hugs the base of the Palisades and ends at the top of Keplinger's Couloir behind the Notch. At this point one could join the next route with a short 4th class stretch into the Notch, but the easiest method goes left across slabs (3rd class, verglas common here) to reach the base of the Homestretch. Five hundred feet of 3rd class grooves finds the summit cairn. Since most of the technical ground on this route faces south, it is an excellent choice in winter (4th class), often free from snow until the wet spring season. FA: The route's name refers to an arrow painted on a rock near the base of the cleft by Longs Peak ranger John Clark — he did not, however, pioneer the route. Jack Moomaw's account of his ascent of **Alexander's Chimney** with J.W. Alexander in 1922 mentions a descent to Mount Meeker, with **Clark's Arrow** being the most likely line traveled. It's probable others took the route before 1922.

2 The Beaver 5.5 ***

This is a delightful line up the left skyline of the east face profile, and for this reason it is sometimes called the Skyline Traverse. Climb to the Loft (via **Lambs Slide** to add ice climbing to the ascent) and hike up the backside of the Beaver until reaching the Notch. Rappel 100 feet from slings on the right to the floor of the Notch (or do **Gorrell's Traverse**), and set up a belay. Move right for thirty feet on the east face to the first weakness encountered. This crux groove is called **Stepladder**, and it leads to the southeast ridge. Take that to the summit (nicely exposed 4th class). FA: The **Stepladder** pitch, at least, was ascended first by Warren Gorrell and Watson, 1935 — see **Kiener's Route**.

3 SE Ridge Variations 5.4-5.6 *

There are several variations near the line of the previous route that are most easily described under one heading. 1. A route known simply as **Slabs** traverses 100 feet right of **Stepladder** and then ascends a prominent crack (5.5) to the southeast ridge. FA: Unknown, though Nesbit's guide claims it was climbed in the 1930s. 2. Further right is **Little Notch**, a gully system (5.4) leading to a slight depression in the skyline; this is still left of a large dihedral just below the summit. FA: A party of seven, which included Carl Blaurock, Mr. and Mrs. Herman Buhl, Dudley Smith,

Herbert Wirtman, John Hart, and Frank Shirmer, made the third ascent of **Alexander's Chimney** in 1922, and finished with **Little Notch**. 3. Climb the large dihedral just below the summit, 5.6 or so. 4. It is possible to avoid these finishes altogether by traversing beneath them, all the way to the top of the Staircase on **Kiener's**. Finish on that route.

4 Gorrell's Traverse 5.4 **

Gorrell's Traverse avoids the rappel from the top of the Notch mentioned in **The Beaver** by down climbing a steep chimney on the west side. This chimney is the northernmost of two that are marked with cairns and separated by a rock prow. It begins with easy scree about 50 yards below the top of the Beaver. Move left (facing down) into a slot with hand crack, and jam to a ledge with slings, (5.4). A short rappel gains the top of Keplinger's Couloir, but the original route traverses up left on flakes to another ledge, and then down climbs off its left side to the scree below. Link up with **Clark's Arrow** or climb back into the Notch with a short 4th class problem and join **The Beaver**. FA: Werner Zimmerman finished his little known ascent of the east face in 1919 with this route that was later credited to Warren Gorrell. Zimmerman began with **Alexander's Chimney** (predating the better known ascent by three years), and linked up with **Eighth Route** (this time beating out a "first" ascent by 21 years). Note: geographically, this route belongs with the climbs of the Palisades, but it is more appropriately included here among the easier routes on the southeast ridge that lead to the summit.

The Palisades

The beautiful cliffs and towers on the west side of the Beaver from the Notch to the Loft are called the Palisades; they rise 400 feet above the head of Keplinger's Couloir. Though much of the rock consists of perfect vertical granite split with several stunning crack lines, the area is seldom visited. A rugged six mile approach is necessary to reach these cliffs, and they remain in the shade until the afternoon (prime storm time, with cold rock in the morning). Still, those who make the journey won't be disappointed — this is a perfect place to practice high altitude cragging.

Approach: The best approach follows **Clark's Arrow** (see previous page) to the base of the cliffs, and coming from this way, **Alexander and the Hawk** is the first route encountered. Due to the topography of the area, it is easier to describe this climb last. Beginning from the Notch and working south, one will notice a broad chimney left of a lichened prow — this is **Gorrell's Traverse**. Right of this is a massive and protruding buttress, the Great White Tower; a deep and obvious chimney (**Great Chimney**) cuts its north wall. The next major formation right is Wisteria Tower, about 200 feet downhill, and one more buttress lies right of this before the cliff band degrades in size and quality.

Descent: The most carefree method of descent for all of these routes simply walks down the southeast ridge (the backside of the Beaver) to the Loft, after which **Clark's Arrow** can be followed back to the base. For the northernmost routes, it is perhaps quicker to rappel from the top of the Notch. One can also descend **Gorrell's Traverse**.

5 Cold Turkey Waltz II 5.10 ★★

Two parallel crack systems run just left of the obvious **Great Chimney**. This route ascends to the base of the left crack, coming in from the left. Jam past two overhangs and continue in the left crack (crux) to a belay in a dihedral. Step right at the dihedral's end to the right crack, but then finish the route with the left line. Rack up to a #4 or 4.5 Camalot. FA: Chip Salaun and Bill Alexander, 1977.

6 Great Chimney II 5.6 ★★

This is the most prominent line in all of the Palisades, a deep, ominous, and ever widening chimney on the north wall of the Great White Tower. Begin down and right near the base of another chimney in a large dihedral capped with a huge overhang. Climb easy, west-facing rock up and left until it is possible to traverse around an arete to gain the base of the main line. Follow this with two or three more leads, passing a high chockstone on the right. FA: Camp Hale climbers, 1957 (associates, perhaps, of Ray Northcutt, who was stationed at Camp Hale from 1953 – 55).

7 Beat the Heat II 5.10d ★★

This is the central dihedral system on the west face of the Great White Tower, climbed in three pitches. The major feature on the route is a large roof two-thirds of the way up the wall — climb through its right side and finish in a left-facing dihedral. FA: Joni Dutton and Mark Howe, 1998.

8 Earth, Wind and Fire II 5.10d ★★

This route climbs the west face of the Great White Tower in two 60 meter pitches, right of **Beat the Heat**. Start at a shallow, right-facing corner forty feet left of a prominent left-facing dihedral (the beginning of **Beat the Heat**), and follow it for a long pitch. The second lead takes a left-facing system, which works through three large overhangs; the final roof is passed to the left on a prow near the top. FA: Doug Byerly and Kath Pyke, 1998.

9 Slumgullion II 5.11d ★★★

This route follows the northwest prow of Wisteria Tower, immediately left of **Autumn Sonata**. Begin at a big pillar that sits at the base of a prominent left-facing dihedral. 1. Go to the base of the dihedral (sharing ground with **Autumn Sonata**?), then angle up and left to a thin crack just right of the arete. Follow the crack into a small, left-facing corner, and continue to a belay stance below a roof (5.11d, 180 feet). 2. Climb through the roof, and up to a prominent crack which ends at a good ledge (175 feet, 5.11a). 3. Take a 5.10 offwidth crack to the top. FA: Kath Pyke and Mark Howe, 1998.

10 Autumn Sonata II 5.10c ★★★

Locate a prominent left-facing dihedral that ends at a small roof in the center of the northwest prow of Wisteria Tower. A large detached pillar sits at its base. 1. Start behind the pillar at a small right facing corner, and lead over a bulge to reach the base of the prominent dihedral. Continue to the uppermost of several stances in the dihedral, 5.10a. 2. Follow the dihedral and pop over the roof at its end (5.10c), and take the crack above to a belay flake on the right. 3. Lead up and left to a wide crack in a right-facing dihedral, and fight up that (5.9) to a nice ledge on the left. 4. Aim for the right side of a small roof and climb through to a section of flakes. Step right again to an easy crack that gains the top. Bring gear through a #5 Camalot. FA: Bill Alexander and Chip Salaun, 1981.

11 Alexander and the Hawk II 5.10 ★

This route is situated on the first large buttress north of the cleft on **Clark's Arrow**, which descends from the Loft to Keplinger's Couloir. Look for a continuous crack line on the southwest face of the buttress and begin at its base. Climb a crack along a large flake, then move into a wide, left-facing dihedral, and jam to a belay stance at its top, 5.10. Continue the line as it widens to an easier chimney and the top of the buttress. Rack up to 5 inches. FA: Salaun and Alexander, 1977.

Ships Prow

Positioned at the southeast edge of the awesome Chasm Lake cirque, Ships Prow is often overlooked due to bigger objectives nearby. It is, however, an attractive cliff, with several worthy routes, early morning sun, a reasonable approach, and good steep rock.

Approach: Hike to the ranger cabin below Chasm Lake (4.3 miles) — Ships Prow rises directly above the surrounding meadows at the east end of the ridge separating Meeker from Longs (Glacier Ridge). The first six routes are most easily approached by leaving the trail at the cabin and following a footpath along a little stream that passes beneath the foot of the wall. The other routes can be accessed from here as well, though a more eco-friendly approach uses the Chasm Lake trail for another 250 yards, and then along a rocky rib to the base.

Descent: The standard descent follows easy terrain west until it is possible to descend north to the back end of Chasm Lake. Hike around the north side of the lake to return to the base (the south side may seem inviting, but there's a dangerous snow slope falling directly into the lake, as well as a 4th class passage named **Dunning's Ledges**, pioneered by Enos Mills in 1924). Another descent heads south along a ramp and gully system (toward Mount Meeker) between the third and fourth routes listed below; this is the preferred method for the first five climbs. The ramp can be down climbed, though a slip may produce a fall of the fatal variety; a two-rope rappel from a horn alleviates the danger. A third option rappels down **Ship of Fools**. The only problem is the first rappel off the edge of the face — there are no established anchors. One could easily fashion an anchor with a couple of #2.5 Friends, or wait for a friendly soul to pop in a couple bolts. Until such time, it is necessary to down climb the last pitch of **Gangplank** (5.7). This protects well, and is only 60 feet to a good ledge and the first of three anchors down the face (see **Ship of Fools**).

The descriptions of several of the older routes modified from earlier guidebooks are rather vague, and don't always match up with the lines drawn on the photographs. Be prepared for on-the-move route finding. The routes are described from left to right, beginning on the south face and wrapping around to the north side.

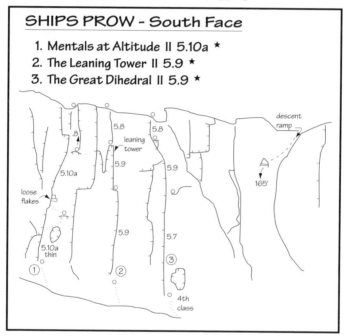

SHIPS PROW - South Face

1. Mentals at Altitude II 5.10a ★
2. The Leaning Tower II 5.9 ★
3. The Great Dihedral II 5.9 ★

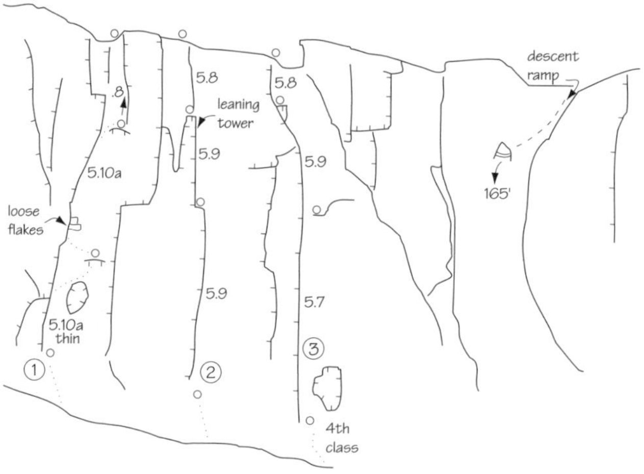

1 Mentals at Altitude II 5.10a ★

This route takes a thin right-facing dihedral to a small saddle in the ridgeline. Begin about 200 hundred feet left of the south face descent ramp below a flake (which lies right of the dihedral) and scramble up to a belay. 1. Climb the dihedral (5.10a) until level with the top of the flake, then traverse right over its top (run out 5.6) to a ledge. 2. Go back left into the dihedral and work past a thin 5.10 crux, then move right to a stance beneath a crack. 3. Jam the crack to a short left-facing corner that leads to the saddle. FA: Mark Ronca and Dave Noble, 1998.

2 The Leaning Tower II 5.9 ★

A perched rock tower (easy to locate from below) lies half way up the wall in a right-facing dihedral right of **Mentals at Altitude**. 1. Climb the dihedral to a stance at the base of the tower, 5.9. 2. Ascend the right side of the tower to a belay at its top, 5.9. 3. A short crack directly above finds the top (5.8). FA: Ronca and Noble, 1998.

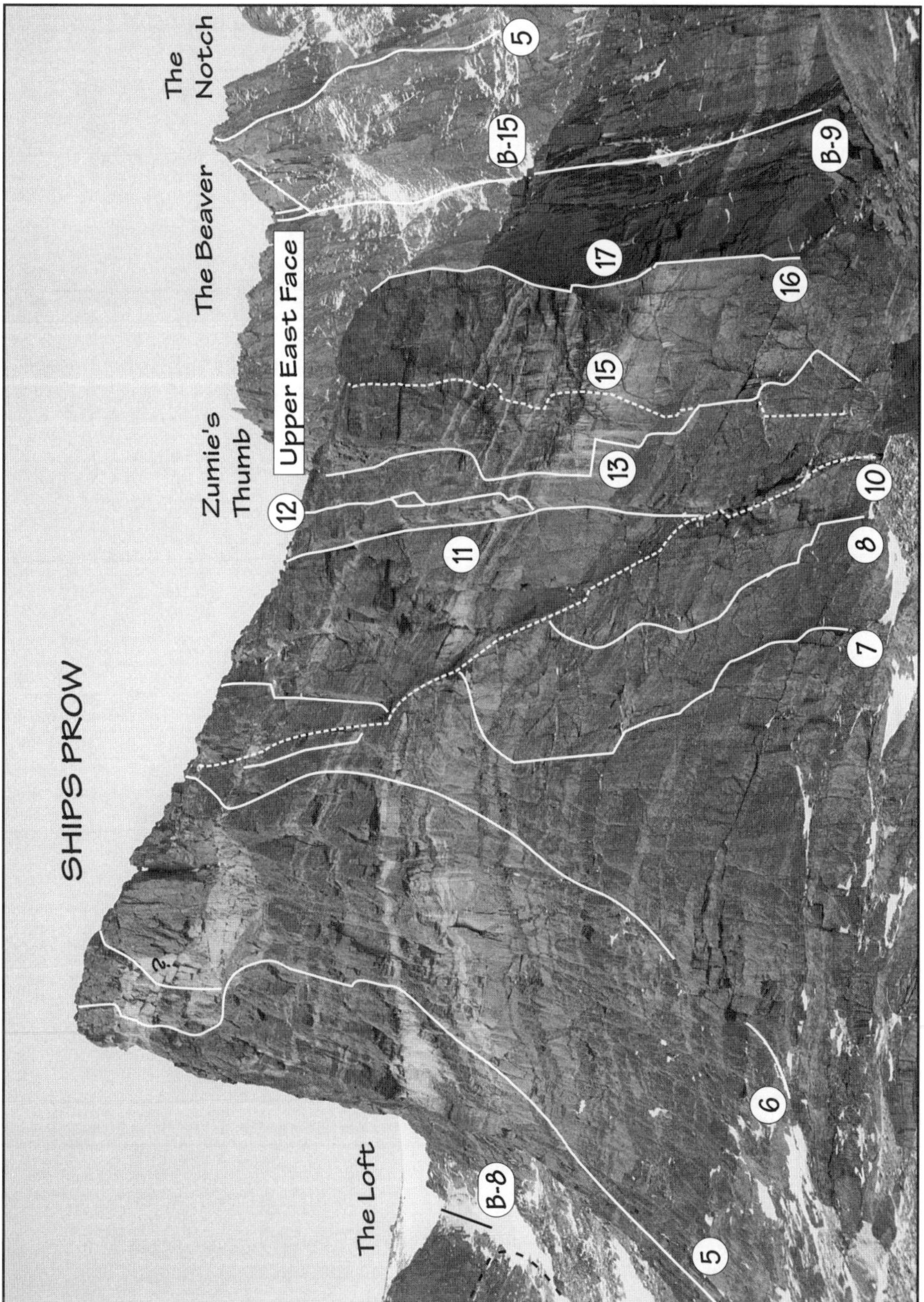
SHIPS PROW
The Loft
B-8
Zumie's Thumb
Upper East Face
The Beaver
The Notch
B-15
B-9
5
6
7
8
10
11
12
13
15
16
17
5
?

SHIPS PROW

6. Nexus Corner II 5.9
7. Half Day's Work II 5.7 A1
8. Old Route II 5.7 (?)
9. Step One II 5.9 A4
10. Stromboli II 5.7
11. Portal III 5.9 ★★
12. Ship of Fools III 5.11a ★★
13. Gangplank III 5.7 A4
14. Gangway! III 5.8 A4
15. The Bilge III 5.8 A3
16. Sarcasm I 5.14a ★★★
17. The Bologna Pony II 5.12c ★★★

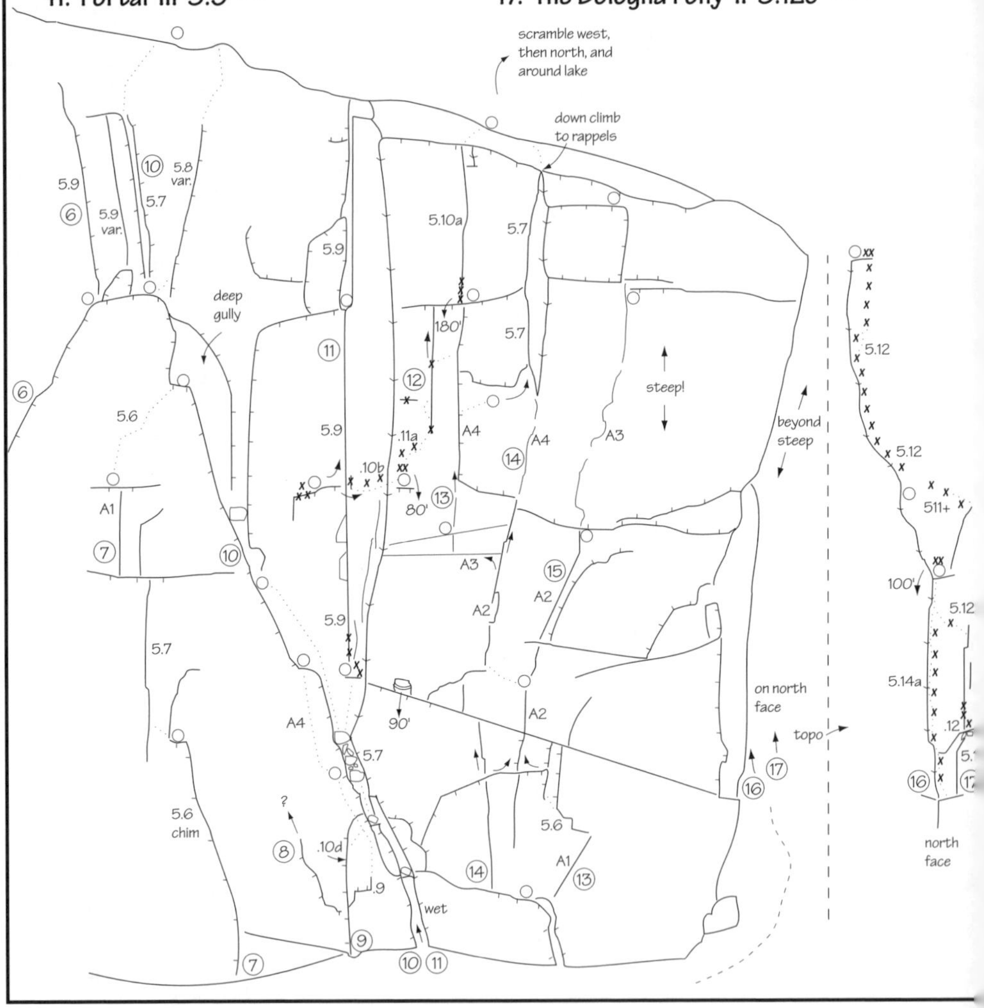

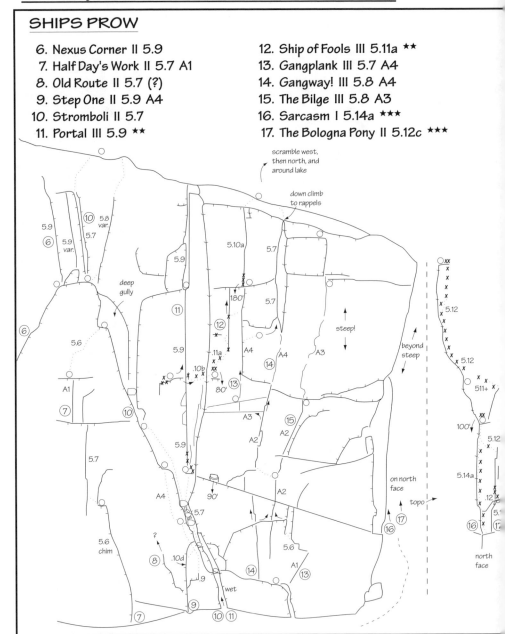

3 The Great Dihedral II 5.9 ★

Begin about 100 feet right of **The Leaning Tower** and scramble up 4th class rock to the base of an obvious right-facing corner. Ascend the corner in three pitches (5.7 to a stance on the right, 5.9 to a good ledge in the corner, and 5.8 to a small notch at the top). FA: Ronca and Noble, 1998.

4 Old Unnamed II 5.8

The final pitch of this route climbs a loose corner system to a big notch on the ridge; the first two follow a line of thin cracks and dihedrals (with a few old pins) directly below the notch.

5 Nose Route II 5.9 (?) ★

Start on the lower angled apron at the juncture of the south and east faces, and climb three easy pitches that diagonal up and right (go around the right side of a large roof band). Finish with a chimney and corner system on the left side of the upper east face — another roof band must be passed on this last pitch, and it looks improbable from below. Fricke's guide states "the route marked on the photograph is a wild guess," and fails to produce said photograph. Whether subsequent authors got it right is beyond my ken. FA: Bob Kamps and Jack Laughlin, 1960.

6 Nexus Corner II 5.9 ★

Scramble up into a gully system just left of a prominent rib. Climb this system for two pitches to a belay near a white band of rock, and then follow a left-facing corner (5.9) 20 feet left of the upper chimney on **Stromboli**. Easier rock finds the top. FA: Stan Shepard and James Burbank with a bit of aid, 1963.

7 Half Day's Work II 5.7 A1

Begin 100 feet left of **Stromboli** at a left-leaning (right-facing) corner and chimney system. Pass through the chimney to a belay (5.6), climb 5.7 rock to a steep headwall with some fixed gear (A1), and then angle right to the third belay on **Stromboli**. Finish on that route. FA: Bob Bradley and Paul Mayrose, 1960.

8 Old Route II 5.7 (?) ★

Early descriptions of this route include a left-leaning dihedral line followed by a chimney, all left of **Stromboli**. This sounds a lot like **Half Day's Work**, but every guide has located the route on the face right of this where there are no chimneys. It's possible that the route begins with **Half Day's Work**, bypassing its aid headwall on the right, or perhaps it goes where previous guidebook photos have shown it (but without any chimney work). I've decided on the latter as it looks like there's a plausible 5.7 route between **Half Day's Work** and **Stromboli**. Start 30 feet left of **Stromboli** and climb a short right-facing dihedral to a ledge on the left. Go left on the ledge to a ramp and belay above the ramp. It appears that a long pitch heads more or less straight up from here to join **Stromboli**; this lead could be broken into two if desired.

9 Step One II 5.9 A4

Start 30 feet left of **Stromboli** and climb a short dihedral to a roof on the right. Undercling the roof, go straight up a 5.9 slab, and move back left to a series of mantles that reach the highest of three ledges. Belay here next to a huge block wedged in the chimney. Nail a thin seam left of the block (RURPs, etc., A4) for 50 feet, then head right into the **Stromboli** chimney. Follow that route. FA: Pat Ament and Fred Pfahler, 1964.

10 Stromboli II 5.7

This route, at least, is easy to locate — it climbs the obvious slanting chimney system that cuts across the entire east face. Snow lingers in the back of the chimney well into the summer, and the lower pitches are often very wet. Climb two pitches (one long and one short) in the chimney proper and then traverse to its left arete. Two leads follow the arete to a big ledge with a large block, and the last pitch climbs a narrow squeeze (5.7). The main chimney line can be followed in the middle portion of the route, but this is dirty and involves a stretch of A1 before reaching the big ledge below the final pitch. FA: George Lamb, Dallas Jackson, and Gorman, 1954. **Variations:** There are several variations to the last pitch that have been added over the years. A thin and attractive 5.9 crack lies just left (still right of **Nexus Corner**); a 5.8 chimney lies 20 feet right; and the wall right of this has been aid climbed.

11 Portal III 5.9 ★★

Portal ascends the huge left-facing dihedral that rises out of the initial section of the **Stromboli** chimney; portions of the climb remain wet until midsummer. The traditional rating is 5.9, but the last stretch may as hard as 5.10a. 1. Climb **Stromboli** for a pitch, but stay right after passing several large chockstones and go to the highest of several grassy ledges (two fixed pins at the belay). 2. Follow the dihedral for 100 feet, using cracks on the right wall when needed (5.9), and belay out left on a nice ledge (three fixed pins). 3. Continue the line to an alcove, 5.8 or 9. 4. A steep chimney and offwidth finale (solid 5.9) finishes the route. The last part of this pitch may be avoided on the left. Bring some big pieces for the last pitch. FA: Stan Shepard and Bob Boucher (with some aid), 1963.

12 Ship of Fools III 5.11a ★★

This climb gains spectacular position as it follows the outer edge of the **Portal** dihedral. Do the first two leads of **Portal**. 3. Traverse straight right past a pin and two bolts (5.10b) to a wild two-bolt belay on the arete — a bit loose, but the views of Chasm Lake more than make up for it. This pitch is short, and can be combined with the previous lead. 4. Climb up left to a fixed wire, then work right past a bolt (5.11a) to a fixed pin in a thin crack. Follow the crack past one more pin (5.10a) and belay on a fine ledge (fixed anchors). It is possible to step right after the last pin (or even earlier) to a nice finger crack in a shallow corner. 5. Follow a thin crack straight above the belay to the top (5.10a). FA: Andy Brown and Rick Guerrieri, 1996. **Variation:** An alternate and drier first pitch begins 30 feet left at a short dihedral (same as **Step One**) and continues straight up a thin corner (5.10d) until it is possible to traverse back into the chimney. This is **Man Overboard** (FA: Mike Schlauch and Bernard Gillett, 1998; bring thin crack gear, including Lowe Balls). The quickest descent from the top of the face begins with a down climb of the last pitch of **Gangplank** (5.7) to the fourth belay. Rappel 80 feet to the third belay, then 100 feet to a cable around a large block which sits on a ledge right of the **Stromboli** chimney. These two rappels can be combined with two 60 meter ropes. One final 90 foot rappel reaches the ground.

13 Gangplank III 5.7 A4

This route starts fifty feet right of **Stromboli** at a sloping ledge some thirty feet off the ground (scramble up and right to gain the ledge). 1. Follow an aid crack off the right side of the ledge, then move up and left to an obvious slanting crack which spans the right half of the east face. Nail a thin, right-facing flake to a small stance. 2. Traverse left 35 feet and aid through a dark band to a flake; follow this to a prominent horizontal crack. Go left on the crack for 25 feet to the leftmost of three white streaks, then move straight up (A3) to a sling belay at another horizontal. A fixed anchor was in place at this location in 1998. 3. Follow the white streak into a hanging, left-facing corner, and aid up to just below a square-cut alcove. Hook right and belay in a big, left-facing corner system. This is the crux pitch. 4 and 5. Free climb the corner to a nice ledge (5.6), and continue with the corner (5.7) on the last pitch. FA: Royal Robbins and Pat Ament, 1963. **Variation:** A more logical finish continues through the square-cut alcove on pitch 3 to a perfect left-facing corner and joins **Ship of Fools** at its fourth belay; whether this has been done is not known.

14 Gangway! III 5.8 A4

This is a major variation to **Gangplank** that straightens out the line. Start on the left side of the sloping ledge and follow a short crack to a good ledge. Go straight up to the obvious slanting crack, and then move left along it until it is possible to go up and back right to join **Gangplank** below the dark band. Follow **Gangplank** to the first horizontal, but continue up through the right edge of a roof band. Some tricky nailing and heading trends left through bulging rock and rejoins **Gangplank** for its last two pitches. FA: Keith Lober and John Gillett, 1989.

15 The Bilge III 5.8 A3

The Bilge climbs the steep wall right of **Gangplank**. Do the first pitch of **Gangway!** to the good ledge, move right to a short, right-facing corner, and nail the crack above it to a small stance. Aid along a slanting crack, which is just left of an obvious arch to a sling belay. The third pitch pieces together several thin cracks, weaving through a continuously overhanging shield (fantastic exposure) to a bolt belay. A final pitch follows the right side of an evident square plaque at the top of the wall. Bring hooks, copperheads, and the like. FA: Lober and Gillett, 1989.

16 Sarcasm I 5.14a ★★★

A direct start to the next route, and the most difficult pitch (by far) in the high peaks. Climb the ultra clean arete at the juncture of the east and north faces, using holds on both sides of the arete (8 bolts plus a large stopper), to the first belay on **The Bologna Pony**. Follow that route or rappel. FA: Tommy Caldwell, 1998.

17 The Bologna Pony II 5.12c ★★★

This follows the outrageous arete where the east and north faces meet. Start at a thin hand crack on the left side of the north face. 1. Jam the crack through a roof (one bolt and two fixed wires, 5.12a), and stay with the crack until a black bolt signals a traverse (5.12) to the arete. Belay at two bolts on a good ledge. 2. Climb an open book corner up and right to its end, then go straight left (three bolts, 5.11+) to a bolted stance on the arete. 3. Clip thirteen bolts along the overhanging prow with two crux sections and a two-bolt anchor. Rappel the route (very exciting; may require some trickery to get to the belays) or use one of the descents described above. Rack up to a #3 Friend; include RPs and several finger sized cams. FA: Jim Redo and Pat Adams, 1997.

B-9 Ships Prow Ice WI 5 M5 (?)

The dark, wet wall right of **Bologna Pony** ices up on occasion. See the ice climbing section.

18 Don't Kick the Bucket II 5.8
Locate a pillar on the north wall of Ships Prow near a cairn (it's unlikely the cairn is still around after 25 years, but you never know). Climb the pillar to a belay ledge on the left. Trend left past several more pillars (loose) to a crack shooting past some roofs, and finish with a short pitch. Descend west and around Chasm Lake. FA: Ron Olevsky, 1974.

Fricke's guide states that most of the obvious one- and two-pitch crack and corner systems on the north side of Ships Prow have been ascended (on aid), probably by climbers stormed off the Diamond. None of them are significant enough to have been named or recorded. Note that the cliffs on the south side of Chasm Lake have also seen some action. Topher Donahue and friends climbed three short routes on a wall due north of the Chasm Lake outlet, finding excellent climbing from 5.9 to 5.12. They also spotted several old pitons in cracks nearby, testament to earlier routes in this area that were never recorded.

The East Face Cirque

The majority of the technical climbing on Longs Peak takes place on the East Face. The routes found here are typically long and involved. Many parties bivouac (permit necessary) above Chasm Lake, on Broadway, or on the ridge near Chasm View, though it is common to finish the free climbs with no bivy.

Climbs are described left to right below Broadway, beginning with the Lower East Face and traversing over to Chasm View Wall, and then left to right above Broadway, starting with the east side of the Beaver (the Upper East Face) and ending at the Diamond. The numbering system begins anew for each of the major sections of the face.

Approach: To reach the cirque, hike 4.5 miles to Chasm Lake, skirt the lake on the right using a footpath that stays about 50 feet above the lake, and head up to Mills Glacier. The glacier is usually hard snow until softened by the sun, and since most parties arrive around dawn, extra care is needed to cross the slope. It is a good idea to bring sturdy boots and a sharp rock to cut steps.

Lower East Face

Overshadowed by the Diamond, the Lower East Face sees little action despite several appealing lines. Because of its position beneath Broadway, the Notch Couloir and upper **Kiener's**, this face is subject to rock fall (although the rock itself is quite sound). Wet sections will be found in all but the driest years as the face drains snow melt from Broadway. As with the Diamond, the sun leaves the face around noon.

Descent: All routes, save the first, end at Broadway, the quarter-mile long ledge system running across the middle of the entire East Face. Descend from Broadway by rappelling **Crack of Delight** (four double rope rappels) or by way of Lambs Slide (bring an ice axe). For many of these routes, it may be easiest to continue to the summit of Longs via upper **Kiener's** (or any of the routes in this area), as the traverse over to **Crack of Delight** can be troublesome.

B-17 Kiener's Route II AI 2 5.3 ***

A splendid mountaineering route. The left side of Mills Glacier sweeps up into a wide, 1,000 foot couloir known as Lambs Slide. Ascend this until it is possible to move right onto Broadway (ice axe and crampons are essential). Broadway can be reached with less ice climbing via Glacier Rib. This is the long band of rock bordering Lambs Slide on the left; it is most easily accessed with a gully 200 feet below the foot of Lambs Slide. Climb on the rib (3rd class, loose) until level with Broadway, then traverse 200 feet across Lambs Slide. Once on Broadway, traverse 1,000 feet to the base of the Notch Couloir, a snow gully left of the Diamond. Most of the traverse is very easy (a spot of 5.1 lies above **Stettner's Ledges**), but tremendously exposed. Cross the couloir and belay at bolts on the right. Two options reach Kiener's chimney directly above. The easiest goes left into Notch Couloir, up for thirty feet, then right over several rock steps (spot of 5.3), and finally back left into a long, low-angled chimney. Belay in the chimney at two pitons. A more difficult and direct method climbs straight above the bolt belay to the chimney (5.5). Head up the easy chimney, then make an unexpected right turn at its end into a narrow passage. This leads onto a long ledge; belay on its right side. Angle back left for a full pitch of steps and corners, 5.0. A short pitch ends the technical difficulties. Wander up 700 feet of talus and gullies (3rd class when free of snow), angling right. The final pitches climb the Staircase, a long section of giant rock steps on the right. Move right at the end of the Staircase, coming very close to the edge of the Diamond, to avoid a huge, steep dihedral below the summit. Turn from the south slopes onto the east slopes and scramble two hundred feet to the top. **Variation:** One can turn left at the end of the Kiener's Chimney (a common mistake) and climb into the Notch Chimneys just right of the Notch Couloir. This is harder, and several run out dihedrals must be negotiated before a rightward traverse regains the line (5.6). FA: Walter Kiener, a climbing guide, pieced together this route in 1924, looking for the easiest way up the east face with an eye toward future clients. Very little new ground was covered on the ascent. It's possible he did this over several visits, with help from Agnes Vaille and Carl Blaurock. Another guide from this era, Guy C. Caldwell, installed cairns all the way up the route and advertised his services in the Aug 7, 1925 issue of the Estes Park paper (an article about his trail building efforts appeared earlier that summer). Note that both Elkanah J. Lamb (in 1871) and Enos Mills (in 1906) descended the east face. It is not clear what route was followed on these intrepid descents, though most authorities put the line near the Notch Couloir, beginning, perhaps, with a descent of **Stepladder** (see **The Beaver**). It is clear that both men traversed south once Broadway was reached, then finished down Lambs Slide, and both nearly perished. Lamb slipped and narrowly escaped a long fall, while Mills was swept away in an avalanche.

1 Glendenning's Arete II 5.4

This takes an indistinct line up the triangular buttress between Lambs Slide and **Alexander's Chimney**. 1. Climb Lambs Slide to the foot of a dihedral near the prow of the buttress, and follow the dihedral to a mossy ledge. 2. Angle right in a gully, and as it narrows, move left below a big block to gain the arete. Climb over the top of the block, then cut back right to a belay at blocks. 3. Go straight up to Broadway. FA: Jack Glendenning, Crowell and Fay, 1953.

LOWER EAST FACE - Overview

15. Grey Pillar IV 5.10d R ★
16. Shining Slab III 5.10a ★
B-14. Field's Chimney II 5.5

17. Craig's Crack II 5.8 ★
18. Overhang Dihedral III 5.10c ★
19. Crack of Delight II 5.7 ★
20. La Dolce Vita VI 5.8 A4

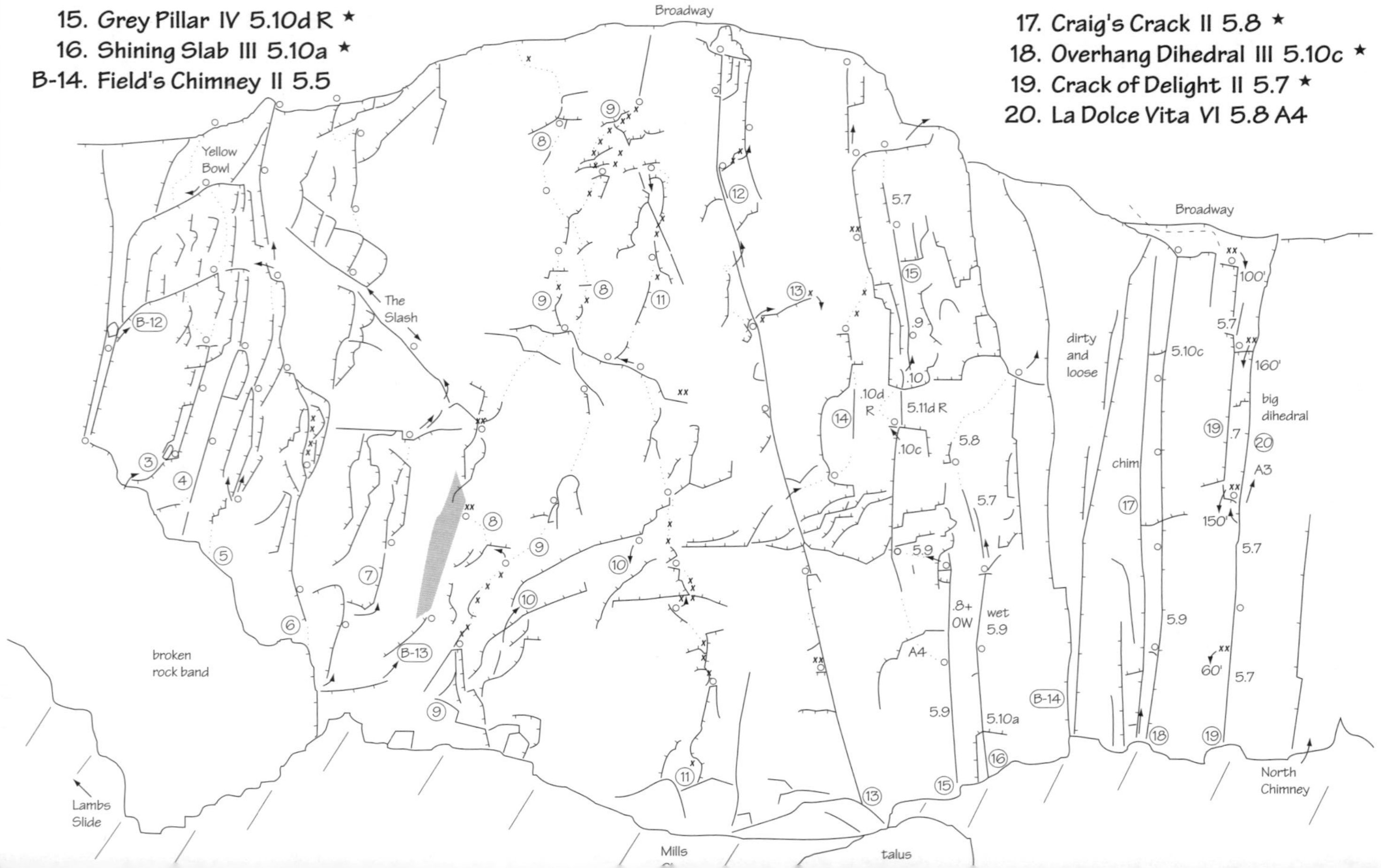

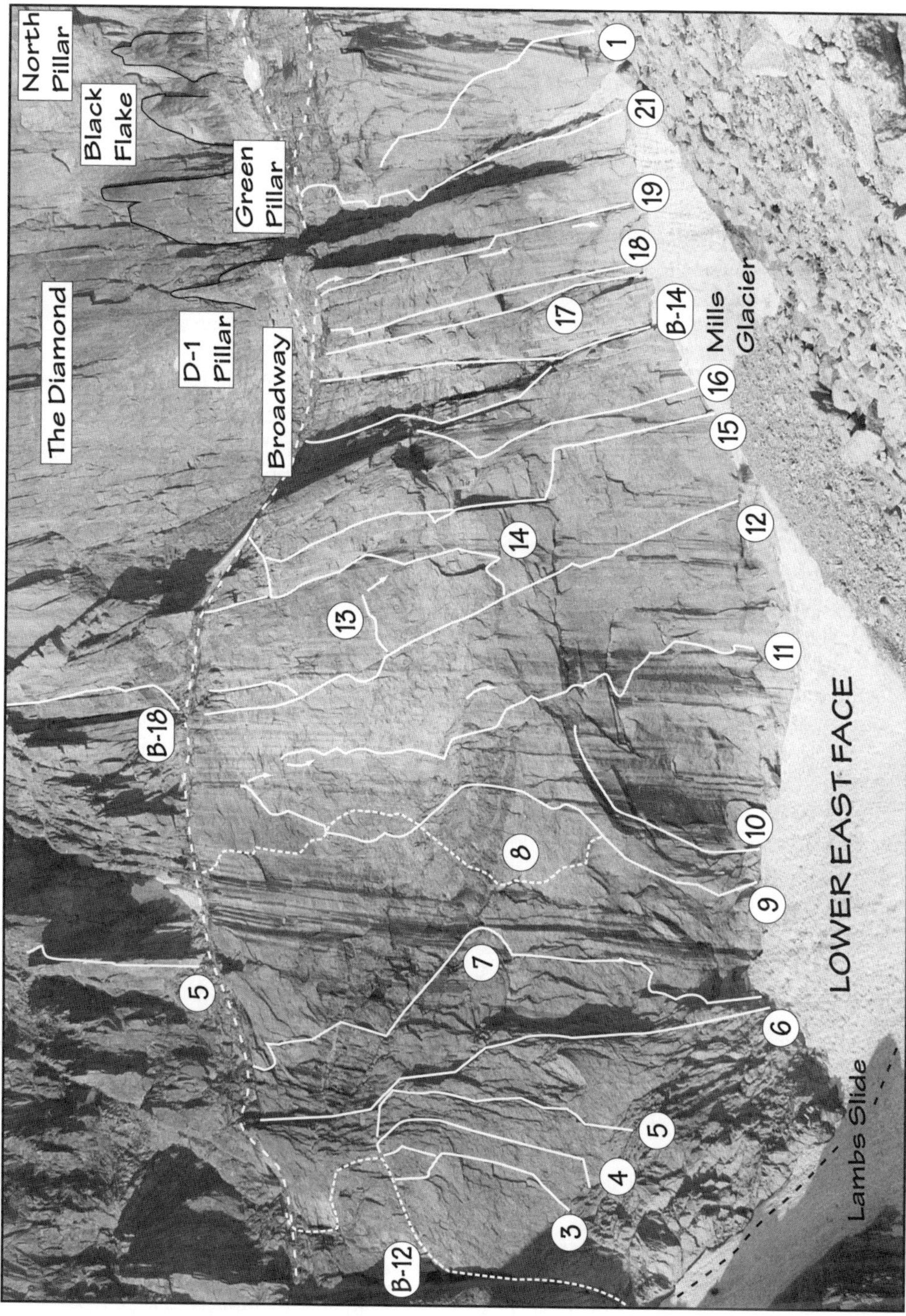
North Pillar
Black Flake
Green Pillar
The Diamond
D-1 Pillar
Broadway
Mills Glacier
LOWER EAST FACE
Lambs Slide
B-18
B-14
B-12
1
21
19
18
17
16
15
12
14
13
11
10
9
8
7
6
5
5
4
3

2 Bongalong II 5.5 A1

This is a variation to the previous line, climbing the first crack left of **Alexander's** (A1) and then switching left higher up. FA: Jerry Brown, Rod Smythe, and others, 1966.

B-12 Alexander's Chimney II 5.5 ★

Alexander's climbs the first major break right of Lambs Slide. It is most appealing as an ice climb in late fall, and is sometimes used as a more direct start to **Kiener's**. The description given here (with all of the variations) is for a summer ascent. Get to the chimney with several hundred feet of Lambs Slide and a traverse across a 4th class rock band (the rock band can be climbed directly to minimize the amount of snow encountered). 1. Go up the chimney to a belay below a huge chockstone, wet 5.5. 2. Move onto the face and traverse right on a long ledge system; belay at Dog Ears Flake on its far right side. 3. Go straight up for 40 feet (5.5), then traverse up and left to a belay flake. 4. Continue traversing left to the Yellow Bowl, cross over to its left side, then up to Broadway. FA: Werner Zimmerman climbed this general line in 1919, though it was named after an ascent by J. W. Alexander and Jack Moomaw, 1922. **Variations: Left Detour** (5.5) traverses left on pitch two instead of right, intersecting **Bongalong** and **Glendenning's Arete**. FA: Melvin Wickens and Sharps, 1930. Or, after reaching the arete on **Glendenning's**, move back onto the left wall of the chimney and take that to Broadway. FA: Glendenning and Bob Frauson, 1950s. **Right Detour** moves right after 30 feet of pitch one and utilizes a small dihedral (5.6) to avoid ice in the chimney. FA: Bill Eubanks and Brad Van Diver, 1948. **Kuncl Direct** traverses right for thirty feet on the second lead before finishing straight up in a fine left-facing jam (5.6). It joins the main line in the Yellow Bowl. FA: Ernie Kuncl and John Deeming, 1959. The headwall between **Kuncl Direct** and the standard third pitch has been climbed in a few other spots. Carl Blaurock and company surmounted the right side of the Yellow Bowl with a triple shoulder stand on the third ascent, 1922. There are at least two other variations, though these are commonly done only in winter — see the ice climbing section.

3 Kor's Door II 5.9 ★★★

A rectangular inset lies about 100 feet right of the base of **Alexander's**. **Kor's Door** climbs up its right side, and over two roofs above. Scramble up the 4th class rock band right of Lambs Slide to a good ledge below the inset. 1. Climb to a leaning flake at the bottom left side of the inset, and belay on the right. 2. Ascend the right side of the inset then through the roof at its top (gorgeous 5.9 hands) to a small stance. 3. Continue the crack to another roof and turn it on the right (5.9). Belay on a good ledge on the left. 4. Follow a thin, right-facing dihedral directly above the belay (5.8), or climb easier flakes on the left, and reach the right end of the long ledge on **Alexander's**. Follow that route to Broadway (5.5), or finish with **Hornsby Direct** (see **Stettner's Ledges**). FA: Layton Kor and Jonathan Hough with some aid, 1958.

4 Malander's Passage II 5.8+ ★★

This route takes the long crack system thirty feet right of **Kor's Door** in three leads, ending on the far right side of the traverse pitch on **Alexander's**. Reach the crack by traversing right on a fading ledge (5.8+), or with a more difficult direct start. FA: John and Jim Malander, 1963. FFA: Michael Covington and John Marts, 1965.

LOWER EAST FACE - Left Side

B-12. Alexander's Chimney II 5.5 ★
3. Kor's Door II 5.9 ★★★
4. Malander's Passage II 5.8+ ★★
5. Tight Squeeze II 5.7 ★

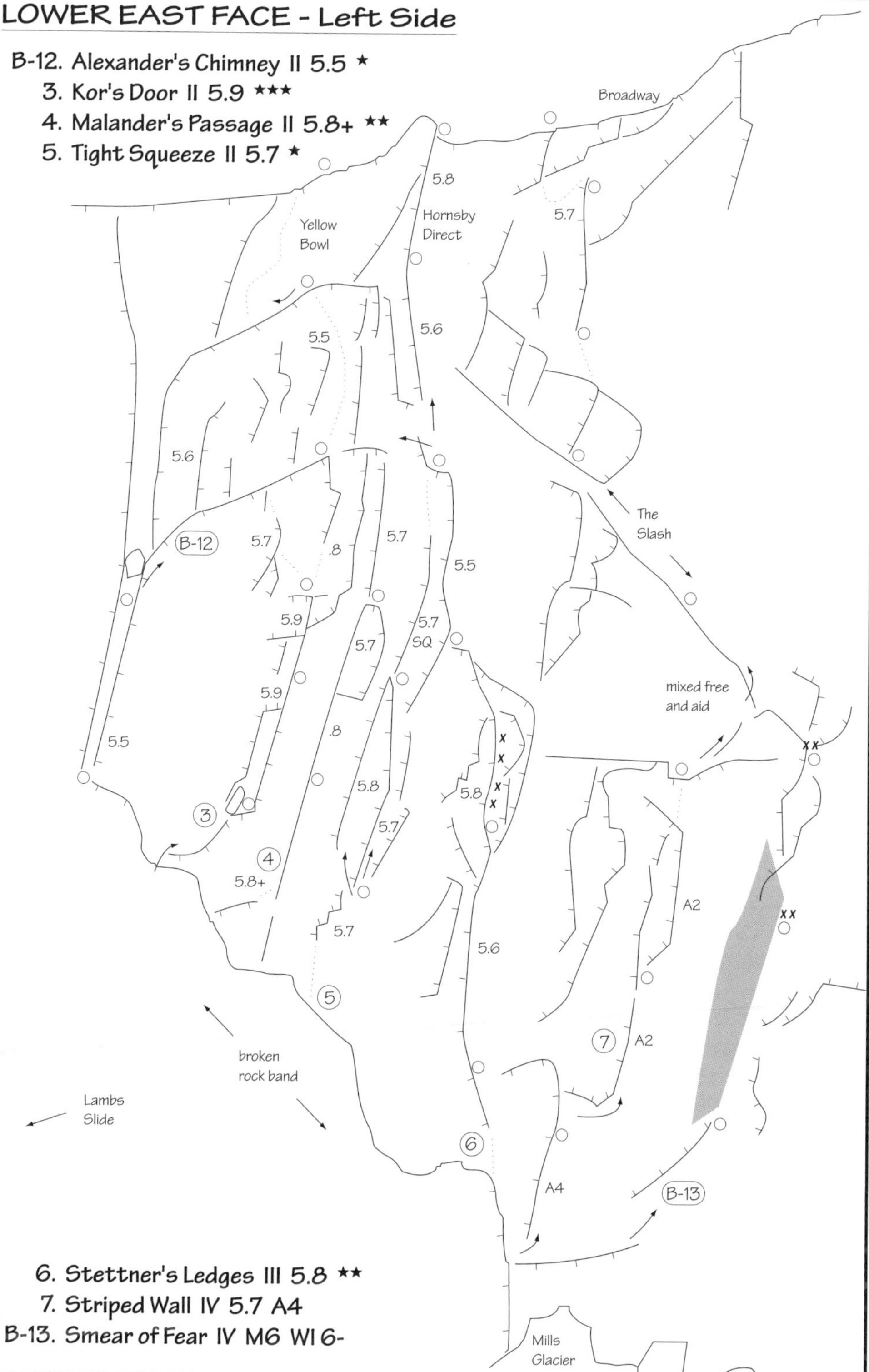

6. Stettner's Ledges III 5.8 ★★
7. Striped Wall IV 5.7 A4
B-13. Smear of Fear IV M6 WI 6-

5 Tight Squeeze II 5.7 ★

Tight Squeeze ascends the next line right of **Malander's Passage**, a flake system leading to a narrow chimney. Above the chimney it joins **Stettner's Ledges**. Start below a double roof in the bottom flake. 1. Good face holds gain the flake. Pass the stepped roofs to the right and belay (5.7). 2. Lieback the flake system (5.8 on the left, 5.7 on the right) then traverse left to the base of the squeeze, 5.7. 3. Thrash up a six-inch crack, 5.7, and merge with **Stettner's**. FA: Paul Mayrose and Bob Bradley, 1962.

6 Stettner's Ledges III 5.8 ★★

A major accomplishment for its time, **Stettner's Ledges** was the hardest climb in Colorado for twenty years, and perhaps the hardest climb in America of such length when it was put up. Its traditional rating is 5.7, though "traditional" is used loosely here — the Yosemite rating system wasn't yet established in 1927. The upper left tongue of Mills Glacier points to a long corner and flake system which angles left; this is the route. The corner faces north and is shaded most of the day, thus extra clothing is recommended. 1 and 2. Follow the middle of the flake system to an alcove 250 feet above the glacier, 5.6. 3. Climb out the right side of the alcove past the Piton Ladder, 5.8 and often wet, and go to Lunch Ledge. 5.8 variations lie to the left and right. 4. Move left on Lunch Ledge and take a steep right-facing corner to another ledge. **Tight Squeeze** joins in here. 5 and 6. Two more pitches straight up the final dihedral provide a fitting finish (5.8, **Hornsby Direct**, FA: Dave Hornsby and Harold Walton, 1949) but the original line diagonalled left on **Alexander's Chimney**. FA: Paul and Joe Stettner, 1927.

7 Striped Wall IV 5.7 A4

This is a particularly dangerous route because it lies below the Notch Couloir in the direct line of falling rock. Begin at a large, right-facing corner just right of **Stettner's** and follow the topo. Bring a helmet. FA: Wayne Goss and Layton Kor, 1965.

B-13 Smear of Fear IV M6 WI 6-

See ice climbing section.

8 Anti Nuclear Tide V 5.10d X A4

Begin with the first two leads of **Endless Summer** (previously difficult nailing, but now tempered with some fixed gear), then make a traverse left along an overhang. Hook over the roof, and climb easy, though run out rock to a bolted stance. From here the route follows the line of **Smear of Fear** until reaching a diagonal system called the Slash (**Striped Wall** climbs along the Slash further left). Angle right above the Slash to arrive at the long ledge on **Endless Summer**, then do a difficult A4+ pitch to its right, reconnecting with it at the undercling flake. Hook up and left to a sling belay. Continue straight up with more hooking and difficult nailing to a single bolt belay beneath a prominent roof. This roof is just right of the water streak coming from the Notch Couloir, and is the most prominent feature on this part of the wall. Nail over the roof, then traverse hard left for forty feet past a bolt or two (5.10d X) until a line of small holds leads to Broadway and the old bolt belay on **Kiener's**. Bring aid gear from hooks to four inches. FA: The first lead might be the line of **Big Bear**, an unfinished route listed in Nesbit's guide with no FA team; it appears that **Big Bear** strayed left toward **Smear of Fear** before reaching its high point. The route described here was done by Jim Beyer, 1987.

LOWER EAST FACE - Diagonal Wall

8. Anti Nuclear Tide V 5.10d X A4
9. Endless Summer IV 5.11a R *
10. Nassawand III 5.7 A3
11. Slippery People V 5.11b R A0 ★
12. Diagonal Direct V- 5.11c or 5.11d R ★★★
13. The Diagonal V 5.11b A0 ★★
14. Directagonal V- 5.11b ★★
15. Grey Pillar IV 5.10d R ★

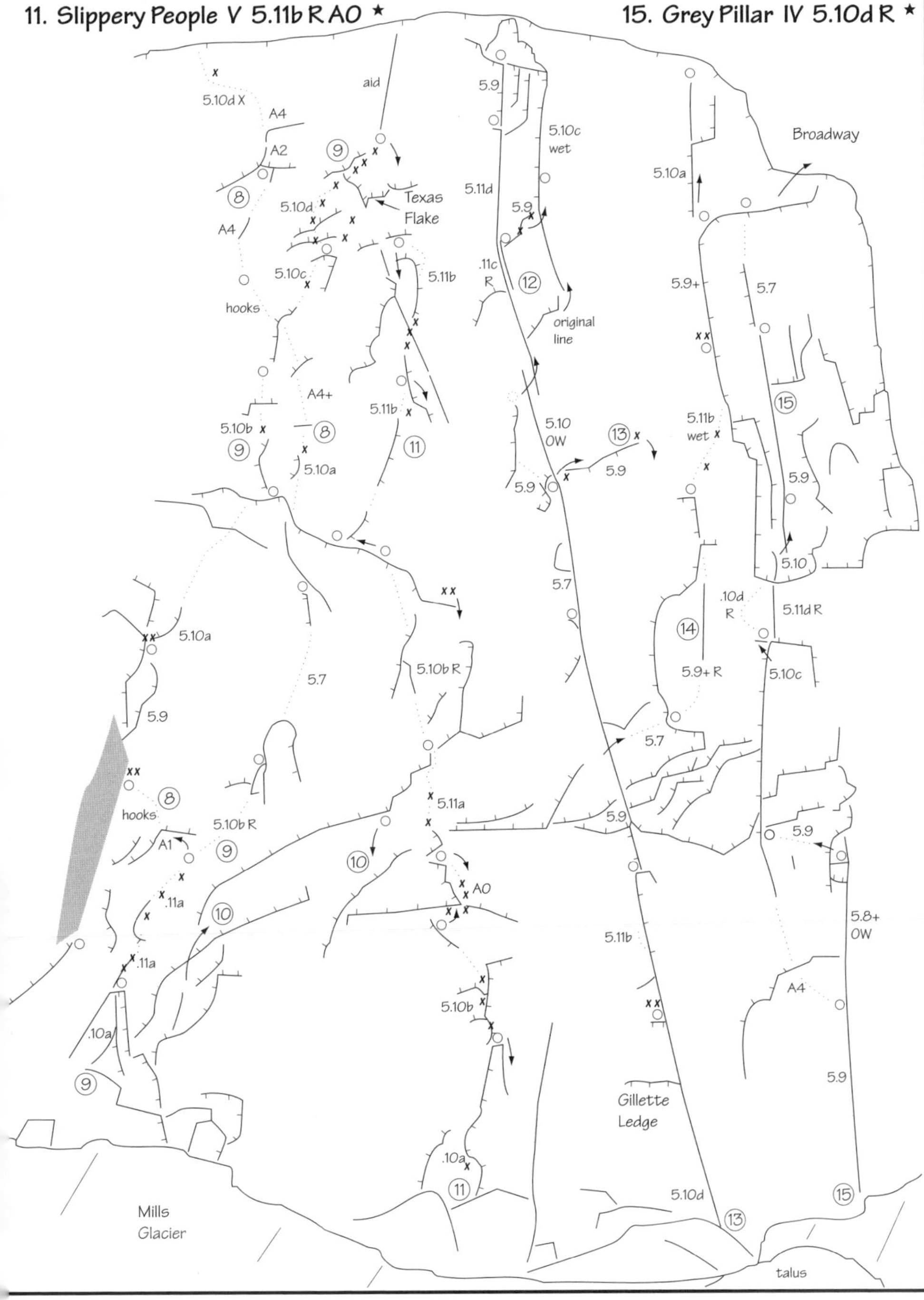

Roger and Bill Briggs on *Diagonal Direct*, Lower East Face.

GLENN RANDALL PHOTO

9 Endless Summer IV 5.11a R ★

In 1987, Layton Kor returned from a 20-year hiatus from climbing to put up (with Dan McGee) a new route called **The Question Mark** (V 5.10 A4, some ground shared with previous route). **Endless Summer** is the free version of that line, involving difficult route finding up a face devoid of continuous features. Begin at a triangular flake located at the left end of a long, arching roof band. 1. Jam the crack in the middle of the flake, 5.10a. 2. Work up an angling slash (fixed pins, 5.11a) and continue past three bolts to a belay even with the roof band. 3. Angle right (5.10b R) toward a black streak, and climb to the top of a flake just left of the streak. 4. Head up left to a long ledge system (using an intermediate belay if necessary), 5.7. 5. Angle left to a bolt half way up the pitch (the bolt out right is on **Anti Nuclear Tide**), then take a right-facing corner to a belay below a small roof, 5.10b. 6. Cut back right, aiming for an undercling flake. Turn the flake on the right and climb past a bolt (5.10c) to a little ledge. Two off-route bolts are seen above the right end of the ledge. 7. Clip a pin on the left, pull through an overlap (bolt), then angle past the left edge of a flake shaped like Texas (more bolts, 5.10d). The wet, vegetated crack above is the last pitch of **The Question Mark**; the free route rappels down **Slippery People**. Rack: RPs, TCUs and a standard rack to #3 Friend. Bring a helmet, and double ropes for the rappels. FFA: Greg Davis and Todd Bibler, 1990.

10 Nassawand III 5.7 A3

An old, unfinished route climbs the underside of the big arch right of **Endless Summer**, then rappels to the ground. FA: Michael Covington and Steve Hickman, 1969.

11 Slippery People IV 5.11b R A0 ★

This route features clean, white rock in its upper pitches, but the lower pitches are usually wet. When combined with the first four leads of **Endless Summer**, it is a two-star route. Start 100 feet left of **Diagonal** at a line of flakes leading to an imposing roof band. 1. Climb past a bolt to a left-facing flake (5.10a) and belay on its top. 2. Pass two overlaps on a left-angling pitch with two bolts and a pin. Belay below the roof. 3. Move right (pitons) beneath the roof, then aid a bolt ladder to a belay atop a pointed flake. 4. Head up and left to the next roof band (5.11a), then pull over on the right to another pointed flake. 5. A left-leaning pitch up small right-facing features (5.10b R) gains the long ledge system shared with **Endless Summer**. 6. Walk left on the ledge and re-establish the belay. Connect a series of left-facing corners to a stance left of a longer, arching dihedral (5.11b). 7. Traverse right past two bolts and a piton, then ascend a thin dihedral system to a small (but long) arching overlap (5.11b). Exit right, then cut back left at a pin to a belay at a roof. This is the high point of the route; three rappels (from the belay anchors) end at the long ledge. Traverse to the right side of the ledge and rappel from bolts to the third belay. Two more rappels reach the ground. Rack: same as **Endless Summer**. FA: Greg Davis and Todd Bibler, 1990.

12 Diagonal Direct V- 5.11c or 5.11d R ***

Diagonal Direct ascends the most obvious line on the Lower East Face, a long leaning crack system that extends all the way to Broadway. On the first ascent, Layton Kor and Tex Bossier endured epic suffering when hit by a savage storm. Start at the prominent crack system below the left edge of the Diamond. 1. Take the crack past Gillette ledge (named for its razor-sharp edge) to a small stance (bolts), 5.10d. 2. Continue up the crack, step left (5.11b) and go to a grassy ledge. 3. Pull over a stepped roof band (5.9) to a belay flake after a full pitch. 4. Follow the line for an easy pitch — the original **Diagonal** traverses right from the belay. 5. Lead through a wide section with a fixed bong, or climb the face on the left to an optional belay stance. Step right, then take a continuously difficult, waning crack to a stance at 160 feet, 5.11c R. 6. Traverse right past fixed pins to the base of a right-facing dihedral, and go up a short distance. 7. Take the dihedral to Broadway, wet 5.10c. Include plenty of thin wires. FA: Layton Kor and Floyd Bossier, 1963. FFA: Charlie Fowler and Jeff Achey, 1980, though Mark Wilford and Pat Adams almost pulled it off in 1977. **Variation:** Instead of traversing right on pitch 6, continue up the same thin crack to a belay below Broadway (spicy 5.11d ***), and complete the route with a short 5.9 pitch. FA: Roger Briggs and Chip Chace, 1987.

13 The Diagonal V 5.11b A0 **

The completion of **The Diagonal** convinced RMNP rangers to lift the ban on Diamond climbs that existed in the late 1950s. Begin at the angling crack system described in **Diagonal Direct**, and climb that route for four pitches. 5. Step out of the **Diagonal Direct** line at a bolt, and traverse a small flake right (5.9). Continue right (5.9 face) to a lone bolt, lower off fifty feet, and pendulum over to a ledge. 6. Angle up right past a bolt and join the free version, **Directagonal**. FA: Ray Northcutt and Layton Kor, 1959.

14 Directagonal V- 5.11b **

A free variation of **The Diagonal**. Do the first two leads of **Diagonal Direct**. 3. Pull through the stepped roofs, then hand traverse right on a good flake to the base of a prominent right-facing dihedral capped with a roof (5.7). 4. Climb an incipient crack out right (5.9+ R) to the right edge of the dihedral's roof, and head up to a ledge with bolts. The pendulum on **The Diagonal** ends at this ledge. 5. Work up right (bolts) to a wet undercling that leads into a left-facing system, 5.11b. Belay at bolts. 6. Climb the corner, 5.9+, and belay on a ledge that extends over to Broadway. 7. Scoot off right, or climb a direct finish up an obvious corner with overhang, 5.10a. Bring extra thin gear. FFA: Roger and Bill Briggs, 1977.

15 Grey Pillar IV 5.10d R *

Start 100 feet right of **The Diagonal** at an obvious crack line (the left of two) leading into some huge roofs. 1. Follow the crack to a bolt belay, 5.9. 2. Struggle up a lengthy offwidth (5.8+) to a big block. 3. Make a long traverse left to the base of a huge corner (5.9). 4. Fire up the corner and over the left edge of the massive roof utilizing cracks on the left wall, 5.10c. 5. Climb poorly protected rock up left (5.10d R), then move back right and pull over an overhang (5.10). Step right into a continuous crack and belay. 6 and 7. Follow the crack and dihedral to Broadway.

FA: Layton Kor and Tex Bossier, 1963. FFA: John Bragg and Bill Briggs, 1977. **Variations:** The original aid line nailed an A4 slab left of the first belay, and then went up to the third belay. Once over the massive roof, it went straight up thin cracks to the second overhang. These thin cracks have now been done free and renamed **A-Wee-Earl Grey** (5.11d R, FA: Derek Hersey and Bobby Campbell).

16 Shining Slab III 5.10a ★

1. Ascend the crack and corner twenty feet right of **Grey Pillar** (sustained 5.9) and crank over a roof (crux). 2. Jam up a fine crack (usually soaking wet) to a good ledge, 5.9. 3. Go up along cracks into a right-facing dihedral and belay. From here the route angles right across a slab (avoiding the huge dirty roof above) into the upper stretches of **Field's Chimney**. FA: Stan Shepard and Burbank, aid, 1963.

B-14 Field's Chimney II 5.5

The fanned-out chimney system right of the main wall of the Lower East Face holds a disagreeable and loose route of poor quality, plus several variations. Its position directly beneath the free climbs of the Diamond further exposes it to rockfall; an ascent in the summer is not recommended. In winter, however, it is a challenging mixed route; see the ice climbing section. FA: Ernie Field and Warren Gorrell climbed the left side of the fan, 1936. **Weeding's Detour** steps left at the initial fork in the chimney and climbs up for a couple pitches to the right side of a roof, then back into the original line. FA: Gale Weeding, Al Auten, and Graves, 1952. Old pitons in the right side of the fan suggest an early ascent; this is the line taken by the mixed winter route.

The next four lines are located on the narrow buttress between **Field's Chimney** and **North Chimney**.

17 Craig's Crack II 5.8 ★

Two long dihedrals in the middle of the buttress face each other. **Craig's Crack** takes the left dihedral (right-facing), which becomes a deep, and usually wet chimney higher up. Some sections of the chimney can be avoided by climbing the face on the left. FA: Robert Craig, Roger and Hassler Whitney (with some aid), 1952.

18 Overhang Dihedral III 5.10c ★

This route takes the right (left-facing) dihedral through two large overhangs in five leads. FA: Layton Kor and Pat Ament, aid, 1964.

19 Crack of Delight II 5.7 ★

An obvious crack and chimney line begins at a large flake fifty feet right of **Overhang Dihedral**. Switch left after two leads (both 5.7) when the crack becomes a right-facing corner, and follow an evident chimney for two more leads (5.7). The route harbors heavy vegetation, and is now equipped with four double bolt anchors (not all of them on belay ledges) to facilitate retreat from Broadway. FA: Kor and Bossier, 1963.

20 La Dolce Vita VI 5.8 A4

The line described here is the bottom portion of a long route that continues up the Diamond. Climb **Crack of Delight** for two pitches. Stay with the same system instead of switching left, and aid up a steep dihedral into the upper reaches of **North Chimney**. FA: Renato Casarotto and Charlie Fowler, 1984.

21 North Chimney II 5.5

The Lower East Face ends at a pronounced cleft on the right. **North Chimney** ascends this cleft (many options available) for three or four loose pitches to reach Broadway. It sees heavy traffic as it is the main line of approach for Diamond routes, and thus it is essential to avoid knocking rocks loose on this route. Listen for the whirring sound of falling ice from the **D-1** exit chimney — in early season, chunks big enough to be lethal can cut loose. The cleanest line begins on slabs just left of the highest tongue of Mills Glacier. Follow the slabs and corners on the right to a huge chockstone blocking the right side of the chimney. In May and June (if the snow is soft), one can kick steps up the snow tongue to this point. Pass the chockstone on the left, then go back right to a left-facing corner above the stone. Angle left (loose slabs) and back right to a short jam crack (5.5) and then head right across grassy ledges to the base of a left-facing corner. Lieback this to a fixed anchor at the base of the **Dunn — Westbay** pillar. Traverse 100 feet across Broadway above the chimney (spot of loose 5.2) to the D-1 pillar and the base of the **Casual Route**. FA: E. H. Bruns (with W. F. Ervin?) 1924 or 25.

Chasm View Wall

The expansive, light colored wall right of **North Chimney** is Chasm View Wall, so named for its position beneath Chasm View. The routes feature steep, high-quality granite, providing a good introduction to the more demanding Diamond climbs. Because the cliff bends from east to south-facing and receives sunlight well into the afternoon, climbing here is decidedly more relaxing than on the neighboring walls.

Approach: Hike past Chasm Lake to Mills Glacier. The first several routes are accessed directly from the glacier. A long ramp and ledge system which runs for several hundred feet up and right (4th class in a few spots, and above the more distinct ramp of **Fifth Avenue**) begins near the right tongue of the glacier, and it is used to gain the base of the remaining routes.

Descent: For routes that end on Broadway, there are several descent choices. Either traverse left on Broadway and rappel **Crack of Delight**, or locate the anchors on top of **Babies Are Us** and rappel that route. One can also traverse right and climb out via **Chasm View Cut-off** (or its variation). This leads to the ridge between Chasm View and Mount Lady Washington, as do the climbs on the right side of the wall. From the ridge top, walk east to the Camel descent gully; follow that back to Mills Glacier (described at the beginning of the Longs Peak section). Extra gear can be left at the base of the Camel gully for pick-up after the climb, provided this is the choice of descent.

1 Near North Unfinished

A picture in Nesbit's Longs Peak guide demarcates this route that climbs all but the last pitch of the slab right of **North Chimney**. It appears to follow the obvious cracks and corners one system left of the next route. Its difficulty and FA team are not listed.

2 Eclipse II 5.10a ★

Eclipse follows the arching dihedral below a huge flake seen midway up the wall about 200 feet right of **North Chimney**. A 4th class ramp leads off of Mills Glacier toward the base of the dihedral. 1. Climb the dihedral for fifty feet (or the slab on the left), then face climb out left for a short stretch. Continue up to and over a roof (5.9+) in the dihedral. 2. Follow the line (sometimes wet) to the end of the arch, 5.10a. 3. Pop over an apex, and go up a shallow dihedral (5.9). 4 and 5. Two pitches (5.7, 5.5) up good rock end at Broadway. FA: Ament and Boucher, 1963. FFA: Beyer and Casey, 1990.

3 Zigzag II 5.7 A2

Begin at the base of the **Eclipse** dihedral. 1. Do the first pitch of **Eclipse** until reaching a belay slot in the corner. 2. Traverse right out of the corner and cross a slab beneath a huge roof; belay at the end of a left-facing dihedral that meets the right side of the roof. 3. Aid through the roof and climb an open book dihedral above to a slanting crack. 4. Follow the slanting crack system to a belay ledge beneath Broadway, then traverse the ledge left to join the last few feet of **Eclipse**. FA: Layton Kor and Floyd (Tex) Bossier, 1963.

4 Babies R Us III 5.12a ★★★ (if dry)

This route climbs the longest and most prominent of several black water streaks between **Zigzag** and **Invisible Wall**. Whenever the streak is wet, so is the route — an August or early September ascent is recommended. Begin five feet right of the streak from a snow belay on Mills Glacier. 1. Smear up a smooth slab (5.9 R) to a sloping, triangular ledge in a pod — the route starts on this ledge in high snow — and ascend past a pin and bolt to a small corner rising up right. Climb the corner (5.7 R) and follow three bolts to a double bolt belay, 5.11a. 2. Work past a flake (TCUs) and a fixed pin, then clip seven bolts (5.12a initially, easing off to 5.11) to a two-bolt belay in the water streak. The crux can be aided if desired. 3. Move left past three bolts toward an arete, then take a thin crack to a pin/bolt stance. 4. Climb right (5.9+, bolt) and place a 3.5-inch cam at the base of a right-facing corner. Follow this (5.7) to a fixed nut belay. 5. Take an obvious zigzag line of cracks to Broadway (5.10a), finishing with a 5.11a section past two bolts, or climb an easy chimney on the left. Include RPs, TCUs, and a #4 Camalot on the rack, as well as 10 long runners and edging shoes. Rappel the route to descend. FA: Bret Ruckman and Randy Farris, both recently inducted into fatherhood, 1998.

5 Invisible Wall IV 5.8 A4

Begin near the right side of Mills Glacier at the base of the approach ramp that leads to the remaining routes. 1. Climb an orange, arching corner (left-facing) and belay shortly after its top at several closely packed cracks, excellent 5.8. 2. Follow the cracks left to a large overhang above a slab, and move around the left side of the roof (tension traverse on FA) to the base of a prominent open book corner. 3. Free climb the corner until forced onto aid (A1) and belay near its top. This is a short lead, and it may be possible to combine it with the next. 4. Finish the corner (A3), tension traverse left to an arch, and set up a belay midway across it. 5. Nail left beneath the arch (A3), and turn its left side into a shallow dihedral; belay at the first available anchor. This pitch is also short, and could be combined with the next. 6. Climb the dihedral to its end at a small roof, step right to a good crack, and

Chasm View
CHASM VIEW WALL
6
7
8
7
10
6
9
5
4

CHASM VIEW WALL

4. Babies Я Us III 5.12a ★★★
5. Invisible Wall IV 5.8 A4
6. Royal Flush IV 5.11c ★★
7. Tip Toe II 5.7 ★
8. Red Wall III 5.10a ★★★
9. The Middle Path III 5.11b ★★
10. Directissima III 5.10a ★★★
13. Fifth Avenue 4th Class
14. Horbein Crack II 5.8
15. Chasm View Cut Off I 5.7

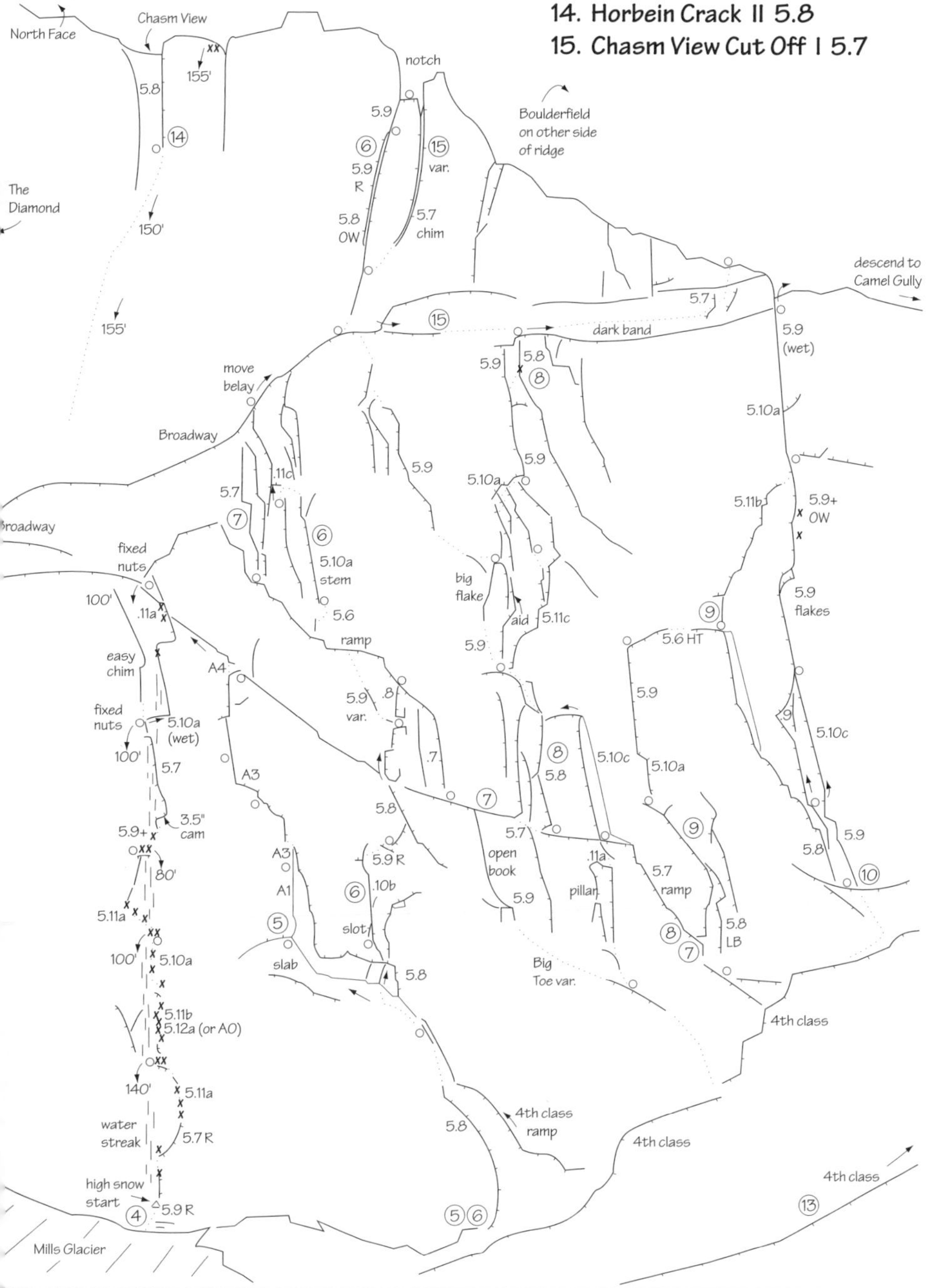

follow it to an alcove belay. 7. Move left out of the alcove to a short A4 section (RURPs and hooks) to a left-slanting ledge. This is near the left end of a long, conspicuous diagonal crack that cuts across the middle portion of the wall. Hand traverse left on this to the right edge of Broadway, and the last belay of **Babies R Us**. Rappel that route to descend. FA: Layton Kor and Larry Dalke, 1965.

6 Royal Flush IV 5.11c ★★

This line starts with **Invisible Wall**, but then climbs straight up through the rightmost of several dihedrals in the middle of the route to a big square notch at the top of the wall (200 feet right of the Chasm View notch). 1 and 2. Do one-and-a-half leads on **Invisible Wall** to the roof, but jam out its right side (5.8) to a belay stance at the bottom of a slot. 3. Squeeze up the slot and jam a strenuous crack (5.10b). When the crack dies, move right on big knobs to a belay flake, 5.9 R. 4. Climb the dihedral above to a slanting roof, and traverse beneath it until reaching a break (5.8). Go straight up a broken corner system and belay on any of several ledges. 5. Continue up to an easy ramp and traverse left for fifty feet, then do a short 5.6 wall to a stance beneath a perfect, leaning dihedral, the rightmost of several such corners. A variation to the left (5.9) is marked on the topo. 6. Stem the dihedral (exquisite 5.10a), exit left, go up fifteen feet, then traverse twenty feet left to a little roof (#2 Friend in roof to protect second). Drop down ten feet and belay. The greenery in the dihedral can be avoided entirely by using a crack on the left wall for protection. 7. Pop over the left side of the little roof and take a thin crack (5.11c) followed by a ramp/corner to the extreme right side of Broadway. 8. Move the belay right and climb a short 5.6 headwall to the base of a dirty chimney, the left-hand of two. 9. Climb the chimney with some unpleasant, loose offwidth (5.9 R) and belay after a full pitch at a ledge thirty feet below the square notch. 10. Climb to the left side of the notch, 5.9. This long route can be made shorter by escaping left on Broadway after the seventh pitch (rappel **Babies R Us**). FA: Bernard Gillett and Scott Ahlgren, with Jerry Hill on the first five pitches, 1993. **Variations:** A 4th class ramp that starts 40 feet above the orange corner can be used to gain the first belay. One can also avoid the loose chimney at the top by climbing **Chasm View Cut-off**, or its variation.

7 Tip Toe II 5.7 ★

Babies R Us and **Invisible Wall** both finish at the left end of a long, conspicuous diagonal crack. **Tip Toe** begins at a ramp leading to the right side of this crack. Scramble up right from the right edge of Mills Glacier along a rising ledge system (some 4th class) for 300 feet to the base of the ramp. 1. Take the left-leaning ramp to its top, 5.7, and belay beneath a classic open book (the second pitch of **Red Wall**) on a good ledge. 2. Traverse the ledge left and step down to navigate an overhang (hand traverse beneath it). Climb a short slab, then delicately move around a corner. Drop down again beneath another overhang, and hand traverse to a good ledge. 3. Step down off the left end of the ledge, then go back up to another. Several short cracks and pillars climb to the right end of an easy ramp (5.7); follow this left (overlapping **Royal Flush**) to a convenient belay. 4. Traverse to the left end of the ramp and set the belay below two wide cracks. 5. Climb the right crack for 25 feet, then take the left crack to Broadway, 5.7. FA: Cecil Oulette and Dick Woodford, 1956. **Variation: Big Toe** (5.9, FA: Harvey Carter and John Auld, 1959)

The incredible sixth pitch of *Royal Flush*, Chasm View Wall.

PHOTO: SCOTT AHLGREN

begins at a big flake on the approach ramp and climbs an easy pitch up left to a short, square headwall at the base of a sweeping dihedral. Surmount the headwall and take the dihedral until intersecting with the normal line near the end of its second pitch.

8 Red Wall III 5.10a ★★★

An overhang in the center of Chasm View Wall provides the crux pitch on this fine route. 1. Begin with the first pitch of **Tip Toe**, and belay below your choice for the second pitch. 2. The open book dihedral on the right is thin 5.10c and was the original line, while the next dihedral left is 5.8. After half a pitch on either option, move left on easy ground to a belay terrace beneath several flake systems. 3. Choose the left-hand of several steep flakes, then move left to a wide crack flush with the wall. Climb this (with bomber liebacks inside) to the top of a huge flake. 4. Climb a right-facing corner toward the left edge of the overhang in the center of the wall, the major feature on the route. Begin a rising traverse from one dihedral to another as the roof nears, then undercling the roof to a hanging belay at its right end, 5.10a. Bring plenty of runners for this sustained section. The traverse can be made forty feet below the roof, also 5.10a. 5. A long pitch ascends the corner system above the right end of the roof (5.9), ending at a dark band. 6. Traverse right on the band (5.7) — this is the last pitch of **Chasm View Cut-off**. FA: Layton Kor and Tex Bossier, with aid, 1963. Walter Fricke and Van Slyke climbed the line described above in 1969. **Variations:** A direct start climbs the right side of a pillar to a thin crack that ends on the first belay ledge, 5.11a. The original aid route on pitches three and four followed an upside-down staircase flake to the right, then slanted back left along a right-facing dihedral to meet the roof. This has now gone free at 5.11c, and was climbed by Topher Donahue and Kim Czismazia in 1995 (after doing the direct start); bring double #0.75 to #1.5 Friends. The steep flake line left of the staircase flake was nailed in 1968 by Mike Donahue (Topher's dad) and Kehmier; this variant joins the standard line at the end of pitch three, atop the big flake. From the top of the big flake, one can make a rising traverse left along right-facing features to reach the rightmost of three flakes. Follow this flake until reaching dark colored rock and the far right side of Broadway, then exit with **Chasm View Cut-off**, or descend left along Broadway. FA: John Allens and Mike Pennings, 1990s.

9 The Middle Path III 5.11b ★★

This interesting route finds a passageway between **Red Wall** and **Directissima**. Begin on the ramp start to **Tip Toe** and **Red Wall** below two right-facing flakes that merge together 40 feet above. 1. Climb the right flake with a dogleg jog (5.8 lieback), then angle left along the top of the flake to its left side. 2. Step right and ascend a short left-facing corner to an overlap (5.10a), traverse left along it, then go up a left-facing, 5.9 flake. 3. Hand traverse straight right on a bomber flake, 5.6, and belay on top of a prominent right-facing dihedral near **Directissima**. 4. Take a right-leaning, stepped flake to the third belay on **Directissima**, 5.11b. 5. Follow **Directissima**, 5.10a. FA: Chip and Monika Chace, 1996. **Variation:** A run out direct start climbs half way up the open book on **Red Wall**'s second pitch, then traverses right to the first belay of this route (5.10 R).

10 Directissima III 5.10a ★★★

Directissima takes the crack and corner system dropping straight down from the right end of the dark band mentioned in **Red Wall**. Approach as with that route (4th class), but continue along the rising ledges for another 150 feet to a U-shaped ledge. 1. Start with a slightly leaning pitch to the bottom of the system, 5.8 on the left or 5.9 on the right. 2. The main line follows a shallow corner to a belay below overhanging flakes (5.10c). Keep the grade at 5.10a by taking the flake out left, 5.9. 3. Big holds lead through the overhanging flakes (5.9), but the tight spot higher up holds the strenuous crux of the route (5.9+ OW). 4. Continue straight up, passing a roof (5.10a) and an often-wet jam crack (5.9). Rack to a #4 Camalot, with emphasis on big pieces. FA: Layton Kor and Bob LaGrange, 1960. FFA: Roger Briggs and Chris Reveley, 1974.

11 Indirectissima II 5.9 ★

Approach as for **Directissima**, then scramble to the right side of the highest ledge. 1. Climb the left side of a flake system for a half pitch, then hand traverse left to a ledge, 5.7. 2. Chimney behind an enormous flake and belay on its top, rewarding 5.2. Fricke called this the "most enjoyable chimney on the East Face (or in the whole Park, for that matter)." 3. The original line traversed twenty feet right (5.7) and nailed a corner (A2) to a wide spot. Step right at this point and face climb to a big ledge. The free version (FA: Larry Dalke and Cliff Jennings, 1967) jams an overhanging flake on the left (crux), then moves right to the big ledge. 4. An easy pitch angles right to the ridge. FA: Walter Fricke and Jock Glidden, 1967.

12 Van Diver's Fantasy I 5.6

This route climbs the extreme upper right edge of Chasm View Wall, finishing near the point where the rim begins to rise again. Start at **Indirectissima** and make a long, slowly rising traverse toward a prominent left-leaning slash, or climb directly to here from **Fifth Avenue**. The last pitch begins left of the slash at a flake which is four feet from the wall; climb more or less straight up to the rim, 5.6 FA: Brad Van Diver, 1948. **Variation: Fisherman's Fantasy** (also known as **Fisherman's Folly**) starts at the base of **Directissima** and makes the slowly rising traverse a bit lower than described above. It continues in this manner all the way to a small notch in the ridge (not the larger saddle of the next line).

13 Fifth Avenue 4th class

This unpleasant route begins at the base of the approach ramp for the previous routes and takes a lower ramp system up and right for several hundred feet before snaking up a gully to a prominent saddle in the Chasm View — Lady Washington ridge. It is reportedly loose, and not recommended.

The next two routes start from the right side of Broadway and climb only the upper portion of Chasm View Wall.

14 Hornbein Crack II 5.8

Hornbein Crack was an important development in high mountain free climbing at the time of its first ascent. It is rarely climbed today. The route starts at the right side of Broadway and climbs to a vertical offwidth crack in a big, left-facing corner that leads to Chasm View. Do two or three pitches of relatively easy rock, with some 5.8 at the end, to reach the base of the crack. Lieback for fifty feet (5.8, bring wide gear) to the lip. FA: Tom Hornbein led it in 1953 with Cary Huston, having top roped it twice previously. **Variation:** The thin crack ten feet right of the crux pitch was nailed in 1953 by Harvey Carter and Clifford Smith, A2.

15 Chasm View Cut-off I 5.7

This is another route that is rarely sought out as the sole objective of the day's climb. It is most often used as an exit from the right side of Broadway, or a finish to several routes on Chasm View Wall. Traverse Broadway to its far right side, and rope up when it seems prudent. Follow narrowing ledges formed by the juncture of the lighter colored rock of Chasm View Wall and the dark band above it, crossing over the top of **Red Wall**, until reaching a small overhang midway between **Red Wall** and **Directissima**. Move up and right around its right side, then angle right to the crest. FA: Bill Eubanks, Tom Hornbein, and Brad Van Diver, 1950. **Variation:** Traverse Broadway to a point directly below a square notch on the rim (**Royal Flush** finishes in this notch). Climb 5.6 rock to the base of a deep, curving chimney on the right (**Royal Flush** takes the more difficult left chimney), then follow the chimney to the right side of the notch (5.7). FA: This appears to be the line of ascent taken by Frank Carey and Jim Gregg in 1950 (**Chasm Chimney**), though it's possible it wasn't done until much later by Roger Briggs.

16 Rollyco Stair I 5.6 R

This is not on Chasm View Wall, but on the bench left of the base of the Camel gully. A deep snow ditch forms on the right side of lower Mills Glacier left of the Camel gully; start inside the ditch at the base of a small, overhanging dihedral. Climb through the dihedral and straight up a gray water streak to a stance at 130 feet. Continue straight up for another pitch to a narrow stance, then walk off left. FA: Pat Ament and Larry Dalke, 1964.

Upper East Face

The mostly broken terrain above Broadway but left of the Diamond goes by the generic label of Upper East Face, though this area is really comprised of two sections: the east side of the Beaver, bordered on the left by Zumie's Thumb and on the right by the Notch Couloir, and the small portion of the mountain between the Notch Couloir and the Diamond. Only this latter slope actually faces east — for the most part, the East Face of Longs Peak faces northeast.

Approach: The climbs on the Upper East Face are most often approached with Lambs Slide and a traverse of Broadway, though some are commonly linked with a route on the Lower East Face.

Descent: For those climbs ending on the Beaver, descend to the Loft and reverse the Ramp (see introductory material on the Southeast Ridge, pages 31-32), or continue along the southeast ridge. The descent from the summit is described at the beginning of the Longs Peak section (page 28).

The routes are described left to right, beginning with Zumie's Thumb and ending at **The Window**, which runs along the left corner of the Diamond.

1 Zumie's Thumb III 5.9 ★

Ascend Lambs Slide beyond the cutoff to Broadway and scramble (first right, then left) onto the lower left corner of the buttress below the thumb. Look for several crack lines that converge together near the base of deep alcove, and belay from a flat rock at the base of the second crack from the left. 1. Take this crack for 125 feet to a sloping stance. 2. Follow a grassy gully to the alcove and the base of two chimneys, and climb the right wall of the left chimney to a big ledge. 3. Scramble up and right for 300 feet to a saddle. 4. Climb the right side of the buttress overhead and belay behind a flake. 5. Work up and left (passing a pointed flake) to a good ledge at the base of prominent crack, about 100 feet below the left side of the thumb. 6. Climb the crack for 25 feet, then switch left to a crack that leads to a terrace on the south side of the thumb. 7. Climb to a jam crack that leads to a sloping shelf (5.9), then take an easier crack to a fixed belay on the small summit. FA of entire buttress: Chuck Schobinger and John Amato, 1959 (with aid on the seventh pitch). Tom Hornbein, Dexter Brinker, and Harry Waldrup did the last pitch of this route in 1951. They hiked through the Loft and rappelled from the rim of the Beaver to the notch behind the thumb, leaving a fixed line. Traversing out to the terrace on the south face, they nailed the last pitch (employing a shoulder stand to reach the sloping shelf), and then rappelled to the notch and prussiked back to the rim. One could also perform a Tyrolean traverse to regain the rim if only the last pitch is climbed. If a rope has not been previously fixed to the rim, it is necessary to make three long rappels south from the notch, landing in the upper right arm of Lambs Slide. Descend this back to Chasm Lake, or descend just the upper arm and climb the last portion of Lambs to the Loft. One scheme that works well with a party of three: send two members up the long buttress while the third climbs to the Loft and rappels from the rim. The team can then rejoin at the terrace below the last pitch. **Variation:** Nail the northwest corner of the thumb on the last pitch, A2 (FA: Harvey Carter and Clifford Smith, 1953).

2 Zumie's Couloir (?)

The gully system immediately right of **Zumie's Thumb** may have been climbed at some point, but if so, its ascent is shrouded in mystery. Walter Fricke writes: "Paul Nesbit [in his Longs Peak guide] shows a dotted line running up this on the photograph of the East Face in his book, but is now unsure why he did so." Godfrey and Chelton's book shows a photo of Ernie Field, Warren Gorrell, Baker Armstrong and an unknown climber, with the caption, "...after an ascent of Zumies Chimney in 1937." Whether the chimney and the couloir are one in the same is not known.

3 4 Pitches, 24 Hours II 5.10a

The only information I have on this route is that it climbs the wall half way between **Zumie's Thumb** and **Eighth Route** for four pitches, with a crux fist crack in a dihedral on the second pitch, and nice position above the Lower East Face. Perhaps it begins with the pretty formation similar in shape to Teeter Totter Pillar (then again, perhaps not). FA: Matt Hobbs and Follari, 1998.

B-15 Eighth Route II 5.6

This route is described in the ice climbing section. As a summer route (5.6), it is somewhat unappealing, climbing a wet and grassy gully in its lower portion.

4 Joe's Solo II 5.6 (?)

This ancient passage is also shrouded in mystery. It begins with the right side of the gully just left of the next route, and climbs easily for 400 feet to a bowl of broken rock. At this point one can traverse left into **Eighth Route** and follow that, but Joe Stettner believes he climbed the difficult headwall above, angling right to the edge of the buttress, then cutting back left at a dark band of rock (with rock climbing as hard as 5.7 or 5.8). Given that he was unroped and alone, later climbers have questioned this line. FA: Joe Stettner, 1936.

5 Teeter Totter Pillar III 5.8 ★

Begin at the base of a striking crack on the east side of the 350 foot pillar just left of Notch Couloir. 1 and 2. Climb the crack for two pitches (both 5.8), stepping right around a corner into a short dihedral near the end of the second lead. 3. Face climb into a left-facing dihedral on the right side (north face) of the pillar, and belay part way up it. 4. Complete the dihedral (5.7) and traverse a ledge at its top to the right, then climb easily into the notch behind the pillar. From here the route finding becomes difficult. Take a chance with the outside arete of the buttress above, or traverse left on broken rock into **Eighth Route**, and finish on that. FA: Michael Covington and Duncan Ferguson, 1977. **Variation:** A direct finish by Gary Neptune and party is said to climb the north wall of the upper buttress via steep crack systems (5.10?).

B-16 Notch Couloir II AI 2+ M3-

See ice climbing section.

The remaining routes on the Upper East Face begin right of **Notch Couloir**. The first of these is upper **Kiener's Route**, described as a complete line in the Lower East Face section (see page 43).

6 Broadway Cut-off II 5.5

A variation to upper **Kiener's Route**. Begin about 200 feet right of the Notch Couloir below a pronounced chimney. Traverse up and left on easy ramps and ledges to the base of a chimney with chockstone. Ascend the chimney and crank over the chockstone (crux), then join **Kiener's**. It's possible the original line continued left beneath the chimney to join **Kiener's** at a lower point. FA: Ernie Field and Warren Gorrell, 1936.

B-18 Schobinger's Cracks II 5.8

This has been done as a challenging mixed climb in the winter (M6), though it was done first in 1958 by Chuck Schobinger and John Amato (5.6 A1, now free at 5.8, and often wet). See the ice climbing section for a description of the line.

B-19 The Window III 5.7 ★

This, too, was first done as a summer rock climb, though even in summer it is common to find ice on the route. See ice climbing section.

The Diamond

The Diamond is the mother lode of high altitude rock climbing in RMNP. Beginning at Broadway (elevation 13,100 feet), the wall rises for nearly 1,000 vertical feet to meet the upper slopes of Longs. **D-1**, the first route established on the Diamond, splits the wall into halves. The left half is characterized by excellent rock and long crack systems, almost all of which have now gone free, while the right half is the aid climber's realm. As with the left side, it is lined with cracks, but these are steeper and generally poorer in quality.

Several landmarks on the wall are helpful in locating various routes. A 200 foot pillar (D-1 pillar) sits above and left of **North Chimney**. The Green Pillar, Black Flake, and North Pillar are similar formations standing in succession right of **North Chimney**. The Obelisk is a slender, 300 foot, left-facing column on the left edge of the Diamond in the middle of the wall; directly below this is the Mitten, a 100 foot flake with a thumb on its right side. Table Ledge Crack extends across the entire upper portion of the Diamond, becoming a ledge on the left side. Many of the free routes escape left along this, joining upper **Kiener's** and following that route. The Yellow Wall Bivy Ledge is situated on top (and left) of the prominent **Casual Route** corners, one pitch below Table Ledge Crack. The Ramp is an unmistakable sloping ledge in the center of the Diamond.

The Diamond faces northeast, and the sun leaves the face by noon during the summer, accompanied by a drastic drop in (apparent) temperature. Storm gear is a must for any route as the weather can change quickly and unexpectedly.

Routes are described from left to right. As with other portions of this book, no stars are assigned to the aid lines. Most of these routes were first put up on aid, and as such, they are grade V climbs. These days, however, almost all of the free climbs are done in a day, and the grades used below reflect this. The grade of "IV+" indicates a good, long day, and "V-" indicates a slow party may not finish in a day. Finally, be aware that free climbing at altitude is difficult for everyone, and especially so for those who aren't acclimated. Cold, wet rock only makes it worse, and 5.10 can end up feeling like solid 5.11.

Approach: The standard approach to the Diamond begins with a hike to and around Chasm Lake, then up to Mills Glacier. From here, most climbers use **North Chimney** (see Lower East Face) to access the base of the wall. Another option hikes through the Boulderfield and up to Chasm View, where one can bivouac (with permit). Rappel three times (double ropes) to reach the right end of Broadway. Traversing Broadway to the base of the various routes is usually a simple matter in summer. However, the exposed step across **North Chimney** (low 5th class) has claimed two lives; neither of the victims was roped.

Descent: The preferred method of descent for those reaching the summit is by way of the North Face (see **The Cables**, page 239). One can bypass the summit in stormy weather (or if the hour is late) simply by traversing over the top of the Diamond to the North Face. Parties that have retreated to Broadway can complete the descent to Mills Glacier by utilizing new bolt anchors established near **Crack**

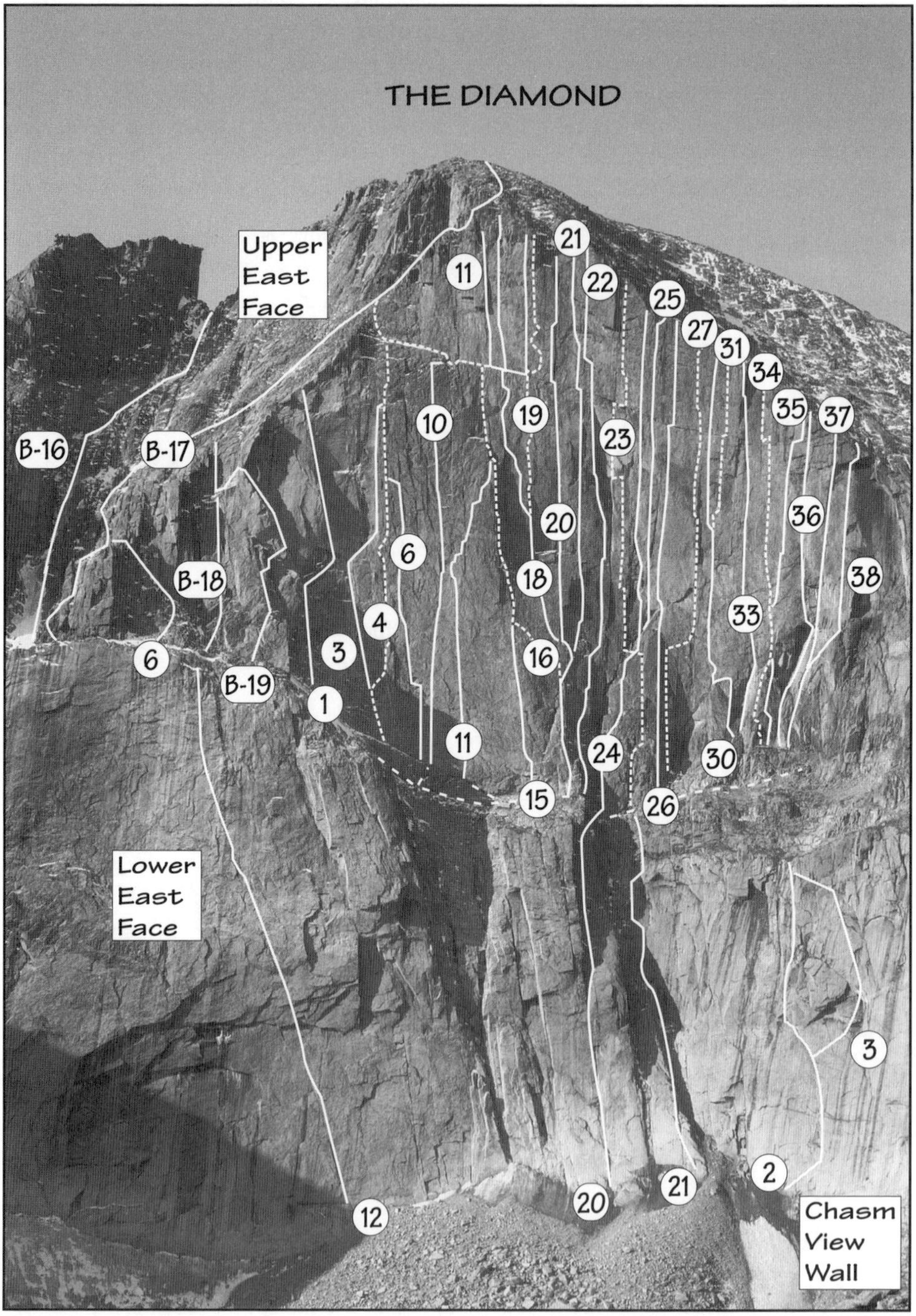
THE DIAMOND
Upper East Face
Lower East Face
Chasm View Wall
B-16
B-17
B-18
B-19
1
2
3
4
6
10
11
12
15
16
18
19
20
21
22
23
24
25
26
27
30
31
33
34
35
36
37
38

of Delight (see Lower East Face, page 53). Carefully scramble down from the base of **Casual Route** to the first of four double-bolt anchors on the wall, and rappel 100 feet to a ledge. Walk 20 feet north, and rappel straight down three more times. Chains should be installed on the three lower stations to avoid wear on the bolt hangers.

There is also a new rappel route down the left side of the Diamond, but climbers should think twice before using it, for several reasons. First, if you've made it to Table Ledge (the beginning of the rappels), it is a simple matter to continue to the summit and descend in the traditional manner. The rappels aren't particularly easy to follow, and experienced climbers who have several Diamond ascents to their credit have reported difficulty in spotting the anchors — first-timers can expect some excitement. Lastly, the rappel route invites people to climb light, and it is only a matter of time before a big storm finds four or five parties strung out in a traffic jam, desperate to get back to gear left on Broadway — this is a bad accident just waiting for the opportunity to happen.

It takes close to an hour for a party of two to make all of the rappels, provided nothing goes amiss and other parties aren't below (add more time if you're unfamiliar with this part of the wall as some of the hangers are of the camouflaged variety). Begin with a short rappel from a bolt and two pitons on Table Ledge to a two-bolt, two-pin and chain anchor on Almost Table Ledge (where **D-7** tops out). Rappel 150 feet and a shade left to two bolts, a wire, and chains in a dihedral on **Soma** (small stance on the left). Rappel 130 feet, angling right (facing in) to two bolts and chains one pitch lower on **Soma**. Now go 140 feet and left to two fat-hangered bolts (chains should be added to preserve the hangers) at a stance just above the traverse on **Hidden Diamond**, then straight down 150 feet to two fat bolts (chains needed) on the first belay of **Curving Vine**. A final rappel goes to Broadway, though it is 190 feet to walking territory — stop at the base of **Curving Vine** for standard length ropes, and down climb the 4th class channel described in **D-7**. Traverse north once on Broadway and rappel **Crack of Delight** (described above, another 30 minutes or more). Note that there are also some fixed anchors and chains on the lower portion of **D-7** that may be of use if the rappel route is crowded.

Consider the following before making the decision to leave gear on Broadway, which in turn locks you into a rappel down the Diamond (or Chasm View) to retrieve gear: A competent party on Table Ledge can scramble to the summit, enjoy the view, and descend the North Face to the Camel gully in an hour and a half, encountering none of the dangers of rappelling down vertical walls, and along terrain which is much easier to negotiate in the face of a storm.

1 Hypotenuse IV 5.6 A3

Start in a north-facing dihedral on the left side of the Diamond; this is the beginning of the direct variation to **The Window** (see ice climbing section, page 239). Climb the Window direct for a long pitch (5.7), then traverse right for 70 feet in dark rock (low 5th class) to the base of the Hypotenuse, an obvious, leaning, right-facing dihedral 100 feet right of the Window. Aid thin cracks on the mossy left

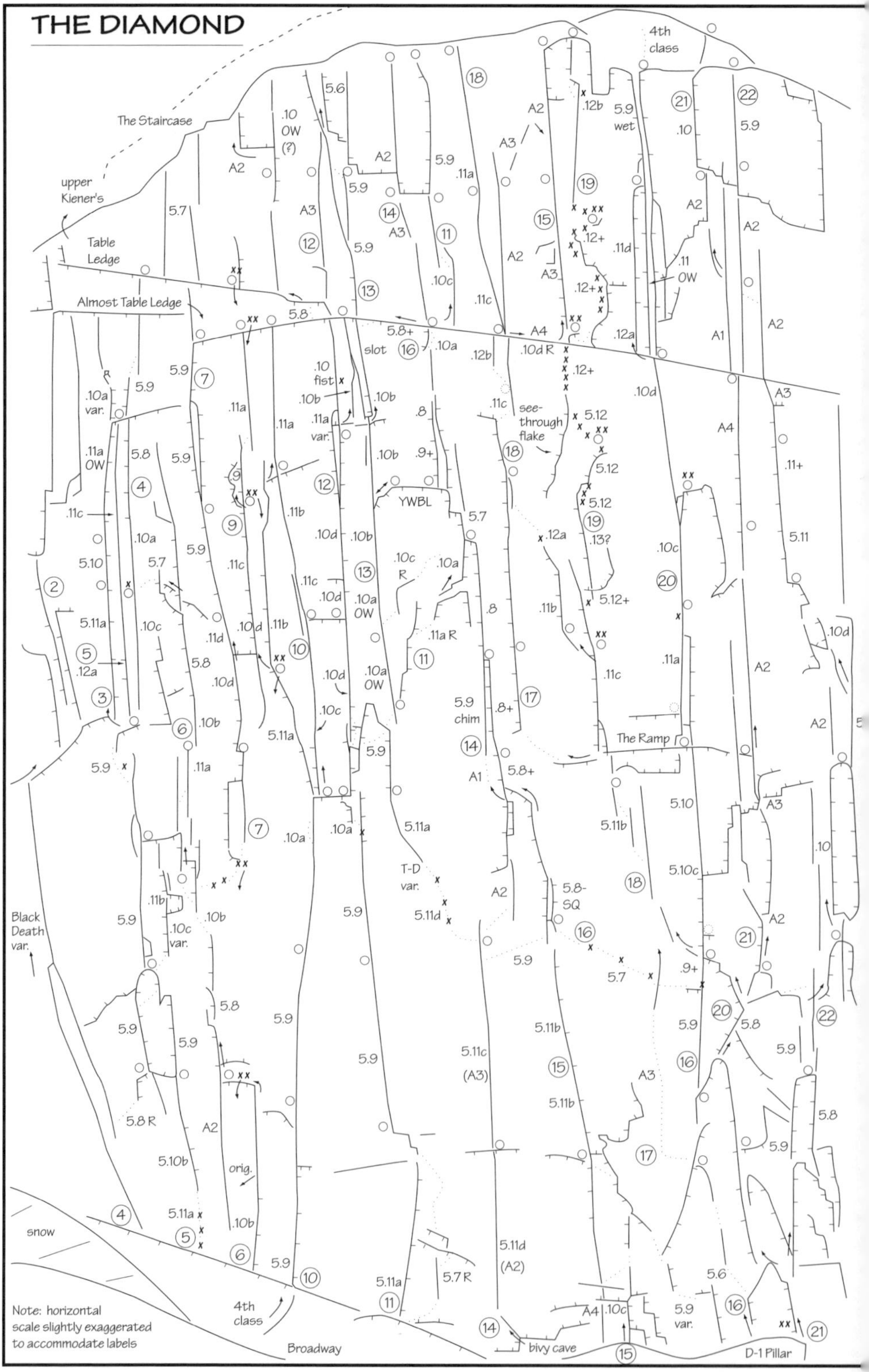
THE DIAMOND
The Staircase
upper Kiener's
Table Ledge
Almost Table Ledge
4th class
slot
fist
see-through flake
YWBL
The Ramp
T-D var.
Black Death var.
chim
orig.
snow
4th class
Broadway
bivy cave
D-1 Pillar
Note: horizontal scale slightly exaggerated to accommodate labels

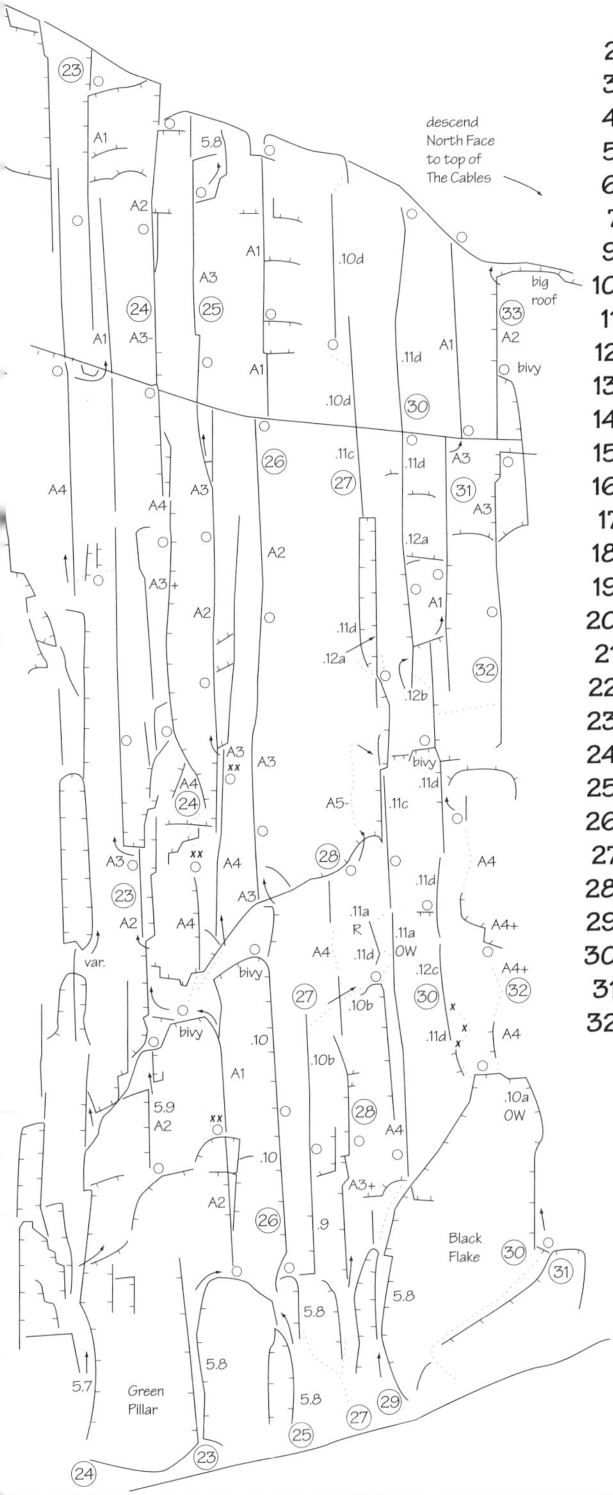

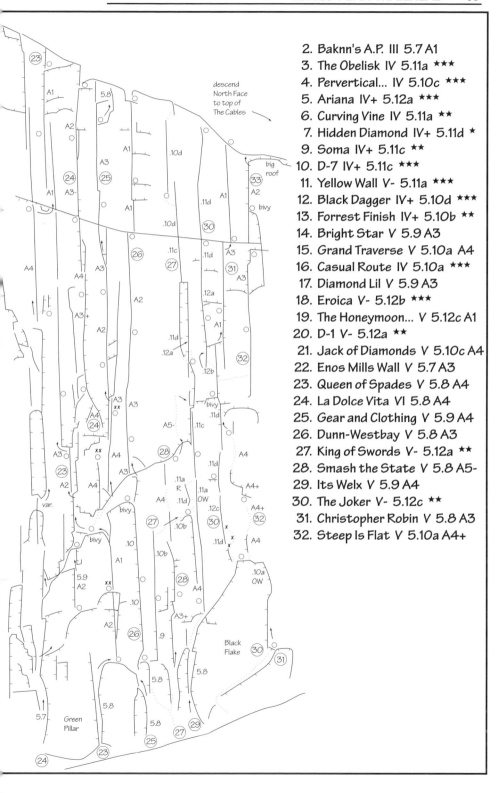

2. Baknn's A.P. III 5.7 A1
3. The Obelisk IV 5.11a ★★★
4. Pervertical... IV 5.10c ★★★
5. Ariana IV+ 5.12a ★★★
6. Curving Vine IV 5.11a ★★
7. Hidden Diamond IV+ 5.11d ★
9. Soma IV+ 5.11c ★★
10. D-7 IV+ 5.11c ★★★
11. Yellow Wall V- 5.11a ★★★
12. Black Dagger IV+ 5.10d ★★★
13. Forrest Finish IV+ 5.10b ★★
14. Bright Star V 5.9 A3
15. Grand Traverse V 5.10a A4
16. Casual Route IV 5.10a ★★★
17. Diamond Lil V 5.9 A3
18. Eroica V- 5.12b ★★★
19. The Honeymoon... V 5.12c A1
20. D-1 V- 5.12a ★★
21. Jack of Diamonds V 5.10c A4
22. Enos Mills Wall V 5.7 A3
23. Queen of Spades V 5.8 A4
24. La Dolce Vita VI 5.8 A4
25. Gear and Clothing V 5.9 A4
26. Dunn-Westbay V 5.8 A3
27. King of Swords V- 5.12a ★★
28. Smash the State V 5.8 A5-
29. Its Welx V 5.9 A4
30. The Joker V- 5.12c ★★
31. Christopher Robin V 5.8 A3
32. Steep Is Flat V 5.10a A4+

THE DIAMOND

30. The Joker V- 5.12c ★★
31. Christopher Robin V 5.8 A3
32. Steep Is Flat V 5.10a A4+
33. Waterhole #3 V 5.8 A3
34. Toiling Midgets VI 5.9 A3+
35. Diamond Star Halo V 5.8 A4

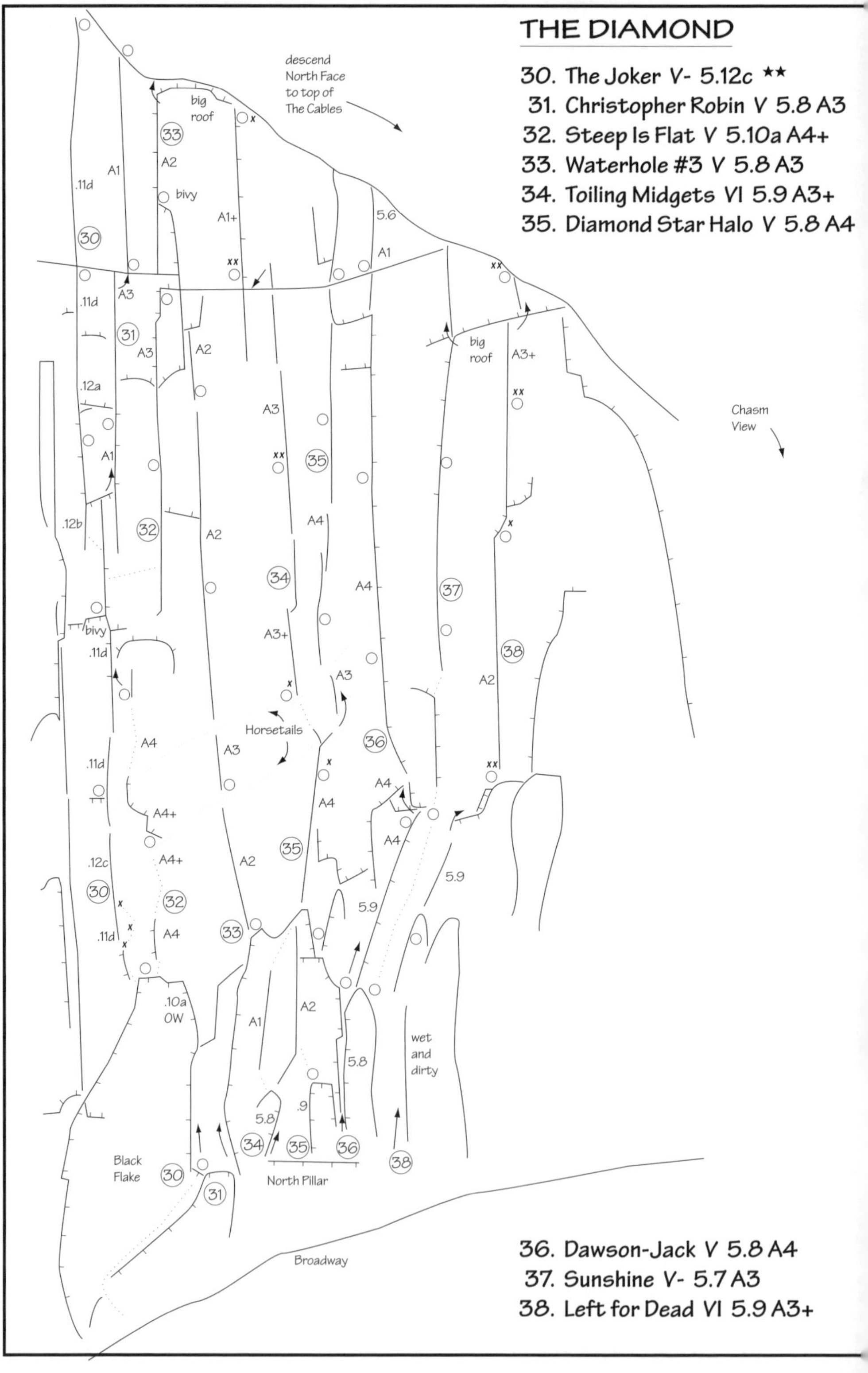

36. Dawson-Jack V 5.8 A4
37. Sunshine V- 5.7 A3
38. Left for Dead VI 5.9 A3+

Several parties basking in the sunlight on the Diamond (climbers are visible on *Pervertical Sanctuary*, *D-7*, and *Yellow Wall*).

THE DIAMOND
11
16
18
33
30
4
6
10
11
16
23
26
27
Broadway

wall of the dihedral for two pitches, belaying at old bolts. A final pitch in the dihedral (A3) leads to a small ledge, after which one can climb up and left on easy ground to join upper **Kiener's**. FA: George Hurley and John Hough, 1966.

2 Baknn's A.P. III 5.7 A1

This route climbs the dirty crack system (which one?) between **Hypotenuse** and **The Obelisk**. Approach as with **Hypotenuse**, but traverse right to the end of the dark rock and the beginning of the crack (5.7). Follow the crack for several pitches with a few sections of aid to the top of the wall, and join upper **Kiener's**. FA: J. Tryda and S. McCallister, 1977.

The next twelve routes tackle the Yellow Wall, a fantastic golden shield of excellent rock on the left half of the Diamond. There are not enough superlatives to describe the climbing found here, and all of these routes could be considered three stars. The climbs begin from a ledge system that extends from a snow patch on the left to the Broadway bivy cave (a small alcove a few paces left of the D-1 pillar). A 4th class channel below the middle of the ledge allows access to the first several climbs. Most of the routes end at Table Ledge crack, and all of them can be cut short here. Traverse this crack left to a nice ledge, and angle up left to escape its left side. This deposits parties on upper **Kiener's**, which is followed (3rd class) to the summit area.

3 The Obelisk IV 5.11a ***

The Obelisk is the distinct column on the upper left side of the Diamond; this route climbs its long left-facing dihedral. 1-3. Do the first three leads of **Pervertical Sanctuary** and move left to the base of the dihedral. The final moves into the dihedral may be tricky and poorly protected (5.11 R?). See note below. 4. Jam double hand cracks in the corner for 100 feet, incredible 5.11a (extra #2.5 and #3 Friends are handy). 5. Stem the corner (5.10) to a stance with a bolt. This is a short pitch and can be combined with the 6th lead. 6. Fight up a classic offwidth in the dihedral (5.11a) and belay on top of the Obelisk column. 7. A thin, 5.9 corner leads off the right end of the column. Step right after 40 feet to a crack and finish on easier ground to Table Ledge. Rack: Include a few big pieces (#4.5 Camalot is key) for the sixth pitch. A thin crack within the offwidth provides the other pro for this lead. FA: George Hurley and Phil Fowler, 1974. FFA: Chris Reveley and partner, 1979. **Variations: Black Death** (5.9, some dirty rock) climbs the double crack system that defines the beginning of **Pervertical Sanctuary** for two long pitches to a ramp system which leads to the base of the Obelisk column. This ramp system can be reached more easily (though not any more aesthetically) by climbing the direct start to **The Window** (5.7), and then traversing below **Hypotenuse** (5.5). Note: A few climbers have reported that moving left from **Pervertical Sanctuary** into the **Obelisk** is scary 5.11 when beginning from the third belay. In the previous edition of this guide, I advised climbers to do just that based on a climb I did with my brother John in 1987. We approached **Pervertical** from **The Window**, and didn't have a difficult time completing the traverse in the reverse direction. We must have done the traverse lower down — be advised to look for an inobvious (though only 5.9?) traverse from the upper portion of the third lead, or just do one of the variations.

4 Pervertical Sanctuary IV 5.10c ★★★

This route climbs the right side of the Obelisk column with a superb jam crack. Begin near a snow patch under the Obelisk at a double crack system angling up and left. This is the line of **Black Death** (see above) 1. Climb the cracks for forty feet, then angle right to the base of the Mitten formation via broken, sparsely protected rock. Belay here or jam up its left side (5.9) to the ledge on top (185 feet). 2. Go straight up a blocky dihedral system to a nice ledge on the right, 5.9. 3. Continue with the system to a small roof. Work up left around the bulge (5.9, manky bolt) then ascend a flake to the right, belaying on its top. This lead can be combined with the previous using a 200 foot rope. 4. Take on the vertical crack on the right side of the Obelisk with strenuous, 5.10c finger and hand jams. Belay at a stance out left (bolt) near a loose block in the crack. 5. Continue up the widening crack to the top of the Obelisk, 5.10a fists. 6. Do the last pitch of **The Obelisk**, 5.9, or chose **Left Exit** (see **Ariana**) to avoid other parties. Rack up to a #4 Camalot, with doubles from #1.5 Friend on up. Note: **Pervertical Sanctuary** actually has another 800 feet of climbing on the Lower East Face that seems to have been forgotten. The first ascent party nailed a line between **Gray Pillar** and **Shining Slab** (beginning with **Shining Slab**) to reach Broadway, then climbed the better known second half. Done this way, it is a grade VI route. FA: Ron Olevsky and Bob Dodds, 1975. FFA: Bruce Adams and Tobin Sorenson, 1975.

5 Ariana IV+ 5.12a ★★★

Ariana ascends the awesome thin crack splitting the Obelisk column. Begin by climbing the 4th class passage below **D-7** and walk left on the grassy ledge to three old bolts. 1. Face climb past the bolts (5.11a, run out until the bolts get replaced) and enter a thin corner which leads to the thumb of the Mitten, 5.10b. 2 and 3. Go to the top of the Mitten and follow **Pervertical Sanctuary** for two leads. 4. Stem left into a thin crack, lieback past the crux section, and belay midway up the Obelisk at a stance. While no move is 5.12, the sustained nature of the pitch warrants a 5.12a rating. 5. Follow the crack to the top of the column, strenuous 5.11c. 6. Finish on **The Obelisk**. Bring plenty of stoppers. FA: George Hurley and R. Bliss, 1975. FFA: Roger and Bill Briggs, 1985. **Variation 1:** From the top of the Mitten, one can work right into a right-facing dihedral. Climb this (5.10c) to a small overhang, pass it on the left, and follow a poorly protected white corner system to the nice ledge at the end of **Pervertical**'s second pitch, 5.11b R. There's a good nut at the crux, but the upper half of this pitch is run out. One could avoid the run out by joining **Curving Vine** above the crux. **Variation 2 (Left Exit,** 5.10a): Step left from the belay on top of the Obelisk (nice exposure) and stem a short, steep dihedral (5.10a) to a section of flakes. Above these, the angle eases, and mellow cracks lead to Table Ledge. Four routes converge at the top of the Obelisk Column, and this is a good option when the area is crowded. Roger Briggs and Bernard Gillett first climbed both of these variations in 1999.

6 Curving Vine IV 5.11a ★★

The original **Curving Vine** contained two pendulums for which the route was named. The free version is described. Start twenty feet left of **D-7** at a thin corner. 1. Climb the corner (5.10b) past a good ledge (**D Minor 7** belay) to a sloping ledge on the left with two fat bolts (part of the Diamond rappel route). 2. Follow the right-facing dihedral off the left end of the ledge, step left at its end to a thinner right-facing dihedral and belay below a flake (5.10b). 3. Go up a short flake, then link together several thin cracks (5.11a) in a lead that angles right to the base of another right-facing corner. Stop short of the corner at a small foot stance. 4. Climb to the corner (5.10b), then follow it to a break half way up (5.8). Hand traverse left along 5.7 flakes to the fourth belay on **Pervertical Sanctuary**, and join that route. Carry a standard rack plus #3 Friend — #4 Camalot for the fifth pitch of **Pervertical**. FA: Michael Covington and Pete Robinson, 1966. FA of free version: Dan Hare and Chris Reveley, 1978.

7 Hidden Diamond IV+ 5.11d ★

Start with the first two pitches of **Curving Vine**. 3. Work up a short corner just right of **Curving Vine**, then traverse right past two pitons (5.10) to gain a crack. Follow the crack past the right end of a small roof and belay. 4. Climb a 5.7 chimney that narrows to fists (5.10d), and work a thin seam in a corner past a couple fixed pins (crux, some marginal pro) to a stance on the left. Bring a good selection of RPs. 5-7. Take a right-facing dihedral to a loose 5.9 chimney, and continue the line (5.9) all the way to Table Ledge. FA: Ed Webster and Robert Anderson, 1985. FFA: Webster and Pete Athans, 1985.

8 D Minor 7 V 5.7 A3 (or 5.11d)

This line is one of the less frequented climbs on the Diamond. All of its pitches have been climbed as part of more recent free routes (**Curving Vine**, **D-7**, **Hidden Diamond**, and **Soma**), but the route is rarely climbed in its original form. Start up **Curving Vine**, then move into **D-7**. Step left when **D-7** gets wide (on its third pitch) and ascend a parallel flake system, which soon arcs left to the base of the chimney on **Hidden Diamond**. Follow that route past its crux, then step right into **Soma**. FA: Bob Bradley and Rick Petrillo, 1967.

9 Soma IV+ 5.11c ★★

This free line connects **D-7** to the last pitch of **D Minor 7**, with one new pitch. Climb the first three pitches of **D-7**, and one pitch of its variation (1) to a bolt belay in a right-facing dihedral. The bolts are just right of a square-edged overhang, a small though conspicuous feature. 5. Traverse eight feet left to the overhang (5.10 face), and climb the hanging dihedral above its right edge (5.10d). The dihedral fades into a flower-filled thin crack — face climb along the flowers (5.11c, a little run out), and follow an emerging dihedral to two bolts and a fixed nut. 6. Move left to a stance, and take a flake that arcs back into the main line. Ascend this for ten feet, then shift right to another crack and jam to Almost Table Ledge, 5.11a. Belay at a four-point fixed anchor on the Diamond rappel route. Bring a full rack, RPs to a #4 Camalot, and climb fast to avoid conflict with parties using the rappel route. FFA: Roger Briggs and Michael Gilbert, 1994.

10 D-7 IV+ 5.11c ★★★

One of the best free climbs on the Diamond, **D-7** is also an excellent clean aid route (mostly A1, with an occasional A2 placement — load up on TCUs when aiding). Start 150 left of the bivy cave at a short channel below a thin, left-facing dihedral. Go up the channel (4th class) to reach the grassy ledge thirty feet above Broadway. 1. Climb the dihedral for half a pitch to a good ledge (5.9) on the right. Continue the lead to a ledge on the left. 2. Climb straight up steep cracks and corners for a long pitch, 5.9. 3. Ascend to a wide section (5.10a, often wet), and face climb along it on the left (5.10a). Climb to a long ledge that stretches right to **Yellow Wall**, and set a hanging belay on its left side. 4. Traverse five feet right on the ledge to a thin right-facing corner (see variation below). Climb this to a stance below two leaning cracks, 5.10. 5. The twin cracks are the crux of the route, but another section of 5.11 must be dealt with before finding a belay stance. 6. Fire straight up a thin crack (5.11a), pass a wide stretch, and follow easier rock to Almost Table Ledge. 7. Go to Table Ledge, 5.8 on the right. 8. Climb either of two 5.7 cracks near the right side of Table Ledge and join **Kiener's**. Rack up to a #4 Friend, with extra stoppers. Many fixed pins are still in place, especially on the lower pitches. FA: Wayne Goss, Larry Dalke and George Hurley, 1966. FFA: John Bachar and Richard Harrison, 1977, though several previous teams had free climbed almost the entire route much earlier (Duncan Ferguson and Bill Putnam in 1972, Roger Briggs and Scott Stewart in 1973, Briggs and Chris Reveley in 1974, and Ferguson, Kevin Donald and Jim Logan in 1974, all contributed. Briggs recalls he may have also made an attempt with Ferguson). **Variation 1:** A common error on this route ascends the inviting right-facing dihedral leading off the left side of the third pitch belay ledge. This was not the original line, but it makes for an easier ascent: 4a. Climb the right-facing dihedral and work left to a short, leaning corner and a double bolt belay, 5.11a. 5a. Continue straight up a thin dihedral (5.11b). Step right when the dihedral fades and join the original line 30 feet below its fifth belay. **Variation 2** (this is sometimes called **Komito Freeway**): In 1975, Wayne Goss and Jim Logan made the first free ascent of the Diamond by linking the first three pitches of **D-7** to **Forrest Finish**, apparently ending with **Black Dagger**'s sixth pitch. This is a great way to climb the Diamond at 5.10, and one can finish with the crux lead on **Casual Route** to avoid the more difficult original line. **Variation 3: Over Thirty Hang** (FA: George Hurley and Jonathan Hough, 1967, 5.7 A2, free at 5.10?) climbs the obvious dihedral-to-overhang line right of the 5.7 cracks on the last pitch.

11 Yellow Wall V- 5.11a ★★★

Yellow Wall was the second ascent of the Diamond. It features excellent rock, varied route finding, and an interesting history. It is the quintessential Diamond climb. Scramble left from the bivy cave along the grassy ledge above Broadway to the first left-facing corner. 1. The original route went up the corner that goes free at 5.11 (RPs). A much easier start heads right on flakes, and rejoins the line above the corner (5.7, some run outs). Belay at stance after 130 feet. 2. Angle left in a fine crack system, 5.9. 3. Stay with the slightly leaning system (often wet near its top) to the long belay ledge of **D-7**'s third pitch. Stem left at a fixed pin to a flake near the end of the lead (5.10a, harder for short people). 4. Go up and right along short corners and ledges, passing beneath **Black Dagger** and **Forrest Finish**, and belay at the base of a red dihedral that rises to the right (the stance is immediately right of **Forrest Finish**). 5. Follow the dihedral to a slanting ledge on the right, then make an exciting traverse right to a short thin corner. Lieback the corner, then move up and right to the alcove belay on **Casual Route**. This section is sparsely protected and continuously difficult (5.11a R). Head to Yellow Wall Bivy Ledge (40 feet) if you have enough rope left. 6. Lead up thin corners off the right end of the bivy ledge (5.9+) to a chimney. Step left at the top of the chimney and go straight up (5.10a) to Table Ledge crack. 7. Hand traverse 15 feet right, and follow cracks and corners slightly left to the base of a big right facing dihedral (5.10c, difficult protection, major exposure). 8. Climb the dihedral, 5.9. Rack from RPs to a #3.5 Friend. FA: Layton Kor and Charlie Roskosz, 1962. FFA: Roger Briggs and Rob Candelaria, 1976, by way of **Forrest Finish**. Briggs also did the FFA of the original first pitch later that summer from a base camp on Broadway while filming *Outside the Arena*. FFA of original A4 traverse (pitch five): Charlie Fowler and Dan Stone, 1978. **Variation:** An easier version of the crux traverse beginning from **Forrest Finish** is marked on the topo (5.10c, also run out, first done on aid by Erb and Summers, 1967). This scary lead is frequently avoided by doing **Forrest Finish** all the way to Yellow Wall Bivy Ledge.

12 Black Dagger IV+ 5.10d ***

This route is named for and climbs through the deep, dagger-shaped chimney fifty feet left of the Yellow Wall Bivy Ledge. Climb three pitches of **Yellow Wall** (or **D-7** if desired) to the right side of the long ledge. 4. Go straight up to a wide slot, then face climb right around the slot. Move left into the dihedral and crack system dropping from the dagger. Follow it to a ledge on the left, 5.10d. 5. Continue up the crack (more 5.10d, sometimes wet) and enter the chimney. Belay high in the chimney on the right. 6. Go right from the top of the chimney, avoiding a wide crack with a bolt (which has gone free at beautiful 5.10 fist). Take the next crack, just left of **Forrest Finish**, and jam to Table Ledge, 5.10b. It is also possible to exit the chimney on the left (5.11a), and continue with the wide crack. 7. Climb to Table Ledge and exit left, or follow the last two pitches of **Forrest Finish**. FA: Wayne Goss and Roger Dalke, 1967. FFA: Duncan Ferguson and Lisa Schassberger climbed it in 1980, as did Jeff Achey and Leonard Coyne. **Variation:** The original line above Table Ledge nailed a thin crack (A3) just left of **Forrest Finish**, rejoining it for the last half of its last pitch.

13 Forrest Finish IV+ 5.10b **

As with **Black Dagger**, **Forrest Finish** begins on **Yellow Wall** but finishes straight up. It was the first route on the Diamond that was soloed (with a rope). Do three pitches of **Yellow Wall**. 4. Continue with **Yellow Wall** to its fourth pitch belay, but keep going up the wide crack at the end of the traverse, and struggle past an offwidth section (5.10a). Arrange a belay on the left above a vegetated alcove. 5. Fight past another wide section (5.10a), then jam a clean, strenuous hand and fist crack. Belay in the crack, or better yet, hand traverse right (5.7) to the left edge of Yellow Wall Bivy Ledge. 6. Traverse back left and continue the crack system through a dark plaque of rock, staying with the right-hand of two cracks to a small shelf, 5.10b. The original aid route stepped left here and nailed a thin crack (which has probably been climbed free). Instead, go straight up a committing 5.10 lieback, and then squeeze up a narrow slot to Table Ledge. 7 and 8. Stay with the same line for a pitch, dirty 5.9. Switch left to a deep groove (5.9), and take it to the top, 5.6. These last two pitches are seldom climbed. Rack to a #4 Camalot, with several hand and fist sized cams. FA: Bill Forrest, 1970. FFA: Wayne Goss and Jim Logan, beginning on **D-7** (see above) did the first free ascent of the Diamond via this route, though they apparently stepped left into **Black Dagger** at the top.

14 Bright Star V 5.9 A3 (or 5.11d R ★)

The first four pitches of **Bright Star** have gone free (5.11d R). As an aid line, it is quite enjoyable, nailing thin cracks on clean rock. Start at the left side of the bivy cave. 1. Aid out the left side of the cave to reach a thin crack that ends at a grassy ledge (A2 or 5.11d R). 2. A similar lead nails the thin crack above with some free climbing to a flake belay on the right (5.9 A3 or 5.11 R). From here it is possible to traverse right along flakes (5.9) to reach **Casual Route**. 3. Angle slightly right to a hanging, right-facing corner (aid or 5.11). 4. Move left from the top of the corner and climb to a perch below a chimney. The free version steps into **Casual Route** at the top of the corner. 5. Ascend the chimney (5.9 A1) to a stance on **Casual Route**. 6 and 7. Follow that line to Table Ledge crack. 8. Go straight up in a discontinuous system that bends left (A3) to a roof. Move left around the roof to a belay in a left-facing corner. 9. Aid over another overhang and follow an exposed crack for a long pitch, 5.8 A2. A short pitch of 4th class ends the climb. FA: Ed Webster, 1984. FFA: Charlie Fowler and Scott Cosgrove, to Table Ledge, 1987. **Tague-Donahue Variation**: Traverse left from second belay to several bolts. Follow these (5.11d) to a pretty finger crack (5.11a) that leads to the right side of a pillar on **Yellow Wall** (see topo).

15 Grand Traverse V 5.10a A4 (or 5.11+ ★)

This old route has been free climbed over the span of several years, though its final two pitches have never been led. Its major feature (the huge right-facing corner in the center of the wall) is now part of the classic **Casual Route**. Start on the right side of the bivy cave at a roof-capped, left-facing dihedral. 1. Climb the dihedral and roof (5.10c with only adequate protection), then continue more easily to a stance at the base of a leaning, left-facing dihedral. The original aid line nailed a thin seam 10 feet left of the dihedral (A4), then traversed right above the roof. 2. Strenuous jams and stems lead up the dihedral (two sections of 5.11), joining **Casual Route** at its third belay. This is a fine pitch with bomber protection. 3-7. Follow **Casual Route** to Table Ledge crack. 8. Traverse the crack right for 90 feet (passing beneath **Diamond Lil/Eroica**), then move up right to a bolted stance at the base of a leaning, rotten crack system. The first half of this traverse is reasonable; the second half has been described as "Eiger Sanction 5.10d — downward lunges with no footholds and crumbly [hand]holds," poor protection included. This is the pitch for which the route was named, and was originally rated A4 (bring hooks). 9. Jam the rotten crack system for a rope length to a good ledge, 5.11+ TR (or A2+). The crux section is continuous and slightly overhanging, with questionable protection opportunities. 10. Continue in the same system with much better rock (5.10c hands and fist, top roped, or straightforward aid). FA: Pat Ament and Bob Boucher, 1964. The free climbing history is complex. Bernard and Robert Gillett free climbed the second pitch in 1992, gaining its base with a 5.9 variant on the right. In 1993, Bernard and John Gillett climbed the first pitch. Chris Reveley and Duncan Ferguson did the middle pitches in 1978 as part of **Casual Route**. Eric Doub, while working on his route **The Honeymoon Is Over**, free climbed the traverse pitch (1993), though Roger Briggs had done it from **Eroica** some years prior, and started up the next pitch but backed off when confronted with rotten rock. In 1994, Bernard Gillett and Shawn Preston rappelled from the top of the

Diamond and top roped the final two pitches. **Variation:** An aid variation connecting **Diamond Lil** (now **Eroica**) with the last pitch of **Grand Traverse** is marked on the topo. My brother John and I failed to traverse far enough on Table Ledge Crack, and started up **Diamond Lil**, but we continued straight up where that route goes left. Realizing our mistake, John nailed up and right on the next pitch to reach **Grand Traverse**, ending with a short pendulum off a hook.

16 Casual Route IV 5.10a ★★★

The **Casual Route** is the easiest and most popular route on the Diamond — expect company. Begin a few paces left of the fixed anchors on top of **North Chimney** at a short, left-facing corner. 1. Ascend the corner and wander up the middle of the D-1 pillar to a convenient belay (5.6). 2. Go up left to a tiny stance below a finger crack. Belay here to avoid getting stranded halfway across the notorious traverse pitch. These two pitches are often simul-climbed. Another option continues to a belay at the flat shelf with fixed pin mentioned in the next lead. 3. Jam up the crack until reaching a fixed pin near a flat shelf on the left, 5.9. Make a long, rising traverse to the left along flakes to a sling belay below a huge right-facing dihedral. Two or three pitons help protect this traverse, which is only 5.7 if the correct line is found. Don't leave the crack too soon; the lower traverse is run out 5.10. 4. Squeeze up a slot (5.8-) and follow cracks up left to a sloping shelf. In early season this shelf holds snow. Climb past the shelf, work along fixed pitons on the left wall of the huge dihedral (5.8+), and stretch the rope out to a broken ledge. 5. A long, continuous pitch climbs the dihedral proper to a belay at an alcove, 5.8+. 6. Finish the dihedral system with a short 5.7 pitch to Yellow Wall Bivy Ledge. 7. Leave the ledge to the right, taking two shallow, opposing dihedrals with several fixed pins (5.9+). Grunt up a chimney (5.8), step left, then go straight up through a bulge (crux) and belay at Table Ledge Crack. This is the same as **Yellow Wall**'s sixth pitch. 8. Hand traverse left for thirty feet (5.8+), drop down to the right end of Almost Table Ledge, then climb back up to Table Ledge (5.8) and move left to a fixed belay. Parties utilizing the rappel route can avoid the last 5.8 move to Table Ledge. FFA: Chris Reveley and Duncan Ferguson, 1977. Note that semi-permanent rappel slings are found at the end of pitch 3; a quick retreat can be made from here by rappelling left to the first belay on **Bright Star**, and then to Broadway.

17 Diamond Lil V 5.9 A3

This aid route has been largely replaced with **Eroica**. The original ascent began on the left side of the D-1 pillar, and took an independent line up the entire wall. 1. Climb to an alcove belay left of the pillar. 2. Start up the loose chimney above, but then switch left at a small ledge, and follow a thin crack to a belay at 150 feet. 3 and 4. Climb a blank-looking wall with thin cracks (some free), crossing over the **Casual Route** traverse, and go straight up to the Ramp (a prominent, sloping shelf in the center of the Diamond). 5. Traverse across a slab from the left end of the Ramp to a chimney (just right of the **Casual Route** dihedral), and ascend to a belay above chockstones. 6 and 7. Continue the chimney line to its end, then angle a bit right to a belay at Table Ledge crack. A party aiding this line can pendulum left to Yellow Wall Bivy Ledge (or the alcove just below it, as per the FA team) for a comfortable overnight stay. 8. Start up the vertical crack above, but take the left fork of the crack at forty feet (the right fork dead ends, though it's been climbed —

Michael Gilbert on crux pitch of *Eroica*, The Diamond
(Yellow Wall Bivy Ledge with climber visible below).

PHOTO: ROGER BRIGGS

see variation on **Grand Traverse**). Continue in the left fork to a stance at a small, left-facing corner. 9. Aid the corner and crack system for a long pitch to a ledge on the right. 10. Finish with a short, 5.6 lead. FA: Michael Covington, Doug Scott, and Dennis Henneck, 1976.

18 Eroica V- 5.12b ***

Eroica is the free version of **Diamond Lil**, and is one of the best free climbs of this grade in RMNP. The route is continuously difficult, requiring a very long day of climbing. Start as with **D-1**, belaying on the grassy shelf at the end of pitch two, or do **Casual Route** to the flat shelf at the beginning of its traverse (belay), and go straight up a pretty 5.9+ finger crack to the grassy shelf. 3. Move left onto the clean wall above **Casual Route**'s traverse and follow a thin crack system up left to a belay below the Ramp, 5.11b. 4. Stem the right-facing dihedral above the left end of the Ramp (5.11c). Step left out of the dihedral at a double bolt belay (**The Honeymoon Is Over**) to the base of a shallow corner. 5. Climb the corner (fixed pins and bolts), then run it out on 5.10 ground to a stance midway up a right-facing dihedral. This pitch contains several sections of 5.11, with a 5.12a move before the run out. 6. Go to the end of the dihedral (5.10). An escape to Yellow Wall Bivy Ledge is possible here with a pendulum. Work up intricate thin cracks and seams, first right, then left, to a belay at Table Ledge Crack (sustained 5.11 with a 5.12b crux; bring long runners). This pitch may have never been redpointed in its entirety; several parties have belayed midway up the lead in an alcove on the right. 7. Climb a vertical thin crack (5.11c) to a fork, stay left, and belay at a stance out left. 8. Take the small, left-facing dihedral and crack directly above, 5.11a. Rack: Standard plus double or triple set of RPs, extra stoppers and TCUs. FA: Covington, Scott, and Henneck, 1976, via **Diamond Lil**. FFA: Roger Briggs and Eric Doub, 1987, though they never linked the sixth pitch.

19 The Honeymoon is Over V 5.12c A1 (5.13b project) ***

This is an exceptionally difficult free climb on the headwall above the Ramp. None of its four (new) pitches have been red pointed, and five aid moves remain. If completed, it will certainly be the hardest route on the Diamond. The climb was originally established as an aid line from the ground (VI- 5.10 A3+), and was later equipped with bolts to allow free climbing — all of this over the span of a few summers, with several belayers, and some rope soloing. Do the first three and a half pitches of **Eroica**, belaying at a foothold and double bolt anchor. 5. Continue straight up the corner where Eroica steps left (5.12b), move right at a small roof, and enter a three-inch, right-facing dihedral (5.12d). Climb this (a few aid points or 5.13?) to three bolts arcing up right (5.12), then jam an arch (5.12a) to a bolted belay stance, 165 feet. The final move has not gone free. An optional belay can be had at the base of the slim dihedral. 6. Climb left to the top of a see-through flake (bolts, 5.12b), then go straight up past Table Ledge Crack (five bolts with one aid move, and a bunch of 5.12) to a double bolt belay at the base of **Grand Traverse**'s rotten crack. 7. Step down and right, then back up along a bolted flake that bends into an overlap. Turn this on the left and go up, then right, to a bolted stance. There are eight bolts on this pitch, and six 5.12 cruxes — when linked, it will be 5.13b. 8. Move left (5.10d, two bolts) to a crack, and follow this to a bolt at its end (5.11d). Traverse left (5.12b), then go up a right-facing dihedral (5.9) to a triple bolt belay and the top of the wall. Rack: Standard plus lots of thin crack gear. FA: Eric

Doub and others, 1993-4. FFA: Roger Briggs and Doub attempted a free ascent in 1996, doing all but a few moves (with hangs on all of the pitches).

20 D-1 V- 5.12a ★★

D-1 fires up the long crack system in the middle of the wall. It was the first route on the Diamond, and is also known as **Ace of Diamonds**. 1. Climb the center of the D-1 pillar as described in **Casual Route**. 2. Move right into a leaning dihedral that ends at a grassy ledge on the left. 3. Climb up to and through a roof (5.10c) and follow a crack to a belay on the right side of the Ramp. With a 200 foot rope, one can continue thirty feet to another ledge. 4-6. Follow the obvious crack system for three leads (or two with a 200 foot rope if starting from the ledge above the Ramp). The first two end at stances with bolts; the third ends in an alcove at the base of a wet (sometimes ice-choked) chimney. All are slightly overhanging with some poor rock. 7. Step left and take a thin crack and corner system to a stance at its top (5.12a). The first free ascent climbed the chimney (5.11 OW, wet and run out), but the thin corner is the original line. 8. Finish in the chimney, wet and funky 5.9. A 200 foot rope is very useful on this route. FA: Bob Kamps and Dave Rearick, 1960. FFA: John Bachar and Billy Westbay, 1978. FFA of original line: Roger Briggs and Jeff Achey, 1980.

The remaining routes on the right side of the Diamond are primarily difficult, grade V aid climbs. The topo for these routes is the result of a collaborative effort between Clay Wadman and the author. Wadman has spent many years researching all of the routes on the Diamond, and has published several poster-sized topos of the entire wall. Much of the information in my right-side topo comes directly from his work. (Wadman's topos are available in many local outdoor shops, and can also be ordered directly from Diamond Productions).

21 Jack of Diamonds V 5.10c A4

The completion of this route was the second one-day ascent of the Diamond (by an abundantly competent team, Layton Kor and Royal Robbins — most parties will take two days). The first one-day ascent took place two days earlier by the same party, who made the second ascent of **D-1**. Begin at the D-1 Pillar, and free climb a right-facing corner on its right side. Climb to the top of the pillar and merge with **D-1**, but continue in a diagonal line of ascent where that route goes left. The next pitch nails a small dihedral leading over the right edge of a roof to a belay stance even with the Ramp. Take the right crack of two to a belay in a dihedral, and then follow that to Table Ledge crack (rotten A4, or free at 5.10?). Move to the left-hand of several cracks, and nail to a hanging belay at the left edge of a stepped roof. The final pitch, rated 5.9 by the first ascent team, jams a beautiful fist crack in a left-facing corner to the top of the wall (5.10 by today's standards). With the exception of the crux pitch, the nailing on this route is moderate in difficulty. Include several fist-sized cams for the final pitch. FA: Layton Kor and Royal Robbins, 1963.

22 Enos Mills Wall V 5.7 (or up to 5.11+) A3

Enos Mills Wall was the first ascent of the Diamond in winter. The line has gone mostly free. Begin at the top of **North Chimney** between the D-1 Pillar and Green Pillar. 1. Climb a minor pillar whose top is even with the D-1 Pillar; 5.9 along its left side, or 5.8 along its right (200 feet, with easy climbing at the beginning).

2. Climb for forty feet above the left edge of the pillar, traverse right, then up a crack to the base of a much more noticeable raised pillar. 3. Take the left side of the raised pillar to a good ledge on top (5.9 or 10 OW). 4. Nail a crack on the left (A2), then traverse left to the base of a terrifically steep right-facing dihedral. Climb thirty feet to a belay ledge (sitting bivy on first ascent), 5.10d or aid. 5. Climb the dihedral to a sling belay short of its top, 5.11+ or very strenuous A2. 6. Nail up to and over a roof to gain Table Ledge, go straight up a rotten crack, then aid left to another crack. 7. Aid through a big overhang to a wide crack, and climb it (5.9). Bring gear to 4 inches, with extra midrange pieces. FA: Layton Kor and Wayne Goss, 1967. **Free Variation:** The standard method of free climbing the route (to the top of the fifth pitch) begins with one and a half pitches of **D-1**, after which a traverse right joins the line described above to the raised pillar. Climb a rotten chimney to the right (5.9) on pitch four. FFA: Jeff Achey and Leonard Coyne, 1980. **Aid Variation:** Climb along the left side of the Green Pillar for two pitches (mixed free and aid), then traverse left to an expanding flake. Go up this to the raised pillar (mixed), then chimney up its right side (mostly free). Aid a vertical wall (the right wall of a the rotten chimney on the free variation?), pendulum left to a good crack, and follow this to a ledge shared with the original line.

The next four routes share a belay and bivy spot on the top of the Green Pillar right of **North Chimney**. They cross over one another on the pillar itself, but become distinct on the upper wall.

23 Queen of Spades V 5.8 A4

A longtime Estes Park local put up this route when he was only 20 years old. Start in a chimney at the center of the Green Pillar. 1. Climb the chimney, then go right to the base of a short corner, 5.8. 2. Aid the corner over a small roof (A2), and pass a ledge with two bolts (optional belay). Continue with a chimney and crack line until it is possible to move left to a good ledge (bivy). 3. Follow the right-facing corner on the far left, exit the corner left at a small overhang, and nail to another overhang. 4. Pass this on the left (A3), then go straight up for 60 feet. 5. Continue in the same crack for a full pitch, then step left to two small left-facing corners. Belay at bolts 6. Swing left to the next crack and follow it to Table Ledge (steep, wide, and A4). 7. Traverse back right for fifteen feet to a small, left-facing dihedral, and follow it for 100 feet. 8. Start in the same crack system, but switch left to the next crack and take it to a good ledge. 9. Traverse right to escape the wall, or do a final pitch off the left side of the ledge. Bring gear from knifeblades to 5 inches; most of the route was done clean on the first ascent. FA: Douglas Snively and Mark Hesse, 1974.

24 La Dolce Vita VI 5.8 A4

Only the second half of the route is shown in the topo; the first half ascends the wall a bit left of **North Chimney** (see page 53). Start with the chimney (5.7) on the left side of the Green Pillar, then move up right and belay below a thin corner facing right. Mixed climbing up this and a more distinct corner above leads to the bivy ledge on the left side of the pillar's top (5.9 A2). A short pitch climbs a right angling ramp to a good ledge on the right (bivy); move back left over a flake to a short right-facing dihedral that is nailed (A4) to a fixed belay below a roof. Aid through the roof and follow the right side of an A-shaped feature (6-inch crack) to a stance above it. From here, the route follows the same crack system for four more pitches. Include hooks, RURPs, lots of KBs and small angles, and a full clean aid rack to 4 or 5 inches. FA: Renato Casarotto and Charlie Fowler, 1984.

25 Gear and Clothing V 5.9 A4

After reaching the top of the Green Pillar, this route runs parallel to **La Dolce Vita**. Start beneath a short slot on the right side of the pillar. Climb the slot (5.8), step left, and aid a crack to the same belay on **Queen of Spades**; follow that route for a pitch to its bivy ledge. Angle right on a ramp as with **La Dolce Vita** (5.9), but nail the next crack to the right (rotten A4) until reaching a bolt belay. Nail a right-facing corner, then move out of it to a belay stance (bolt) at the base of a left-facing dihedral. Now follow the same system to its end, stepping left at a wide section just below a spectacular roof at Table Ledge. Bring three sets of Friends and some tube chocks (or equivalent), as well as the standard fare of pitons. FA: Kyle Copeland and Marc Hirt, 1984.

26 Dunn-Westbay V 5.8 A3

This route starts in the large right-facing dihedral on the right side of the Green Pillar and takes a very direct line up the wall. 1-3. Climb the right side of the pillar (5.8, 5.10, 5.10) to a bivy ledge at its upper right side. 4. Nail a crack off the right side of the ledge and hook to a flake arcing left. Nail the flake to a crack and belay. 5-7. Follow this crack to Table Ledge, A3. 8-9. Step right a few feet and aid for two pitches (both A1) to the North Face. Rack from KBs to three inches, including a hook and quarter-inch bolt hangers (with nuts). FA: Jimmy Dunn and Billy Westbay, 1972. **Variation: Tail of the Tiger** nails the S-shaped roof right of the hook move on the 4th pitch (A4), then joins **Its Welx**. FA: Kris Walker and Walt Walker, 1973.

27 King of Swords V- 5.12a ★★

This route and its neighbor on the right (**The Joker**) are the only free climbs on the right side of the face. After two new pitches, the route free climbs **Its Welx** (see below). Though none of its pitches (on the original free ascent) are rated 5.12, the route is considerably more strenuous than other 5.11s on the wall — five of its eight pitches overhang. Start in a crack just right of the prominent **Dunn-Westbay** dihedral. 1. Jam the crack for 130 feet to a sling belay (5.9). 2. Follow the crack until it fades, move right to the next crack (**Smash the State**), then move right again to a ledge on **Its Welx** (5.10b). 3. Head right again into the main crack system which defines the route, struggle past an offwidth (5.11a R), then belay at a foothold just below (and right of) the S-shaped roof. The original free line avoids the offwidth by moving left (5.11d) to a crack facing left, up that for 20 feet (5.11a R), then back into the main line. 4. Follow a long fist crack above the roof to the base of a raised column, 5.11c. 5. Step left and fire up the left side of the column (a thin, clean corner), excellent 5.11d. This was the original line, but the right side of the column goes free as well (5.12a). 6. Climb to Table Ledge crack in the same system (5.11c hands), then follow the crack until it dies (5.10d). Move left to the next crack and belay. 7. Jam the crack, 5.10d (wide and wet). FFA: Roger Briggs and Dan Stone, 1985. The offwidth variation on pitch 3, and the right side of the column on pitch 5 were first climbed free by Michael Gilbert.

28 Smash the State V 5.8 A5-

This difficult aid route was soloed in the winter on the first ascent. After four independent pitches, it pendulums right into **Its Welx**. Start between the Green Pillar and the Black Flake at the base of two chimneys separated by a rib. 1 and 2. Climb the left chimney leading into a serious right-facing dihedral (A3+). 3. Aid up to a belay below the S-shaped roof, zigzagging as necessary to link small features, A4. 4. Surmount the roof with a KB crack, then labor up the right side of the improbable blank wall above, using all of the tricks of the trade (beaks, hooks, copperheads, and RURPs, A5-). Escape right when the opportunity presents itself with a pendulum from A1 anchors to join **Its Welx**. The second ascent of this route questioned the A5 rating, but it's still among the most difficult artificial pitches on the Diamond. FA: Jim Beyer, 1990.

29 It's Welx V 5.9 A4

With the exception of the first two pitches, **Its Welx** has been free climbed as **King of Swords**. Start at the base of two chimneys on the left side of the Black Flake. 1. Climb into and up the right chimney (5.8) to the base of a right-arching crack. 2. Nail the crack (A4) to a bolt (optional belay), and continue with the main crack system described in **King of Swords** (climbed at 5.9 A1 on the first ascent). FA: Dan McClure and Mark Hesse, 1973.

The following three routes all begin with a pitch on the right side of the Black Flake. Scramble up and right from its bottom left corner to the right-facing dihedral that defines its right edge, 3rd class.

30 The Joker V- 5.12c ★★

This is currently the most difficult free climb on the Diamond (though **The Honeymoon Is Over** will surpass it if completed). It begins with the first few pitches of **Christopher Robin**, climbing to its bivy ledge, then takes a crack and corner system on the left straight to the top. 1. Climb the right side of the Black Flake (5.10a OW near the top). Move left to belay. 2. Step down to a short corner, climb it, then angle right past two bolts. Head back left past a pin to a bolt at the base of a steep crack; climb this to a small ledge on the left (5.12c). There are several fixed nuts on this sustained pitch. 3. Go straight up (5.11d, somewhat rotten) to a perfect, bi-level ledge on the left (the **Christopher Robin** bivy ledge). 4. Climb off the right side of the ledge to a fixed pin, and traverse left to the next crack; this is where **The Joker** and **Christopher Robin** diverge. Follow the difficult left crack (5.12b) to a sling belay at a fixed pin. 5. A long and strenuous pitch climbs a right-facing to left-facing dihedral to a belay at Table Ledge, 5.12a. 6. Continue in the same crack, 5.11d. This final pitch is known as the Last Laugh, and it is usually wet. Bring a standard double rack to a #3 Friend, and a #3.5 – 4 Friend. FFA: Roger Briggs, Chip Chace and Steve Levin worked on the route on several occasions in 1993, but were unable to bag the free ascent. Briggs returned in 1994 with Pat Adams for an all free ascent.

31 Christopher Robin V 5.8 A3

This fine route follows a series of mostly A1 and A2 cracks in a direct line from the left side of the Black Flake, and is a good introduction to the right side aid climbs. Walker comments that "**Christopher Robin** has all of the elements of ... a Diamond classic," including a perfect minimalist bivy ledge for two, solid belay stances, and a great line. Due to the overhanging nature of its middle pitches, the hauling is very easy, and with the addition of several bolts, pins and fixed nuts (on **The Joker**), some of the difficult aid has been tempered. Follow the first 3 pitches of **The Joker**. 4. Aid the left-facing dihedral on the right, step right a few feet, and go to a belay below a small roof. Walker suggests making this pitch as long as possible to avoid a belay in the A3 section at the end of the next pitch, but he was using a 150 foot rope. 5. Continue in the same corner system to Table Ledge with a stretch of A3 at the end. Traverse right (5 or 10 feet) to a perfect A1 crack and set a hanging belay. 6 and 7. Follow this beautiful crack (with flowers). Walker used two pitches here; a party equipped with a 165 foot rope can do it in one. Rack: most of the gear should range from very thin to 2.5 inches, with a few pieces up to 4.5 inches. This might be a good line to try all clean. FA: Kris Walker (solo), 1972.

32 Steep is Flat V 5.10a A4+

This route climbs incipient cracks along the left edge of the Horsetails, two wisps of dark rock that slant up right about 100 feet above the North Pillar. It then joins **Christopher Robin** briefly, but ends in the next crack right, perhaps joining **Waterhole #3** for its last pitch. 1. Do the first pitch of **The Joker**. 2. Aid up right and pass a right-facing flake (A4), then angle left and up (A4+) to a belay even with the lower left Horsetail. 3. Nail past the upper left Horsetail (A4+), then turn a small overlap on the left (A4) and up to belay. 4. Head left into **Christopher Robin** before reaching an overhang, and go to the bivy ledge. 5. Stay with **Christopher Robin** for about 30 feet, then traverse straight right for 30 feet to the next crack system. 6. Follow the crack to a belay in a right-facing dihedral, short of Table Ledge. 7. Aid straight up past Table Ledge and enter a big roof-capped dihedral; belay at the bivy spot on **Waterhole #3** (?), and finish on that route. FA: Jim Beyer and Pat McInerney, 1991.

The final six routes on the right side of the Diamond are often very wet due to snowmelt from the North Face. Some pitches remain dry because the wall is very steep here, but windy days make for constant "rain showers" originating from a small waterfall. Bring a good waterproof shell.

33 Waterhole #3 V 5.8 A3

This was the first climb done on the right side of the Diamond, as well as the first complete route established on rope solo. Walker states, "...it was, in most other respects, a very unremarkable route." Given that it climbs a sheer, overhanging wall with no stances, and moves through a tremendously exposed overhang at the top, most parties will find it remarkable enough. The name is derived from three wet bivouacs experienced on the first ascent (one a thunderstorm, the others due to a persistent stream near the route). Start by scrambling up between the Black Flake and North Pillar, and climb the left side of the North Pillar to its top. From here the route is well-defined: nail a leaning crack system that sweeps to vertical for several pitches, and enter a large, right-facing dihedral capped with an enormous overhang at the top of the wall. Exit this on the left. All of the belays are hanging except for the first on the North Pillar, and the last, a small bivy ledge below the big roof. Rack up to 4 inches, with an emphasis on thin gear. FA: Kris Walker, 1971.

34 Toiling Midgets VI 5.9 A3+ (see below)

This difficult aid climb (rated modern A3+, which likely translates into standard A4+ or harder) branches left from **Diamond Star Halo** in the vicinity of the Horsetails. It also has an independent start. Scramble up to a long, flat ledge at the base of the North Pillar (approach from the right), and walk to its left side. 1. Climb the right side of a small finger (5.8), then angle left to an A1 crack on the left side of the pillar. 2. Nail a right-angling crack to a bolt, then angle left to a forked crack at a roof. This stretch is shared with **Diamond Star Halo** (rated modern A3 by Takeda). Take the left fork to a belay at a bolt just above the Horsetails, A3. 3. Follow discontinuous cracks to a bolt belay, A3+. 4. Continue in the same crack system past Table Ledge (A3), then pendulum left to a shallow left-facing dihedral, and go up to a double bolt belay. This is opposite **Waterhole #3**'s right-facing dihedral and roof. 5. Go straight up (A1+) to a belay bolt on the right. 6. A short stretch of free climbing (5.9) goes to slabs on the North Face. Rack: heads, beaks, extra KBs, Bugaboos, long-thin LAs, 60 meter ropes, in addition to the standard wall rack. FA: Pete Takeda and Dave Sheldon, 1996.

35 Diamond Star Halo V 5.8 A4

This route climbs through the right half of the Horsetails with continuously difficult nailing. Scramble to the middle of the flat ledge at the base of the North Pillar, and begin at a left-facing dihedral (left of a chimney). Climb the dihedral, then nail a crack to a belay in a slot (5.9 A2). Go out the left side of the slot and nail a crack to a bolt, then angle left (A4) to a sling belay below a small roof and the Horsetails. Now follow the right-hand of a forked crack through the Horsetails (the left is **Toiling Midgets**) for a long pitch to a hanging belay, devious A4. The next pitch begins straight up, but then performs a double pendulum to reach the exit crack, which leads to an angular roof (A4). Belay at a ledge below the roof, then climb past the right edge of the roof along a crack, which leads to the top. FA: Kyle Copeland, Charlie Fowler and Mike Burke, 1986.

36 Dawson-Jack V 5.8 A4

The right side of the Horsetails angles into the bottom of a big left-facing dihedral. **Dawson-Jack** swings into this from the right and follows it to the top. Start in a chimney on the right side of the North Pillar and climb it (5.8) to a belay on the right. Face climb to a crack (5.9) and nail (easily at first, but turning to A4) to a bolt on the right side of an intimidating overhang. Nail right and then up to avoid the biggest part of the overhang, tension left into the big dihedral, and nail to a bolt belay, A4. Nail thin cracks on the left (A4) to avoid a rotten slot, then pass a hollow flake and belay below a set of overhangs. Aid out the overhangs on the right to Table Ledge crack, and traverse left to a good stance. The final pitch goes up and right via easy aid and free climbing (A1 followed by 5.6). Be prepared for much difficult nailing and rotten rock. Rack to 3 inches with lots of thin gear, as well as hooks, copperheads, and RURPs. FA: Lou Dawson and Rich Jack, 1975.

37 Sunshine V- 5.7 A3

Sunshine takes the loose and wet chimney/dihedral system that originates at the right side of the intimidating roof on **Dawson-Jack**, and goes through the left edge of the obvious overhang at the top. Start just right of the chimney on **Dawson-Jack** and climb an easy pitch to a grassy ledge; belay at a big flake. Climb the flake, and head for a trough on the right. A right-facing crack above the trough ends at a ledge below the right edge of the **Dawson-Jack** roof. Move up right to a left-facing corner that leads over the roof and enters the chimney system defining the route. Follow the chimney, pass a long overhang on the right, and go up to a good belay ledge. Continue the line to a stance in a slot (belay), then climb to an overhang, which is turned on the left, go up 15 feet and step right to the lip of the large overhang at the top of the wall. Aid through the left edge to a sling belay. The last pitch takes short, double cracks to the North Face slabs. Gear up from knifeblades to 4 inches with a few hooks. FA: Jim Beyer (solo), 1974.

38 Left for Dead VI 5.9 A3+ (see below)
The thin crack/seam dropping down from the middle of the final overhang on **Sunshine** is the major feature of this route. 1. Begin right of **Sunshine** and climb broken rock (wet and dirty) to a belay next to a short, slanting, right-facing dihedral. 2. Ascend up and right to gain a left-facing corner, and climb this (5.9) to double bolts left of a small pillar and at the base of the upper crack. 3. Aid the crack and a shallow, right-facing dihedral (clean A2) to an arching overlap; belay at a bolt. 4. Nail straight up to a double bolt belay. 5. Difficult aid leads to the middle of the big roof at the top of the wall (modern A3+, could be as bad as A4+/A5-). Move right and aid though an obvious break in the roof, then go 35 feet higher to belay bolts on the left. Scramble up and right onto the North Face and over to the next route to descend. Rack to three inches, with KBs, lots of LAs, and some heads, beaks and hooks. Sixty meter ropes are recommended as one pitch is long. FA: Dave Sheldon, Pete Takeda and Shane Wayker, 1998.

North Face

The North Face is a gently sloping talus field above the left end of the Boulderfield, with a diagonally rising cliff band along the lower border. On its flanks reside many old and easy routes that see almost no traffic in modern times, with the exception of **The Cables**, which is almost certainly the most traveled technical route on the peak. The snowfield below the cliff band is called the Dove as it resembles a diving bird for most of the summer.

Approach: All routes are approached with a hike of six miles to the Boulderfield, and then a scramble up talus or snow to the base of the North Face. An ice axe is recommended for the routes above the Dove.

Descent: The quickest descent reverses **The Cables**, though one can also bag the summit and descend **The Keyhole** or **Clark's Arrow** for a nice tour of the peak.

B-20 The Cables I 5.4 ⋆
This route is described in the ice climbing section (see page 239), and a summer ascent follows the same line (5.4, usually wet). **Variation: Moss Chimneys** continues the right-slanting line of the first two pitches for several hundred feet of 4th class until easy ground leads to the upper reaches of **Keyhole Ridge**. The danger of rolling rocks onto the normal route outweighs any desire to climb it, and therefore it is not recommended.

1 Ev's Chimney I 5.2

Follow a wet chimney with an overhang at the top about 150 feet right of **The Cables**. FA: Ev Long and Melvin Wickens, 1931.

2 Webb's Walk-Up I 5.4

Begin fifty feet right of **Ev's Chimney** and follow a crack for two long pitches to the top of a block, then scramble left along a flake system to the top of **The Cables**. FA: Peter Webb and John Koch, 1963.

3 Zumie's Chimney I 5.0

Climb a long corner/chimney left of a protruding buttress for about three pitches. FA: Clerin Zumwalt and Ev Long, 1932.

4 Mary's Ledges I 5.2

Climb the right side of the protruding buttress in the middle of the lower North Face. FA: Wickens and Gilman, 1930.

B-21 Left Dovetail II 5.4 and easy snow

This route is described in the ice climbing section; the summer rating is given here.

B-22 Right Dovetail II 5.0 and moderate snow

Described in the ice climbing section. In late summer or fall, the snow will be much more challenging (AI 2+).

5 Keyhole Ridge II 5.5 ***

This is an enjoyable and exposed jaunt on the northwest ridge of the mountain. Start near the Keyhole (the opening on the ridge though which the summit trail passes) and traverse left above a slab along an exposed ledge on the east side of the ridge (4th class), then go up to a saddle. This saddle is the False Keyhole; it can also be accessed from the west by ascending slabs above the Ledges section of **The Keyhole**. Climb on the ridge until a steep section blocks progress, then ascend a ramp on the left. When it peters out, climb to the top of the tower above, 5.4. Descend ten feet to a ledge on the west side, then traverse over to a notch (the second major notch on the ridge). This notch can be reached from the False Keyhole by staying on the west side of the tower the entire way (also 5.4). Head left from second notch along a ramp on the east side, pass beneath a prominent crack system (which is 5.6), and continue with the now narrow ramp until it is feasible to climb straight up to the ridge (5.5). Follow the ridge, with one short detour on the west side. FA: J. W. Alexander and Smith, 1924.

6 The Keyhole 2nd class ***

Though some climbers may not be interested in an ascent of **The Keyhole** for its own sake, it would be unjust to give it anything but three stars. It is a remarkable route, climbing several improbable stretches that just barely pass as hiking, and it affords views of all sides of the mountain as it circumnavigates the summit block. Note that in any but perfect conditions, this route is 3rd class or harder; in fact, it often remains "technical" well into July. Hike to the Boulderfield and climb through the Keyhole. From this point on, the route is periodically marked with red and yellow painted targets. It begins with a traverse of the Ledges, going up and then down over the top of a large slab. A short distance beyond, the route enters a long gully called the Trough. This drops all the way down into Glacier Gorge, and can be ascended from there if desired. A short wall must be negotiated at the top of the Trough to reach a benchmark on the southwest corner of the mountain (13,850'). Turn left and traverse the Narrows, a sidewalk perched above a considerable drop. At the end of the Narrows the route makes a shallow turn around a minor rib, then ascends a long groove (polished by thousands of climbers) in a slabby area known as the Homestretch. On a busy day, 200 people or more may be on the route. FA: Brown, 1870.

West Face

The West Face of Longs is quite impressive: a quarter mile wide, 600 feet high, and clean, light-colored granite as good as one could hope for, all at a comfortable angle. Its lofty position above the Trough on **The Keyhole** and the whole of Glacier Gorge affords commanding views of the surrounding peaks. Despite these positive attributes, the West Face routes are guarded by a long approach, and thus are seldom climbed. Realize that any rocks rolled off these routes will cascade onto the throngs of hikers below — be extra cautious.

Approach and Descent: Hike through the Keyhole and traverse across the Ledges and the Trough to gain the various routes. It is also possible to approach from Glacier Gorge by hiking east from Black Lake and up through the Trough. Descend by reversing **The Keyhole** (see previous page).

1 Northwest Couloir I 4th class
This route climbs the wide couloir that ascends left of the rib that defines the left edge of the main face. Scramble up from the Ledges, and climb along the left side of the couloir, tunneling through a cave at one point to avoid more difficult ground on the right. Gain the crest and follow **Keyhole Ridge**. FA: Enos Mills climbed it in 1896, but found signs of a previous ascent.

2 Northwest Rib II 5.5 ★
This climbs along the rib that forms the border between **Northwest Couloir** and the main wall. Begin as with the previous route, and climb up and right onto the rib, then follow it to **Keyhole Ridge** for several pitches of increasing difficulty.

3 Dialogue on Zen II 5.7 ★
This route follows cracks and corners in the narrow concave face just right of **Northwest Rib**. Hike to the base of the Trough and scramble up to a 4-inch crack on the left. Climb the crack and belay on the second of two ledges after 100 feet. Take a thin slab crack to a right-facing dihedral (the left-hand of two such dihedrals on the left side of the concave face), and follow it to a stance. The next pitch finishes the dihedral, then steps right to the next corner (belay), and the last pitch takes a chimney and face. FA: Tim Hogan and Richard Rossiter, 1986.

4 Far Left II 5.6
A prominent left-facing dihedral marks the left side of a slender column that stretches most of the way up the left side of the face. **Far Left** climbs a continuous system of left-leaning cracks near or on the column's right side for four pitches.

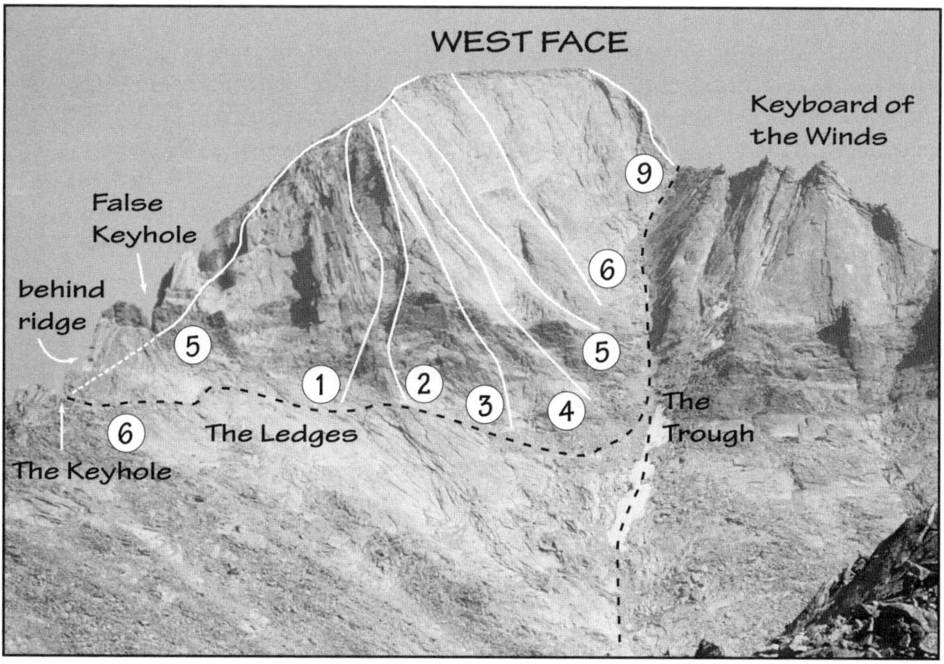

5 Van Diver's West Wall II 5.2 (?)
Previous guidebooks give varied ratings for this route, from 4th class to 5.4. It climbs a left-angling, shallow depression in the face, beginning from a gully on the left side of a triangular buttress. Hike up the Trough for 200 feet, then traverse left into the gully, and commence climbing. As with most routes on this face, only the general line of ascent is known; the right-facing dihedral right of **Far Left**'s column is the probable line. FA: Brad Van Diver and Bob Working, 1956. They noted the route is similar to Boulder's Third Flatiron.

6 West Wall II 5.4 ★
Hike several hundred feet up the Trough and traverse left to the base of the wall. Climb the middle of the West Face to a break in the summit ridgeline. FA: Bill Eubanks and Brad Van Diver, 1950.

7 Fourth of July II 5.4
The whereabouts of this route is uncertain. It begins at a nice belay flake forty feet below an obvious open book crack and climbs to a ledge at the base of the crack (a very short pitch). Lieback and jam the flake that forms the crack (possibly encountering an old piton) to a big ledge (belay), then go up the face, step right, and follow a crack. Given its length (it was described as three pitches with a forty foot first pitch in Fricke's guide), it probably ascends the short part of the West Face, i.e. near the top of the Trough. FA: Kenyon King and Clarence Gusthurst, 1963.

8 Bruns West Face (?)
This is an even more obscure route, reported in Nesbit's guide as having an indefinite location somewhere on the west face. FA: Bruns, 1924.

9 Southwest Ridge II 5.4 ★★

This route takes a nice line with fine positions and good belays. Hike to the top of the Trough and scramble up the ridge for forty feet to a big belay flake. Head up left (5.4) across ledges to a gully that leans back right, and follow that to a belay on the ridge. Climb through an overhang to an exposed belay, then head for the top, but escape the last headwall on the right. FA: J. W. Alexander (solo?), 1924, though Enos Mills may have made an earlier unrecorded ascent. For a complete ascent of the southwest ridge, hike past Black and Green Lakes in Glacier Gorge to the base of a long gully left of Pagoda Mountain's northwest face. Ascend the gully to a saddle between Pagoda and the Keyboard of the Winds, then scramble along the backside (east side) of the Keyboard to the top of the Trough (3rd class). Brown pioneered this route in 1870, though he finished on the Narrows and Homestretch.

The next two routes are on the south face above **The Keyhole**.

10 West Chimney I 5.2

Two chimneys ascend to the summit beginning from the Narrows on **The Keyhole**. This is the left chimney; it is short and on good rock. FA: Ev Long and Clerin Zumwalt, 1932.

11 East Chimney I 5.2

The right chimney, with several big flakes. FA: Greeley solo, 1932.

GLACIER GORGE

The giant U-shaped valley of Glacier Gorge runs along the west side of Longs Peak. Many feel this is the most beautiful area in Rocky Mountain National Park, and it's hard to argue against such an opinion. The southern rim of the gorge is lined with huge mountain faces — an almost continuous wall of superb, glaciated stone goes from one side to the other. Mount Pagoda is on the left, connected to the west face of Longs Peak by the Keyboard of the Winds; the northeast face of Chiefs Head sits adjacent to Pagoda on the right; and the northeast face of Spearhead towers above in the foreground. Hidden behind Spearhead is the northwest face of Chiefs Head, which dwindles in size as it nears the saddle between Chiefs Head and McHenrys Peak (Stone Man Pass). The big walls start in again right of the Stone Man, and continue unabated across the east face of McHenrys and over to the south wall on Arrowhead. Myriad lakes, streams, waterfalls and wild flowers add to the beauty — it is difficult to imagine a better place to climb.

Travel Directions: All of the routes in this area are accessed via the Black Lake trail, which begins at the Glacier Gorge Junction trailhead. To get to the trailhead from Estes Park, drive west on Highway 36 (Elkhorn Avenue in downtown Estes Park, turning into Moraine Avenue at a traffic light), and pass into Rocky Mountain National Park at the Beaver Meadows Entrance Station. Turn left soon after the entrance booth onto Bear Lake Road. The parking lot, located inside a hairpin turn one mile before the end of the road (about 8.5 miles from the entrance station) is small, and fills up early. Additional parking can be found 0.1 mile down the road, or at the Bear Lake trailhead (the end of the road). A short trail (0.3 mile) leading southeast from the Emerald Lake trail connects the two lots (or use a 0.25 mile trail from the east end of the Bear Lake parking lot).

Approach: The main trail heads south from the lot toward Alberta Falls. It passes the North Longs Peak trail at 1.5 miles, and then hits a junction at 2.0 miles. Take the left fork, which leads into Glacier Gorge, passes Mills and Jewel Lakes, and continues to Black Lake at 4.5 miles. The right fork leads to Loch Vale (described in the next section). A third trail very near to this junction traverses over to Lake Haiyaha, and then drops into Tyndall Gorge just below Dream Lake; all of these trails are signed.

HALF MOUNTAIN

The summit of Half Mountain is directly east of Mills Lake, and at the end of the long north ridge of Longs Peak. This ridge forms the eastern border of Glacier Gorge, and upon it lie several rock towers. Only two climbs have been recorded here, on a single buttress called Astro Tower, which is the third major formation on the ridge (starting at the summit of Half Mountain and counting south). Although the rock is excellent, the approach is tedious.

Approach: Hike to the south end of Mills Lake, and begin a long diagonal tack up to the tower, gaining about 1,000 feet in elevation.

Descent: Descend from the top of the tower by walking off its backside. If no gear is left at the base, it may be easiest to return to the trailhead by way of the North Longs Peak trail — consult a map.

FERN LAKE, BEAR LAKE, and GLACIER GORGE

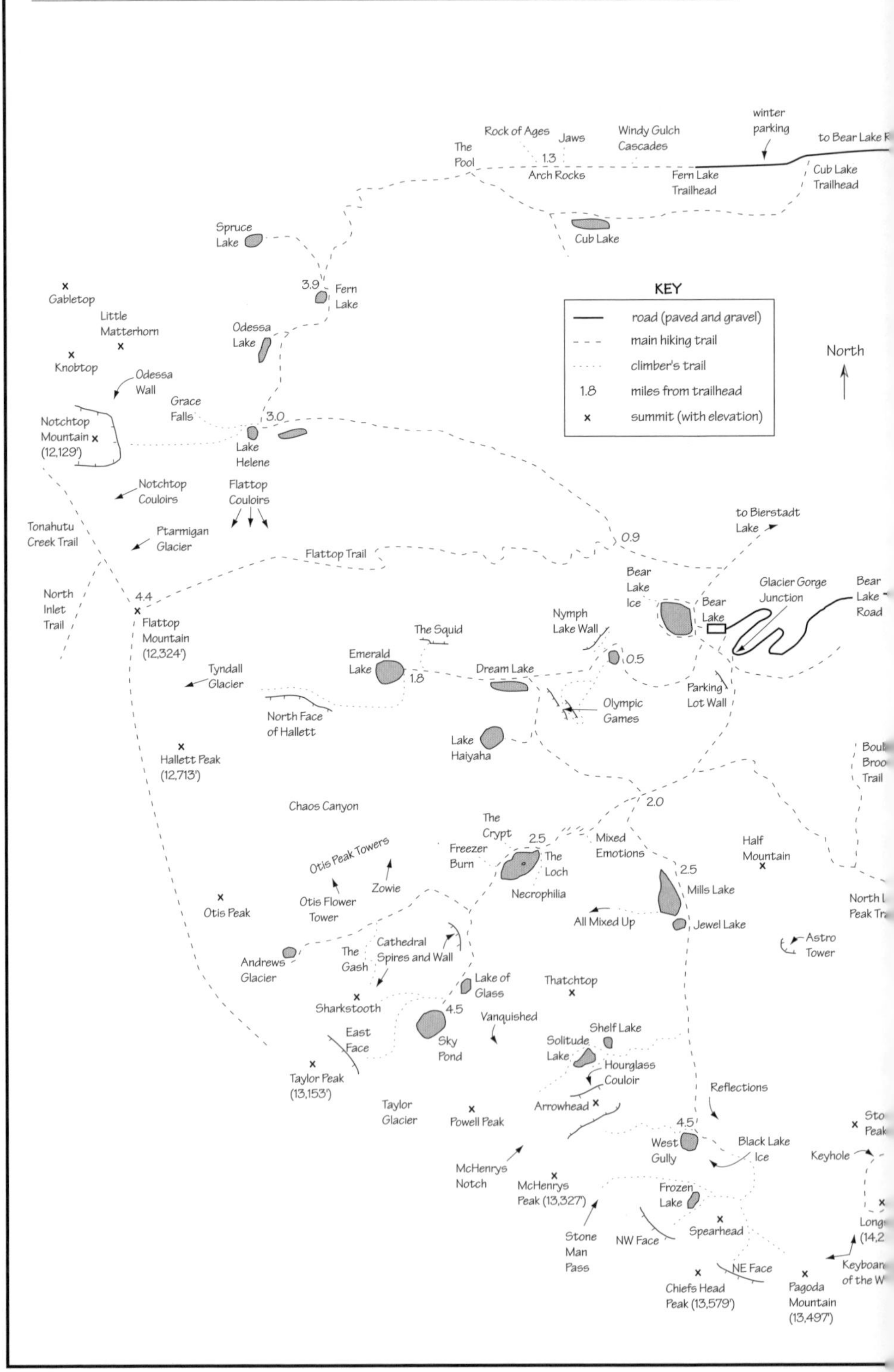

winter parking
Rock of Ages
Jaws
Windy Gulch Cascades
The Pool
1.3
Arch Rocks
Fern Lake Trailhead
Cub Lake Trailhead
Cub Lake
Spruce Lake
3.9
Fern Lake
KEY
road (paved and gravel)
main hiking trail
climber's trail
1.8
miles from trailhead
summit (with elevation)
North
Gabletop
Little Matterhorn
Knobtop
Odessa Lake
Odessa Wall
Grace Falls
3.0
Notchtop Mountain (12,129')
Lake Helene
Notchtop Couloirs
Flattop Couloirs
to Bierstadt Lake
Tonahutu Creek Trail
Ptarmigan Glacier
0.9
Flattop Trail
Bear Lake Ice
Glacier Gorge Junction
Bear Lake Road
North Inlet Trail
4.4
Flattop Mountain (12,324')
Bear Lake
Nymph Lake Wall
The Squid
Emerald Lake
1.8
Dream Lake
0.5
Tyndall Glacier
Parking Lot Wall
Olympic Games
North Face of Hallett
Lake Haiyaha
Hallett Peak (12,713')
2.0
Chaos Canyon
The Crypt
2.5
Mixed Emotions
Half Mountain
Freezer Burn
The Loch
Otis Peak Towers
2.5
Zowie
Necrophilia
Mills Lake
Otis Peak
Otis Flower Tower
All Mixed Up
Jewel Lake
Astro Tower
The Gash
Cathedral Spires and Wall
Andrews Glacier
Lake of Glass
Thatchtop
Sharkstooth
4.5
Vanquished
Shelf Lake
East Face
Sky Pond
Solitude Lake
Hourglass Couloir
Taylor Peak (13,153')
Reflections
Taylor Glacier
Powell Peak
Arrowhead
4.5
West Gully
Black Lake Ice
Keyhole
McHenrys Notch
McHenrys Peak (13,327')
Frozen Lake
Stone Man Pass
NW Face
Spearhead
NE Face
Chiefs Head Peak (13,579')
Pagoda Mountain (13,497')

1 Central Buttress II 5.11 ★★

The exact location of this route is not known — Douglas pointed out the general line (15 years after the fact, and from 1,000 feet below the face), but it's difficult to tell how much of the route is shared with **Space Walk**. Climb cracks near the center of the southwest face to a belay ledge, 5.9. Jam a hand crack to an overhang and pull through to a belay, 5.11. The third pitch tackles thin cracks, 5.11. FA: Douglas Snively and Billy Westbay, 1983.

2 Space Walk II 5.11a ★★

A big, right-facing dihedral (perhaps the line of **Central Buttress**) runs along the left side of the southwest corner of Astro Tower. **Space Walk** begins 100 feet right at a left-facing corner that arcs left into a roof. Climb around the left side of the roof, and continue to a ledge at 75 feet (5.9). The next pitch climbs a nice left-facing corner formed by a pillar; belay on its top below a dihedral. Jam the right wall of the dihedral with a 5.8 finger crack and belay at a small stance (70 feet). Step right and follow a difficult dihedral (5.11a) toward the right side of the overhang at the top of the wall, but traverse left a good distance below it to a sloping ledge. Jam up to the roof from here (5.10c), turn it on the left (5.10a), and go straight to the top. Rack to a #4 Friend. FA: Richard and Joyce Rossiter, 1983. **Variation:** An alternate start left of the normal route is marked on the photo (5.9).

KEYBOARD OF THE WINDS

Several striking towers known as the Keyboard of the Winds grace the southwest ridge of Longs Peak. Most of the "keys" have technical routes on their Glacier Gorge side, and all are approached from Green Lake (see Pagoda Mountain, page 100, for the hike to Green Lake).

Approach: From the lake, scramble up the gully that leads to the col between Pagoda Mountain and the southernmost key (Sievers' Tower). Pass a slabby rock band (which lies on the left), and then scramble left to the base of the keys. The approach is long, and it may be worthwhile to climb more than one tower once on site.

Routes are described right to left from the Pagoda col, as an approaching climber would encounter them. A portion (in some cases the entire line) of all of these routes except the first can be viewed from Green Lake (a convenient bivy spot). A stiff hike of about 45 minutes reaches the base of the towers from Green Lake, which is six miles from the trailhead.

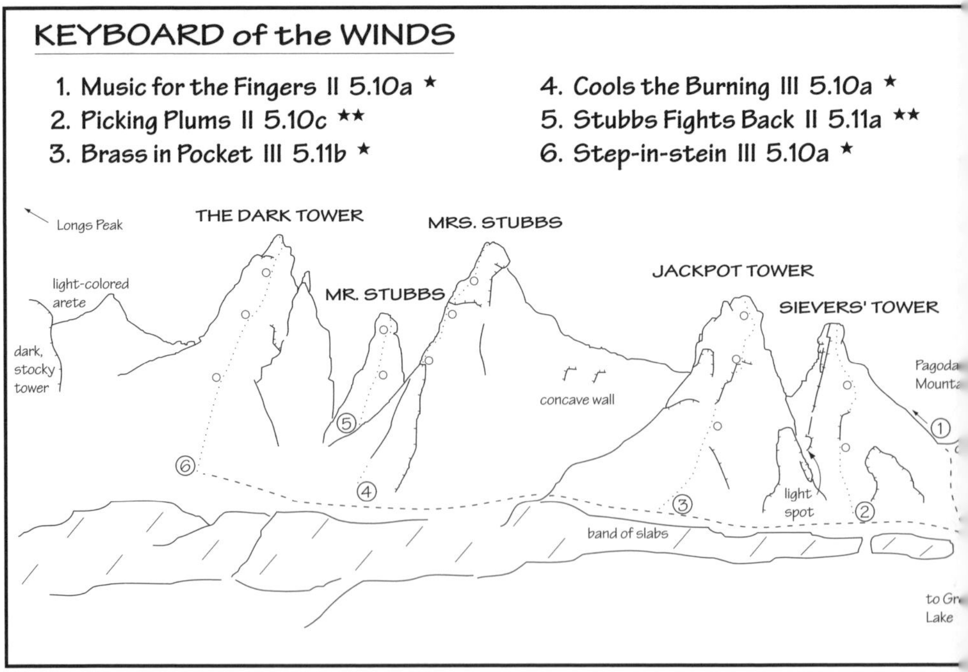

KEYBOARD of the WINDS

1. Music for the Fingers II 5.10a ★
2. Picking Plums II 5.10c ★★
3. Brass in Pocket III 5.11b ★
4. Cools the Burning III 5.10a ★
5. Stubbs Fights Back II 5.11a ★★
6. Step-in-stein III 5.10a ★

Longs Peak   THE DARK TOWER   MRS. STUBBS
light-colored arete   MR. STUBBS   JACKPOT TOWER
dark, stocky tower   SIEVERS' TOWER
concave wall   Pagoda Mountain
band of slabs   light spot
to Green Lake

Sievers' Tower

This is the first tower on the left from the Pagoda col.

Descent: Scramble off the backside to descend, and then hike down the approach gully.

1 Music for the Fingers II 5.10a ★
Start 30 feet right of the tower's prow on the south face. The first pitch pieces together several small dihedrals, trending right and ending on a small ledge split by a four-inch crack (5.8, 150 feet). Go up a shallow, four foot wide chimney, and then face climb along small cracks in an orange band. Master a 5.10a lieback crux off a right-facing edge, then weave left ten feet and back right to straight up cracks leading to the summit, 5.8. FA: Greg Sievers and Rob Cassidy, 1994.

2 Picking Plums II 5.10c ★★
This route essentially follows the prow of the tower's northwest face. 1. Begin at a shallow left-facing dihedral that switches to right facing, then angle left to a right-facing arch, 5.8 and 100 feet. 2. Climb the arch to its apex, go up a crack, and make an obvious rightward traverse. Face climb straight up at the first opportunity to a good crack and belay (5.10c, 100 feet). 3. Jam the crack with some thin face work for fifteen feet, then move right around an arete. Head up left toward the center of the face (passing over several large, loose flakes) and follow a crack system to a six-inch slot splitting the summit block (5.10c). A #5 Camalot or Big Bro is useful for the final wide crack. FA: Nigel Gregory and Dave Sheldon, 1999.

Jackpot Tower

Jackpot Tower is adjacent to Sievers' Tower on the left.

Descent: Hike off the back to descend.

3 Brass in Pocket III 5.11b ★
Locate a right-leaning, low-angled groove on the northwest face that leads into a huge roof-capped, right-facing dihedral (the dihedral is very prominent). 1. Climb the groove for 200 feet, 5.2. 2. Lead over blocky territory to the big dihedral, angle right near its top and pull over the overhang (5.11b, 100 feet). Belay in a small, right-facing corner. 3. Step right and jam an overhanging crack for fifty feet, then move right again around an arete. Go up and back left to the middle of the wall, then straight up through a dihedral. Crank over a small overhang and belay (5.11a, 180 feet). 4. Go for the top, 5.6. FA: Gregory and Sheldon, 1999.

Mrs. Stubbs

This is the next formation to the left, across a large, concave wall from Jackpot Tower.

Descent: Scramble over the top and down the tower's left side to begin the descent, then locate a small ledge with a slung chockstone. Rappel 120 feet, and hike down the notch between Mrs. and Mr. Stubbs.

4 Cools the Burning III 5.10a ★
A prominent (and loose) right-facing dihedral at the base of the tower forms the right side of a prow of sorts. Begin 100 feet left of this at a crack and corner system on the face of the prow. 1. Climb the crack system to a left-facing dihedral leading to a small roof. Undercling left, then follow a loose crack to a small ledge atop the prow (5.8+, 200 feet). 2. Angle up right via finger cracks for a half pitch and belay beneath a large overhang, 5.10a. 3. Turn the overhang on the left, then go up right to a big ledge, 5.9, 80 feet. 4. Climb blocky terrain on the right side of the tower to the summit (200 feet of 5.6). FA: Gregory and Sheldon, 1999.

Mr. Stubbs

This is Mrs. Stubbs companion on the left, set back from the main towers of the Keyboard.

Descent: Rappel from fixed slings on the summit to the gully between Mrs. and Mr. Stubbs, and follow that to the base.

5 Stubbs Fights Back II 5.11a ★★
This route is obvious from the base of the tower. 1. Pass several steep overlaps followed by a tricky set of moves to an overhanging crack. Jam up, undercling five feet left, then reach for an undercling on a large flake. Head right from the flake to a small dihedral (facing left), climb up that, then move right to a small stance (5.11a, 120 feet). 2. Go up a steep, right-facing corner, move right under a roof, then up to a belay at the base of the summit block (5.10a, 100 feet). 3. Work up the short northwest face of the block to the top, 5.10a. FA: Gregory and Sheldon, 1999.

The Dark Tower

Hike left from Mrs. Stubbs to the next large formation on the ridge, easily identified by an unclimbed satellite spire right of the true summit.

Descent: Walk off the back and traverse over to Mrs. Stubbs, then follow its descent.

6 Step-in-Stein III 5.10a ★
Start below an obvious left-facing dihedral in gray rock near the base of the main tower. 1. Climb into the dihedral and lead up to a small roof. Undercling left, then climb cracks to a big left-facing dihedral; follow that up left to a small stance (5.9, 200+ feet). 2. Move right to another left-facing corner, then go straight up and over a roof on good holds. Angle left to a sharp arete, climb its left side, then swing back right onto the main face, great exposure. Continue up right to a sloping belay on the right side of the tower, 5.10a, 180 feet. 3. Step left, master a twenty foot headwall, walk ten feet to another headwall and climb to its top (awkward, and with a loose chockstone). Walk ten more feet to a wide crack angling right, and follow that to a ledge (5.9+, 160 feet). 4. Traverse 80 feet around the right side of the tower and climb a steep crack up the summit block, 5.10a. FA: Gregory and Sheldon, 1999.

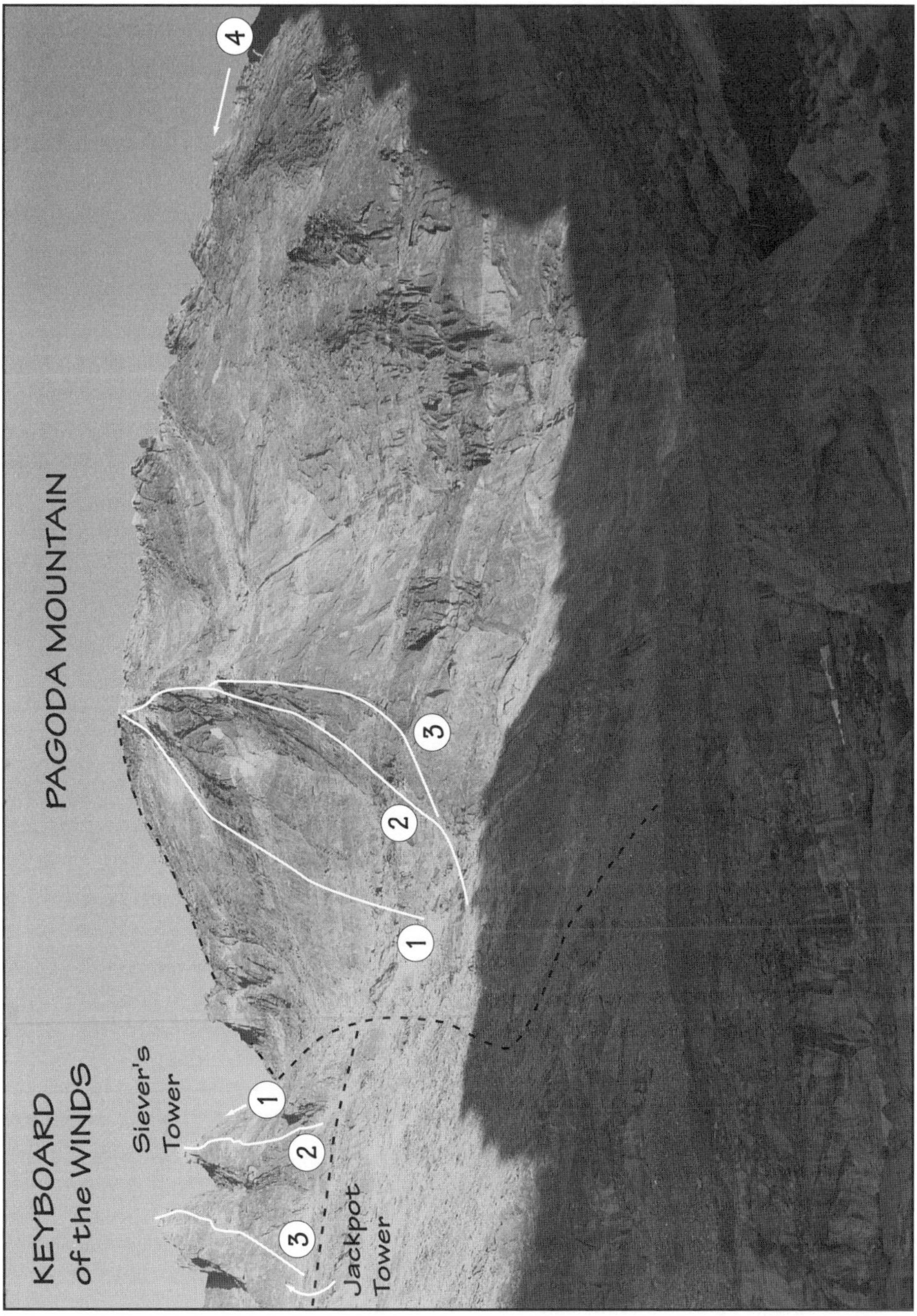
PAGODA MOUNTAIN
KEYBOARD of the WINDS
Siever's Tower
Jackpot Tower
1
2
3
4

PAGODA MOUNTAIN

Pagoda Mountain is the triangular peak at the back (southern) end of Glacier Gorge, connected to Longs Peak by the Keyboard of the Winds. Its mammoth northwest face is immediately left of the northeast face of Chiefs Head, and the crenelated ridge connecting the two peaks is a classic alpine traverse. Though the northwest wall is well over 1,000 feet high, it doesn't see much action — most of it is lower-angled than it appears.

Approach: The approach to Pagoda is long but simple. Hike to Black Lake (about 4.5 miles) and go around the left side of the lake to a steep path that follows the inlet stream. The path levels out as it enters upper Glacier Gorge, and at this point, one could take a beeline to the mountain. However, this involves a fair amount of bushwhacking through krummholz colonies. The best method crosses the stream and travels toward Spearhead on a trail of sorts, then passes left of Spearhead to reach Green and Italy Lakes. At this elevation, there is no longer any bothersome vegetation, and a quick scramble over rocks and tundra leads to the bottom of the face.

Descent: The descent is also straightforward: walk down the northeast ridge to the saddle between Pagoda and the Keyboard of the Winds, then turn northwest and follow a steep gully along the side of the face.

1 Northeast Face II 5.5

This route climbs slabs and shallow corners in the big bowl left of the obvious central prow (**North Buttress**). Hike about half way up the descent gully, and then climb straight up the middle of the bowl for seven pitches, joining the next route near its top. There are several possible lines of ascent here, all about the same level of difficulty. FA: J. Johnson, 1975.

2 North Buttress II 5.6 ★

North Buttress climbs along the left side of the obvious prow in the middle of the wall for half its length, then works up onto the prow itself for the remainder of the way. Begin a short distance up the descent gully above a low-angled slab, and traverse right across grassy ledges. Climb slabs up to a dark band of rock in the lower part of the face, and then follow a set of dihedrals left of the prow for several pitches (5.6). Work onto the prow at midheight, and follow that, moving right occasionally to avoid difficulties. FA: Bill Buckingham, Brook, Catwood, and Cox, 1958.

3 Silk and Satin III 5.8 R ★

This climbs the central prow a little more directly, and on its right side. Approach as for **North Buttress**, but move farther right to the base of the prow. Follow a chimney above the dark band for a pitch, then move up and right on easy ground to the base of a right-facing dihedral on the right side of the prow. Climb the dihedral in a long pitch, passing an overhang, and belay on a nice ledge. Continue the dihedral to its end, then move up and left (5.8 R) to a left-facing corner, which is followed to a belay below a steep section of dark rock. Move left on a ledge, then up right on white rock, and turn a small roof on the left to a stance above it (belay). Follow a trough and crack system to join the upper part of **North Buttress**. FA: Dan Hare and Jeff Bevan, 1984.

4 West Ridge II 5.7 ★★

This traverse along the west ridge of Pagoda achieves some spectacular positions, and includes a delightfully exposed and tilted sidewalk near its end. Begin with an ascent of the narrow snow gully leading to the notch between Pagoda and Chiefs Head, easy in early season, but becoming icy later in the summer. Most of the snow can be avoided with rock scrambling on the left, though ice gear is recommended. From the pass, the route simply follows the ridge, with short crux sections at several gendarmes and vertical steps.

5 Southwest Face II 5.4 ★

This climb makes for a good winter mountaineering adventure. Start with the first part of **West Ridge**, up the snow gully to the pass between Pagoda and Chiefs Head. A long traverse from the pass of nearly 1,000 feet walks along a level ledge system and leads onto the southwest face. The route makes a big switchback at the end of the traverse, climbing up 20 feet (5.3) to the right end of a diagonal ramp that slants up and left. Follow the ramp for another 1,000 feet (3rd class), but stop short of a wet chimney, and climb a left-facing dihedral just right of the chimney for 200 feet, 5.6. Finish with 100 feet of mellow slab work (5.2). This route has been reported as easy as 5.2, and as hard as 5.6 — there may be a better line from the ramp than the route described here.

CHIEFS HEAD PEAK

Chiefs Head stands at the very end of Glacier Gorge, immediately behind Spearhead, and sandwiched between Pagoda and McHenrys. Its northeast and northwest faces are among the biggest in the Park, each about 1,000 feet high and twice that wide. The two faces are separated by the ridge of Spearhead, but both are similar in the type of climbing offered: committing, run out, and difficult.

It may be wise to carry pitons when climbing on Chiefs Head. Good protection is scarce, and a marginal belay in this remote area could lead to disaster.

Approach: Hike to the base of Spearhead (see page 115), and pass along its left side to reach the Northeast Face. Bear right of Spearhead, passing Frozen Lake, to reach the Northwest Face. Both of these walls face northeast, and thus are cold in the afternoon. Snowfields at the base guard both walls. Allow several hours for the seven mile approach, and pick up a rock for step cutting before venturing onto the snowfields.

Northeast Face

The main feature of the Northeast Face is a huge, sometimes sloping shelf that cuts across almost the entire right half of the wall. The photo does not show the broken, left half of the face — the shelf goes across almost the entire photo. Though the shelf doesn't have a formal name, this book uses "Long Ledge" in the route descriptions. It holds snow for much of the season, and some degree of moisture will exist on all of these routes until August. Aside from Long Ledge, there are very few continuous cracks or flakes, and route finding is a constant challenge. The rock on this side of the mountain is not as clean as that found on the Northwest Face, yet the free climbing is enjoyable. Bear in mind, however, that these routes are every bit as exciting as their Northwest Face counterparts — check your adrenaline levels.

Two slanting snow gullies run along the margins of the wall; the left is the standard descent line while the right is the site of a moderate ice climb. At bottom right is a low-angled tongue of rock reaching into the snowfield at the base of the face. This tongue provides access for several of the routes, as well as a dry belay for the first pitch.

Descent: The standard descent for the Northeast Face is the aforementioned gully on the left side of the wall. It drops from the notch between Pagoda and Chiefs Head, and is easy enough in early summer, but becomes icy later on. The ice can be avoided for the most part by staying right (facing down) on moderate rock. Avoid it altogether by using the alternate descent (easier, but much longer): Walk over the top of Chiefs Head, hike along the northwest ridge, and enter a steep gully with rock walls on either side, descending to Stone Man Pass. A disheartening 200 feet of elevation must be regained to get into the pass, and there is a snowfield on the other side to contend with, though this is not as steep as the standard descent gully. Once below the pass, it is an easy matter to return to the trailhead (or contour around Spearhead to get back to the base of the wall).

1 Tenderfoot IV 5.10a

The prow of a protruding buttress drops down from the left edge of Long Ledge in the middle of the wall. **Tenderfoot** takes a line to the right margin of this buttress, climbs through the overhang above the left side of Long Ledge, then takes easier and lower-angled rock to the east ridge of Chiefs Head. The buttress shades the lower half of the route, so one can expect cold climbing and wet rock. 1. Begin about 100 feet left of the next route, and climb cracks and flakes to the first of two closely spaced horizontal faults, 5.8. Traverse left and go up to a belay on the higher fault, below a left-facing flake. 2. Follow the flake to a stance below a wide crack on the left side of a column (5.9+). The belay is level with a thin strip of dark rock that stretches across most of the face. 3. Climb past the wide section and up to the top of the column, on which is perched a tilted finger (the finger is visible from the ground). Climb above the finger past a ramp to a large ledge below a long overhang (5.8) and belay. 4. Traverse 100 feet left on the ledge to a hand crack by a block, re-establish the belay, and climb the crack (5.10a) to the next ledge — this is the left side of the first large ledge on **Northeast Face**. 5. Follow the right-facing dihedral formed by the top of the buttress (5.8) to the left side of Long Ledge. 6. Move the belay 100 feet right, and then cut back left on broken ground to a thin flake that leads into the left corner of the big overhang above. Hand traverse left through the lip of the overhang (5.9+), and belay on a ledge. Two or three easier pitches follow flakes up and right to the top of the face. FA: Greg Davis and Eric Winkelman, 1983.

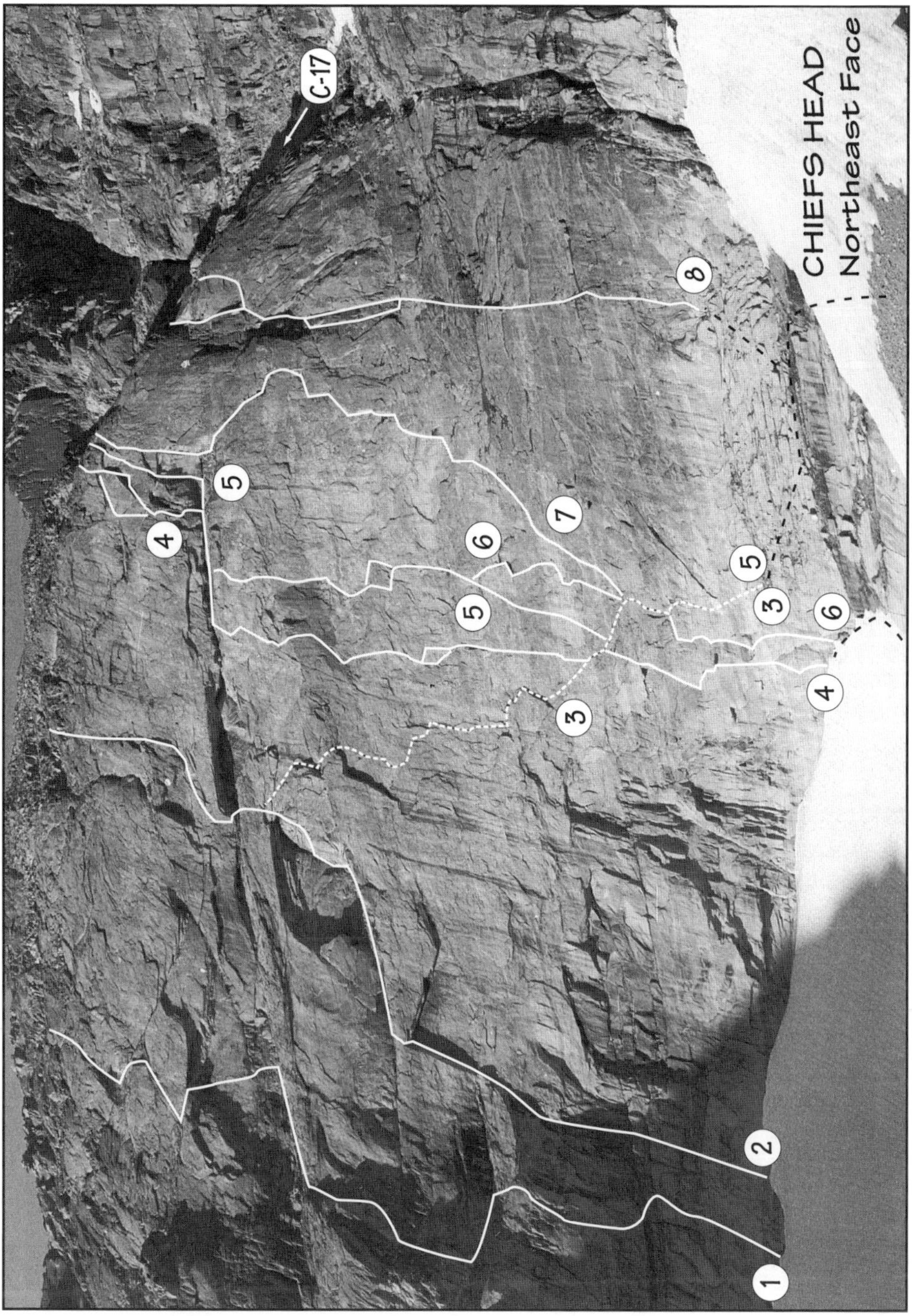
CHIEFS HEAD
Northeast Face
C-17
1
2
3
3
4
4
5
5
5
6
6
7
8

CHIEFS HEAD - Northeast Face

1. Tenderfoot IV 5.10a
2. Northeast Face IV 5.8 A3

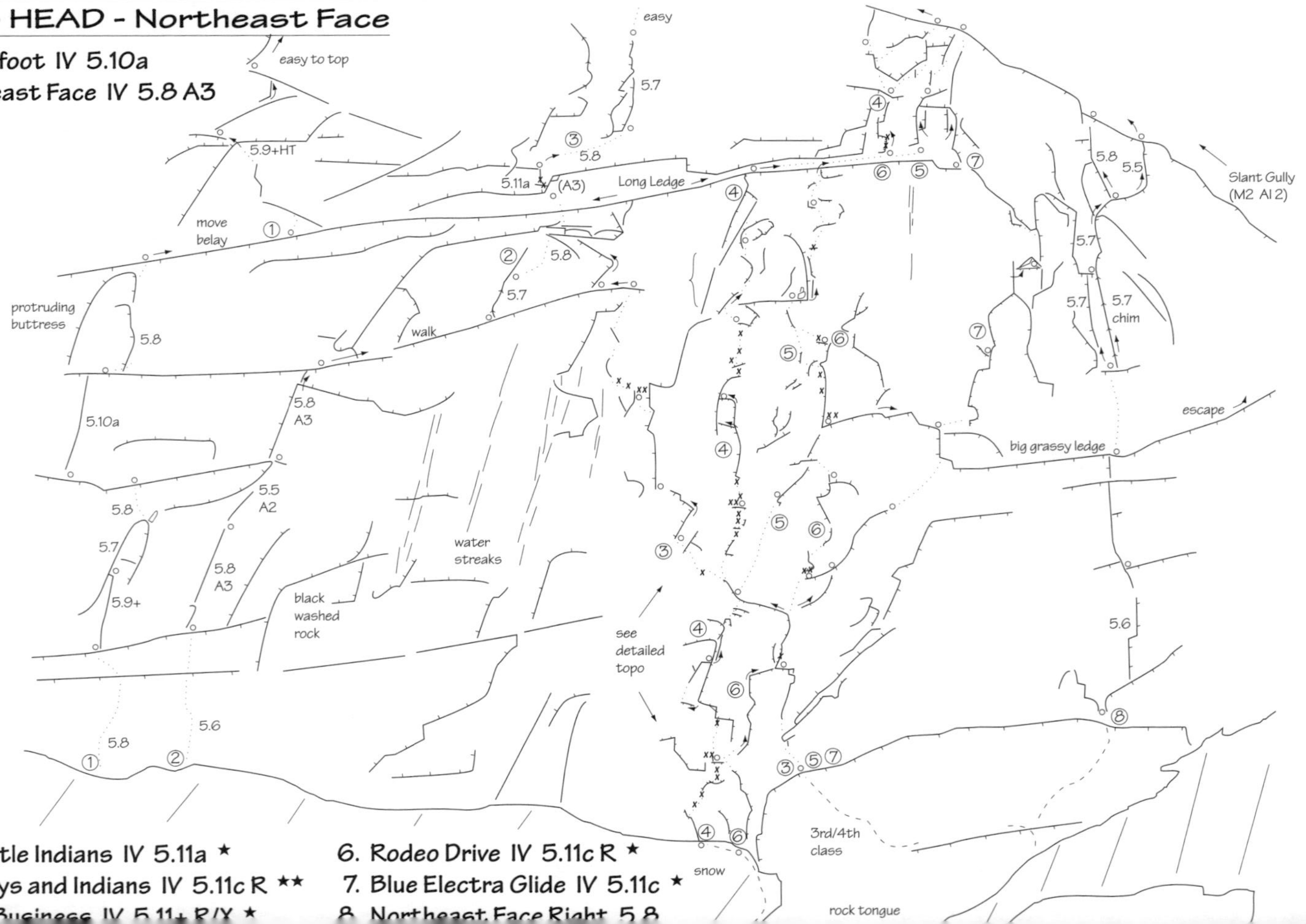

3. Ten Little Indians IV 5.11a ★
4. Cowboys and Indians IV 5.11c R ★★
5. Risky Business IV 5.11+ R/X ★
6. Rodeo Drive IV 5.11c R ★
7. Blue Electra Glide IV 5.11c ★
8. Northeast Face Right 5.8

CHIEFS HEAD - Northeast Face Detail

3. Ten Little Indians IV 5.11a ★
4. Cowboys and Indians IV 5.11c R ★★
5. Risky Business IV 5.11+ R/X ★
6. Rodeo Drive IV 5.11c ★
7. Blue Electra Glide IV 5.11c ★

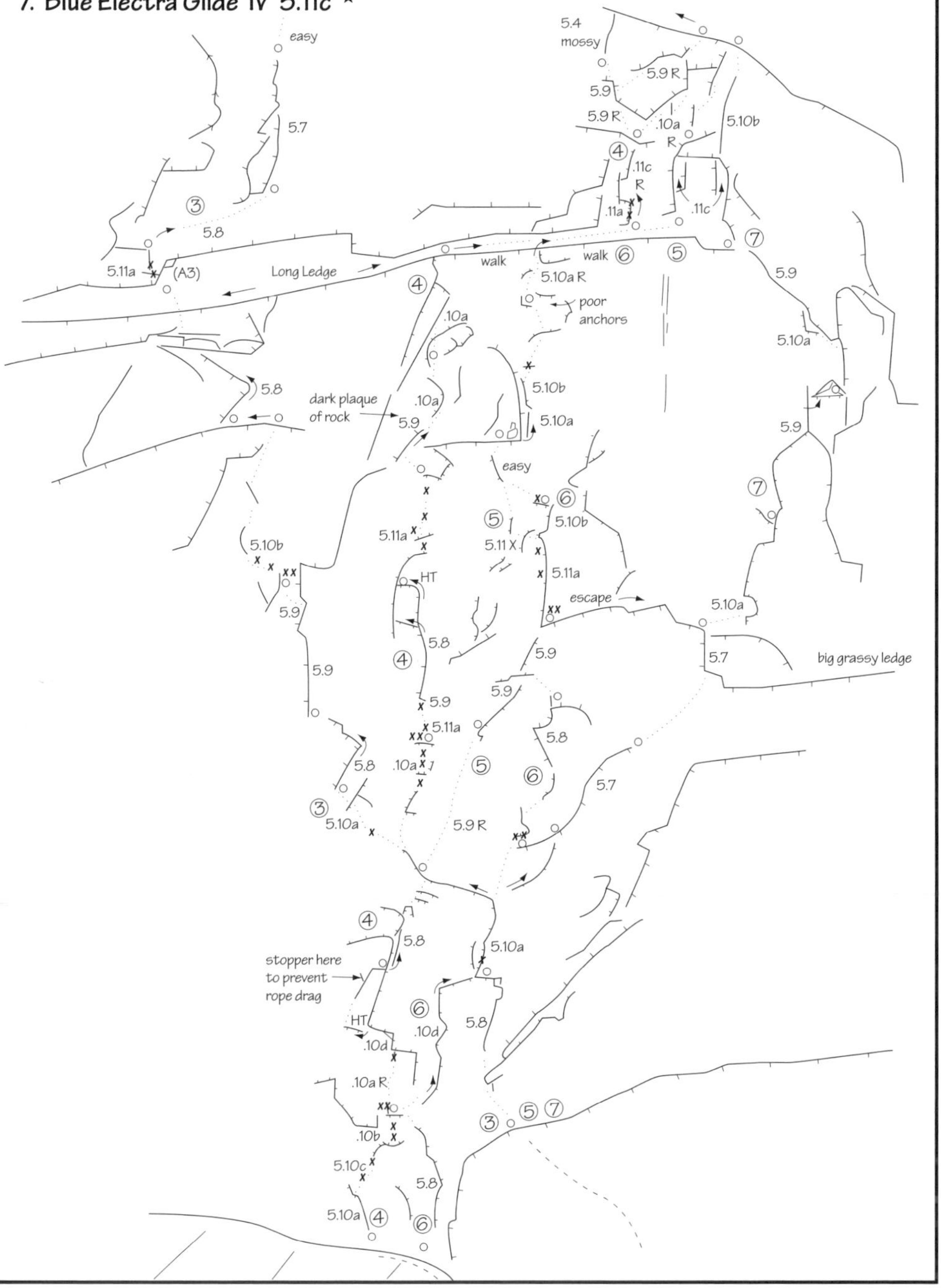

2 Northeast Face IV 5.8 A3

This old aid line begins in the middle of the wall below a very prominent angular ceiling that slopes down right, some 400 feet off the deck. Two more big roofs lie up and right, and **Northeast Face** climbs through all three of them. 1. Climb easy rock to the higher of two horizontal faults. 2-4. Follow the corner and crack system dropping down from the left edge of the angular ceiling, going straight through the roof to a big ledge, 5.8 A3. 5. Walk right on the ledge for 200 feet, passing beneath the second big overhang, and belay at a ramp leading up right. 6. Do a short pitch up the left side of the ramp with a chimney at the bottom, 5.7. 7. Continue up and right on the slab formed by the ramp, climbing near the right edge of the second roof, 5.8. Belay in the middle of Long Ledge below the left edge of the third big roof. 8. Nail through the left end of the overhang, originally A3. The fixed pins found here should not be removed as they provide protection for **Ten Little Indians**. Belay as with that route, just over the lip of the roof, or keep going up and right on shaky flakes to a belay behind a large flake, 5.8. 9 and 10. Moderate free climbing along a right-facing feature leads to the top. FA: Layton Kor and Bob Bradley, 1963.

3 Ten Little Indians IV 5.11a ★

This route traces a long diagonal line across the wall and joins **Northeast Face** at the third big overhang. Begin on the right side of the wall and scramble up the rock tongue described above (3rd class). 1. Angle left to the base of a striking wide crack, and climb to its top, 5.8. 2. Step left to the right-hand of two small corners (facing right), and climb past a fixed pin to a ledge (5.10a). Traverse left fifty feet, and belay where the ledge turns into a steeper ramp. This stance is common to routes 3, 4, and 5. 3. Go up the ramp to the end of the ledge, then make a slowly rising traverse (5.10a, bolt) to a leaning, right-facing dihedral. 4. Climb the dihedral (5.8), and traverse the ledge on its top to the left; belay below a long, right-facing flake system. 5. Climb the flake system to a stance in a corner, then step left and ascend to a double bolt belay, 5.9. 6. Traverse left past two bolts (5.10b), connect small flakes straight up to the right edge of a prominent roof-capped dihedral, and move right through a bulge to a grassy ledge. 7. Move the belay left and climb a right-facing dihedral to a ramp, then angle left on the ramp and join **Northeast Face** midway through its seventh lead. Belay in the middle of Long Ledge below the left end of a huge horizontal roof. 8. A short pitch takes the left edge of the roof past two pins (5.11a) to a stance. 9. Traverse up and right on flakes to a right-facing feature, 5.8. 10 and 11. Climb that (5.7) to finish. The last four and a half leads are the same as **Northeast Face**. Rack up to a #4 Friend. FA: Davis and Winkelman, 1991.

The next four routes overlap one another to some extent. All are long, continuously difficult free climbs that end with steep corners off the right side of Long Ledge.

4 Cowboys and Indians IV 5.11c R ★★

Hike up the snowfield along the left side of the rock tongue, then traverse left in the bergshrund until beneath a stepped roof 200 feet above. Start at a tiny crack slanting left. 1. Jam the crack to a bolt (5.10a), then move right to a fixed pin, 5.10c. Continue up and right along an arching flake, then pop over a roof at a bolt and climb past another (5.10b) to a stance at two fixed pins. Back up the belay with a #2.5 Friend. 2. Face climb to a fixed pin in the stepped roof, 5.10a R, and follow the roof to its left edge, 5.10d. Hand traverse fifteen feet left, then follow a leaning crack to a broken ledge in a roof-capped, left-facing dihedral. A directional stopper can be placed near the leaning crack to avoid rope jam in the roof. 3. Step right out of the dihedral to a nice hand crack, 5.8. Jam to the top of some big flakes, then belay on the highest of three grassy ledges (belay shared with **Ten Little Indians** and **Risky Business**). 4. Head left on the ledge, then go up to a little leaning corner (RPs) at the top of a white band of rock. Clip three bolts above to a two bolt belay on a great ledge, 5.10a. 5. Balance left past a bolt (5.11a), then run it out to another bolt just below a right-facing flake. Follow the flake to a ledge, and either continue straight up to a hand traverse left, or go left on the ledge and then up. Either way ends at the same tiny stance in a right-facing flake (small cams for the belay). 6. Continue up the flake line and climb through several overlaps, 5.11a. There are three bolts here, though the first is camouflaged and difficult to see until you get close (the other two are pretty obvious). Continue past one more bolt and find a belay anchor on a small ledge — don't go too high, or you'll end up on the big belay ledge of **Risky Business**. 7. Step left into right-leaning arch that forms the bottom edge of a dark section of rock. Follow the arch, face climb up right to a right-facing corner, and take that to a belay on the left. 8. Move left into the upper half of a long crack. Follow it to its end (5.10a), go left, then up and belay on Long Ledge. 9. Traverse the ledge right for 130 feet to a series of right-facing corners, and set up a belay under the second — look for a couple pins. 10. Climb the corner past two fixed blades to a stance on the left (5.11a), then stem a butt-kicking corner to a good ledge, 5.11c R with difficult pro. 11. Move up right to a prominent right-leaning corner and place gear at its base before it pinches off to a seam. Traverse straight right, then go up to where the leaning corner becomes vertical, 5.10a R. Follow this to an overhang, step left, and climb to the top. FA: Winkelman and Davis, 1993. **Variation**: Move left from the tenth belay, and climb a slab to the top of a left-leaning corner (the mirror image of the right-leaning corner in pitch 11), 5.9 R. Turn an overhang on the right, and either traverse up and right beneath an overhang (5.9 R) to join the last part of the standard last pitch, or move left to a belay below a mossy crack and follow that (5.4) to the top of the wall.

5 Risky Business IV 5.11+ R/X ⋆

This was the first free line on the Northeast Face. Following Rodeo Drive for a pitch avoids the scariest section. Begin as with **Ten Little Indians**, and do its first two pitches. 3. Angle right on a poorly protected slab, climbing through a light colored band followed by a darker band, 5.9 R. Belay on top of the dark band at a flake. 4. Continue up and right along small flakes to a double bolt-belay on a long ledge. 5. Climb a right-facing flake with two bolts (5.11a, bolts placed when **Rodeo Drive** went up) to a small overhang in the flake. Traverse left, passing over another flake to the base of a third (5.11 X), and take that up to a ledge. Move right to the belay bolt on **Rodeo Drive**, or stretch out the lead up an easy corner to a big ledge. The crux traverse was protected with hooks and knifeblades on the first ascent. 6. A beautiful hand crack in a leaning dihedral rises off the right end of the big ledge. It is, however, perpetually soaked and mossy. Step right out of the dihedral to a thin crack, and jam to a flake, 5.10a with excellent exposure. Continue up

Don Otten on *Rodeo Drive*, Northeast Face of Chiefs Head.

the flake, devious 5.10b, then move up right to a fixed pin. Wander up above the pin, and belay whenever a good anchor presents itself. There are several small ledges suited to belaying in this section, but bomber anchors are hard to find — a few pitons or a bolt kit is advised. It is a mistake to stretch the lead out to Long Ledge; there aren't any good anchors here either (not near the lip, anyway). 7. Angle up and right to an overhang with a left-facing dihedral on its left, 5.10a R. Take the dihedral to Long Ledge, then traverse 80 feet to several right-facing dihedrals; set up a belay below the middle (and largest) one. 8. Climb in from the left and work through an A-shaped alcove, then crank over several ceilings to a belay, 5.11+. 9. Move up right to a right-facing dihedral. Rack up to four inches, with hooks and pitons. FA: Mark Wilford and Jeff Lowe, 1984.

6 Rodeo Drive IV 5.11c R ★

This line climbs alongside **Risky Business**, and usurps several of its pitches. Begin about thirty feet right of **Cowboys and Indians** at a left-facing flake (the right-hand of two). 1. Climb the flake until it is possible to move left to the first belay on **Cowboys and Indians**. 2. Move back right into the flake system, and follow it to the first belay of **Risky Business**, 5.10d. 3. Take the right-hand of two small corners (5.10a, fixed pin) to a ledge, and then continue straight up to a belay at two pitons. 4. Move up right to a leaning, right-facing dihedral that spans a dark band of rock. Follow the dihedral to a roof, then climb around it on the right to another roof, and pop over to a belay. 5. Traverse left into **Risky Business**, and climb to its two-bolt belay. 6. Follow that route to the spot where it makes its dangerous traverse (5.11a), but continue up the flake system to its top, 5.10b. Step left to a ledge with a bolt. 7. An easy pitch goes left, then up to the big ledge on **Risky Business**. Belay on the right side of the ledge at stacked blocks. 8 and 9. Follow **Risky Business** for two pitches to Long Ledge. 10 and 11. Join **Cowboys and Indians**. FA: Davis and Winkelman, 1993.

7 Blue Electra Glide IV 5.11c ★

This route also starts with **Ten Little Indians/Risky Business**, but then takes an independent line on the right side of the face. Climb one and a half pitches on **Ten Little Indians** to the ledge, then step right and climb a flake to the right end of another ledge (**Rodeo Drive** belays on the left side). 3. Do an easy ramp up right. 4. Continue up to a nice right-facing corner, and climb to its top. 5. Traverse right across a slab and climb a left-facing dihedral to an alcove, 5.10a. 6. Continue along the dihedral, jogging right at mid-pitch, and exit right near the end of the pitch to a good ledge, 5.9. 7. Climb the corner off the right end of the ledge to a shelf on the left, then angle left along a corner and crack system to the extreme right side of Long Ledge, 5.10a. 8. Tackle the steep dihedrals directly above through the right edge of an overhang, 5.11c. 9. Continue in the same crack system, 5.10b. Bring pitons and a standard rack. FA: Greg Davis and Kevin Cooney, 1989.

8 Northeast Face Right II 5.8

This is a comparatively mellow route with easy escape on the far right side of the wall. Scramble to the upper right portion of the rock tongue, and belay below a nice crack one pitch up the wall. 1. Follow moderate flakes to a long grassy ledge at the base of the crack, 5.6. 2. Jam the crack for a full pitch to a big grassy ledge. 3. Move up to the base of an obvious chimney. 4. Follow the chimney (or the dihedral to its left) to a ledge, 5.7. 5. Continue up the chimney, then exit right to a belay below a big, right-facing dihedral. 6. Climb the dihedral (5.8) to a ledge at its top, then work right into **Slant Gully**. The gully is loose 3rd class in summer; it leads all the way to the east ridge of Chiefs Head. **Variation:** from the right end of the fifth belay ledge, climb a corner up right, 5.5.

C-17 Slant Gully III M2 AI 2

See the ice climbing section.

Northwest Face

The 1,000 foot slab of the Northwest Face is home to some of the scariest lines in the Park. Its low angle allows climbing on featureless rock, but this absence of crack systems makes for dangerous run out climbing and devious route finding. For the experienced climber willing to execute 5.10 moves with little protection, this wall provides exceptionally clean slab climbing in a beautiful setting.

All routes end on a long ledge system just below the west ridge. The ledge holds snow late into the season — expect to encounter wet spots along each climb, especially near the top.

Descent: To descend, walk right on the ledge until reaching a 3rd class gully that drops down to a long (often snow covered) ramp, and then follow the ramp east to the snowfield at the base of the wall. One can also gain the west ridge and follow it down to Stone Man Pass, dropping down into the Spearhead plateau further north. This is longer, but easier.

C-18 Central Rib II M4- (?)

The approach to this route is the same as the hike into the Northwest Face, but the climb is located on the rib that becomes Spearhead — see the ice climbing section.

1 Papoose III 5.9 R ★

This route climbs the left side of the wall (shaded and cold) for five leads, with several opportunities to escape left. Begin left of a jagged, right-facing dihedral in the center of a gray section. 1. Start down and left of a short, right-slanting corner, and climb through it to a ledge; move up and right to belay. 2. A long pitch goes straight up the face, linking small flakes to a belay at a slot, 5.9. 3. Climb the short slot, then continue up a right-facing dihedral to a long ledge with two stubby rock towers. 4. Climb straight up a thin slab (5.9 R) to the next ledge, or follow two left-slanting ramps on the left to the same ledge (easier). 5. Go up, then angle left along a slanting crack to a belay on the left edge of the wall. Scramble up and right from the end of the route to join the descent ledge. FA: John Harlin and Kent Wheeler, 1980. **Variation:** Continue straight up on the last pitch (5.9 X).

2 Kachina Winds IV 5.10a X

This climb begins below the right side of an obvious ramp that slants up left to a roof band cutting back right, half way between **Papoose** and **Seven Arrows**. 1. Climb over the right end of the ramp, then up and right to a pinnacle (5.8, optional belay), and continue along a left-facing flake to a sloping ledge, 5.9. 2. Go straight up, passing the right edge of the roof band, and belay amongst right-facing flakes, a long pitch of run out 5.9. 3. Pass the right end of **Papoose**'s long ledge, and angle

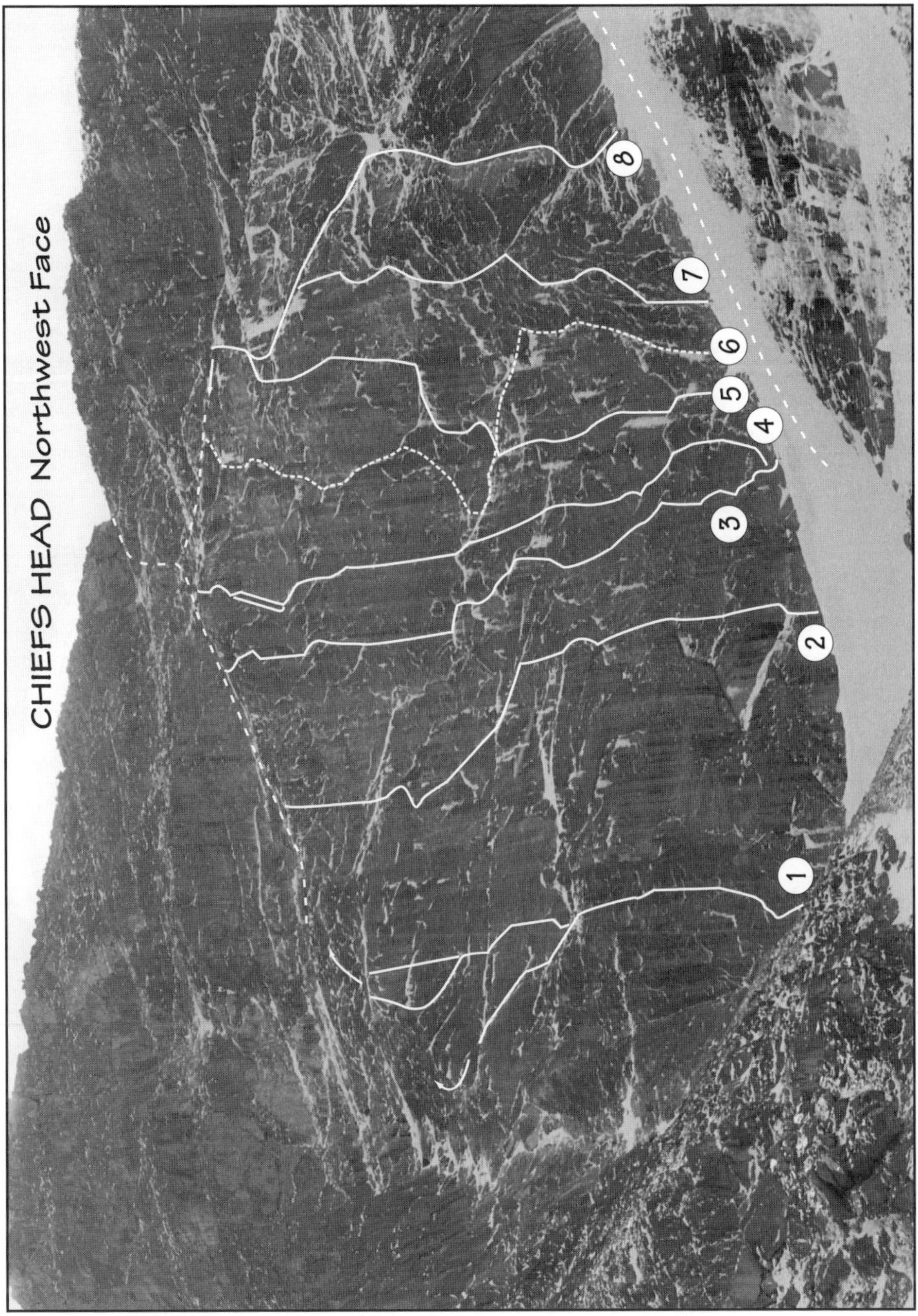
CHIEFS HEAD Northwest Face
1
2
3
4
5
6
7
8

CHIEFS HEAD - Northwest Face

1. Papoose III 5.9 R ★
2. Kachina Winds IV 5.10a X
3. Seven Arrows IV 5.10b R/X ★★★
4. Birds of Fire IV 5.11a ★★★
5. Screaming Eagle IV 5.10 X
6. Path of Elders IV 5.10a R ★★
7. As You Like It IV 5.10 R
8. Much Ado About Nothing III 5.8

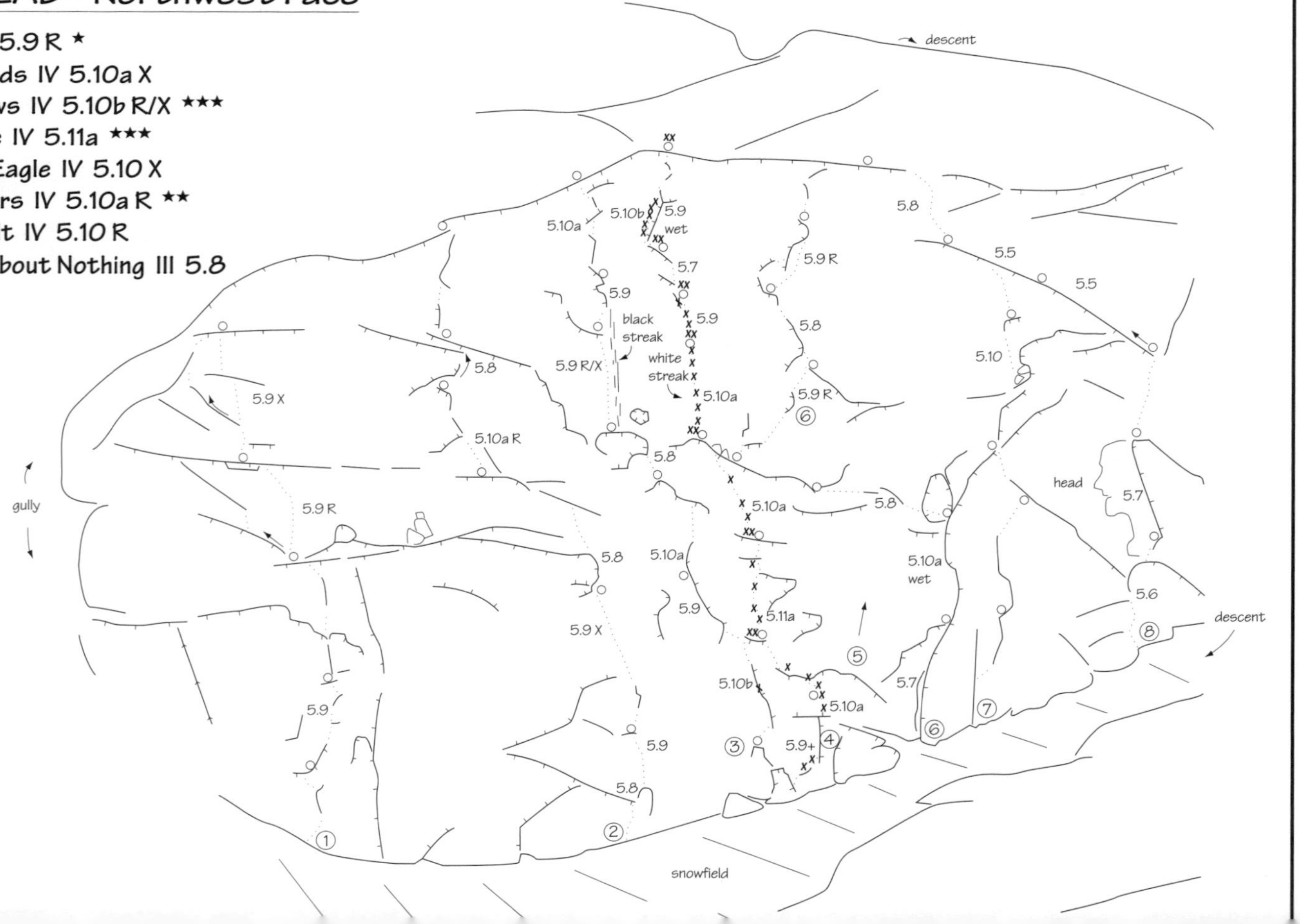

left along a ramp to the next ledge, 5.8. 4. Move left on the ledge, then diagonal left up a slab, aiming for the left end of an overhang, 5.10a R. 5. Traverse under the roof and climb around its right side to the middle of a big ledge, 5.8. 6. Step left and climb easy flakes to the top of the face. Work right along a ledge over the top of **Seven Arrows** and gain the descent ledge. FA: Bob Horan and John Baldwin, 1993.

3 Seven Arrows IV 5.10b R/X ★★★

Direct and highly aesthetic, **Seven Arrows** climbs the center of the northwest face, beginning at a rectangular-shaped flake with its upper right corner missing. A faint, black water streak trickles down from the descent ledge; the upper part of the route climbs along its left edge. 1. Climb to the top of the rectangular flake and lead up left to a right-facing flake. Belay here to avoid simul-climbing on this long pitch. Angle back right to a faint left-facing corner (5.10b) and stretch the rope out to a ledge on the right which is shared with **Birds of Fire**. One can also belay in the corner at a horn. 2. Angle left to a similar left-facing corner and find a belay. 3. Continue with the corner (5.10a), then step right to a good ledge. 4. A short pitch heads left around the right side of a distinct flake, then crosses the bottom of the black streak to a good belay on the flake. 5. Face climb along the left side of the streak, beautiful (though run out) 5.9. A belay can be had after 120 feet, but most parties simul-climb for a bit to reach a better stance 180 feet out. Better yet, bring a long rope. 6. Step right to a right-facing dihedral and maneuver around the right edge of a protruding flake, 5.9. 7. Climb a waning corner and over a roof (5.10b), then angle left to the long descent ledge. Rack: Lots of thin gear up to a 2.5 Friend. FA: Charlie Fowler and John Harlin, 1980.

4 Birds of Fire IV 5.11a ★★★

This bolt-protected route is relatively safe compared to the other lines on Chiefs Head, although it still has run out sections. It parallels **Seven Arrows** on the right, climbing an ultra-clean white streak high on the wall. Each pitch except the first ends at a two-bolt belay. 1. Move right from the rectangular flake on **Seven Arrows** past two bolts, and follow a shallow corner to a roof, 5.9+ (optional belay). Spring over the roof (5.10a) and belay at a stance with a bolt. 2. Climb to a grassy ramp, then angle left along it to a higher ledge. 3. Boulder up past two bolts (crux) and fire straight up to a stance. 4. Weave back and forth beside two bolts and a piton to a belay at the left end of a long, angling ramp, 5.10a. 5. Climb straight up the white streak, phenomenal 5.10a. 6. Continue with the streak, 5.9. 7. A short pitch runs left to the base of a right-facing dihedral. 8. The original line took the dihedral (wet 5.9), turned a roof at its top, and jammed a crack to the descent ledge. A much better finish steps left and climbs along the outer edge of the dihedral with five bolts, 5.10b, rejoining the original line at the jam crack above the roof. Belay in the crack, or stretch the rope out to bolts on the descent ledge. Bring a light rack up to a #3 Friend. Seven rappels, utilizing the belay anchors, end at the optional belay flake on the first pitch of **Seven Arrows** (down climb from there), though it doesn't take any longer to walk down. FA: Richard and Joyce Rossiter and Rob Woolf, 1988.

5 Screaming Eagle IV 5.10 X ★

This audacious line crosses **Path of Elders** at its long traverse and continues up on nebulous ground. The first ascent team used a 300 foot rope and little protection, and they suggest a bolt kit (as well as pitons and keyhole hangers) for any further attempts. The approximate line of ascent is marked in the photo; it begins with the leaning ramp mentioned in the next route. It seems that the first portion of the route follows the original Kor-Culp line on **Path of Elders** (an old bolt was found); but be advised that little information is known about the exact line of ascent. FA: Charlie Fowler and Dan McGee, 1987.

6 Path of Elders IV 5.10a R ★★

A ground breaking route for its time, **Path of Elders** was the maiden voyage on the wall (it was originally called **Center Route**). The second ascent wasn't completed until fourteen years later, testimony to the difficult and dangerous climbing that Layton Kor was famous for. Begin in a left-facing system about 100 feet right of **Seven Arrows**, just right of a leaning ramp. 1. Climb the dihedral for a pitch, 5.7. 2. Continue with the corner over a roof (5.10a, usually wet), or find a run out 5.9 variation on the right. Belay on the right side of a big flake**. 3 and 4.** Cross beneath the flake and gain a long ledge that slants all the way over to the fourth belay on **Birds of Fire**. Traverse along this ledge for two pitches (spots of 5.8). 5. Move up to a good ledge (bring pitons for pro here), then arc right on run out 5.9 to reach the base of a series of right-facing corners; a long pitch. 6. Climb to a stance near the top of the corners, 5.9. 7. Another long right-angling traverse (5.9 R) ends at a shallow corner. Go up the corner (fixed pins) to a belay, 5.8. It is also possible to finish the last fifty feet of the sixth pitch corners, then traverse right along an overhang, eventually reaching the same belay (5.9 R). 8. Easier cracks lead to the descent ledge. Rack: Include a plentiful selection of small wires; thin pitons are helpful. FA: Layton Kor and Bob Culp, 1961. FFA: Billy Westbay and Dan McClure, by a less direct line (described above), 1975.

7 As You Like It IV 5.10 R

Begin fifty feet right of **Path of Elders** at a crack in a shallow, left-facing corner. Follow the crack for sixty feet, then step right to another crack, and take that to a ledge. A moderate pitch climbs to the end of the second crack, then moves right to a diagonal crack coming in from the right. Follow that to begin the third lead, then climb up and left to the base of a left-facing dihedral. The next pitch takes the dihedral to a blocky corner. Go up the blocky corner, then friction up a smooth slab (5.10) to a small ledge — it may be possible to avoid the crux by taking the blocky corner to its top, and moving right into **Much Ado**. A final pitch climbs straight up to the ramp on the next route. FA: Eric Doub and G. Russel, 1980.

8 Much Ado About Nothing III 5.8

This route climbs up to a left-leaning ramp on the upper right side of the slab, and follows that to the top. Begin below a 150 foot high, light-colored patch of rock. The patch looks like the head of an Easter Island statue. 1. Climb moderate and broken ground to the base of the head, 5.6. 2. Climb the left-facing dihedral that borders the head on the right, 5.7. 3. Go up and right on easy ledges to the base of the ramp. 4 and 5. Follow the ramp left for two pitches, 5.5. 6. Go more or less straight up along flakes (5.8) to a ledge that leads left and joins the descent. FA: Dan McClure and M. Kleker, 1980s.

THE SPEARHEAD

The 800 foot northeast face of Spearhead stands in a commanding position at the head of Glacier Gorge, and at the end of a broad ridge extending north from the top of Chiefs Head. Its clean, light colored granite is among the best rock found in the alpine regions, featuring flakes, thin cracks and face climbing. With routes of every grade, Spearhead heads the list of the must-do walls in RMNP. A long, grassy ledge, known as Middle Earth, extends clear across the bottom of the northeast face. The Eye of Mordor peers out 50 feet above Middle Earth, directly below the summit block, and the prominent sickle-shaped dihedral/roof up and right is the landmark feature on **Sykes Sickle**.

Only one of the routes ends on the actual summit block; the others finish at a ledge 100 feet below it, or on the north ridge. If weather and time permit, a quick jaunt to the top comes highly recommended. A tight passage on the west side with a hole dropping out onto the northeast face worms up to the tiny summit, which affords a panoramic view of Glacier Gorge.

Approach: Hike to Black Lake, then head east (toward Longs Peak) out of the Black Lake basin along the inlet stream, and arrive on the plateau below Spearhead after a half mile. Cross the stream and pick your way across granite slabs and krummholz, passing a number of cairns. Some parties bivouac near the base of the face, but all routes can be completed in a day.

Descent: The easiest way down from the summit area scrambles along the northwest slopes, avoiding any steep gullies to the west. This is the standard descent for routes ending on the north ridge, though the next option can also be used. It begins on the loose ledge below the summit tower (routes **2** through **10** end at various points along this ledge, and it can be traversed right to gain the summit area). Traverse the ledge to its far left side, being careful not to roll rocks on parties below, then turn south toward Chiefs Head and walk down grassy shelves past the first steep gully on the left. Descend the second gully, down climb a short 4th class wall, and move right (toward Chiefs Head again) until a 3rd class ramp leading down left is reached. The ramp looks as though it will cliff out in several spots, but it goes all the way to the talus at the base of the southeast face.

1 Border Patrol II 5.8

This is a short route that climbs the left side of the southeast face. Begin about 100 feet right of the 3rd class descent ramp described above. Follow a slab crack that is right of a large, right-facing dihedral. Belay on the left side of a grassy ledge. Climb a long pitch up a right-facing corner system; this ends on the descent route, below the 4th class wall. FA: Dan Hare and Jeff Bevan, 1974.

2 East Direct III 5.10d ★

This route goes along a set of overlapping left-facing flakes directly below a prominent stepped dihedral high on the wall. Begin left of a dark dike that rises up right — this dike continues around the corner onto the northeast face and becomes Middle Earth Ledge. Climb thin cracks to a ledge on the right. Step right into the corners, and follow these for two or three pitches to a belay below the right edge of the stepped dihedral; take that to the top (crux). FA: Michael Colacino and Ron Kirk, 1988.

3 Awesome III 5.10a R ★

Awesome is a two-pitch direct finish to **East Prow**. Do three pitches on that route, but set the belay 15 feet down and left of **East Prow**'s horn belay. 4. Climb into the big, hanging dihedral above, and go up cracks on the left wall to a hanging belay on the arete, 5.10a R. 5. Continue with thin cracks on the left wall of the dihedral (5.9+) to the overhang at its top. Traverse left for ten feet, around the arete, and pull over the roof at a short dihedral leading to the descent ledge. FA: Eric Bader and Paul Hauser, 1980.

4 East Prow III 5.10a ★★

As its name implies, this line climbs along the juncture of the northeast and southeast faces, but only for its first three and a half pitches. It then traverses right onto the northeast face, and shares its final three leads with **Age Axe**. Begin below a pointed, right-facing flake (with a tooth of rock wedged beneath it), about 100 feet left of **Age Axe**. 1. Climb over a dike, then friction right to the tooth (5.7). Pull through an overhang onto the pointed flake, and climb a knobby slab to a left-slanting crack; follow that to a good ledge. Another nice belay ledge sits forty feet higher (200 feet from the ground). 2. Undercling a flake from the higher belay and climb along thin flakes to a double roof. Pull through the first (5.8 with marginal gear) and turn the second on the left; set a sling belay in a left-facing dihedral. 3. Follow the dihedral over another roof, and take a thin crack (5.8+) to an area of ledges. Stretch the lead to a good belay at a horn, directly below a prominent fist crack on the left edge of the northeast face. 4. Jam the fist crack (5.8), stem past a loose section, and clip two old bolts for a directional. Continue right for twenty feet to a belay at the end of a big ledge. 5. Climb an easy ramp off the right end of the ledge to a gaping flake. Either squeeze up the slot behind the flake (5.7), or move right to a nicely exposed 5.8 flake. Both end on a long, grassy ledge — belay on its left side. 6. Climb a steep crack past two small roofs, 5.10a. Three wires were fixed at the crux in 1996. FA: Dan Hare and Jeff Bevan, 1974.

5 Age Axe III 5.10a ★★

Two obvious right-facing dihedrals, with low-angled ramps beneath them, mark the left side of the wall just above Middle Earth. **Age Axe** takes the left dihedral, which is capped with a large roof. Begin at a serrated flake near the left side of the northeast face. 1. Follow a thin RP crack on the left side of the flake (5.7) and continue up to a big sloping ledge below the dihedral. 2. Go up the dihedral for fifteen feet, then face climb left to a crack with fixed pin. Step left from the pin and climb to an old bolt (exciting 5.10a), then move back right to the crack. Angle left from the end of the crack to a cramped belay in a horizontal slot. 3. Step right, then stem opposing dihedrals to a bolt on the left. Move left at the bolt and climb past loose corners to a good belay at a horn (same as third belay on **East Prow**). Follow that route to the ledge 100 feet below the summit. FA: Ajax Greene and Chris Reveley, 1975. **Variation:** One can also begin the route with twin finger cracks twenty feet left (5.8), or traverse in on the dike mentioned in **East Prow** (5.5).

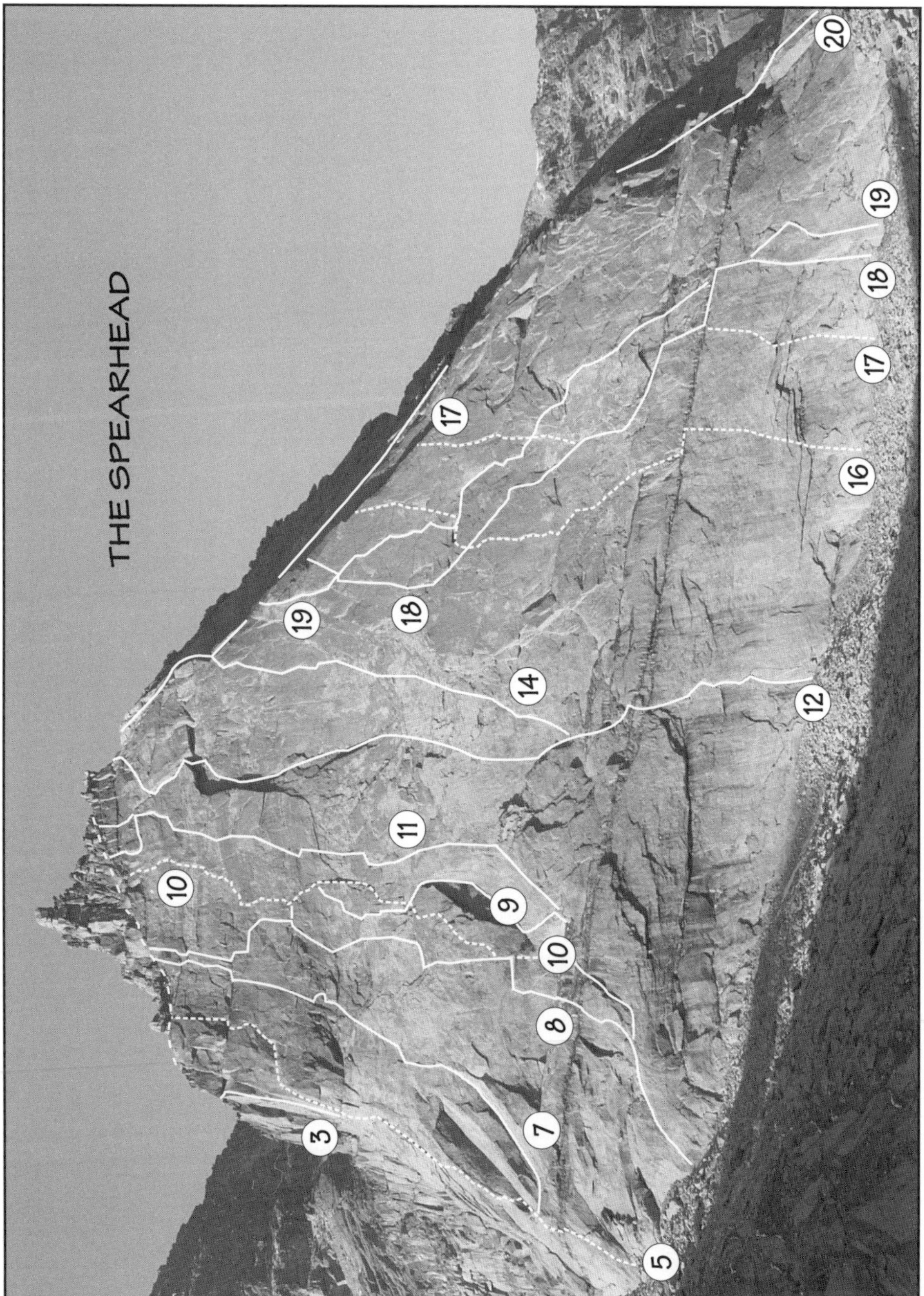
THE SPEARHEAD
3
5
7
8
9
10
10
11
12
14
16
17
17
18
18
19
19
20

SPEARHEAD

3. Awesome III 5.10a R ★
4. East Prow III 5.10a ★★
5. Age Axe III 5.10a ★★
6. Unbelievers III 5.10b ★
7. Stone Monkey III 5.12a ★★★
8. Three Stoners IV 5.11a ★★
9. Obviously Four Believers IV 5.11a ★★
10. All Two Obvious IV 5.11d ★★★
11. Spear Me the Details IV 5.11d ★★
12. Sykes Sickle III 5.9+ ★★★
13. Atmospear III 5.10d ★★
14. Stratospear III 5.11c R ★
15. The Ten Essentials III 5.8 ★
16. Burning Spear III 5.10c R ★
17. Barb Gnarly III 5.11b ★★
18. The Barb III 5.10c ★★★
19. Barbarella III 5.10d ★★
20. North Ridge III 5.6 ★★★

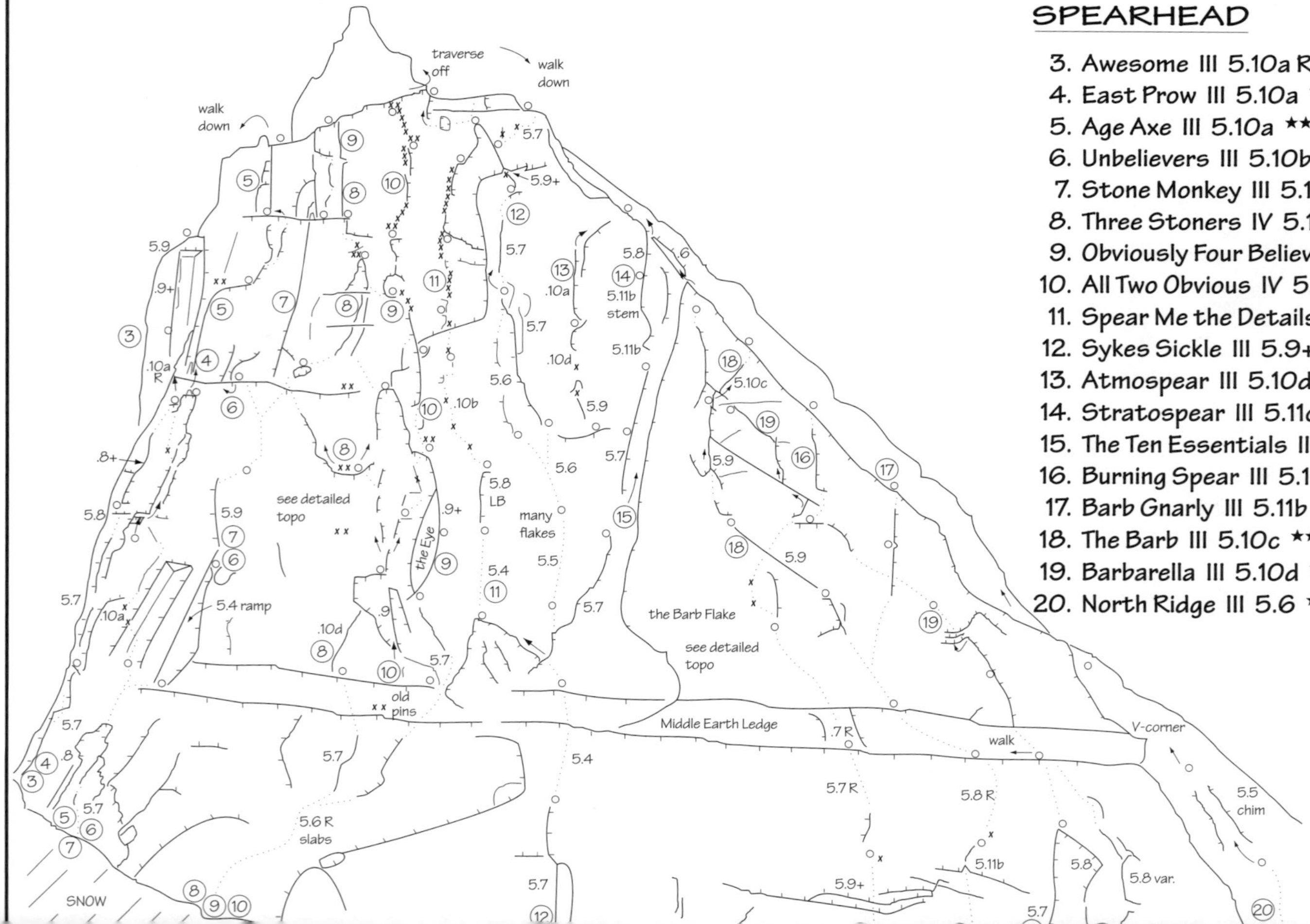

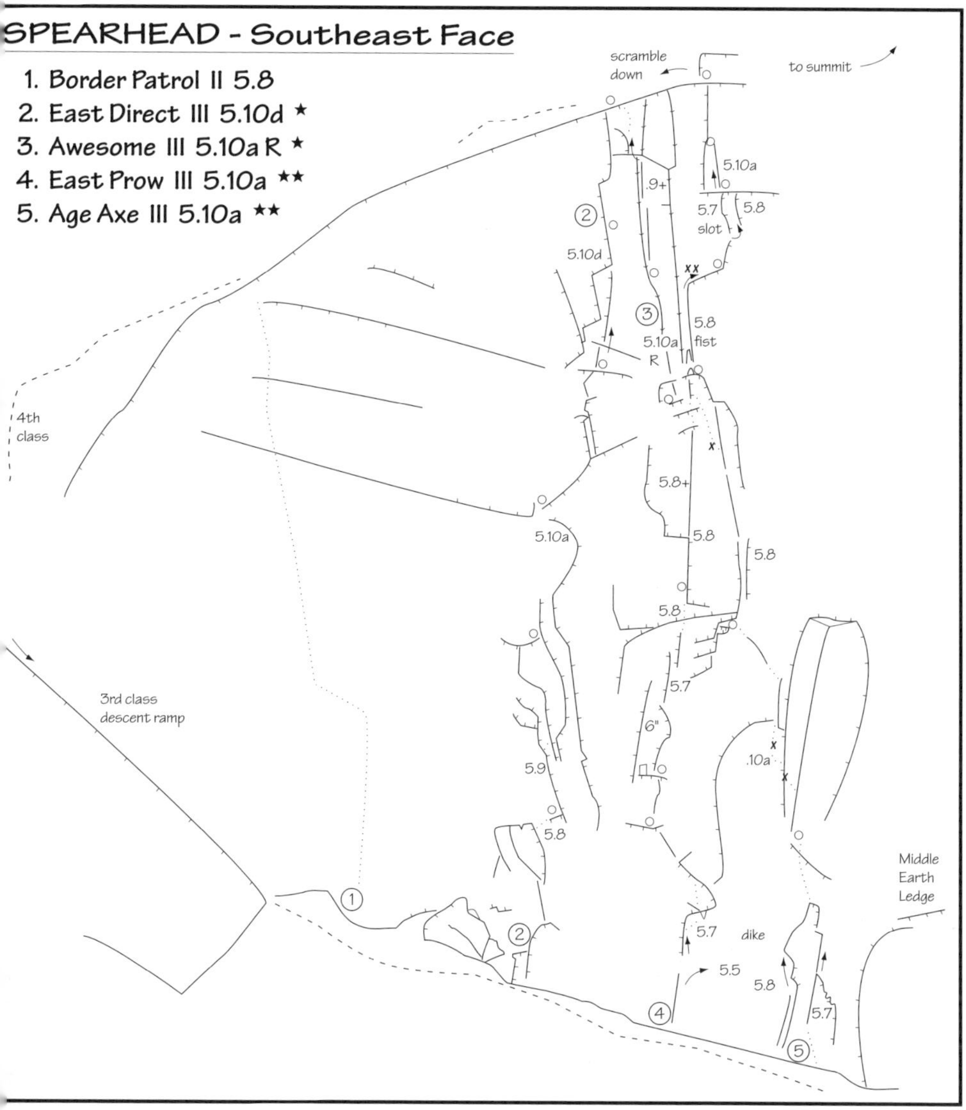

6 Unbelievers III 5.10b ★

This is the continuation of an incomplete route called **Scimitar**, which rappelled after three pitches. It shares the first three and a half pitches of **Stone Monkey**, then hand traverses left (5.9) to the edge of the wall and joins **Age Axe**. FA (of **Scimitar**): Scott Woodruff and Dan Hare, 1975.

7 Stone Monkey III 5.12a ★★★

This route climbs the right dihedral of the two mentioned in **Age Axe**, and then works up the wall to a fantastic thin crack. Only the fifth pitch is original (the first four were done as **Scimitar**, and the last with **Obviously Four**...). 1. Do the first pitch of **Age Axe**, or climb the curving dihedral to the right and pull over a bulge(?); belay at the base of the right dihedral. 2. Climb the easy ramp along the dihedral.

3. Work into a right-facing flake and lieback to near its top (5.9). Make an exciting 5.10 traverse (poor pro) twenty feet right to a sling belay. 4. Climb flakes up right to a grassy ledge, then go straight up to a belay on a rectangular plaque. 5. Undercling left to gain an angling corner (5.9), continue to its end, and jam a desperately thin crack (crux) to a block in an alcove on a grassy ledge. Routes **4** through **9** belay along this ledge. 6. Walk fifteen feet right to another alcove and do the last pitch of **Obviously Four Believers** to the descent ledge. FA: Chip Chace and Dan Stone, 1985. **Variations:** Begin between the two alcoves on the fifth pitch belay ledge at a short, right-leaning corner. Follow that to a flake (5.9+), go up the flake and step right, then traverse back left along the lip of a little roof (5.9+ R). Turn the roof on the left and jam a crack straight up. FA: Bernard Gillett and Don Otten, 1996. The crack leading out of the left alcove (with big block) may have also been climbed. Another short, though difficult lead can be had after the descent ledge is reached: Locate a tiny crack on a 35 foot block and climb to a big ledge, 5.12a (FA: Jeff Lowe and George Lowe on top rope, 1983).

The following five routes all begin with the same approach pitches to Middle Earth Ledge. They can be done in one long lead when the snowpack is high, but simul-climbing or an intermediate belay is usually required. Locate two short, right-facing dihedrals with an S-crack between them; all lead to Middle Earth below and left of the Eye of Mordor. Angle up to the S-crack from the left (easy slabs), and take that (5.7) or either of the dihedrals to the ledge. The ledge is two-tiered here, and these routes begin from the second tier.

8 Three Stoners IV 5.11a ★★

This route begins from the left side of the upper tier described above, below a tiny crack, and joins **Obviously Four Believers** for its final two pitches. 1. Jam the crack (5.10d, strenuous gear placements) to a little left-facing corner, and follow the corner to a ledge. 2. Follow flakes on the left to a big scooped out ledge with a fixed anchor, 5.9. 3. An easy pitch goes up left to another grassy ledge, then continues to the fourth belay on **Stone Monkey**. One can also climb straight up a left-facing system to the first ledge and belay at a rappel station. 4. There are several ways to climb the bottom half of this pitch; the basic strategy is to head up to the right side of a big triangular flake, and belay on its top. 5 and 6. Do the sixth and seventh leads of the next route to the descent ledge below the summit block. 7. Work up a roof-capped chimney on the northeast face of the summit block, 5.8. Descend from the summit block by dropping into a hole and wriggling west out a slot. FA: Nichols party, early 1980s.

9 Obviously Four Believers IV 5.11a ★★

This was the first route up the left side of the northeast face. It climbs the right side of the Eye of Mordor, zigzags up for two pitches, and then traverses left to a prominent triangular flake, where **Three Stoners** joins in. Start on the right side of the upper tier described above. 1. Scale a short wall and angle left to the Eye of Mordor. 2. Jam a finger crack along the right side of the Eye to a belay at fixed slings. 3. Continue the crack (wet 5.9+) and head left past a piton belay on the next route to a right-facing flake; belay on top of the flake. 4. Go back right to a short crack, then up into a right-facing corner, 5.9. Clip three pins and belay in a "half-circle" (two #3 Friends). 5. Traverse straight left to the right side of the triangular flake,

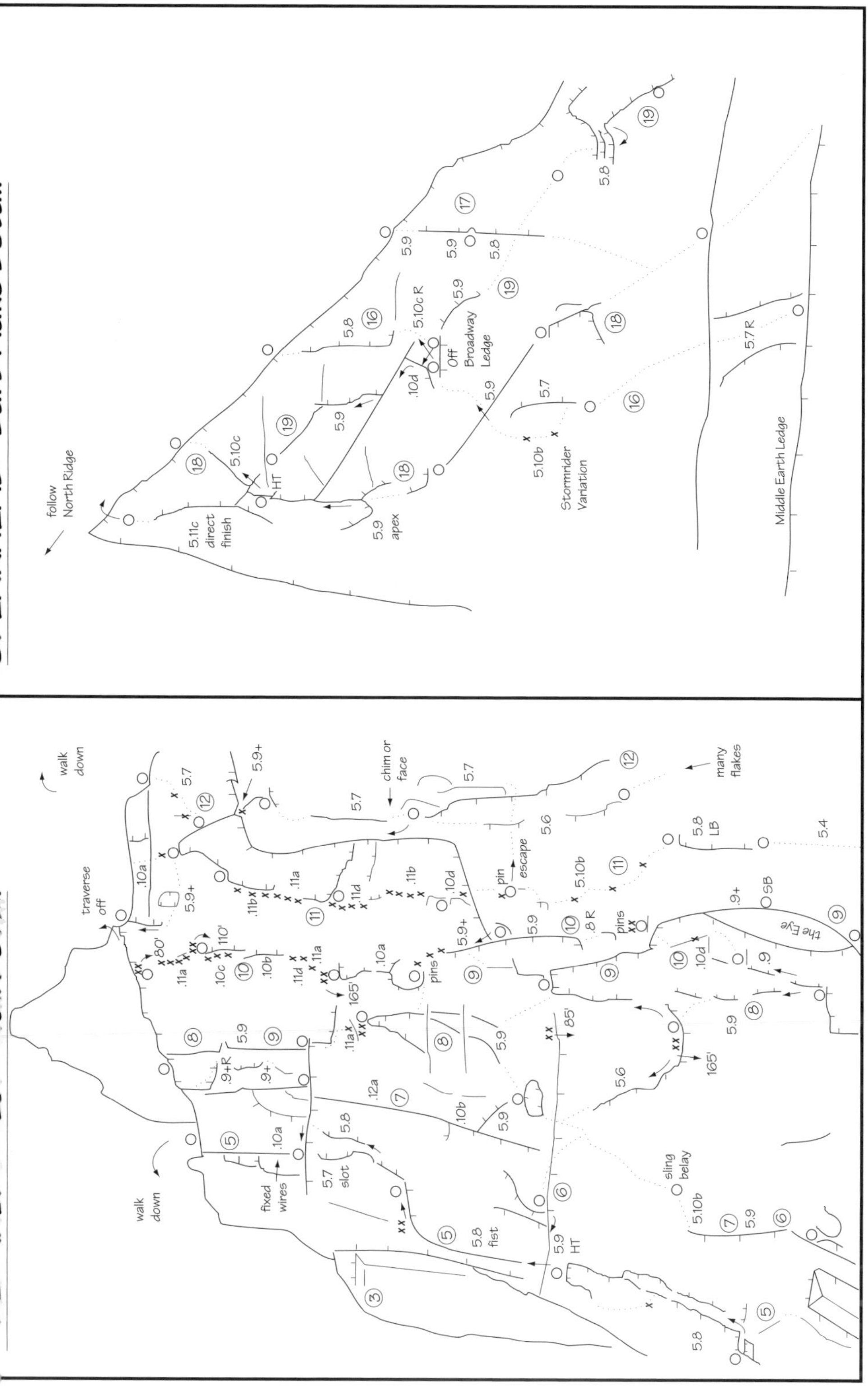
follow North Ridge
5.11c direct finish
Broadway Ledge
Stormrider Variation
Middle Earth Ledge
walk down
traverse off
chim or face
many flakes
escape
sling belay
fixed wires
the Eye

Hidetaka Suzuki on the crux pitch of *Three Stoners*, Spearhead.

PHOTO: DOUG SNIVELY

and belay on its top. 6. Step off the top of the flake and crank through a small overlap (5.11a), then work left to another, much longer overlap. Two old bolts protect this section. Undercling left along the upper overlap for thirty feet, turn up into a short corner, and follow that to an alcove on the right side of a grassy ledge. 7. Climb a 5.9 crack, step left around a small roof, and go straight up to the descent ledge. FA: Mike Covington, John Marts, Rick Petrillo and Jim Stanton, as an aid line in 1967. **Variation:** A more direct version of the route goes left from the third belay, then up and right as in **Three Stoners** to the right side of the triangular flake (one pitch).

10 All Two Obvious IV 5.11d ***

This stellar route ascends left of the Eye of Mordor, and then crosses **Obviously Four Believers**, finishing to its right. Start in the middle of the upper tier described above at a left-facing flake. 1. Climb this to the first belay on **Three Stoners** (60 feet), but continue up and right along left-facing flakes to a belay at a perfect, short finger crack, 5.9. 2. Move up right to a tiny, angling seam (fixed pin). Climb to the pin (5.10d, RPs), then step right at the end of the seam to a fixed pin belay. 3. Move up left and undercling right into an obvious right-facing flake system. Go about half way up and belay at a stance on the right, 5.8 R. 4. Continue up the flake system (5.9+, RPs), and clip three pins to the "half circle" belay on the previous route (two #3 Friends for the belay). 5. Make a difficult entry move into the crack above the circle (5.10a), then jam a left-facing corner to a bolt belay, 5.8. This is a steep pitch, and one of the best on the wall. 6. Face climb past increasingly difficult ground (three bolts, foot intensive slab work, 5.11d), then follow shallow, left-facing flakes (three more bolts) to a bolt belay. 7. Weave past four bolts (5.11a), and climb to a crack ending at a bolt belay just below the descent ledge. FA: The first part of pitch one was climbed by Charlie Fowler and Kent Lugbill, 1981. Dan Stone and Jeff Achey did the second pitch, 1985. The rest of the route was done by Greg Davis and Eric Winkelman, 1993.

11 Spear Me the Details IV 5.11d **

As with **Four Believers**, start on the right side of the ledge below the Eye. 1. Scale a short wall and angle right on easy ground to the top of a broken mass of flakes. 2. Continue with moderate rock to the base of a left-facing pillar, then jam and lieback the pillar, 5.8. The base of the pillar may also be reached from the right via **Sykes Sickle**. 3. Angle left past two pitons and an old bolt (5.10b) then go up to a flake. Traverse right 15 feet and move up a shallow crack to a stance (fixed pin) below a long, small roof band. An escape is possible here with a 90 foot traverse to **Sykes Sickle**. 4. Climb to the roof band, and breach it at its narrowest point with a mantle (bolt). Hand traverse left, then up to a belay below a roof-topped corner, 5.10d. 5. Pop over the roof, then work right along three bolts and a pin, 5.11b. Ascend a thin flake and scratch past four more bolts (5.11d) to a belay at the base of a left-facing corner. 6. Follow the corner, move right (5.11a, bolts and piton), and take another corner with fixed pins to its top, 5.11b. 7. Continue with the left-facing dihedral system to a belay on top of a column. 8. Face climb straight left past a shallow dihedral (5.9+) and go up the next dihedral. FA of first three pitches: Ed Webster and Joe Frank, around 1986. FA of complete line: Greg Davis and Neal Beidleman, 1991. **Variation:** A straight up version of the last pitch clips two bolts, and then climbs a seam to a short, right-facing corner, 5.10a.

Sean McMahan on *All Two Obvious*, Spearhead.

12 Sykes Sickle III 5.9+ ★★★

A time honored classic, **Sykes Sickle** breaks through the obvious feature for which it was named. Start in the middle of the face directly below the sickle at two parallel cracks. 1. Take the left crack in a corner, 5.7. 2. Go to Middle Earth ledge, 5.4. 3 and 4. Two moderate pitches wander up flakes and cracks to the base of a slanting, right-facing dihedral. 5. Climb into the dihedral and jam up steep cracks (5.7) to a belay level with the bottom of the sickle. The flakes and face left of the dihedral provide an alternate route. 6. Head up left into the sickle and chimney up its left side for a short distance (often wet). The jam cracks immediately above the belay can also be climbed; either way it's 5.7. Traverse right to a wonderful belay ledge directly below the notch in the sickle's roof. 7. Climb to the notch (pitons) and stem out the roof, 5.9+ (harder for short climbers?). Belay above in a trough. 8. Work right across a smooth slab with a piton and bolt for protection, exciting 5.7. Step down from the piton and go right around a bulge to find the bolt. FA: Richard Sykes, Dave Rearick, David Isles and John Wharton, 1958. FFA: Royal Robbins and Steve Komito, 1964.

13 Atmospear III 5.10d ★★

This is a two-pitch variation of **Stratospear**. Climb **Sykes Sickle** to a ledge system below and right of its slanting dihedral, and belay in the middle of the ledge. Follow a thin crack up left, then go up past a couple bolts and a piton to a belay beneath a left-facing flake, 5.10d. Climb the flake (5.10a), then traverse right to **Stratospear** above its crux pitch.

14 Stratospear III 5.11c R ★

Stratospear is the free version of an old aid line named **Believe It or Not**. Most of the route is straightforward, with only one pitch of difficult climbing. Start with the first three leads of **Sykes Sickle**. Break right for two more pitches along a mostly continuous, left-facing flake system. The sixth pitch is the crux: Work into another left facing flake (5.11 R) and stem up on very thin ground, also 5.11. A pitch of 5.8 flakes joins **North Ridge**. Bring many tiny nuts for the crux pitch. FA: R. Osborn and B. Fargo, 1981. FFA: Tim Coats and Bret Ruckman, 1987.

15 The Ten Essentials III 5.8 ★

This route threads a line between **Stratospear** and the gully on the left edge of the Barb Flake. Start with three pitches of **Sykes Sickle** and head right for three more pitches of discontinuous flakes and cracks to gain the **North Ridge**. Some care is needed to find the best line. FA: Chris Reveley and Jim Erickson, 1974.

The next four lines weave up the Barb Flake, a huge triangular shield on the right side of the northeast face. Many thin cracks are etched into the flake, forming an intricate lattice of intersecting lines. A study of the topo and photo should clear up any confusion.

16 Burning Spear III 5.10c R ★

Several overlapping flakes run along the wall right of **Sykes Sickle**'s first pitch. **Burning Spear** starts under the middle of the overlaps at a mushroom-shaped flake. 1. Climb a crack in the center of the flake, then pull through two overlaps (and touch the left end of a third, 5.9+) to a bolt. Find a belay (at the bolt?). 2. Run out 5.7 slabs lead to Middle Earth. 3. Angle left (5.7 R) then go up to the base of a left-facing corner. 4. Climb the corner and cross The Barb, ending at a good ledge

(Off Broadway Ledge). 5. Face climb off the right end of Off Broadway Ledge (5.10c R) to a slanting crack. Take the crack for a short way to the first left-facing dihedral, and climb that to the right side of the Barb Flake. Follow **North Ridge**. FA: Steve Grossman and Larry Coats, 1987. **Variation: Stormrider** (5.10b, FA: Ed Webster and Curt Fry, 1987) steps left out of the fourth pitch corner and clips two pins before returning to the corner at its top.

17 Barb Gnarly (and the Flailers) III 5.11b ★★

Begin 100 feet right of **Burning Spear** near the right side of the overlaps, below a small, raised pillar 1. Climb past the pillar up to the first overlap. Pull through below a notch in the second overlap, and then go out the notch at a leaning crack, 5.11b. Belay (at a fixed pin?). 2. Climb a 5.8 R slab to Middle Earth. 3. Walk left on the ledge for nearly 100 feet, then climb to a good ledge. 4. Go more or less straight up for a pitch, aiming for the base of a left facing, hanging dihedral. Belay a short way up the dihedral in a little pod. 5. Follow the dihedral, 5.9, and join **North Ridge**. FA: Bret Ruckman and Tim Coats, 1987.

18 The Barb III 5.10c ★★★

The Barb is another of the main attractions on Spearhead. It diagonals to the top of the Barb Flake in seven pitches, the last three being the most difficult and best. Both **The Barb** and **Barbarella** begin right of **Barb Gnarly**, but they both end left of **Burning Spear**. 1. The long band of overlaps mentioned in **Burning Spear** and **Barb Gnarly** ends at a left-facing dihedral. Climb the dihedral for a pitch, 5.7. 2. Continue to Middle Earth. 3. Walk left for 70 feet, then angle across easy rock to a wide crack, which is followed to a belay. 4. Go up and left to a prominent right-facing dihedral, and climb it or the corner to its right to a belay. 5. Take a thin, left-leaning crack to a belay below a little roof, 5.9. This is even with Off Broadway Ledge. 6. Step left and climb a leaning corner, then up to an apexed roof. Jam through the roof and continue in a left-facing system. Belay after a rope length; a comfortable stance is hard to find. 7. Step down right from the top of the left-facing system and gain a thin crack that shoots to the crest of the Barb Flake. Jam the tips crack (5.10c, RPs) and belay on the north face. FA: Walter Fricke and Charlie Logan, 1970. FFA: Dan McClure and Robert Gulley, 1974. **Variation:** Instead of stepping down at the start of the crux pitch, continue left into a steep, left-facing dihedral that ends at the very top of the Barb Flake (5.11c, FA: Bill Feiges, 1970s). Scramble down into the gully behind the flake and join **North Ridge**.

19 Barbarella III 5.10d ★★

1. Climb the right side of a big flake (5.8); the left side of the flake is the first pitch of **The Barb**. 2. An easier pitch ends at Middle Earth. 3. Move left a few paces and climb into a long, left-leaning flake system. 4. Continue with the system until reaching an apex below several overlapping roofs. Step down around the apex and barge through the tiered roofs, 5.8. 5. Cross the bottom of the hanging dihedral mentioned in the fourth pitch of **Barb Gnarly**. Angle up left to a left-facing dihedral that curves up to Off Broadway Ledge. 6. A short thin crack shoots out of the right end of a roof above Off Broadway Ledge. Take this (5.10d) to where it intersects another crack, step left along that crack, then go up a curvy dihedral. Continue the thin crack above the dihedral to a stance below the crux pitch of **The**

Barb. 7. The first ascent party angled left to the direct finish of **The Barb** (5.11c). To keep the grade at 5.10d, do the crux pitch of **The Barb** (5.10c). FA: Steve Grossman and Larry Coats, 1987. **Variation:** The flake and crack system 20 feet right of the first pitch goes at 5.8.

20 North Ridge III 5.6 ***

The **North Ridge** climbs the broad slab just right of the Barb Flake, and is one of the best routes of its grade in the Park. The final pitches climb along the very edge of the northeast face, providing a great deal of exposure. Scramble around to the northwest side of Spearhead and start below a deep and obvious chimney (the left-hand of two slots) near the left edge. 1. Angle up and left to a slab beneath the chimney, and skirt this on the left to a belay, 5.4. The slab can be climbed directly, but this is much more difficult and run out. 2. Climb through the steep chimney (5.5) to a sheltered ledge at the base of an acute dihedral. 3. Follow the dihedral (nice 5.4) and belay on any of several suitable ledges. 4 and 5. Two long leads go up pleasant slabs and cracks, with several possible lines and mostly easy climbing. Angle left near the end of this section to a horn belay level with and behind the top of the Barb Flake. 6. Lead up a thin crack into a left-facing dihedral that hangs over the edge of the northeast face, 5.6. Move right at its top to avoid a little headwall, then climb a beautiful crack just left of another corner to a perfect seat on the arete. 7. Move right into a blocky slot, and climb to the base of a square chimney, 5.5. It is also possible to do this pitch left of the ridge via short walls and ledges (5.6, not as clean as the standard route). 8. Jam a crack in the back of the chimney to a large terrace and belay, 5.4. From here, 200 feet of 3rd class scrambling leads to a ledge below the west side of the summit block. Wriggle up a tight passage up the middle of the block (as described in the introduction to Spearhead) or step right into an extremely exposed, 4th class corner. This corner hangs out over the southeast face of Spearhead, and while the climbing is easy, a rope is recommended as a slip here would produce quite a fall. FA: Pete Soby and Charles Schobinger, 1958. **Variation:** Take a left-facing dihedral immediately left of the first pitch (5.8) to a belay, continue up corners to a good ledge with a pillar (belay), and then follow an arete to a big ledge above the acute dihedral.

21 Revenge 5.12b **

Revenge is not located on Spearhead, but on a short cliff nearby. The approach is long for such a short route, but it may be of interest to climbers bivied in the cirque with time to burn. Walk east from Spearhead (ten minutes) to a band of cliffs below the Trough and the Keyboard of the Winds, and locate a north-facing cliff matching the topo (it's fairly apparent). A slanting roof half way up the right side is pierced by a hand crack; this is the route. 1. Climb thin, 5.10 cracks to a belay beneath the roof. 2. Jam out the roof, and up the short, but awesome thin hand crack above, 5.12b. FA: Randy Joseph and Mark Wilford, early 1990s.

22 Rain Delay 5.9+ ***

This excellent pitch is on the left side of the wall described in **Revenge**. As the name suggests, it's a great diversion when inclement weather threatens ascents on the big walls of the cirque. Start below the right edge of an overhang pierced by a finger crack. Step up to the overhang and place gear, then walk up and right to a ledge leading to the lip of the roof. Traverse left on perfect knobs to reach the finger crack (5.7), and jam to a grassy ledge. The roof can be pulled directly, but this is much more difficult. Climb the left side of a flake above the ledge (or do the leaning dihedral to the right, 5.9), and jam an obvious hand-to-fist crack to a big ledge, 5.9+. Rack to a #4 Friend, and walk off left. FA(?): Bernard and John Gillett, 1999. **Variations:** At least two more attractive leads could be had between this route and **Revenge**. The steep chimney on the right side of a massive overhang leads to an intimidating lieback (looks like 5.11 or harder), and the obvious overhanging wide crack just to the right has the look of 5.12 OW — bring a couple #5 Camalots, or top rope it. Several large rocks at the base of this wall provide some good bouldering.

CLIFF EAST OF SPEARHEAD

21. Revenge 5.12b ★★
22. Rain Delay 5.9+ ★★★

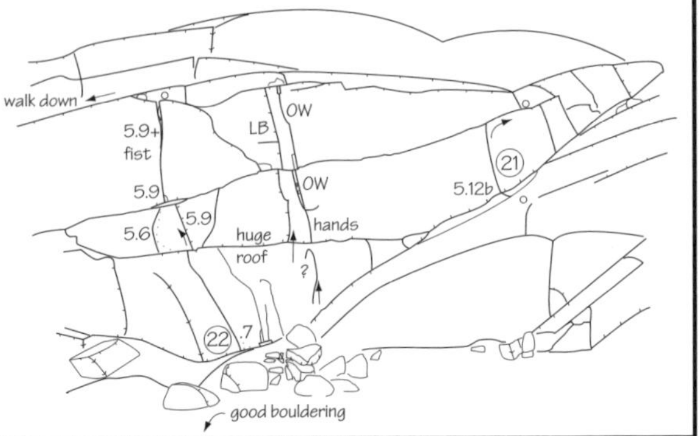

MCHENRYS PEAK

McHenrys Peak is one of the more majestic mountains in Rocky Mountain National Park. It sits at the back of Glacier Gorge, northwest of Chiefs Head Peak. Though the east face is somewhat broken, this is the main attraction for climbers. The triangular buttress beneath a subpeak on the southeast ridge holds several rock climbs, while the main wall below the summit is home to three quality mixed routes. The gendarmed ridge on the right leads to Arrowhead; it is a favorite of the Colorado Mountain Club for a hair-raising outing to a beautiful summit. The north side of the peak, above Shelf and Solitude Lakes and on the other side of the McHenrys-Arrowhead ridge, is much less frequented, though two alpine routes have been done here.

Approach: There are two approaches to the east face, each equally time consuming. The first passes easily beneath Spearhead after hiking east from Black Lake and proceeds directly to the bottom of the face. The second option takes a path around the north shore of Black Lake — begin by crossing the outlet stream on rocks and logs, and seek out a trail near the edge of the lake that wanders through tight trees. Cross a marsh on the north side and follow a boulder-filled gully to a maze of steep krummholz. Zigzag up ledges toward Arrowhead, then turn left on a grassy slope and go straight for McHenrys. The route is fairly obvious, and perhaps a half-mile shorter than going under Spearhead, but it is also steeper with some 3rd class, and may be blocked by snow in early season.

The best way to reach the north face follows Shelf Creek into the Shelf Lake cirque. Hike about 3.75 miles from the Glacier Gorge trailhead toward Black Lake, and look west for a cascading stream — this is Shelf Creek, and it spills into Glacier Creek where the trail exits a small grove of trees and enters a jumbled mass of boulders. Wade across Glacier Creek at this point, or find a boulder crossing 200 yards downstream during periods of low water (this is difficult to find if you've not done it before). Seek out a footpath on the north (right) side of Shelf Creek and follow it to a stream crossing just below Shelf Lake, then ascend slabs to the mouth of the cirque. The path is steep and hard to follow in spots; it stays within earshot of Shelf Creek the entire way but always on its north side. This description may be of no use during the winter when snow covers all; in that case, just hike up a tree covered slope passing beneath the north side of Arrowhead.

Descent: To descend from the summit, follow the southeast ridge to Stone Man Pass, which is marked by an obvious rock pillar (the Stone Man) between Chiefs Head and McHenrys. The ridge can be tricky in spots (3rd class), especially in off-season, and it is easy to wander into 4th class territory if care is not taken in selecting the best line. Turn north into Glacier Gorge at the pass and descend back to the east face — the steep snow pillow below the pass is prone to avalanche.

1 Constellation Prize II 5.7

This climb follows ramps and corners on the left side of the triangular buttress. Start about 150 feet left of **Dogstar** at a leaning chimney and corner combo. Follow this for two leads, then head right to the left side of a slabby area in the middle of the wall. Cross the easy slabs to a good ledge (two pitches), and then traverse left beneath several right-leaning corners to a gully that leads to the ridge. FA: Rich Page and M. Taliaferro, 1979.

2 Dogstar III 5.8 ★

Dogstar starts 200 feet left of the central prow at a big block. Walk right on grassy ledges to a point beneath a broken dihedral. Climb the dihedral and go left at its top along a grassy ramp; set the belay below a black, right-facing dihedral. Jam the dihedral and a short wall above and belay at the base of a low-angled section — this is the right side of the slabby area mentioned in the previous route. Angle right across the slab for a pitch, and then climb straight up to a ramp — belay near its right side beneath a roof-capped corner. Follow the corner, turn the roof, and go straight up to a big ledge (two pitches). One can escape left on this ledge to the ridge, but the route takes the headwall for a bit before angling left on small ramps and corners. FA: Larry Hamilton and Dakers Gowans, 1974.

3 Dream of Babylon Burning IV 5.10d (R?) ★★★

This route begins directly beneath the summit of the triangular buttress near its low point. Scramble over broken rock to a series of right-facing corners just left of the prow of the buttress. 1. Climb the right-facing corners in three steps, 5.9+. 2. Follow a black, right-facing corner through a 5.10 pod. 3. Ascend to a thin seam splitting a slab, 5.10d, and belay on the right side of a ledge. 4. Angle left for 50 feet, then back right along a right-leaning flake (5.8), or climb more directly (5.10) to a belay stance. 5. Angle right toward a large, left-facing dihedral just left of the prow, and climb a thin, 5.10d flake just left of the dihedral's base. Join the dihedral

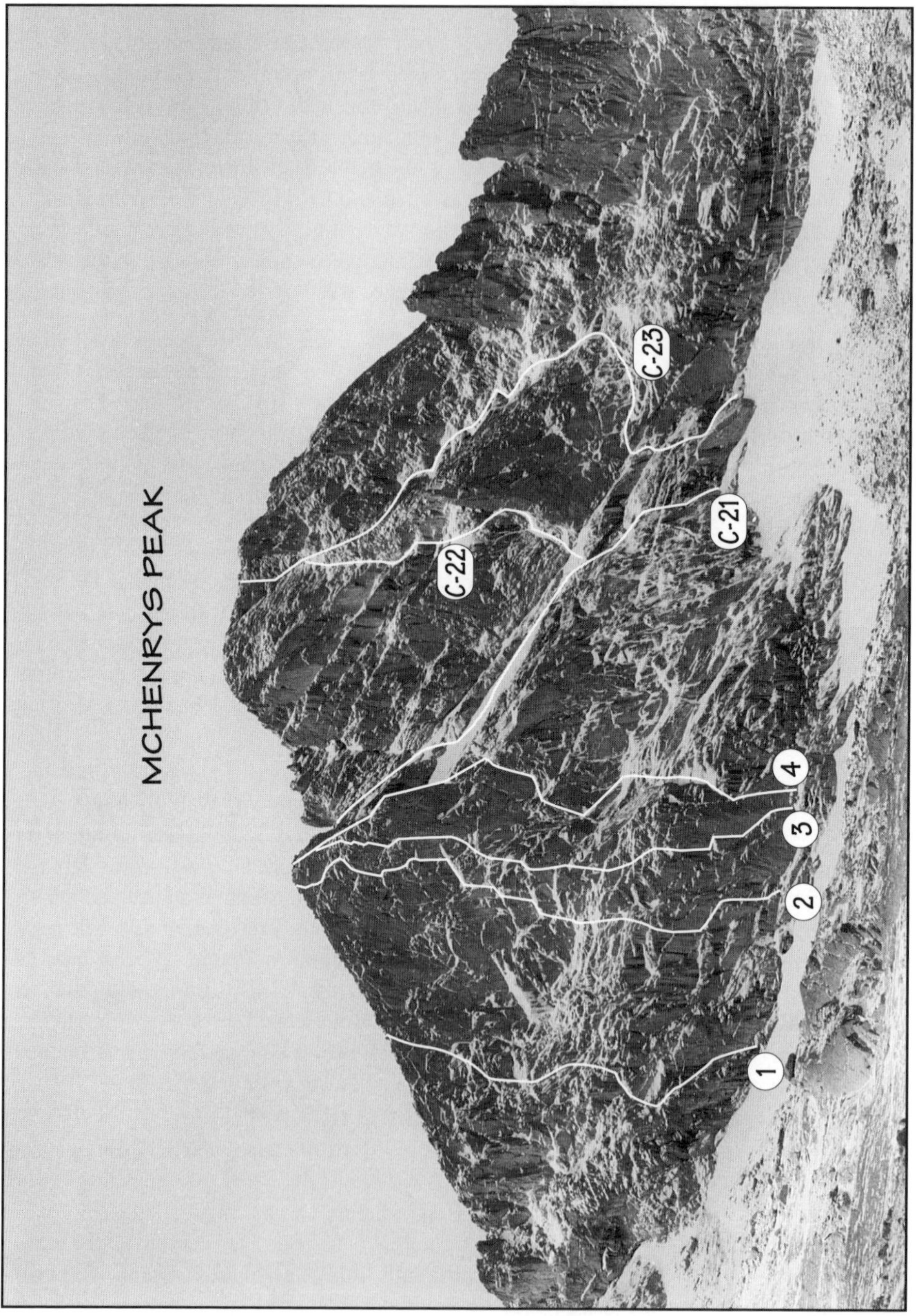
MCHENRYS PEAK
C-23
C-22
C-21
1
2
3
4

McHENRYS PEAK

1. Constellation Prize II 5.7
2. Dogstar III 5.8 ★
3. Dream of Babylon Burning IV 5.10d (R?) ★★★
4. LV 426 III 5.11b ★★

C-21. Snow Bench II M3 AI 2
C-22. Big Mac Couloir III M4- AI 4-
C-23. Right Gully III M4 AI 4+

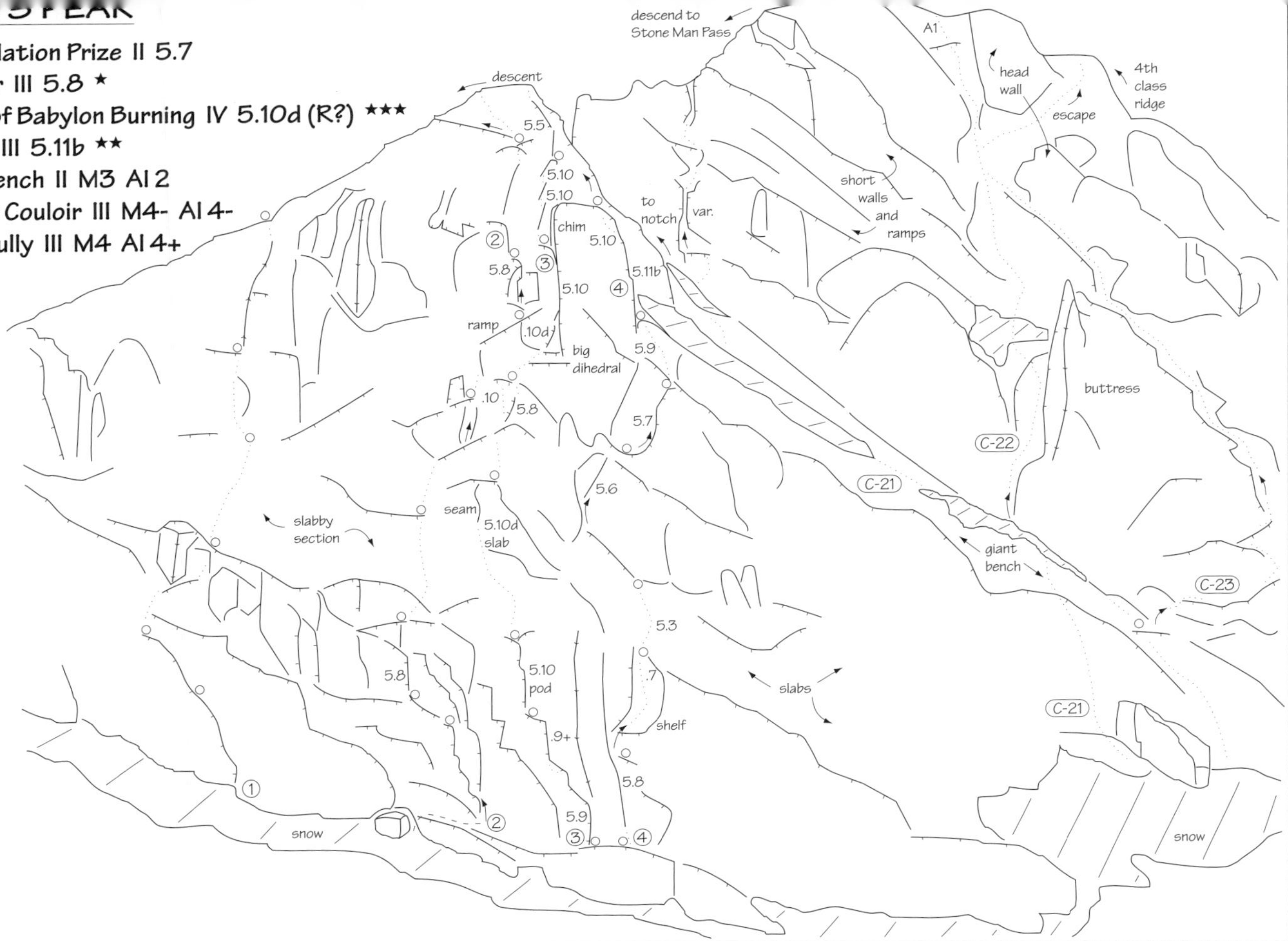

and jam until reaching a belay ledge on the left; the dihedral turns into a chimney above this. 6. Stay left of the chimney with triple, right-leaning cracks (two 5.10 sections to connect the cracks). 7. Go up then left on easy ground. FA: Jon Allen and Doug Byerly, 1998.

4 LV 426 III 5.11b ★★

This route climbs right of the central prow of the triangular buttress. Start directly under the summit of the buttress (a bit right of the previous route) and climb along a crack splitting the prow, 5.8. Escape right from the crack and follow a large 5.7 corner to a slab. An easy pitch crosses the slab to the base of a left-leaning ramp. Take the ramp to its top, and ascend straight up to the left end of scoop (belay), then climb a flake off the scoop's right side to another belay. The climbing up to this point is relatively easy, though pleasant and on good rock. A short 5.9 slab gains the base of a stunning right-facing corner on the upper wall — belay at the left edge of a snowy ramp (the left margin of **Snow Bench**). Follow the corner (5.11) to an exit move left that leads to a crack and belay ledge. An easy pitch finishes the route. FA: Jeff Lowe and Teri Ebel, 1994.

C-21 Snow Bench II M3 AI 2

Snow Bench climbs the obvious snowed up ramp that forms the right border of the triangular buttress; it is described in the ice climbing section.

C-22 Big Mac Couloir III M4- AI 4-

This too is described in the ice climbing section.

C-23 Right Gully III M4 AI 4+

See the ice climbing section.

5 Right Chimney II 5.7

Start at the extreme right margin of the east face and follow a chimney system to a notch on the ridge (east of the first major gendarme) in four pitches, then follow the ridge (see next route).

6 Northeast Ridge 5.6 or 4th class ★★

This is the exciting ridge that separates the east and north faces of McHenrys; it continues to Arrowhead. There are two ways to gain the low point of the ridge: the first begins with a route known as **The Shaft** (5.6, see Arrowhead below) while the second starts at a small pond above Solitude Lake and climbs 3rd class ramps for several hundred feet before tapering off to easy boulder hopping. Two major gendarmes must be negotiated once on the ridge; both are passed on the right. Steep and exposed slabs (4th class) above the second gendarme lead to the summit. FA: Charlie Ehlert, Philip Ritterbush, Charles and Prentiss Sawyer, 1957.

C-8 North Face Direct III M4 AI 4+

This route is described in the ice climbing section.

C-9 McHenrys Notch II AI 2 4th class

See the ice climbing section.

ARROWHEAD

Arrowhead is the name given to the long northeast ridge of McHenrys Peak — when viewed on a contour map, the ridge does indeed look like the tip of an arrow. The authors of the book *RMNP High Country Names* (a delightful title which gives the history of the appellations in the region) believe this is how the mountain got its name, but they also cite consistent nomenclature as a reason, with Spearhead and Chiefs Head just across the gorge.

From Black Lake and points nearby, the peak doesn't look much like an arrowhead, but rather a broad, cliffy ridge. The west end of the ridge remains hidden from view when approached directly from Black Lake; it harbors a beautiful south facing wall right of the low point on the McHenrys/Arrowhead ridge. Right of this wall the mountain is broken into three features: a long ramp system (**Summit Ramp**) diagonals directly beneath the summit tower; a double-topped pinnacle with a notch stands front and center; and a triangular prow juts out on the right. Much of the vertical relief here consists of low angled rock, with the last few hundred feet being the most interesting. Although Arrowhead hasn't received much notice from climbers in the past, recent activity on the west end puts it among the list of must-do walls in the Park. Arrowhead also has an interesting northern aspect above Shelf and Solitude Lakes. Two mixed routes ascend obvious gully systems; these are described in the ice climbing section.

Approach: To approach the rock climbs, use the second option described under McHenrys Peak (page 128), straight up from Black Lake. A longer approach circles the gorge while passing beneath Spearhead; it is useful in early season when the direct approach is snow-laden. The ice climbs in the Shelf Lake cirque can be gained from Black Lake as well simply by contouring beneath the east shoulder of Arrowhead. A more direct approach fords Glacier Creek about a mile below Black Lake, after which Shelf Creek is followed (see details under McHenrys Peak).

Descent: There are three descents in common use. The first two are convenient for the rock climbs on the south and east sides of the mountain, and though the third option is best suited for the ice climbs on the north side, it provides a splendid tour of the peak as well as a trip down the seldom visited Shelf and Solitude Lakes cirque, a serene hanging valley of unparalleled beauty.

Descent One- Use with routes **1** through **10**. Look for a sling and stopper anchor on the edge of the wall about fifty yards west of the low point on the McHenrys/ Arrowhead Ridge, and rappel 195 feet to slings on a sloping ramp. Rappel an additional 160 feet to 3rd class scrambling which leads to the base of low angled slabs and an extensive ledge system. Another rappel route begins below the low point at two fixed wires (difficult to locate). Down climb to this anchor and rappel 120 feet to slings around a block; the slings are visible from the low point. A long rappel (200 feet) finds easy slabs and the ledge system. Those climbing the first seven routes can leave gear directly below the rappels and traverse the ledge system to the beginning of the climbs. Parties climbing with 165 foot ropes are advised to bring extra rappel gear (or use the second or third descent).

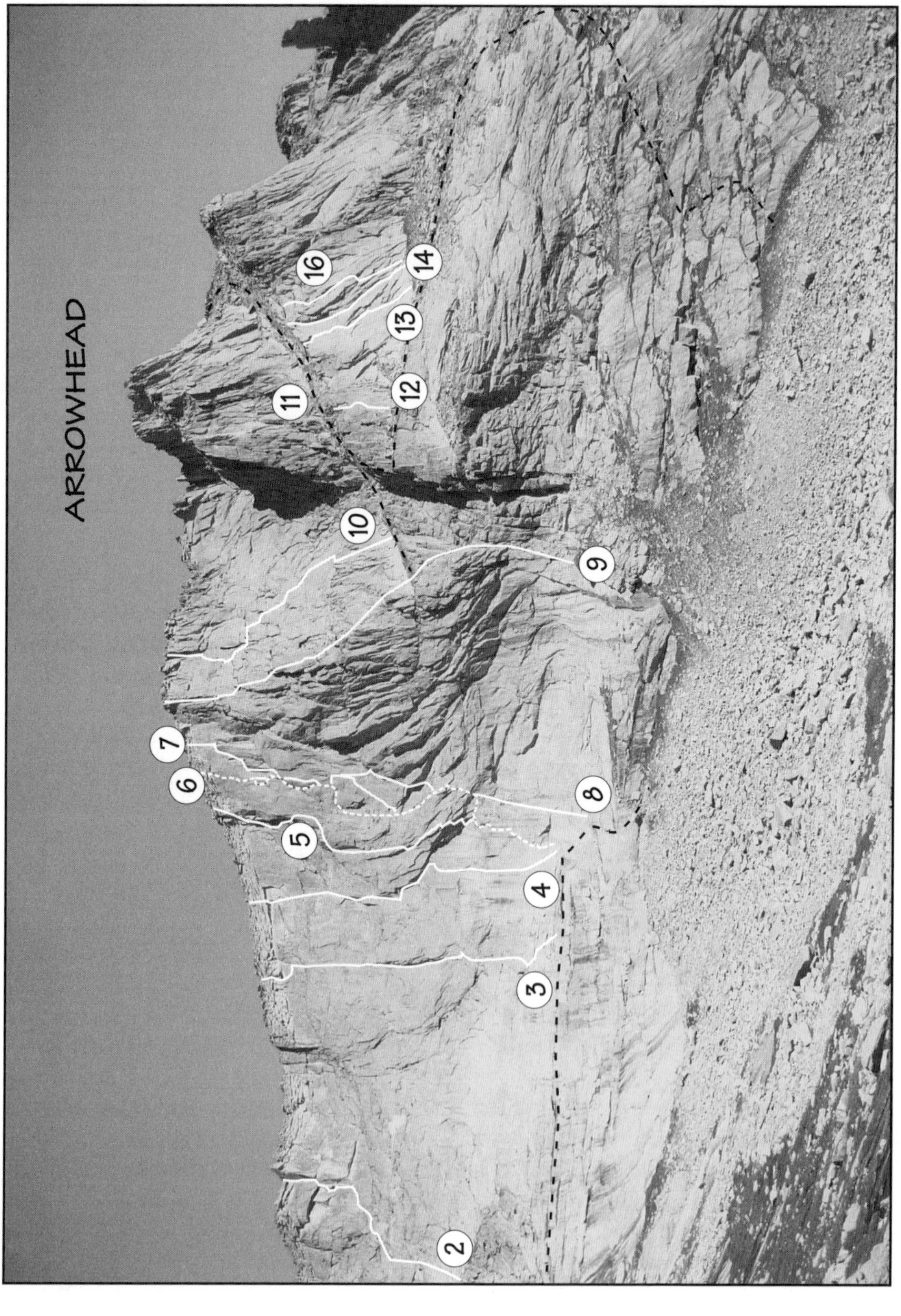
ARROWHEAD
2
3
4
5
6
7
8
9
10
11
12
13
14
16

ARROWHEAD - South Face Overview

1. The Shaft II 5.6
2. Artemis II 5.9+ ★
3. Airhead III 5.11d ★★★
4. Ithaca IV 5.12a ★★★
5. Crooked Arrow III 5.11b R ★
6. Arrowplane III 5.11a ★★★
7. Lost Arrow III 5.10d ★★★
8. Medusa III 5.11a ★★
9. Refugium III 5.10a ★★★
10. Rain Dance III 5.9 ★★★
11. Summit Ramp 3rd Class ★★★
12. The Ear I 5.9 ★
13. Orange Pillar III 5.9 ★★★
14. Eloquence I 5.11a (?) ★★★
15. Ramp Tramp I 5.9 ★★★
16. Romper Ramp I 5.9 ★★
17. Warhead III 5.9 ★
18. Goldfinger III 5.11d ★★★

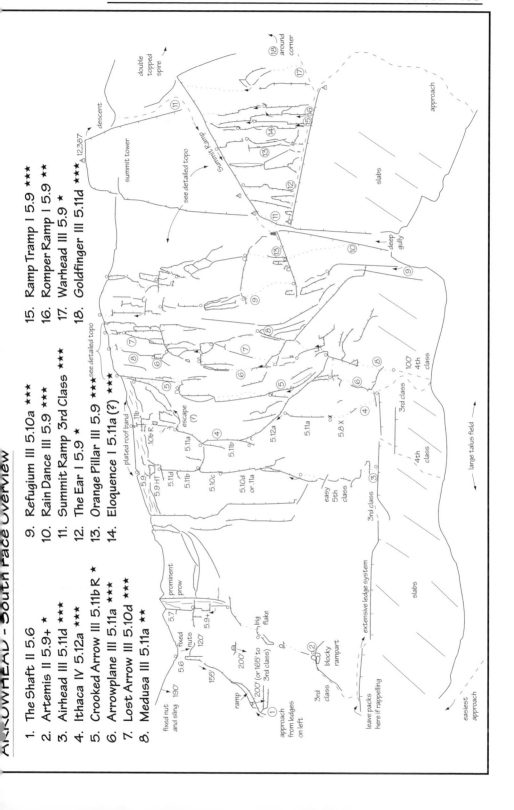

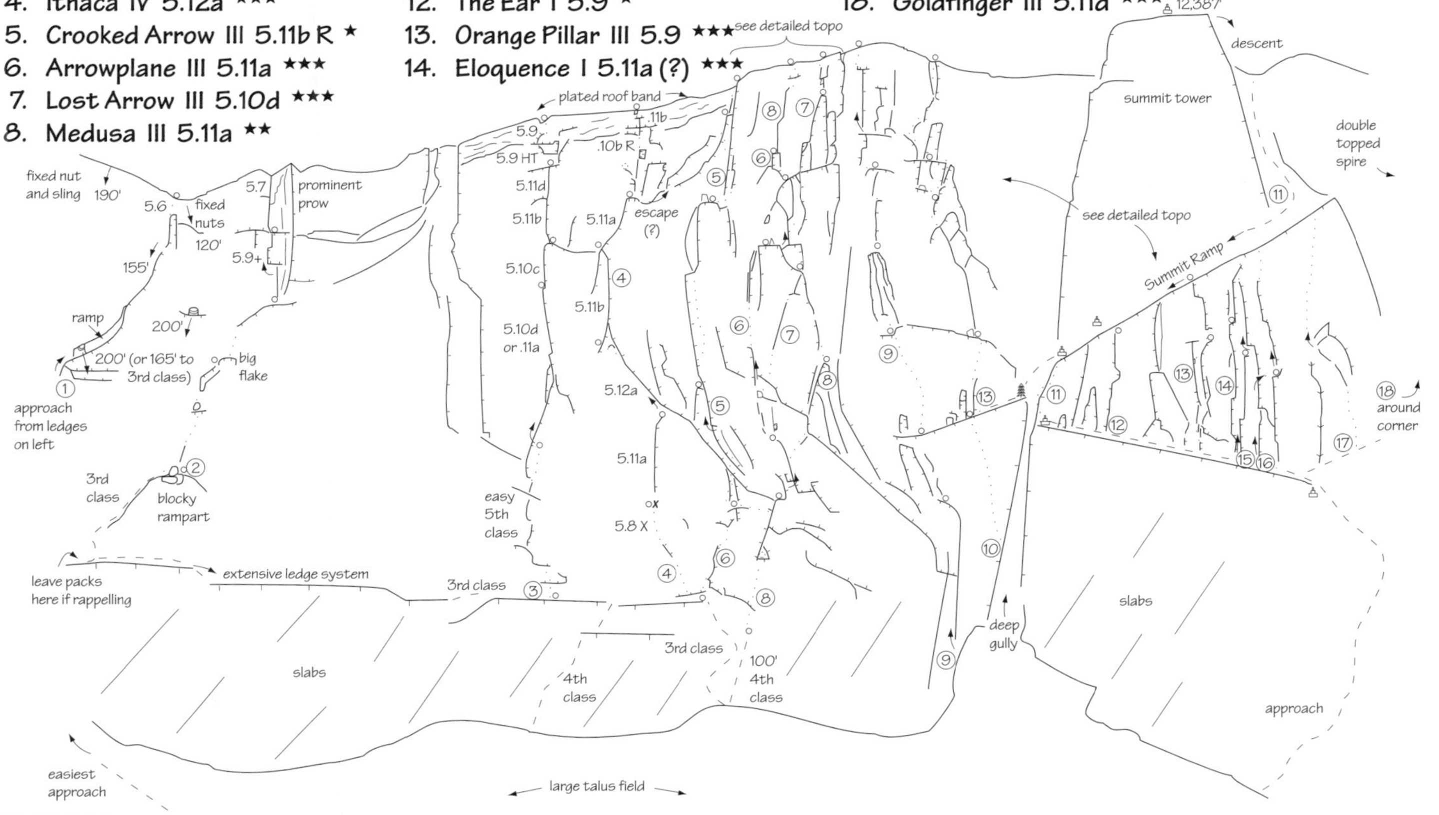

Descent Two- Use with routes **1** through **20**. Reverse **Summit Ramp**, described below. This method is especially convenient for climbs beginning near **Summit Ramp**, or for those wishing to bag the peak after any of the rock climbs. It is also advised for parties using ropes less than 200 feet in length.

Descent Three- Use with ice climbs **C-6** and **C-7**, or any of the rock climbs for a tour of the peak. Hike down from the summit into the Shelf Lake cirque about a half-mile above Solitude Lake. The route is tricky unless two key features are located: a grassy gully descending northwest from the summit (the only significant vegetation on this side of the mountain) and a shallow pond above Solitude Lake. Boulder hop to the grassy gully and hike down to a cairn at its base; look for the pond as you descend. A series of ramps and ledges (3rd class), all west of the pond and marked with occasional cairns, leads to the floor of the cirque just above the pond. Hike past Solitude and Shelf Lakes, then down the north side of Shelf Creek to the Black Lake trail. Bring all gear along when using this descent after a climb from the south.

The long ledge system mentioned in Descent One spans the lower portion of the south-facing wall on the west end of Arrowhead; it gives access to the first seven routes. 250 feet of slabs lead directly to the ledge (4th class in the middle, 3rd class on the right); an easier method traverses in from the far left side.

1 The Shaft II 5.6

The low point on the ridge between McHenrys and Arrowhead is the logical division between the two peaks, even though the south-facing wall joining them is continuous. Scramble along grassy ledges left of the low point (3rd class) and angle up right along a ramp and chimney system to reach the ridge, 5.6. An easy scramble over boulders leads to the summit of Arrowhead, though the first ascent team used this route to access the northeast ridge of McHenrys. The exact line of ascent taken in 1957 is not known; a likely line uses the rappel station shown in the topo as a belay, then climbs to a chimney on the left side of a huge flake. A short, steep headwall finishes the route. FA: Charlie Ehlert, Philip Ritterbush, Charles and Prentiss Sawyer, 1957.

2 Artemis II 5.9+ ★

A very prominent hanging corner sits left of a prow which is 100 feet right of the low point on the McHenrys — Arrowhead ridge; this is the line. The final two pitches are quite good, and could be climbed after the next several routes by rappelling in from the top. Begin beneath the low point of the ridge and take a third class ramp up and right to the rope-up spot. 1. Climb flakes for 100 feet (5.6, several options) to a right-angling ramp leading to a large flake. 2. Go up and right from the flake (5.4) and traverse a narrow, rising ledge to its right side; belay at the base of the hanging corner. 3. Lieback a one-inch crack to an overhang and turn it on the left (crux). Continue past a ledge with a balanced flake to another ledge just right of a big roof. (In certain light, the big roof appears as the brow of a man's face, and the dihedral below his nose. Perhaps this is Apollo, Artemis' brother). 4. Go straight up the hanging corner (two sections of 5.7). The thin cracks on the right look very inviting and climbable. These last two pitches are short, and could be combined with proper rope management. Rack to a #4 Friend. FA: Larry Hamilton and T. Griese, 1975.

3 Airhead III 5.11d ***

Locate a prominent left-facing dihedral in the middle of the south face, about 100 feet right of an also prominent left-facing flake system that reaches the top of the wall at a jog in the ridgeline. The dihedral and thin crack above it feature excellent rock and awesome climbing. 1. Do an easy pitch of flakes (beginning from any of several suitable ledges) to a stance below and right of the dihedral. It is tempting to climb the initial portion of the dihedral to a shelf, but the anchors here are poor. 2. Lieback and stem the corner past the first shelf to a smaller stance at 150 feet, using the right wall when necessary (5.10d or 5.11a). 3. A short pitch of 5.10c up the final forty feet of the corner ends at a nice ledge. These two pitches can be combined with a 200 foot rope and lots of gear. 4. Lieback a left-facing dihedral to a tiny roof (5.11b) and follow a thin, sustained crack through a headwall to a big ledge (5.11d, or enjoyable C1). 5. Start up a corner off the right end of the ledge, then hand traverse left on a horizontal crack to a rising flake, 5.9. Pull through a bulge above the flake, angle right around a roof, and weave up and left to the ridge (loose 5.9). Rack to a #4 Friend with extra small pieces. FA: Eric Winkelman and Michael Bearzi, 1994.

4 Ithaca IV 5.12a ***

This appealing line delivers sustained climbing on excellent rock. Start 150 feet right of **Airhead** on the right side of the access ledge beneath a long, slanting ceiling. 1. Cross a fantastic slab (5.8 X), aiming for the base of a left-facing pillar dropping down from the middle of the ceiling; belay at a fixed pin amongst broken ledges. Early morning sun reveals abundant holds, but almost nothing in the way of protection. It appears feasible to traverse left from the first belay of the next route to reach the fixed pin; this may be a safer approach. 2. Climb the pillar to a belay below the ceiling, 5.11a. 3. Undercling left along the ceiling past a fixed wire (crux), and continue on easier ground to a cramped belay stance on the left. 4. Follow a hanging, left-facing corner to a sloping ledge, 5.11b. 5. Stay with the dihedral system to a good ledge, 5.11a. 6. Move left, then up along the left side of a big detached flake. Run out face climbing (5.10b R) leads to an obvious left-facing dihedral capped with a big roof. Pull through the roof (and several more above) with awesome exposure, 5.11b. This long pitch can be broken up with an optional belay left of the detached flake. Include plenty of small wires and camming units. FA: Andy Donson and Dave Light, 1997. **Variation:** A hypothetical escape from the top of the fifth pitch (leading to the last pitch of the next climb) is marked on the topo.

5 Crooked Arrow III 5.11b R *

This route features attractive climbing on each of its pitches, but lacks the overall quality of nearby lines. Tricky route finding and some run out sections add a fair amount of spice to the day. Start on the extreme right side of the access ledge below a left-facing flake. 1. Climb through an overlap and angle right into the flake. Step right at the flake's end and go straight up a water streak to an undercling (5.8 R), then move right (5.8+) to a short, left-facing corner. Belay below a series of slanting, left-facing corners that breach the right side of **Ithaca**'s long ceiling band. 2. Start up the underside of **Ithaca**'s roof, then traverse right into the first leaning corner at a jug (committing 5.10). Follow the corner past two jammed

ARROWHEAD - South Face Detail

4. Ithaca IV 5.12a ★★★
5. Crooked Arrow III 5.11b R ★
6. Arrowplane III 5.11a ★★★
7. Lost Arrow III 5.11a ★★★
8. Medusa III 5.11a ★★

Note: The J-shaped crack mentioned in the text description of **Crooked Arrow** was top roped in 2000 (FA: Bernard Gillett). Look for bolts leading to the crack in the future.

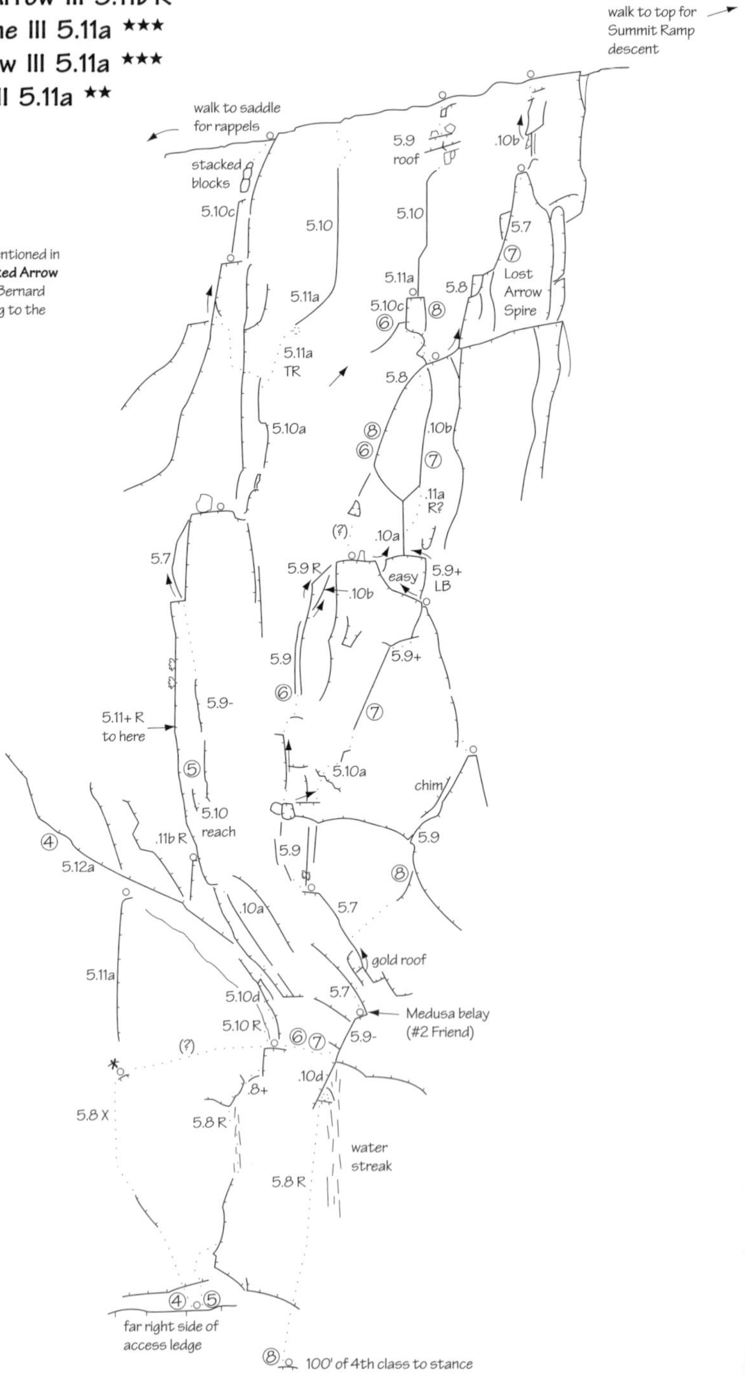

flakes, and crank right to a hidden hand crack and the second corner, 5.10d. Move right again at the top of the hand crack to a beautiful finger crack in a slab. Go left when this crack dies (5.9+ R) to a stance at the base of a long, left-facing dihedral (similar in appearance to **Airhead**'s dihedral). 3. Stem up the dihedral for fifteen feet to a foot prong (5.11 R), and exit right to a jug on the face. Follow easier flakes up the face and finish with a dogleg hand crack on the left to a big ledge. 4. Climb right over the top of a thin pillar to reach a finger crack in a beautiful orange headwall. Step left at the crack's end to a big left-facing dihedral, go up twenty feet, then move left to another dihedral. Follow this up and right past broken rock to a good ledge. 5. Jam an obvious and easy looking crack that gets difficult near its top (5.10c, great pro). Follow stacked blocks up right, and tread carefully past loose, jumbled blocks to the top. Bring a standard rack from RPs to a #3 Friend, and 200 foot ropes (the first four pitches are long). FA: Roger Briggs and Bernard Gillett, 1998. **Variations:** Several possible options should be noted. The first left-leaning corner on pitch 2 appears as though it can be climbed directly. The more obvious line on the third pitch up the left-facing corner was abandoned after two good stoppers at fifty feet allowed retreat from hard, run out 5.11 (looks hard above). A few bolts added to the fourth pitch would allow safe access to the sweet J-shaped crack on the orange headwall (this variation was top roped in 2000). If this last option is added, it might bump the route to two-star status.

The next three routes were established within weeks of each other, and they share common ground. Those wishing to climb the wall at 5.10b can piece together a natural line with only two short sections of 5.10 (see topo).

6 Arrowplane III 5.11a ***

This route finishes with the stellar lightning bolt crack slicing through the orange headwall right of the J-shaped crack noted in **Crooked Arrow**; these features are visible from below. The headwall crack is **Arrowplane**'s best pitch, though the entire route is superb, perhaps the best on Arrowhead (add another star to the route by climbing **Lost Arrow**'s fourth pitch seam and crack). 1. Do the first pitch of **Crooked Arrow** (5.8+ R, 175 feet). 2. Traverse twenty feet right (#4 Friend) to a slanting crack on the right edge of the **Ithaca** ceiling (hidden nut placement at knee level), and follow it to a ledge (5.9-). Work up through the right side of a small, gold roof, and follow a nice 5.7 crack to a stance at the base of a thin crack with a bush. 3. Move left and link thin seams to a jammed flaked on the left edge of a long overhang, 5.9. Pass the flake and climb straight up for sixty feet to double finger cracks left of a prominent, left-facing dihedral. Reach right when the cracks die at a lieback flake leading into the dihedral. Several tense moves (5.10b with blind cam placements) gain the dihedral and a big ledge at its top; belay at a spike. One can also climb straight up past the dying cracks, and then angle right to the belay ledge (5.9, poor pro). This lead is a stretch with a 165 foot rope, though it could easily be broken into two pitches. 4. Walk right to a thin crack and jam to a seam splitting off right, 5.10a. Stay left, leading into an easy wide crack, which thins near its top (5.8), and belay on a ramp at the base of a giant pillar. 5. A short pitch works through a left-facing crescent to the left edge of an obvious rectangular block. Lieback the block (5.10c) to a perfect stance beneath the lightning bolt crack in the headwall. 6. Jam the crack (5.11a at its base, easing to 5.10) and angle right to a thin crack splitting an overhang (0.75-inch cam). Pull over the roof to a good ledge (5.9); thirty feet of buckets lead to the top. Rack to a #4 Friend with extra finger crack gear. A 165 foot rope is sufficient, though a bit of simul-climbing is necessary on the first pitch (and maybe the third). FA: Bernard Gillett and Bill Briggs, 1998.

7 Lost Arrow III 5.11a ***

This line is named for the giant pillar (Lost Arrow Spire) seen high on the wall right of **Arrowplane**'s lightning bolt crack. Begin with the first two pitches of **Arrowplane**. 3. Start up the third pitch, but move right on a ledge after passing the jammed flake. Climb through overlapping flakes on the right (tricky 5.10a) and aim for a slanting finger crack; traverse right at the crack's end (5.9+) and jam to a belay stance in a right-facing dihedral. 4. Lieback a short flake to the right (5.9+), or climb easy corners up left to a good ledge. Take a thin crack on the left side of the ledge (5.10a) to a seam branching right, place an RP in the seam, and back it up with good stoppers in the main crack — the seam opens up to a beautiful crack after ten feet, but it looks difficult to gain the crack this way. Instead, down climb fifteen feet, and follow knobs up right, then back left (daring 5.11a, perhaps with an R-rating) to bomber jams in the crack. Follow the awesome crack to a belay at the base of Lost Arrow Spire (the fourth belay on **Arrowplane**). 5. Climb the left side of the spire to its top, 5.8 hands and fists. A 5.8 leader will want several large pieces for this excellent pitch. 6. Take the obvious steep crack (with jammed flake) just behind the spire (5.10b), step left, and go straight for the top along a thin slab crack followed by steep buckets. Rack to a #4 Friend with a few RPs. FA: Gillett and Bill Briggs, 1998.

8 Medusa III 5.11a **

This was the first route up this section of the wall; its final two pitches feature brilliant crack climbing. It was established with a 200 foot rope, and the description below reflects this, but a standard rope length suffices if the belays of the previous two routes are incorporated (see topo). Start at the high point of the talus field below the wall and climb 100 feet of 4th class to a rope-up ledge that lies down and right from the beginning of **Arrowplane**. 1. Climb a run out slab past an overlap to reach the obvious right-leaning dihedral (often wet) below the right side of **Ithaca**'s ceiling (5.8 R, 150 feet, optional belay at a triangular inset). Ascend the bulging dihedral (5.10d), which leads into **Arrowplane**'s slanting crack, and belay just after it (#2 Friend, 250 feet from rope-up ledge, simul-climbed on first ascent). 2. Climb right to a gold roof and the nice crack above it (same as **Arrowplane**), then angle up right to a wide crack through the right end of a long overhang. Pull through (5.9) to a broken chimney that leads to the top of a belay pillar (180 feet). 3. Step left and take a flake system to the right side of a good ledge (finishing with the 5.9+ lieback described in **Lost Arrow**). Move left and do the thin crack that is common to all three of these climbs (rated 5.10d by Pyke and Donson), and continue to **Arrowplane**'s 4th belay. 200 feet total. 4. The last pitch combines **Arrowplane**'s fifth and sixth pitches, but it takes the flared crack on the right side of the rectangular block. Rack up to a #4 Camalot. FA: Kath Pyke and Andy Donson, 1998.

9 Refugium III 5.10a ***

The wall on which the previous eight routes reside juts out to an obvious, broad prow on the right. **Refugium** takes a line up the right side of the prow in four long pitches (bring 60 meter ropes, or use intermediate belays). **1.** Climb the right margin of the low-angled slab below the prow and skirt several overhangs to the right. Belay on the right side of a pillar. **2.** Climb 5.7 cracks just right of the prow, and then link together several cracks on the face of a large pillar, 5.8. **3.** Take the left-facing flake directly above (5.8), step left to a short crack, then back right to a good ledge (with huge block) below a steep headwall. **4.** Move off the left end of the ledge to a thin 5.10a flake, lieback right around an overlap, then move left into a prominent dihedral at the top of the wall. Follow the dihedral (steep 5.9 jugs) through a roof. FA: Jon Allen and Doug Byerly, 1998.

10 Rain Dance III 5.9 ***

This route takes a beautiful crack system on the lower-angled wall left of the summit tower. Begin with the 3rd class pitch of **Summit Ramp** (see below), then walk down and left over the top of a deep gully (passing a curious tree, way above timber line!) to the middle of a grassy ledge. Set a belay below opposing corners. It is also possible to climb a long, easy pitch beginning in the deep gully, fifty feet right of the previous route. 1. Follow the corners and angle right to a big ledge (5.6); belay on the right side of a block below an amazing finger crack. 2. Jam the leaning finger crack to a fork (stunning 5.8), stay left with a wide section to another fork, and go left again along a tiny crack, 5.9. Step around left near its top to a left-facing dihedral and follow this to a good ledge — belay here if using 165 foot ropes. 3. Climb twenty feet to another ledge, from which there are three options. A) The best option hand traverses left along a flake to a steep slot with finger crack (5.9+); belay on a big ledge. B) The easiest and original line stays right, climbing over stacked blocks to a short 5.6 squeeze. C) In between these is a dead end seam with a difficult entry move from the highest stacked block (5.11a, top roped, blind #5 RP placement at its base). 4. A fifty foot orange pillar, which is visible from the ground, rises off the belay ledge. Climb a tricky corner ten feet to its left, follow an easy ramp left, then go back right to a short slot leading to the base of a large, left-facing dihedral (the most prominent feature on the upper wall). Work up the dihedral to a wedged spike (5.9), then take disjunct hand cracks up the right wall (steep 5.8 with wild chicken heads). Bring a standard rack with extra thin gear, and descend the next route to retrieve packs left at the base. FA: Byerly and Pyke, 1998. The variations on pitch 3 were climbed by Bernard Gillett and Chris Hill (see **Orange Pillar**).

A deep chimney/gully on the left side of the summit tower divides the south wall from the rest of Arrowhead. The next eight routes begin on a long ledge system right of this gully. Reach this ledge from a point directly beneath the summit by angling up and right for several hundred feet, then back left. The lines on the one to three pitch wall below the left half of **Summit Ramp** are short; taken alone, they don't justify the long approach necessary to reach them. The climbing, however, is excellent, making this a worthy high-country crag. Plan on doing a few lines in a row, or hit them after descending from one of the longer routes.

ARROWHEAD - Summit Area Detail

9. Refugium III 5.10a ★★★
A. Gimme Shelter II 5.11a ★★
10. Rain Dance III 5.9 ★★★
11. Summit Ramp 3rd Class ★★★
12. The Ear I 5.9 ★
13. Orange Pillar III 5.9 ★★★
14. Eloquence I 5.11a (?) ★★★
15. Ramp Tramp I 5.9 ★★★
16. Romper Ramp I 5.9 ★★
B. Gimme a Break I 5.8+ ★
17. Warhead III 5.9 ★
18. Goldfinger III 5.11d ★★★

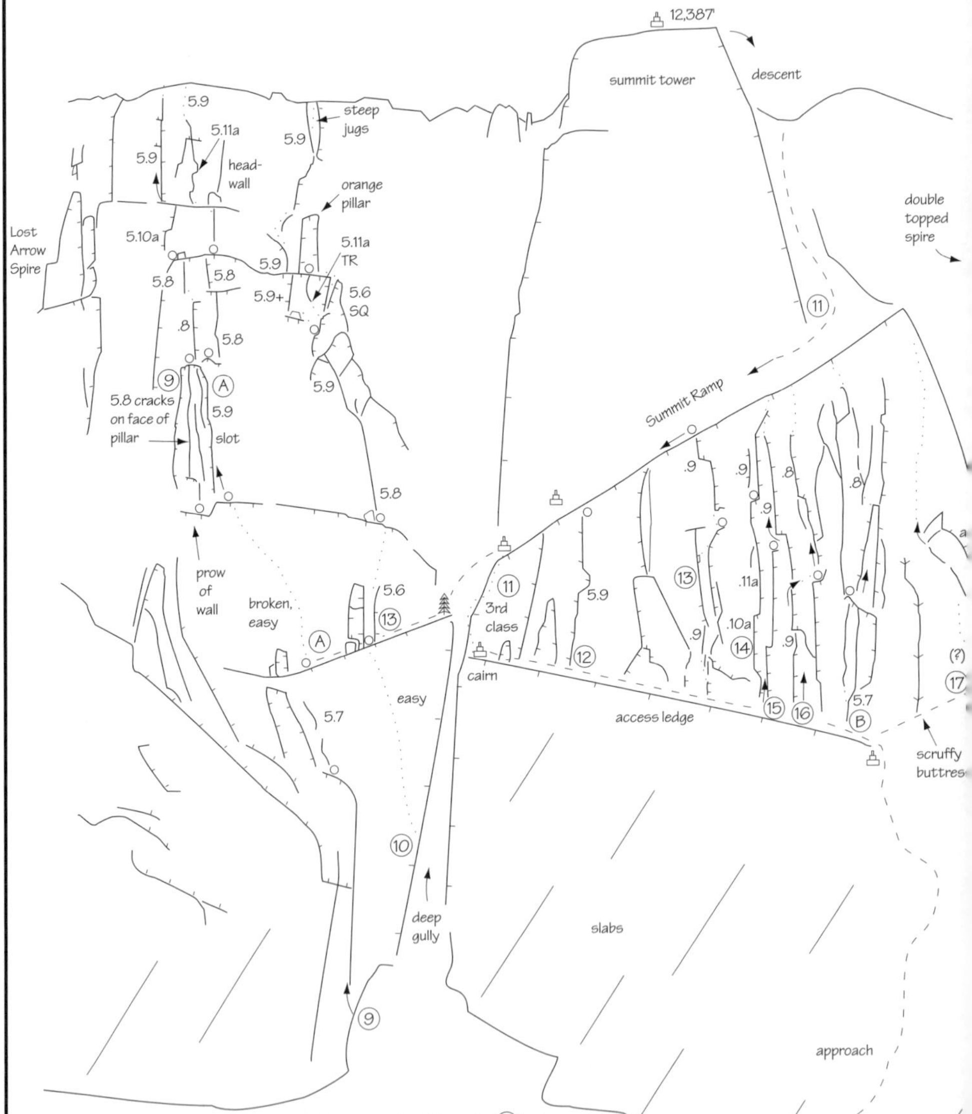

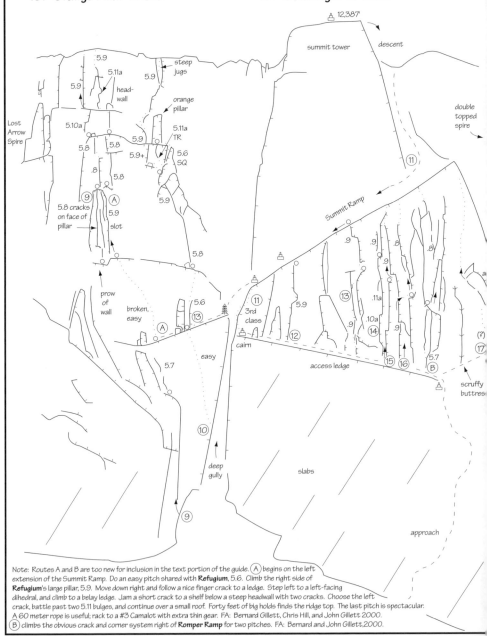

Note: Routes A and B are too new for inclusion in the text portion of the guide. (A) begins on the left extension of the Summit Ramp. Do an easy pitch shared with **Refugium**, 5.6. Climb the right side of **Refugium**'s large pillar, 5.9. Move down right and follow a nice finger crack to a ledge. Step left to a left-facing dihedral, and climb to a belay ledge. Jam a short crack to a shelf below a steep headwall with two cracks. Choose the left crack, battle past two 5.11 bulges, and continue over a small roof. Forty feet of big holds finds the ridge top. The last pitch is spectacular. A 60 meter rope is useful; rack to a #3 Camalot with extra thin gear. FA: Bernard Gillett, Chris Hill, and John Gillett 2000. (B) climbs the obvious crack and corner system right of **Romper Ramp** for two pitches. FA: Bernard and John Gillett, 2000.

11 Summit Ramp 3rd class ★★★

An excellent peak bagging route, **Summit Ramp** takes the most obvious feature on the wall beneath the summit tower. Though it looks improbable from below, there's only one pitch of 3rd class. It was reported as 5.4 in the DuMais guide (with the generic name of Southwest Face); perhaps the first ascent followed the low angled right-facing dihedral immediately right of the line described here, or climbed the deep gully. Walk to the far left edge of the access ledge, (tunneling beneath a fallen spike) to a cairn — the deep gully dropping from the summit lies immediately left. Climb flakes for thirty feet on the left edge of an arete, then switch right to grooves leading to the left side of the route's namesake (100 feet of 3rd class, though an unroped fall here would be lethal). Hike up the ramp to a saddle, turn left and go to another saddle on the ridge. One hundred feet of scrambling on the north side of the peak reaches the summit. If descending the route for the first time: go east from the summit to the first saddle on the ridge, turn right and descend to a saddle at the top of the ramp, then follow the ramp to its end (look for a few cairns). You've gone too far if you encounter the tree on **Rain Dance**. Scramble down from the westmost cairn staying just left of an arete, then switch to its right side at a big flake; take that to the access ledge. Tunnel beneath the fallen spike and hike along the ledge for several hundred feet to a cairn on a large boulder. Easy gullies lead down from here; move right to avoid slabs at the bottom.

12 The Ear I 5.9 ★

Locate a forty foot finger of rock leaning against the wall near the left side of the access ledge. The right-facing dihedral to its right (with an obvious undercling ear) is the line. One pitch (crux at the ear) ends on the huge ramp of the previous route. Descend that to return to the base. Bring RPs. FA: Bernard Gillett and Chris Hill, 1998.

13 Orange Pillar III 5.9 ★★★

The name of this line refers to the obvious orange pillar on the last pitch of **Rain Dance**. The two pitches described here were used by the FA team to access the upper wall; it was later discovered that the higher pitches had already been climbed. Locate a striking, left-leaning finger crack directly below the summit; begin a few paces right. 1. Climb a short corner to reach triple thin cracks right of the leaning crack. Take the leftmost crack, move right at its top toward a left-facing dihedral, then step left to another finger crack. Move back right at a wedged spike and belay at a small stance beneath a left-facing, roof capped dihedral (5.9-, 180 feet, lower belay possible). 2. Follow the dihedral (place gear on the right to enter it) and belay on a huge ramp, 5.9. 3. Hike 400 feet left and continue with **Rain Dance**, or descend **Summit Ramp**. FA: Gillett and Hill, 1998.

14 Eloquence I 5.11a (?) ★★★

Start forty feet right of **Orange Pillar** at the leftmost of several left-facing dihedrals. Follow this ultra clean corner for 180 feet to a small stance (200 foot rope recommended), and continue the corner on pitch two (5.9+) to the huge ramp (descend **Summit Ramp**). The first pitch is difficult to rate with no well-defined crux, and it may warrant an R-rating as the middle section is protected with tiny nuts (nothing bigger than a quarter-inch for seventy feet). A rest ledge (and possible escape right) exists half way up this pitch. Bring double RPs and tiny camming units plus gear to a #3 Friend. FA: Gillett and Hill, 1998.

15 Ramp Tramp I 5.9 ★★★
Climb the left-facing flakes immediately right of **Eloquence** to a belay below a roof. Turn the roof on the left and follow the nice left-facing dihedral above. Descend **Summit Ramp**.

16 Romper Ramp I 5.9 ★★
Start just right of **Ramp Tramp** and climb through the left side of an obvious, square overhang. Exit right before the line bends left into the roof on **Ramp Tramp** and belay. The second pitch takes the evident left-facing dihedral past another square roof and ends on the huge ramp.

17 Warhead III 5.9 ★
The location of this route is uncertain. A prominent left-facing arch graces the longer wall right of the previous five climbs; **Warhead** apparently passes beneath this arch via a pretty slab crack, but the exact line of ascent up to this point is difficult to discern from DuMais' High Peaks guide. Start near the right side of the access ledge and aim for the bottom of a left-leaning arch via a flake. Climb the arch to a ledge, then exit at a black flake. Angle left beneath the more obvious left-facing arch above, climbing a thin crack to a stance. Keep going left to avoid the steep headwall at the far end of the arch, and climb a rotten section just left of the headwall to a ledge. Follow a corner for a stretch, then face climb to its right to a belay — this is even with several pinnacles to the left. Take a small corner leading through an overhang and go up a headwall to the first saddle described in **Summit Ramp**; descend that route. The DuMais guide includes two pitches of low angled slabs at the beginning of this route, but there's not much in the vicinity that would require a rope. FA: Larry Hamilton, Griese and J. Byrd, 1975.

18 Goldfinger III 5.11d ★★★
This route begins on the far right side of the access ledge and climbs the wall below the ramp's top. Begin below a left-facing corner. 1. Climb to the corner and follow it over a roof (5.10a fingers and stemming) to a 5.11a hand crack. Belay on the left after 200 feet. 2. Take a curving, left-facing feature to a belay at the base of a right-leaning crack (5.10a, 100 feet). 3. Jam the crack past a thin section (crux), pass an overhang on the right, and go for the top. Bring 200 foot ropes (or choose different belays). FA: Doug Byerly and Kath Pyke, 1998.

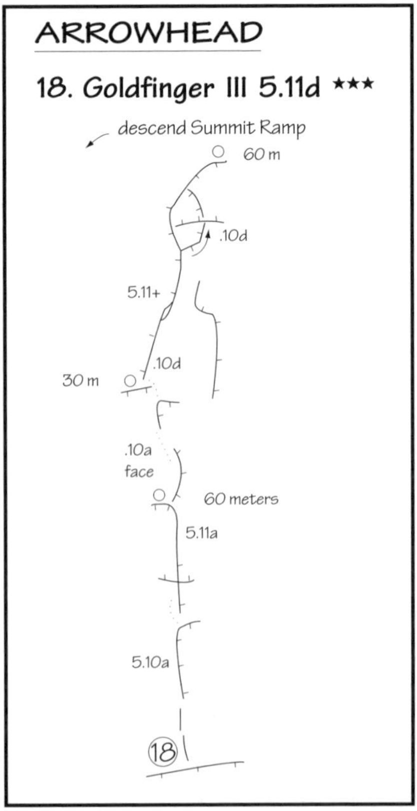

The double-topped spire right of **Goldfinger** does not have a recorded ascent, though the 1971 Fricke guide hints at an early route on the back side — in any case, it appears the crack systems on its south and west sides are climbable. As with all features on this part of the mountain, several hundred feet of lower angled slabs must be negotiated before reaching the base of the spire, though its higher summit can be reached easily from the upper part of **Summit Ramp**.

19 Independence III 5.9+ ⋆

This route may share ground with the next line, in spite of its name, which was inspired by a Fourth of July ascent. Climb low angled slabs (4th/5th class) to the large terrace mentioned below, and then follow an obvious dihedral system just right of the **Manic Laughter** "face" directly to the top for three pitches. The last pitch, at least, appears to be independent of **Manic Laughter**'s line, and it's possible the entire route is separate. FA: Kath Pyke and Dylan Taylor, 1998.

20 Manic Laughter III 5.9 ⋆

This climbs the southeast-facing wall of the triangular prow right of the double-topped spire. The name may have been inspired by the visage near the lower left corner of the buttress — look for slanting eyebrows, a long nose and a slightly maniacal grin. Climb 300 feet of easy slabs to a large terrace at the base of the triangular buttress. Follow a right-facing system just right of the "face", then chimney behind a flake to a ledge beneath an overhang. Pass the overhang on the left with a wide crack and belay after 100 feet. Go straight up to a grassy ledge and move the belay 40 feet right, then finish with a dihedral to a chimney. Scramble along the ridge to the summit and descend **Summit Ramp**. FA: T. Brink and R. Warren, 1980.

21 East Face III 5.4 ⋆

This route climbs the east facing slabs right of **Manic Laughter** for several pitches to the large terrace. Work up right from here to gain the northeast ridge, and follow that all the way to the summit. This is a long route with a mountaineering flavor; descend into the Solitude Lake cirque or reverse **Summit Ramp**.

C-6 Hourglass Couloir AI 3 M3

A deep chimney system (with several huge chockstones) in the middle of the north face marks this line. It is described in the ice climbing section under Glacier Gorge Trailhead.

C-7 Sister Sweetly M4 AI 4

The chimney right of **Hourglass Couloir**, also described in the ice climbing chapter.

POWELL PEAK

Climbers and hikers seldom visit the secluded east and southeast faces of Powell Peak, at the very end of the Solitude Lake cirque and right of the north face of McHenrys. The east face is home to two routes on dark rock, and two more are housed on the cleaner southeast wall to the right. A long, sloping ledge system (sometimes snow-covered) at the base of the wall allows access to all of the routes.

Approach: Hike for a mile past Solitude Lake (see McHenrys Peak) and swing right to gain the right side of the access ledge, then walk left to the chosen route.

Descent: The easiest descent from the summit goes around the backside of Taylor Peak to Andrews Glacier, but this is a long walk and comes nowhere near the base of the wall. The best descent for the first two routes heads north along the ridge toward Thatchtop, then east into a gully system — climb down to a double rope rappel that ends at the base of the gully and the east face. The next two routes utilize a snow gully right of the prow mentioned in **The Corporate Ladder**; no rappels are needed. Other descent options from the summit are described in the ice climbing section (see **Vanquished** and **Thatchtop-Powell Icefield**).

1 Snark III 5.6

Locate a pronounced pillar on the left side of the east face and scramble up to an obvious crack system below its right side. 1. Climb the crack to a good ledge at the base of the pillar. 2. Angle right up a dying crack, then go left to the base of a black gully. 3. Climb the left side of the gully to a ledge. 4. Go straight up a crack to a ledge, walk right, then move up left to a stance. 5. Work right across good rock and then follow the line of least resistance up a headwall that ends on easier ground and the top. FA: Dakers Gowans, J. Byrd and Larry Hamilton, 1974.

2 Early Retirement III 5.10

Start about 300 feet right of **Snark** at two parallel and vegetated cracks. 1. Climb the left crack (5.10) and traverse right to a belay ledge at the end of a full pitch. 2. Ascend between the cracks for 150 feet to a long ledge, 5.9. 3. Work up left to the right side of a detached flake, then traverse right (5.10) to a prominent left-facing dihedral; climb this to a belay among blocks. 4. Go straight up for a long pitch to a big ledge thirty feet shy of the ridge (5.8). 5. An easy pitch goes up and left. Bring a few thin pitons along with a standard rack. FA: Bob Monnet and Terry Murphy, 1996.

3 Pyke's Route (?)

This route climbs the same clean wall on which **The Corporate Ladder** is located, but details were not available at press time. FA: Kath Pyke and partner, 1998.

4 The Corporate Ladder II 5.11 **

This route climbs the right side of the clean, southeast face of Powell in three long pitches. Look for a left-facing system dropping down from the left side of a large prow that rises above the ridge, and begin to its left at a seam in a slab. The seam is about 100 feet right of a large, detached flake that sits fifty feet above the grassy ledge at the base of the route. 1. Climb the seam (5.10) and move right to double cracks. Go up the right crack (5.7), then angle left (loose) to a 5.10c finger crack that leads to a belay in an alcove (#3.5 Friend). 2. Take the nice left-facing dihedral directly above (sustained fingers, 5.11), and continue to a belay at 150 feet. 3. Work up and left along broken rock to a deep slot above a slab; follow the slot to the ridge. Bring extra stoppers. FA: Bob Monnet and Terry Murphy, 1996.

LOCH VALE

Loch Vale, western neighbor to Glacier Gorge, is the beautiful valley backed by Taylor Peak. A great many alpine pinnacles are located here, with Cathedral Spires in the southern fork of the vale and Otis Peak towers in the northern fork. These towers are the main attraction for rock climbers, though the sizable Cathedral Wall at the eastern terminus of Taylor's northeast ridge also affords good climbing.

Approach: The approach to Loch Vale begins at the Glacier Gorge Junction trailhead (see Glacier Gorge for travel directions to the parking lot, page 93). Hike south out of the lot toward Alberta Falls, pass the North Longs Peak trail junction at 1.5 miles, and veer right at a signed fork (2.0 miles; the left fork leads to Glacier Gorge). Twenty yards beyond this fork is another path originating from the Bear Lake trailhead. Stay on the main trail to The Loch (2.5 miles), and go around the north side of the lake to a footbridge across Andrews Creek (3.5 miles) and yet another fork. The majority of the climbs in Loch Vale are accessed with the left trail to Sky Pond; only the Otis Peak towers and a few routes on the north side of Cathedral Spires use the Andrews Creek (right) trail.

THATCHTOP and POWELL PEAK

The long ridge joining the summits of Thatchtop and Powell Peak separates Loch Vale from Glacier Gorge. Thatchtop is the eastern and much more prominent of the two peaks, appearing just as its name suggests it should. On the other hand, Powell Peak is nothing more than a bump on the Continental Divide, named only recently (1961) for the leader of the team who made the first recorded ascent of Longs Peak.

With the exception of the short wall described below and a six-pitch rock climb further up valley, all of the routes on Thatchtop are ice climbs, and are described in that section. Powell Peak also boasts several snow and ice routes on its Loch Vale side, as well as a few rock climbs on its east face. These are described in the previous section as Glacier Gorge is the path of approach.

Lakeside Wall

A substantial cliff band wraps around the northwest face of Thatchtop, site of two desperate mixed climbs (**Deep Freeze** and **Necrophilia**). Lakeside Wall is a summer attraction below and left of the much larger buttresses on which the mixed climbs are located (see photo in ice climbing section, page 251). Only a few pitches have been established, though the topo points to several logical lines that could be added.

Approach: Hike to the Loch (2.5 miles), go around the left side of the lake, and cross the outlet on logs and rocks. Seek out a break in a short rock band, scramble through the break, and hike over talus to the base of the wall (about ten minutes from The Loch).

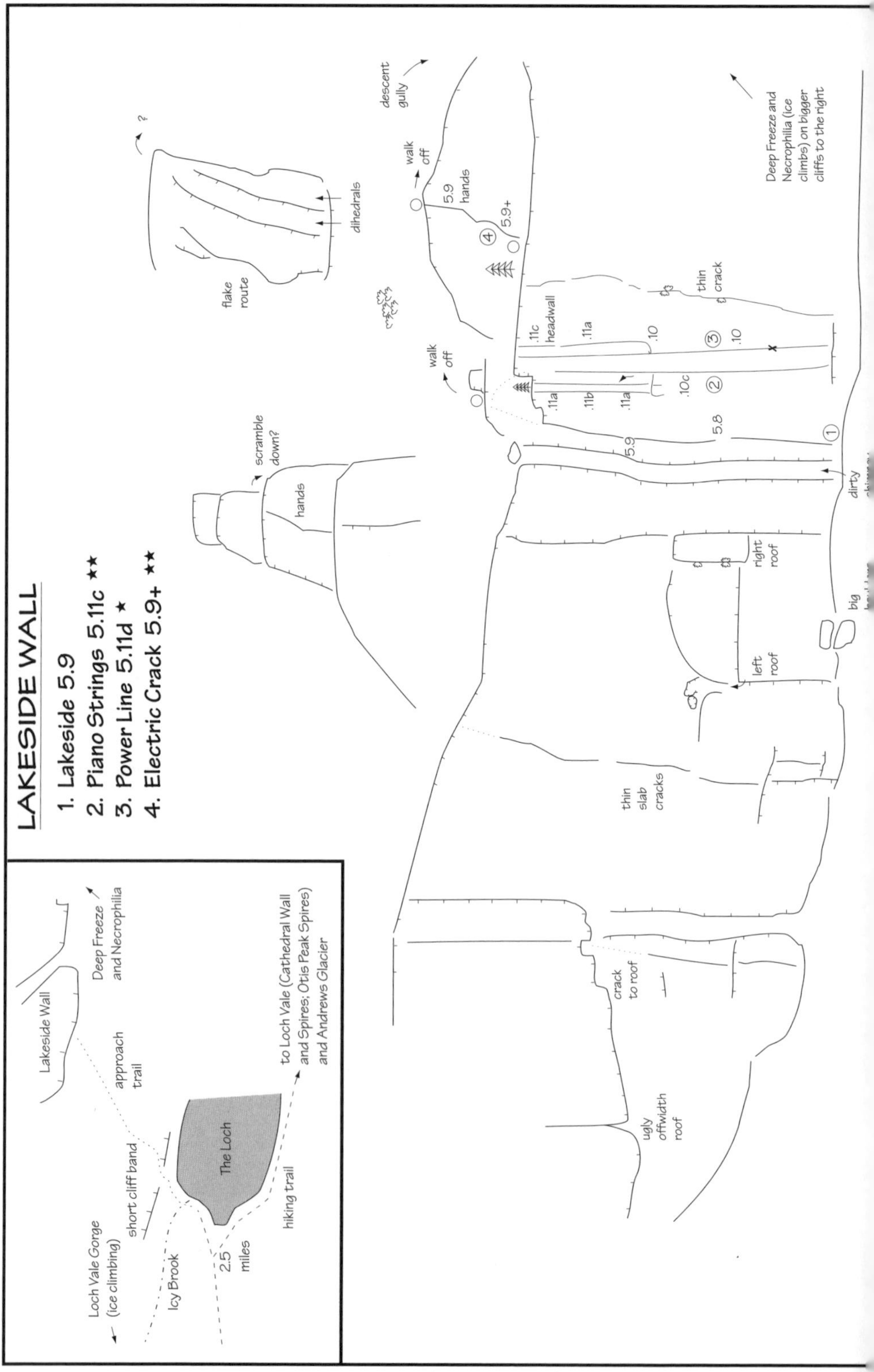
LAKESIDE WALL
1. Lakeside 5.9
2. Piano Strings 5.11c ★★
3. Power Line 5.11d ★
4. Electric Crack 5.9+ ★★
Lakeside Wall
Deep Freeze and Necrophilia
approach trail
The Loch
short cliff band
Loch Vale Gorge (ice climbing)
Icy Brook
2.5 miles
hiking trail
to Loch Vale (Cathedral Wall and Spires; Otis Peak Spires) and Andrews Glacier
flake route
dihedrals
descent gully
walk off
5.9 hands
5.9+
Deep Freeze and Necrophilia (ice climbs) on bigger cliffs to the right
thin crack
.11c
headwall
.11a
.10
.10
.10c
.11a
.11b
.11a
5.8
5.9
scramble down?
hands
dirty
right roof
left roof
big
thin slab cracks
crack to roof
ugly offwidth roof

THE SABER

20. The Pocketknife III 5.11a R ★★★
21. Snively-Harlin III 5.10b ★
22. Southwest Corner III 5.10a ★★
23. Southeast Corner III 5.10d ★★
24. Kor Route III 5.8+ ★★★

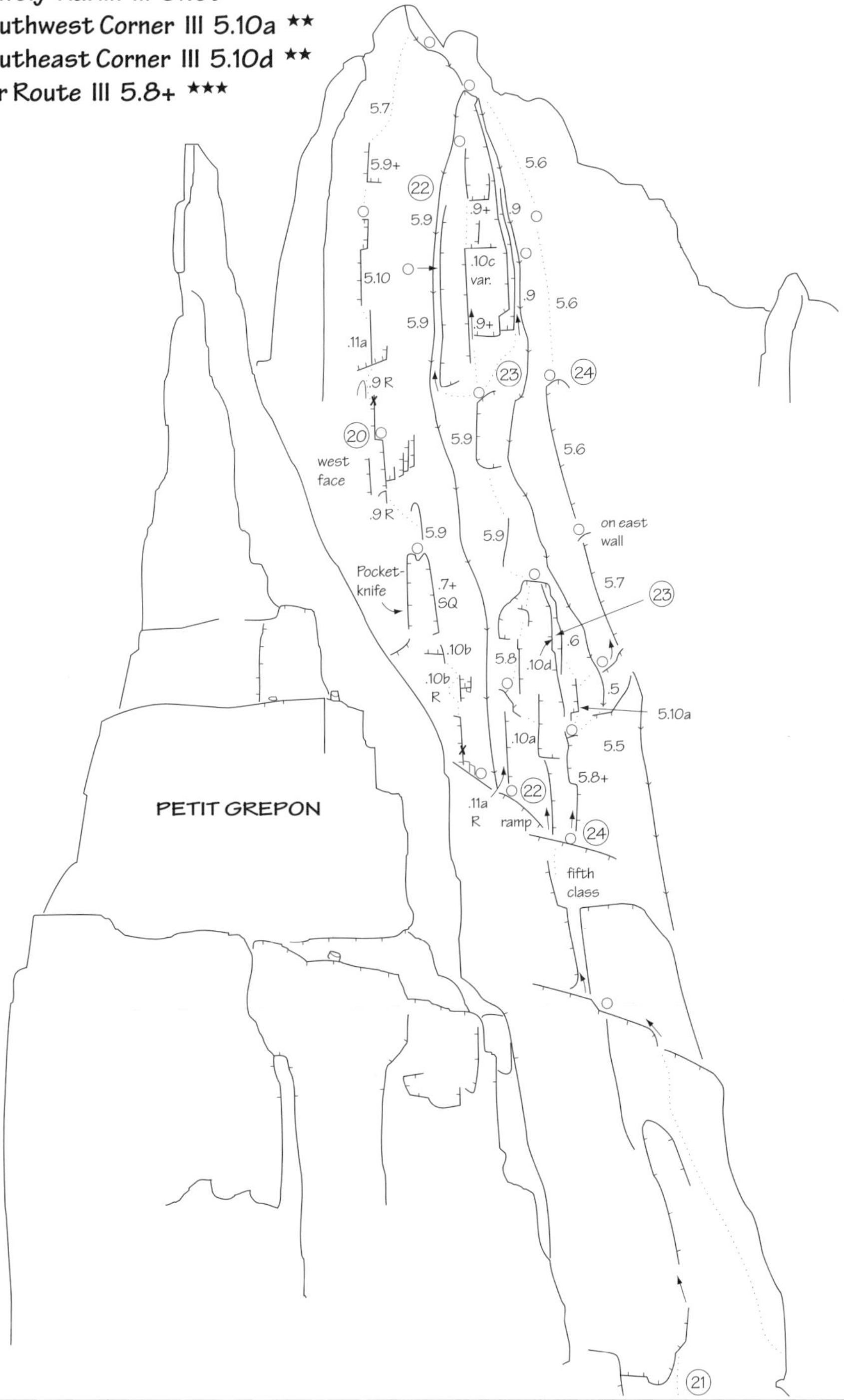

ridge to the true summit. FA: Chris Reveley and Bob Wade, 1974. **Variation 1:** Climb a steep, left-facing corner (5.11a R) left of the second pitch, beginning from the top of a ramp (the left end of the second big ledge). **Variation 2: Mother Mica** (5.10c R *, FA: Richard Getz and John Marrs, 1988). Directly above the hanging dihedral of pitch four is another hanging dihedral. It is much longer, faces right, and has two overhangs. Climb through the overhangs (5.10c R) and continue to yet another hanging dihedral (facing left with a big roof at its base), then go up this to the sixth belay on the standard line, 5.9+. Two pitches.

23 Southeast Corner III 5.10a or 5.10d **

The upper half of this route is the mirror image of the previous one, climbing the hanging, right-facing dihedrals seen high on the southeast corner of the Saber. Begin by climbing the first two pitches of the **Kor Route**. 3. Step left and ascend a thin, right-facing dihedral to the pillar belay (third belay) on **Southwest Corner**, 5.10d. One can also climb the 5.10a variation on the **Kor Route**, then move left to an easy, right-facing corner that also leads to the top of the pillar (this corner is just right of the 5.10d version). 4. Follow **Southwest Corner** for a pitch, to the top of its hanging, left-facing dihedral. 5 and 6. Traverse up right past a few ledges to the base of the upper dihedrals, and follow them for two pitches, both 5.9. 7. Climb up and left to the false summit, and finish as with **Southwest Corner**. **Variation:** This keeps the grade at 5.9, but it moves through some nebulous territory and poor rock. Do the first three pitches of the **Kor Route**, then head up left to the right margin of the south face. Climb through white streaked rock via cracks, corners and some overhangs, going more or less straight up, and gain the upper dihedrals.

24 Kor Route III 5.8+ ***

The **Kor Route** climbs the south and east faces of the Saber. 1. Do the first pitch of **Southwest Corner** to the second big ledge, 5.6. 2. Climb the prominent, left-facing dihedral off the middle of the ledge, stepping left through a small roof (crux, 5.8+). 3. Traverse right to a right-facing dihedral on the east face, and follow that to a big ledge, 5.6. A more direct line takes the thin corner continuation of the crux pitch (5.10a, and right of **Southeast Corner's** 5.10d pitch), then moves right to the big ledge on the east face. 4. Move the belay to the right end of the ledge, and climb an obvious open book dihedral for a long pitch, 5.7. Belay at a small pillar. 5. Continue up the corner to another good belay ledge, 5.6. 6 and 7. Climb moderate (though exciting) terrain directly to the false summit, 5.6. The last of these two pitches can be done to the right (in a deep, right-facing corner). This avoids the down climb from the false summit (see **Southwest Corner**), making for an easier escape off the summit ridge. FA: Layton Kor and Dean Moore, 1962.

The Foil

Two routes have been established on the Foil, the skinny pinnacle east of the Saber. The Foil's diminutive summit rivals Petit Grepon, and its airy perch is worth reaching.

Descent: To descend, rappel north 85 feet to the notch behind the summit, walk north, and set up a belay. Traverse right and climb a loose crack in a big dihedral to the ridge top (5.5), then scramble down to the talus below. Walk out via the Gash,

THE FOIL

25. South Face III 5.9+ R ★
26. The Poc Club III 5.11+ ★★★

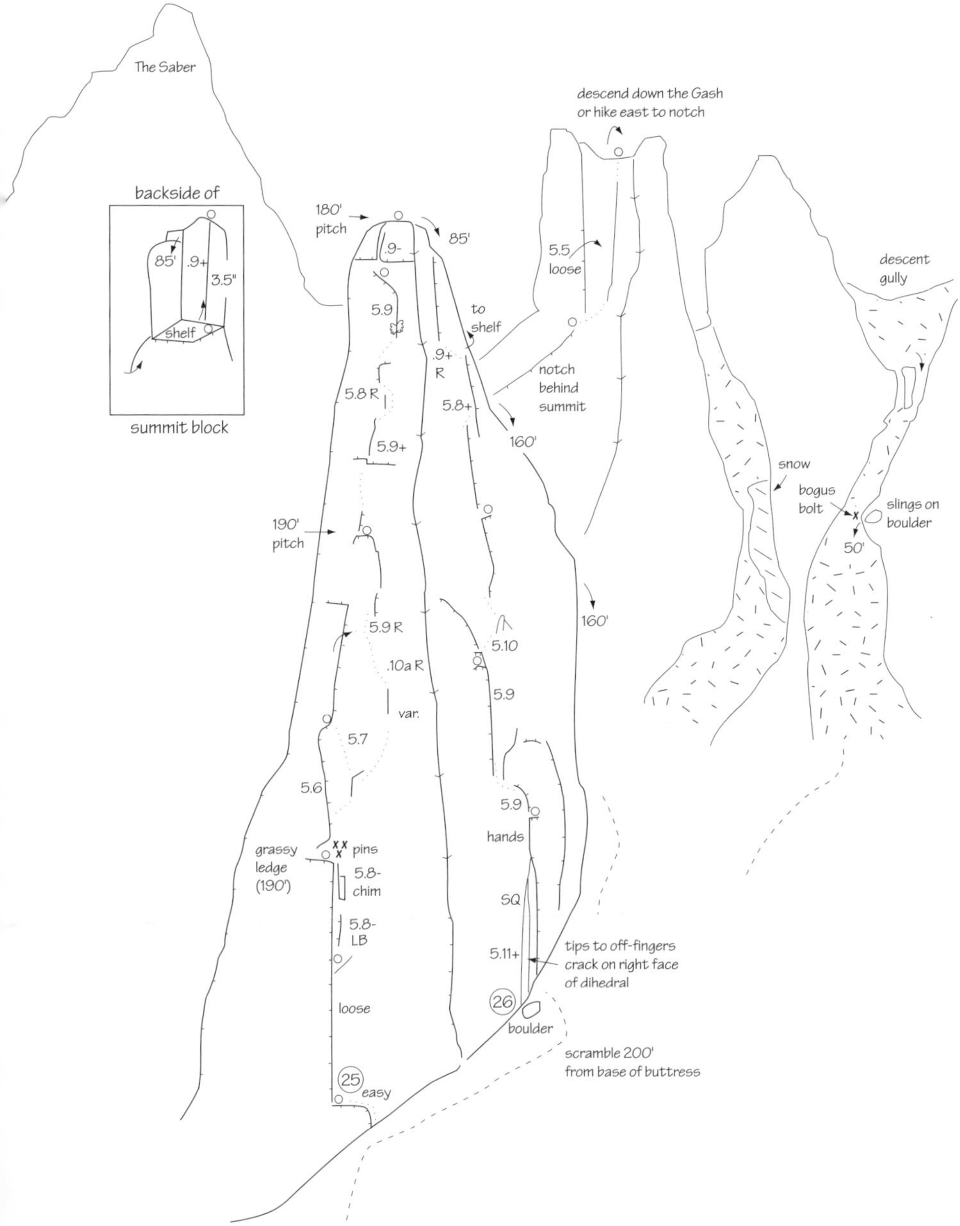

or hike east behind the bulky tower north of the Foil to a notch in the ridge. Descend the gully beneath this notch; a fifty foot rappel from slings around a boulder (bogus bolt nearby) ends the technical difficulties.

It is also possible to descend more directly: Do the 85 foot rappel from the summit to the notch, then make two double-rope rappels to the east. This puts the party just uphill from the base of **The Poc Club**, and avoids the gully scramble of the traditional descent.

25 South Face III 5.9+ R ★

Climb easy rock to the base of a huge, right-facing dihedral in the center of the south face. 1. Go up the loose dihedral to a sloping belay at a flake. 2. Lieback to a chimney in the corner, and continue to a big ledge on the left, 5.8- (three fixed pins). 3. Follow a blocky, left-facing dihedral directly above the belay to a step in the dihedral (5.6), or move right onto the face to a small corner, then go up to the same belay, 5.7. 4. Continue up the left-facing dihedral, but exit right before reaching the overhang at its top. Work through an unprotected bulge (5.9 R) and continue with easier cracks to a ledge. 5. Start with a short corner on the left, then climb through an overlap at a pretty finger crack (5.9+). Zigzag up to a crack with a bush, and stretch the pitch out on a ramp below the summit overhang. 6. Step left and climb a wide crack through the overhang (5.9-). FA: Duncan Ferguson and Mark Hesse, 1973. **Variation:** A line of ascent right of the third and fourth pitches is marked on the topo (5.10a R). It climbs clean, but run out rock with no obvious belay opportunities for some distance, and joins the normal route at the unprotected bulge. A 200 foot rope is recommended. FA (?): Bernard, John, and Robert Gillett, 1996.

26 The Poc Club III 5.11+ ★★★

This route climbs the southeast face of The Foil. Begin two hundred feet up from the base at a dihedral with a thin crack on its right wall. 1. Climb the crack (burly 5.11+), squeeze through a slot, and finish with a hand crack to a ledge (160'). 2. Move left along a left-facing arch (5.9), then traverse left to a right-facing system. Climb this to a belay on the left, 5.9, 140'. 3. Traverse right (5.10), then climb up through a left-facing corner to a belay ledge (100'). 4. Link two long, left-facing dihedrals, stepping right after half a pitch, and then traverse around to the north side of the summit block. Belay on a big shelf below a fist crack. 5. Jam the crack to the top, 5.9+. Rack from RPs to four inches, with extra finger crack gear. FA: Topher and Patience Donahue, Simon Fryer, and Melissa McManus, 1999. **Variation:** It is also possible to move left from the two dihedrals on pitch 4 into another left-facing dihedral (5.9+ R). Follow that to the summit (longer ropes are useful if this variation is taken — it's a 170' pitch from the third belay to summit).

The Moon

The Moon and The Jackknife are located at the east end of the Cathedral Spires. The Moon is on the left, and is considerably taller. The actual spire, which is cut by a prominent wide crack on its south side, sits atop a larger buttress.

Descent: Down climb northwest to a gully, and follow that back to the base, or rappel west to the gully.

27 Tantric Pickle III 5.11a ★
Scramble up 3rd class rock to the toe of the buttress, then go up the west gully for 200 feet, reaching a 4th class traverse (right) which leads to a grassy ledge. Establish a belay under the corner that is closest to the prow of the buttress. 1. Climb the corner, which fades into a face crack above some overhangs, and belay on an exposed projection of rock, 5.11a, 130 feet. 2. Jam steep hand and finger cracks, then move right onto the prow when possible. Continue right to avoid loose rock and belay. 3. A short pitch finds the summit. Bring extra finger crack gear. FA: Patience Donahue, Melissa McManus, and Topher Donahue, 1999.

28 South Face II 5.9
Begin on the left side of the buttress' south face, and climb two pitches (5.8) to a grassy ledge, moving right near the end. The next lead climbs up some corners (5.8) to a ledge beneath an overhang, which in turn is below the wide, prominent crack mentioned above. Avoid the overhang with a short pitch on the right; belay at the base of the crack. Follow the crack to a ledge, and continue up a hand crack. FA: Molly Higgins, L. Manson, and Stephanie Atwood, 1975.

The Jackknife

The Jackknife is the easternmost spire of the group, a square-topped pinnacle right of The Moon.

Descent: Rappel from slings near the northeast corner (or find a devious down climb), and then scramble down the east side.

29 South Face II 5.9
Go up to a chockstone in the gully west of the spire and commence climbing. 1. Move right along grooves to the middle of the south face and belay. 2. Climb a crack on the left, and tackle an overhang near the end of the lead, 5.9. 3. Head right to a steep crack, pop over another roof, and continue to the top, 5.9. FA: Scott Kimball and Wildberger, 1979.

30 The Jackrabbit III 5.11b ★
This route climbs the furthest system to the right when viewed from Sky Pond. Gain the base of the tower by traversing on ledges from below the Moon. 1. Climb a small, left-facing system for a full pitch to a grassy ledge, 5.11a. 2. Step left, go up a 5.7 crack on the south face, and belay below an imposing and arching thin crack. 3. Jam the crack, 5.11b. 4. Move up left to a 5.9 corner in the summit block. FA: Topher and Patience Donahue, 1999.

CATHEDRAL WALL
1
#1 Buttress
C-56
5
6
4
7
#2 Buttress
#3 Buttress

CATHEDRAL WALL
#3 Buttress
#4 Buttress
#2 Buttress
#1 Buttress
1
4
7
8
9
10
11
12
13

CATHEDRAL WALL

5. Winchester III 5.10 R ★
6. Lever Action 5.10a R ★
7. Pillar East III 5.9 R ★
8. Altar Boy III 5.9 R ★
9. Kor Route III 5.9 R ★
10. The Pew III 5.9 R ★
11. Garden Wall 5.10

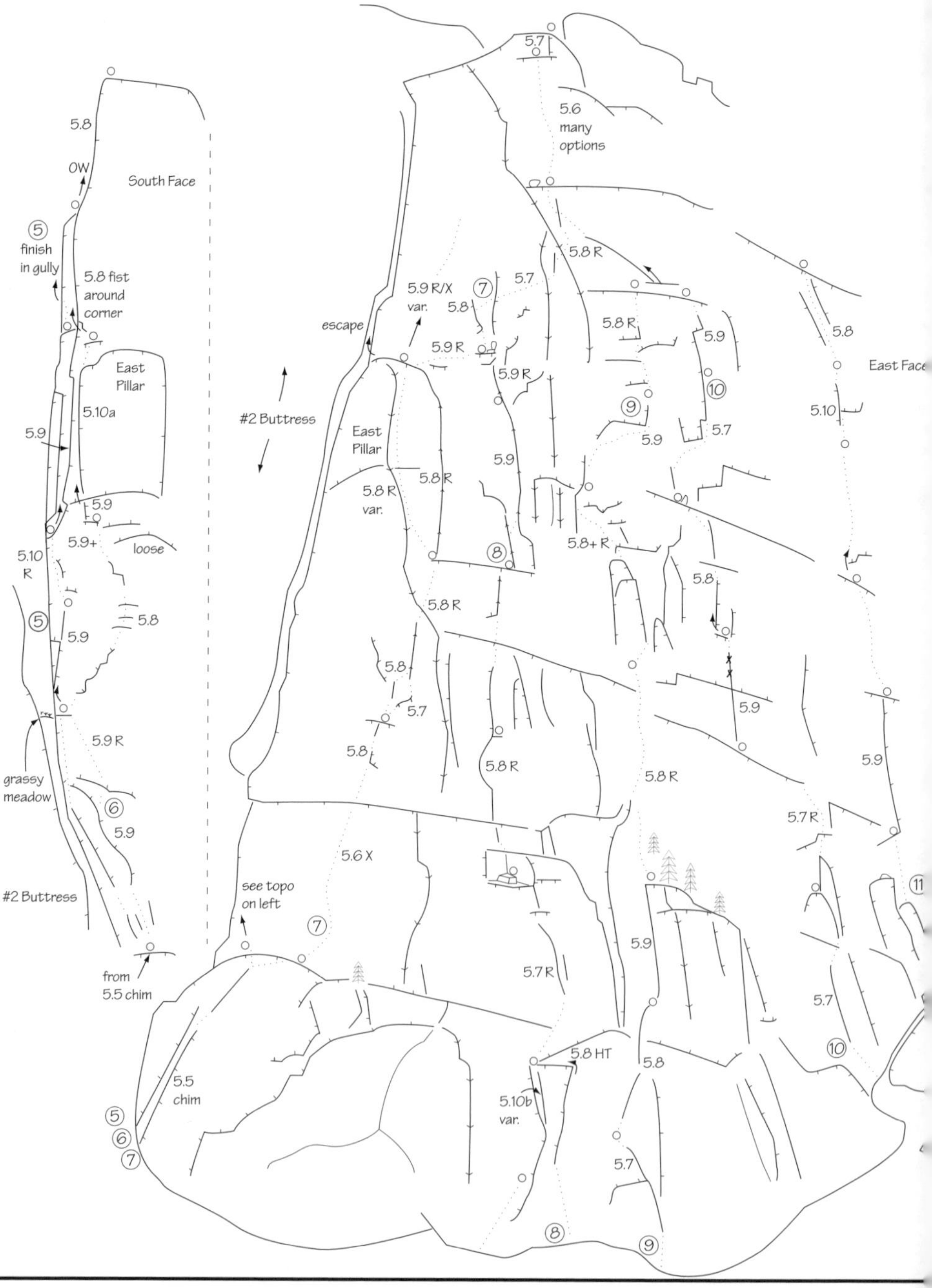

CATHEDRAL WALL

Cathedral Wall forms the eastern end of the ridge that separates the upper forks of Loch Vale (i.e. the northeast ridge of Taylor Peak, site of the Cathedral Spires). Four closely packed buttresses constitute the whole of Cathedral Wall, though the name originally referred to a route on the largest of these (the #3 Buttress). The #1 Buttress, on the south side of the wall, is sectioned off by an offwidth crack (see **Blackstar**) and a more prominent chimney on the right (see **Womb with a View**). The last three buttresses are more apparent, separated from each other by deep chimneys and gullies. While most of Cathedral Wall's routes ascend good rock, the compact nature of the crack systems thwarts attempts at protection. As a result, these lines are quite serious.

Approach: The approach is simple and fast. Take the trail past The Loch and toward Sky Pond, but break right at about 3.7 miles to the base of the wall (before Lake of Glass is reached). The descent from each buttress is described below.

#1 Buttress

Descent: Walk southwest until it is obvious to scramble down talus to Lake of Glass.

1 Blackstar II 5.7+ ⋆
This is an enjoyable route, the upper half of which climbs through the offwidth crack on the left edge of the buttress. Begin about 150 feet left of a black water stain below a roof up on the wall. 1. Angle up right toward the stain. 2. Cross the stain and belay on a ledge with tree. 3. Work back left on moderate cracks to a good ledge below the chimney/offwidth of the upper route. 4. A short lead up the chimney ends at a stance, 5.6. 5. Continue up cracks alongside the chimney to a big ledge at the base of the final offwidth section, 5.7. These last two pitches can be combined. 6. A quick thrash up the offwidth (with chockstone) ends the climb, 50 feet of 5.7+. FA: Dan Bradford and Angelo de La Cruz, 1985.

2 #1 Buttress II 5.6
This route starts from the lower right corner of the buttress and climbs four pitches of mostly easy going to the top.

C-56 Womb with a View III WI 5 M6-
This is the mixed route between the #1 and #2 Buttresses — see the ice climbing section.

#2 Buttress

Descent: Maneuver across the top of the #1 Buttress, and then follow its descent to escape from the top of the next two routes.

3 #2 Buttress II 5.7

Prior descriptions of this route are just as sparse as that given for **#1 Buttress**. Begin at the lower left corner of the narrow buttress (left of a large, right-facing dihedral), angle into the middle of the wall, and head for the top, apparently crossing over the next route at some point. Five pitches with plentiful ledges and several options.

4 Tourist Tragedy III 5.9 ★

This route begins near the middle of the buttress, but then angles left to a line near the left side. Start right of the large, right-facing dihedral on the lower left side of the buttress. 1. A long pitch climbs to a right-facing corner leading to a roof; pull through the roof and step right to a belay, 5.9. 2. Go left past a tree, then follow a right-facing dihedral to a big ledge, 5.8. 3. Angle left on an easy ramp to another long ledge. 4. Take a right-facing feature to a belay about 100 feet below a prominent right-facing dihedral, 5.8. 5. Follow easy ground to the base of the right-facing dihedral — this is the most obvious feature of the route; it is capped with a roof. 6. Climb the dihedral and roof, and continue to a ledge below a steep headwall, 5.6. 7. Begin with a crack on the left, hand traverse right, then go straight up to a ledge with a huge block, 5.8. The initial crack can be climbed directly to the same ledge, 5.10a. 8. Go up the right side of the block, pass a small overhang, and reach easy terrain at the top of the buttress. FA: Richard and Joyce Rossiter, 1984.

#3 Buttress — Main Wall

Descent: Traverse north (toward Otis Peak) along ledges to the end of the wall, then descend northeast to the backside of the #4 Buttress. Walk around the east end of this (passing beneath its two routes) back to the base.

5 Winchester III 5.10 R ★

Winchester climbs the left edge of the #3 Buttress. Begin at a chimney just right of the huge cleft that separates the second and third buttresses. 1. Climb the chimney and crack above (5.5) to a large ledge — a short stretch of simul-climbing may be necessary. 2. Move left to the edge of the wall and take a leaning dihedral past the left end of an overhang, then continue up to a ledge even with a grassy meadow in the huge cleft. 3. Climb a short, left-facing corner and go over a roof, then follow a short crack to a small ledge, 5.9. 4. Angle left along some overhangs, and run it out to a stance on the left edge of the face and at the base of the large dihedral forming the left side of the East Pillar (see below), 5.10 R. 5. Climb the large dihedral (5.9), then move left around the corner to a steep face ending on a good ledge. 6. Traverse right with the ledge, then angle back left with moderate face climbing to a big ledge. 7. Take a crack from the left end of the ledge than leads into the upper portion of the huge cleft and follow that. FA: John Harlin and Kent Wheeler, 1980.

6 Lever Action III 5.10a R ★

This route begins with the initial pitch of **Winchester**, and then stays just to its right. It's possible the two routes overlap to some extent on the second pitch, and the last two pitches seem to correspond to a variation of **Pillar East**. 1. Do **Winchester** to the big ledge. 2. Face climb along a thin crack to an arching, left-facing dihedral, then step right and over a roof at its end, 5.9. Head up and left to the belay on **Winchester**, 5.9 R. 3. Diagonal up right for 50 feet and climb through a small staircase (5.8). Aim for the left edge of a large roof, and climb an orange face (5.9+ R) to a good stance. 4. Climb a short left-facing dihedral on the left edge of the East Pillar, then continue along the left arete of the pillar to a sloping ledge at its top. 5 and 6. Step left around the corner and follow fist and offwidth cracks to the top for two shorter pitches, 5.8. Easier options exist left, deeper in the huge cleft, but these are littered with loose blocks. FA: Greg Sievers, John Dorman, and Dan Capellini, 1996.

7 Pillar East III 5.9 R ★

This route climbs the right side of the huge pillar (the East Pillar) on the narrow south face of the #3 Buttress. It is also known as the **Dalke Route**. 1. Do the first pitch of **Winchester** to the big ledge, and move right toward a tree to belay. A variation climbs past the left edge of the huge roof on the right to the same belay, 5.6. 2. Wander up an easy face (5.6 X) to a horizontal crack, and climb a headwall to a ledge, 5.8. 3. Traverse right (5.7 low, or up then right, 5.8) to a groove, and climb past its end to a good ledge at the base of the East Pillar, 5.8 R. 4. Follow the vague corner on the right side of the pillar to a big sloping ledge at its top, 5.8 R. Good anchors are difficult to find on this ledge. 5. A short pitch traverses almost straight right (5.9, no pro) to a shelf with two stacked blocks. 6. There are several possibilities on this devious and poorly protected pitch. One option angles left from the blocks through a short, right-facing flake, then makes a long rising traverse around the prow of the wall; zigzag up to a ledge with a block, 5.8 R. 7. An easy pitch up broken cracks leads to a shelf near the top, and one more thirty foot lead finishes the route. Bring RPs to a #4 Friend, and plenty of long runners for the sixth pitch. FA: Larry and Roger Dalke (with some aid), 1966. **Variation 1:** Climb left of pitches 3 and 4 near the right arete of the East Pillar, sustained 5.8 with poor protection. Go straight up on the fifth pitch (5.9 R/X) on the steep south face, and then bend right on the final two leads. **Variation 2:** It is also possible to escape left from the top of the East Pillar, joining up with **Lever Action**.

8 Altar Boy III 5.9 R ★

Begin beneath the right-hand of two large roofs at the base of the wall, at the left end of the east face, and scramble up a slab. 1. Climb to a break on the left edge of the big roof, and hand traverse left to pass the roof, 5.8. 2. Follow faint corners to a good ledge with a square block, 5.7 R. 3 and 4. Climb grooves and corners for two pitches to the good ledge at the end of **Pillar East**'s third lead, 5.8 R; belay to the right. 5. Climb into the open book corner that parallels **Pillar East**'s fourth lead, and jam to a stance, 5.9. 6. Continue with the corner for a short, steep lead to the ledge with two stacked blocks (**Pillar East**'s fifth belay). 5.9 R. **7.** Follow **Pillar East**. FA: Billy Westbay and Douglas Snively, 1981. **Variation: Flying Nun** (FA: Greg Davis and Charlie Fowler, 1986, 5.10b ★★). A thin crack splits the arete leading to the left edge of the big roof at the base of the climb. Access this crack from the right, belaying from the top of a slab, then jam it to the first belay. The rest of the route is the same, though the fourth and fifth leads may have been climbed first by Davis and Fowler (Westbay and Snively might have joined **Pillar East** after three pitches).

9 Kor Route III 5.9 R ★

This line climbs through the obvious left-facing dihedral (trees on top) near the left side of the east face. Higher up, it weaves though several black overhangs. Start below the right end of the big roof mentioned in **Altar Boy**. 1. Climb a short pitch up left to a piton belay below the big roof, 5.7. 2. Move up right to a ledge at the base of the obvious dihedral, 5.8. 3. Climb the dihedral with a steep crack on its left wall, and move right to the trees above, 5.9. 4. Climb past the right end of an arch, and angle up left to the right end of a grassy ledge, 5.8 R. Belay as high as possible (beneath a groove/corner). 5. Move right out of the groove into the next dihedral on the right. Climb this (fixed pins) to a roof, then traverse left and up for 40 feet (5.8+ R) to a roof-capped corner. Work out the right side of this roof and belay on a pedestal below a black overhang. 6. Move up right to the black overhang, and traverse around its right end to a tiny stance, 5.9. 7. Climb straight up (passing along the edge of two more overhangs, 5.8 R) to easier ground and belay when convenient. 8 and 9. Clamber up moderate terrain (two more pitches). FA: Layton Kor and friend, 1963. **Variation:** Move left from the fourth belay and climb directly through the black overhang on pitch six (5.11c R, FA: John Marrs and Chris Ann Crysdale, 1987).

10 The Pew III 5.9 R ★

Hike up the gully on the right side of the main face to the point where it constricts. Two opposing dihedrals in an inset with a crack between them mark the beginning of the route. 1. Follow the crack past a ledge (dead tree) to a pedestal belay in a prominent left-facing dihedral, 5.7. 2. Head up right, then angle back left to a long, grassy ledge, 5.7 R. 3. A nice crack splits the long, narrow roof above. Follow this over the roof (two fixed pins), then step left to a belay in a left-facing dihedral, 5.9. 4. Move left again to another left-facing corner, and follow that to a long horizontal crack, 5.8. Step left to a ledge with a perched flake. 5. Go up left with a short crack, then move back right to a jagged, right-facing dihedral. Take this to a belay. 6. Stem up to an overhang and climb through its right side (5.9) to a good ledge. Easy climbing up and left leads to the top. Bring plenty of small nuts. FA: Tim and Larry Coats, 1988.

11 Garden Wall III 5.10

This route climbs a long, thin, left-facing dihedral on its second pitch, then takes a less defined route above. Scramble up the gully beyond **The Pew** and begin below the thin dihedral. 1. Climb to the base of the dihedral. 2. Follow the dihedral to a ledge on its top, 5.9. 3. Follow moderate cracks up left to a stance below an overhang. 4. A long pitch goes past the overhang and ends a ways below a bigger overhang. 5. Turn the big overhang on the left (5.10) and go to a belay. 6. Take a slab between two dihedrals (5.8) to broken terrain at the top of the face. FA: Joe Hladick and Scott Kimball, 1979.

#4 Buttress

This is the large, though mostly broken dome-shaped buttress right of the main wall. Two short climbs have been established on its east face.

12 Spider Web I 5.11b ★

Begin right of some large overhangs low on the wall near the left end of the east face — look for some obvious thin cracks in excellent, orange rock. Climb the cracks to a ledge (5.10), step left, and work up difficult seams (crux) to hand jams. Go five more feet, then move left into a right-facing corner. Follow that to a loose gully and belay at a tree. The gully leads to a big ledge with more trees — traverse the ledge toward the main wall, and down climb a short, 5.0 face to walking territory. FA: Bernard and John Gillett, 1995.

13 #4 Buttress I 5.8 R

This route follows a few left-facing corners 300-400 feet uphill from **Spider Web** (nice, clean and compact rock, but less than memorable climbing). Belay on a grassy ledge after a long pitch, and escape right along the ledge to the base. FA: Gilletts, 1995.

OTIS PEAK

The south side of Otis Peak forms the nearly two mile long northern boundary of Loch Vale. The mountain itself looks very much like a loaf of bread from the east, stretching from The Loch to Andrews Glacier and the Continental Divide. Running deep beneath the mountain's southern slopes is the Alva B. Adams Tunnel, a man-made shaft big enough to accommodate a Jeep convoy. It carries water to the east side of the Divide and surely must be the envy of ice farmers the world over — imagine the routes that could be created by tapping into that source!

All of the climbing covered in this book is concentrated on the towers and buttresses above Andrews Creek on the south side of the peak, though both the spire on the northwest corner (The Turkey Monster, FA: Charlie Logan and Larry Van Slyke, around 1975) and the scruffy cliff at the end of Otis' east ridge have been ascended. No information on the latter routes is available.

Approach: The hike to all of these formations is the same: Go past The Loch for one mile, cross Andrews Creek on a foot bridge, and turn right at a trail junction, heading along the creek (the left branch of the trail leads to Cathedral Wall and Spires — see previous section). After a short grade, the trail bends left with the creek, and goes up to Andrews Tarn and Glacier. To approach the Otis towers, leave the hiking trail at various points and scramble to the day's objective — none of these exits is marked, nor are there any established climber's trails, but the towers are easily viewed from the trail. Climbs are described right to left, up valley.

Loch Vale Pinnacle

Loch Vale Pinnacle is the square-shaped block perched above a lower-angled buttress several hundred feet right of Zowie and Wham. A long, though straightforward scramble up the southern slopes of Otis gains the base of the buttress.

Descent: To descend from the upper block, make a seventy foot rappel north, and then follow a gully to the bottom.

LOCH VALE PINNACLE
WHAM
ZOWIE
SOLAR WALL
1
2
3
4
5

1 South Face II 5.8

Begin in the middle of the lower buttress at a rotten chimney, and follow that for two pitches to a terrace. Two more moderate leads ascend over ledges to the south side of the square block. The final pitch climbs a dihedral system near the center of the block, then moves left on a ramp to the southeast arete; follow that. FA: Michael Covington, Shambu Tamang, and J. LaSage, late 1970s (?).

Wham

This is the narrow, knob-topped rib up and right of Zowie. Approach with the gully between Wham and Zowie.

Descent: Rappel into the notch on the north side, then make several more rappels west (two ropes), reaching the upper portion of the approach gully.

2 South Face II 5.7

Tack back and forth as needed up the narrow south prow of the buttress for several pitches, and skirt the summit overhangs on the right. FA: Bob Culp and Ken Parker, around 1961.

Zowie

Zowie is the most striking of the Otis Peak towers, similar in shape to Petit Grepon in the Cathedral Spires. In fact, its south face looks so much like Petit Grepon that one hapless party, having made a wrong turn in the hour before dawn, mistook Zowie for the Grepon when the sun rose. Not until they were halfway up the face did they suspect their mistake, and it wasn't confirmed until later that night. The south face routes have become increasingly well traveled, and Zowie is a good choice on weekends (or any day) to avoid crowds on the Grepon.

Descent: A new rappel route has been established to accommodate the increased traffic. It begins with an 85 foot rappel from two bolts on the summit. Walk north to the next set of bolts and rappel to the saddle behind the summit spire (85 feet). Scramble down the gully on the west side (reversing **Standard Route**), and locate two Metolious Rap anchors on the right (west) side of the gully; a final rappel of 90 feet reaches the ground.

3 South Face Direct III 5.8+ R ★★

This variation (5.8 R) to the normal south face route provides additional climbing at a grade more consistent with the rest of the route. Begin in the center of the triangular buttress abutting the southeast corner of the tower, and follow a left-facing dihedral for two pitches. Step over to the main mass and ascend to the right end of the long ledge on **South Face**, then join that route. FA: Dougald McDonald and Kate Bartlett, 1996.

4 South Face III 5.8+ ★★

Start at the big chimney in the middle of the tower, directly below the summit. 1 and 2. Do two easy pitches along the chimney, beginning with the face to its left, and then entering the chimney on the second lead to reach a long ledge. 3. Walk right on the ledge for 250 feet, stopping before the right edge of the south face.

OTIS PEAK - Solar Wall

6. Solar Arete III 5.11a ★★

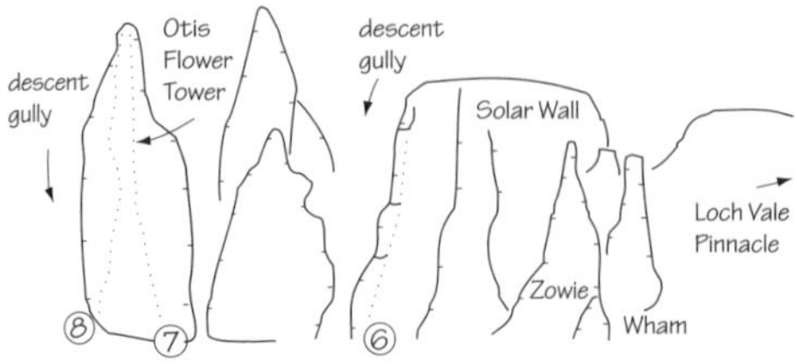

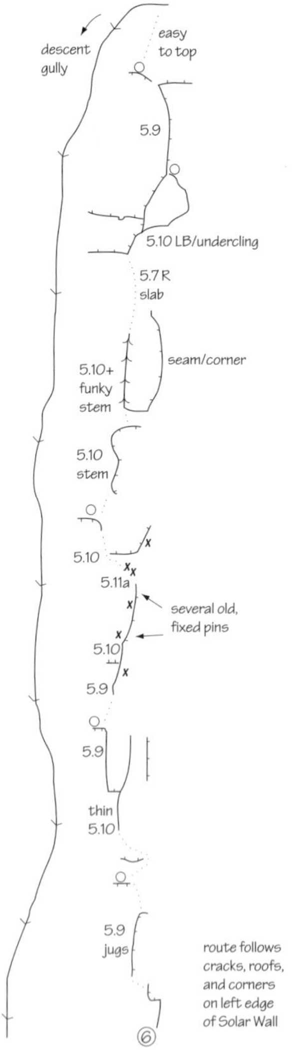

OTIS FLOWER TOWER

8. Heat Wave IV 5.11c ★★★

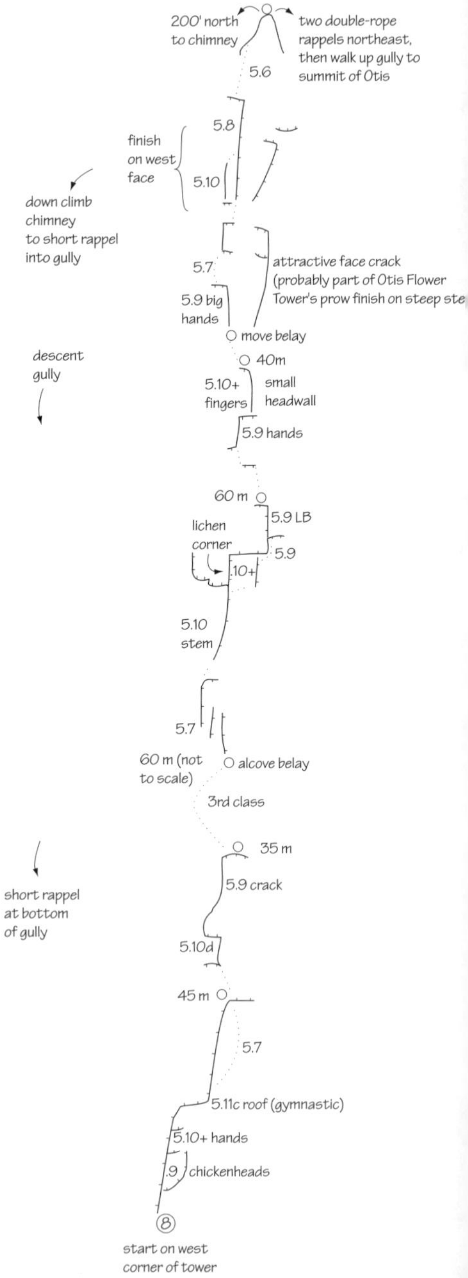

4 and 5. Ascend to the southeast ridge and climb it for two pitches, both 5.6. This section can be made easier by climbing further right (on the east face). 6. Continue up the ridge to a shelf that leads to the southwest corner. Move left on the shelf to a belay below the final chimney. 7. Lead up the chimney past one overhang (crux, poor pro) and up to another. Turn the second roof on the right and move right to the summit. One can also traverse out of the chimney about half way up and climb 5.9 face on the right, or avoid this pitch altogether by doing the last lead of the next route. FA: William Buckingham and S. Boucher, 1961 (DuMais), or Brian Poling and Barry Harper, 1968 (Fricke). **Variation:** A prominent crack shoots up the center of the face from partway across the long traverse on pitch three. Jam up this to a belay, then move over easy ground up and left for a pitch. Follow a dihedral and the cracks above it to arrive at the shelf below the final crux chimney. The exact location of this variation is uncertain, though it is reported to be 5.8.

5 Standard Route II 5.8 ★

This route takes a spiraling line to the top. Begin at the base of the descent gully on the west side of the tower and climb one moderate pitch on the left to a belay near or at two big bolts (the final station on the rappel route). Scamper up the gully for several hundred feet to the grassy notch behind the summit spire and set a belay. Climb a broken chimney to the big ledge at the base of the spire (belay, perhaps at the new rappel bolts), then traverse over to a steep jam crack (5.8) on the east face and follow that. FA: Jack Glendenning, H. Walton, and Cary Huston, 1952.

Solar Wall

This is the parent cliff that gave birth to Zowie and Wham. One route has been established on its left side.

Approach and Descent: Approach by scrambling left of Zowie to the foot of the wall. Descend with a gully on the west side, adjacent to the route.

6 Solar Arete III 5.11a ★★

Solar Arete ascends the southwest edge of Solar Wall. The climb is characterized by face climbing along cracks and corners (expect some run out sections). Begin just right of the arete at a short crack leading into a small overhang. 1. Move up to the overhang, go around its left edge, and then traverse left to a left-facing dihedral. Ascend this (5.9 jugs), then move up to a belay beneath a roof. 2. Avoid the roof on the right, then move back left over its top to a thin crack. Climb this to a small overhang (5.10), then step left to a 5.9 crack. Belay at a stance on top of the crack. 3. Angle right to a left-facing corner, and follow that past several old pitons to an overhang (5.11a), then move left and up to a ledge. 4. Climb the left side of a flake into a funky stemming groove (5.10+), and go up a run out slab (5.7 R) to a flake overhang. Lieback and undercling up right (exciting 5.10) to a belay at the base of a left-facing dihedral. 5. Follow the dihedral (5.9) to the end of the climb, then scramble several hundred feet to the top of the descent gully. Bring 200 foot ropes. FA: Unknown, but apparently an old aid route. FFA: Doug Byerly and John Allen, 1998; the team found six old pitons on the third pitch.

Otis Flower Tower

This creatively named tower is west of Zowie and Wham, two formations left of Solar Wall and roughly opposite Sharkstooth and the Gash (but still below Andrews Tarn). Two routes have been established here, and each party chose a different method of descent from the summit.

Descent: The easier of the two descent routes makes two long rappels (from slings — bring your own) to the northeast, and then hits walking territory in a gully that leads to the summit of Otis. Go southwest from the summit to the top of Andrews Glacier, and descend that to Andrews Tarn and the trail. The second method is quicker, and has the advantage of ending at the base of the climbs, but it is more technical: rappel 200 feet north, then down climb a chimney for several hundred feet (4th class) to the gully on the west side of the tower. Enter the gully with a short rappel, and scramble down to another short rappel near the bottom.

7 Otis Flower Tower IV 5.9+ ★

This line begins at the toe and low point of the buttress, and basically climbs the southern rib of the tower for seven pitches. The lower portion of the route is mostly 5.8; the crux consists of very enjoyable straight in cracks on the prow itself at a few steep steps near the top. FA: Topher Donahue and John Thieschafer, 1995.

8 Heat Wave IV 5.11c ★★★

Heat Wave ascends the south face of Otis Flower Tower, beginning on the west side beneath an obvious overhang, about 250 feet left of the previous route. The two routes converge in the middle portion of the tower (it's possible they even share a pitch), but **Heat Wave** stays left of the prow for the most part, and finishes on the west face. Bring 200 foot ropes. FA: Doug Byerly, Matt Hobbs, and Sari Niccols, 1998.

BEAR LAKE AREA

Bear Lake is perhaps the most popular destination in all of RMNP. It is located only 100 yards from the Bear Lake trailhead, and thousands of tourists make the handicap-accessible walk to and around the lake each week. Climbers come for the same views that attract all the tourists: the narrow canyon of Tyndall Gorge stretches west from the lake, rimmed by the north face Hallett Peak, Tyndall Glacier and Flattop Mountain. These three features combined with the west side of Longs Peak and the eastern summits of Glacier Gorge form a tremendous alpine vista.

Though not visible from Bear Lake, the upper portion of Odessa Gorge on the north side of Flattop gives climbers and hikers alike another reason to visit the area. The distinctive Notchtop Mountain is found here, along with Little Matterhorn and Tourmaline Spire.

Approach: Several trails originate from the Bear Lake trailhead (located at the end of Bear Lake Road — see Glacier Gorge for travel directions, pages 93-94). All of these begin with the boulevard leading west from the parking lot. Hallett and Flattop are reached from Emerald Lake: turn left before Bear Lake (big sign), then follow the right option at a fork a short distance beyond (the left trail descends to Glacier Gorge Junction). This leads to Nymph Lake (0.5 mile), Dream Lake (1.1 miles) and Emerald Lake (1.8 miles), with an option to ascend to Lake Haiyaha just before Dream Lake is reached. Climbers headed to Notchtop and Odessa Gorge should turn right at Bear Lake, follow the lakeside path for 100 yards, and then turn right onto the Flattop Mountain trail. Make a switchback left at 0.5 mile, and take the right option at one mile (the left continues to Flattop, and is the descent route for climbs on that mountain). Lake Helene is reached after three miles, and the approach from there to the various points of interest in Odessa Gorge is described below. The Bear Lake parking lot often fills up by 9:00 or 10:00 am, though climbers making an early start should have no difficulty finding a spot.

HALLETT PEAK

The somber north face of Hallett Peak is one of the more famous walls in RMNP. Situated above beautiful Emerald Lake in the middle of Tyndall Gorge, it offers several long routes of moderate difficulty and excellent quality. The approach is the shortest of the alpine walls (a quick two miles), contributing to Hallett's popularity. The only disagreeable aspect of this fine wall is its general lack of protection. All the routes are rather sporty and deserve extra respect — it would not be unreasonable to attach an R-rating to most of the routes, though tradition dictates otherwise. Be prepared for some run outs and difficult route finding. The sun leaves the face early in the day; bring extra clothing.

Due to the "climb anywhere" nature of the north face, myriad variations have been completed, often by parties off-route. In fact, at least one climb was established in this fashion. Though all of the variations I am aware of are listed at one point or

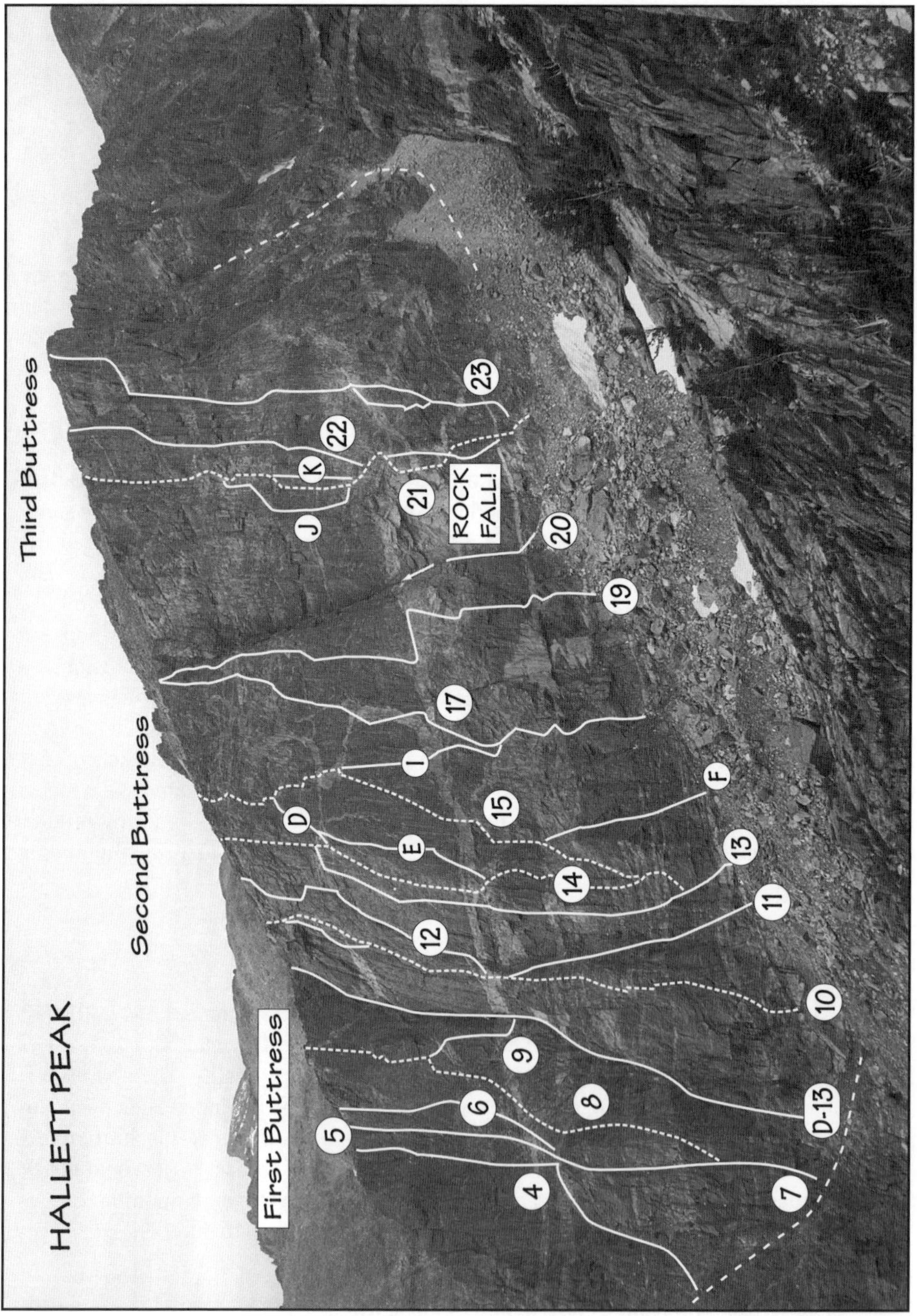
HALLETT PEAK
First Buttress
Second Buttress
Third Buttress
ROCK FALL!
4
5
6
7
8
9
D-13
10
11
12
13
14
15
17
19
20
21
22
23
D
E
F
I
J
K

1. South Ridge I 5.5 or 3rd class

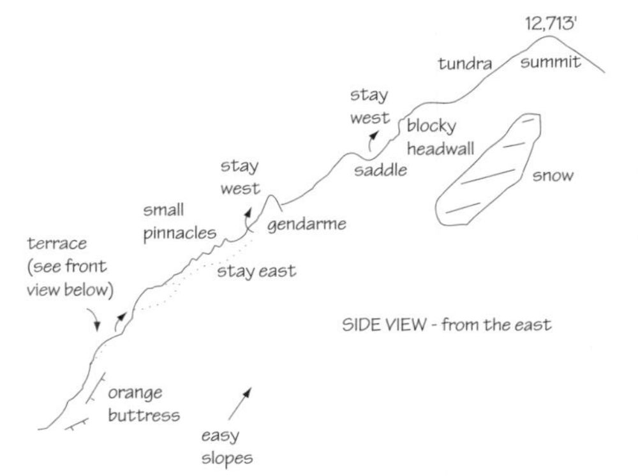

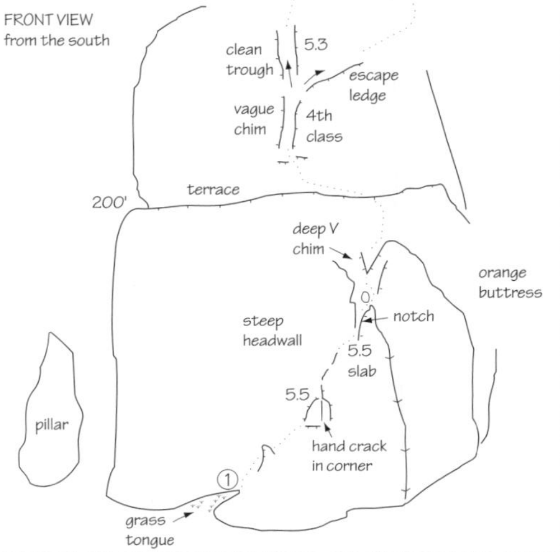

3. East Ridge 4th class
4. Standard Route II 5.5
5. Finch Route II 5.8
6. Center Route II 5.5
7. Great Dihedral II 5.7 ★
8. Magistrate II 5.7
9. Dunrite Flake II 5.7

D-13. Hallett Chimney IV AI 5 M5

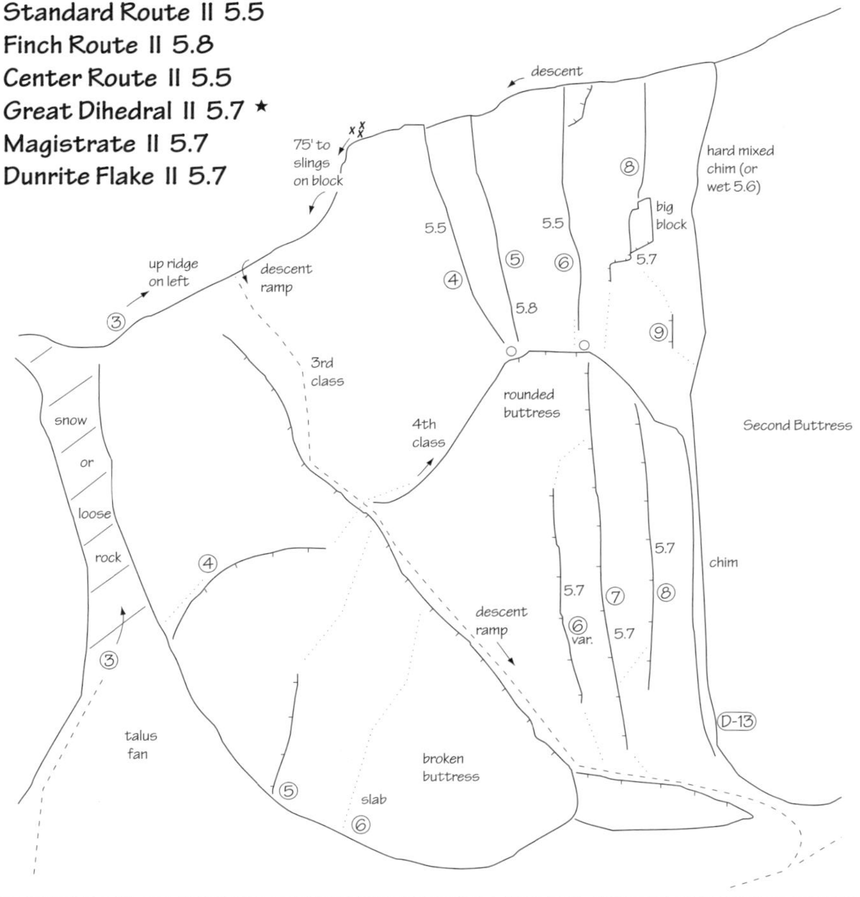

another, they are not always duplicated for each of the routes that may use them. To facilitate an easy reading of the topo, some of the variations are listed as A, B, C, etc.

The north face is sectioned off into three buttresses by two deep chimney lines (**Hallett Chimney** and **The Slit**). The First Buttress is farthest east, and while several routes run up its face, they are broken and not very appealing. The Second Buttress is blessed with excellent rock and longer periods of sunshine as its left half faces northeast. It sees the most traffic. The expansive Third Buttress houses **Northcutt-Carter**, one of the area classics.

Approach: Drive to the end of Bear Lake Road and walk to Emerald Lake. Cross the outlet on boulders and hike directly up a short talus step to reach a long, wide shelf. Turn west and follow a faint path along the shelf to the loose scree slope below the face. Patches of snow remain along the base until midsummer.

Descent: Two options are available for the descent from the north face. The most-used descent drops down a scree gully at the west end of the Third Buttress. Switch left through a notch halfway down the gully and continue to the base. Some snow may be encountered in early season. The second option hikes east from the top of the face until a drop-off necessitates a rappel. Locating the bolt anchor on top of the drop-off is easy if one stays near the edge of the north face — don't wander south into Chaos Canyon. Two single-rope rappels (the second from slings around a block can be avoided with 4th class down climbing) end in a gully. Turn left (north) at the bottom of the gully, go over a short rise (cairn), and hug the cliff past trees with rappel slings — don't rappel! This improbable passage leads to a steep ramp cutting across the lower half of the First Buttress and ends at the base of **Hallett Chimney**. Nothing harder than 3rd class is encountered if done correctly. The second option is not recommended for parties leaving gear at the base of the Third Buttress, but it is the preferred descent for all routes on the First and Second Buttresses.

Climbers wishing to bag the summit can hike to the top of Hallett from the end of any of these routes, and then join the Flattop Mountain trail. This is the long way around, and all gear should be carried up the route as the Flattop trail comes nowhere near the base of the wall.

South Side

The first two routes begin from Chaos Canyon on the south side of the mountain.

1 South Ridge I 5.5 or 3rd class

This route might appeal to mountaineers. It begins in the upper reaches of Chaos Canyon, and ascends the south ridge of the peak (which is visible in its entirety as one drives up Bear Lake Road). There are two ways to reach the base; both are tedious. The first hikes to Lake Haiyaha from Dream Lake, and then navigates through the jumbled boulder fields that give rise to the canyon's name (1.5 miles, very slow-going). The second makes an ascent of **East Ridge** as far as the saddle (see below), and then drops into Chaos Canyon, joining the first option for the last mile. It is best to stay on the north side of Chaos Canyon for either choice. The base of the route can be identified by an orange, east-facing buttress at the bottom of the long south ridge. Walk around to the south face of this buttress, and locate a grass tongue reaching into the left side (a 100 foot pillar sits further left, across a talus gully). Climb up and right from the grass tongue and jam a fine hand crack in a big corner (5.5). Continue up right and cross a 5.5 slab, aiming for a notch. Climb through the notch, then move up and left to a deep, V-shaped chimney, and follow that to a big terrace. Walk left, then go up a vague chimney to a ledge leading right. Continue up the chimney/trough line for another 100 feet, or escape right on the ledge to easy scrambling on the east side. This first section of the route is about 350 feet long on good rock, and all of the technical difficulties can be avoided simply by hiking up slopes to the east. The second portion weaves up the ridge for 1,000 feet (3rd class and easier, see topo). Descend via the Flattop Mountain trail, or hike down to the top of the north face and choose one of its descents. FA (?): The line described here was climbed by the author in 1998, beginning with **East Ridge** and descending via the Third Buttress gully for a nice tour of the peak. I was searching for a route that Glen Porzak enjoys climbing (my brother John told me about it) — I'm not sure whether I found it.

2 South Buttress III 5.8

This route climbs the prow of the steep and impressive buttress one mile down canyon from the previous route. Use either of the approaches described above (via Lake Haiyaha is best) to reach the base of the wall. Climb cracks and corners just left of the prow for seven pitches (some short). Descend by reversing the next route to the saddle, at which point one can go back to the base of the wall, or continue down to Emerald Lake. It might be better to walk west from the top until it is possible to hike down the open slopes between this route and **South Ridge**. Or, one could hike to the summit and walk out with the Flattop trail. FA: Duncan Ferguson.

3 East Ridge 4th class and snow

This route is normally approached from Emerald Lake, though an ascent from Chaos Canyon is also possible. Hike past Emerald Lake toward the north face, but turn left at the huge talus fan emanating from the gully on the left side of the First Buttress. Follow the gully to a saddle (Chaos Canyon version joins here), then turn west and climb along the ridge (4th class, mostly on the left) for a few hundred feet to the slopes above the north face. Continue to the summit, or use the second descent option described above — the technical portion of the route ends near the rappels. The initial gully is a loose and disgusting 4th class choss pile once the snow melts out (as it does by mid to late summer); climb it in early summer and bring an ice axe, or reverse the descent ramp on the First Buttress and gain the ridge that way.

First Buttress

As mentioned above, the First Buttress consists of broken rock and ledges for the most part (so broken, in fact that one of the north face descent routes walks right down the middle of it). The upper headwall (beginning from the highest white band) is more continuous, though it hardly compares to the Second and Third Buttresses. Below the center of the headwall is a rounded buttress with several parallel, right-facing dihedral systems. The aforementioned descent ramp borders this buttress on the left, and separates it from another buttress of sorts on the lower left half of the wall.

4 Standard Route II 5.5

This route traverses over the top of the lower left buttress (coming in from the bottom part of **East Ridge**), then follows a trough up right to the top of the rounded buttress. Nothing more severe than 3rd or 4th class is encountered up to this point. From here, follow the left-hand of two similar chimney/dihedral systems on the upper left headwall for two or three pitches.

5 Finch Route II 5.8

Finch Route apparently climbs the lower left buttress more directly (begin at a right-facing dihedral), then joins **Standard Route**'s trough to the top of the rounded buttress. Climb the right-hand chimney/corner system described above for three or four leads.

6 Center Route II 5.5

This climb also starts with the lower left buttress, climbing a slab and broken ground above. As with the previous two routes, the lower portion of the climb can be avoided simply by reversing the descent ramp, though a better choice takes the right facing dihedral just left of **Great Dihedral** (5.7). Once above the rounded buttress, the route follows the obvious left leaning, right-facing dihedral about fifty feet right of **Finch Route** (5.5).

7 Great Dihedral II 5.7 ⋆

Follow the big, right-facing dihedral in the middle of the rounded buttress (several pitches, 5.7), then climb any of the upper headwall routes.

8 Magistrate II 5.7

This route begins with the first lead of **Great Dihedral**, and then angles up to the next corner on the right (also facing right). Follow that to low-angled rock near the top of the rounded buttress, then head up right to a huge block above a prominent roof band. Climb through the middle of the roof, the left side of the block, and the obvious crack/corner leading straight to the top. FA: Jeff Bevan and friends, 1972.

9 Dunrite Flake II 5.7

Dunrite Flake is a variation that connects **Hallett Chimney** with **Magistrate**. Climb **Hallett Chimney** as far as the high white band, then go left to a big right-facing flake and follow that to the roof band on **Magistrate**. FA (?): This route may duplicate an earlier effort by Herbie Keishold, Erwin Hegewald, and Ernie Kuncl — the Fricke guide credits this party with a left-hand variation (no other details available) to **Hallett Chimney**, done in the late 1950s. Ken Duncan and B. Ebrite climbed the route described here in 1975.

D-13 Hallett Chimney IV AI 5 M5

Hallett Chimney is the dividing line between the First and Second Buttresses, and though it can be climbed in the summer as a wet and dirty 5.6 rock route (as it was first done), it is described in the ice climbing section.

Second Buttress

Clean rock and excellent climbing characterize the Second Buttress. Extra gear can be stowed near the base of **Love Route**, thereby facilitating easy pickup if the second descent option is used.

10 Better Than Love III 5.8 ***

This is an awesome direct start to the **Love Route** — the description includes a variant finish to keep the grade at 5.8. Scramble up left to a grassy ledge from the base of the huge, right-facing corner defining the first half of **Love Route**. 1. Two right-facing dihedrals mark the right, outside face of the protruding buttress on **Love Route**. An indistinct pitch wanders up short cracks to the base of the left dihedral, 5.6. 2. Climb the dihedral to a good ledge at its top (5.8 with bomber pro), passing an intimidating overhang midway up the pitch. This is one of the best leads on the north face. Belay on the left at an old piton. 3. A steep headwall looms overhead. Either go up right with disjointed finger cracks (5.7), then step left to a right-facing dihedral on the edge of the headwall (belay on any of several ledges above it), or bypass the headwall far to the left, swinging back right near the end of the rope, 5.5. 4. A short and easy pitch may be needed to reach the highest ledge on top of the protruding buttress (third belay on **Love Route**). 5. Do the fourth pitch of **Love Route**. 6. Start up the fifth pitch of **Love Route**, but make a rising traverse to the right near the end of the lead and find a tiny stance in a left-facing corner, 5.7. This corner parallels the standard crux pitch on **Love Route** (about thirty feet right). 7. Continue up the corner, and when it ends, traverse a 5.8 slab up left to the base of a left-facing dihedral. Step left and belay in a groove. 8. A short pitch shared with **Love Route** finishes the climb. FA (?): The old piton at the top of the second pitch suggests an early ascent, though its possible this was left by a retreating party; the variant finish was described in the DuMais guide. The above information comes from a 1993 climb by Bernard, Robert and Sally Gillett.

11 Love Route III 5.9 **

A fun climb on the left side of the Second Buttress, **Love Route** begins in a huge right-facing dihedral. The dihedral forms the west side of a protruding buttress that ends half way up the wall. 1 and 2. Climb into the big dihedral (many variations possible, low 5th class, somewhat loose). 3. Exit left onto the face of the buttress and climb to its top. Stretch the rope out past a tiny tree to the highest of several ledges. 4. Climb the left side of a large pillar, then angle slightly left to a small ledge with an old bolt, 5.6. 5. Work through a left-facing flake, then weave up toward a big, black roof (excellent face climbing, 5.7). Belay at a sloping ramp below the right edge of the roof. 6. Lead up the left-facing corner dropping from the right edge of the roof (often wet). Several fixed pins protect this steep section, the crux of the route. Angle left above the roof in a groove and belay. 7. Do a short pitch up left. FA: Carl Love, William Hurlihee and Dean Egget, 1957 (with some aid).

HALLETT PEAK - Second Buttress

10. Better Than Love III 5.8 ★★★
11. Love Route III 5.9 ★★
12. Englishman's Route III 5.8 ★
13. In Between III 5.9 ★ (★★★ with Var. B)
14. Culp-Bossier III 5.8 ★★★
15. Jackson-Johnson III 5.9 ★★
16. Bliss-Carlson III 5.7 ★
17. Second Buttress Direct III 5.10a ★
18. Kor-Benneson III 5.9 R
19. The Vaults IV 5.11+ R ★
20. The Slit III 5.8 R

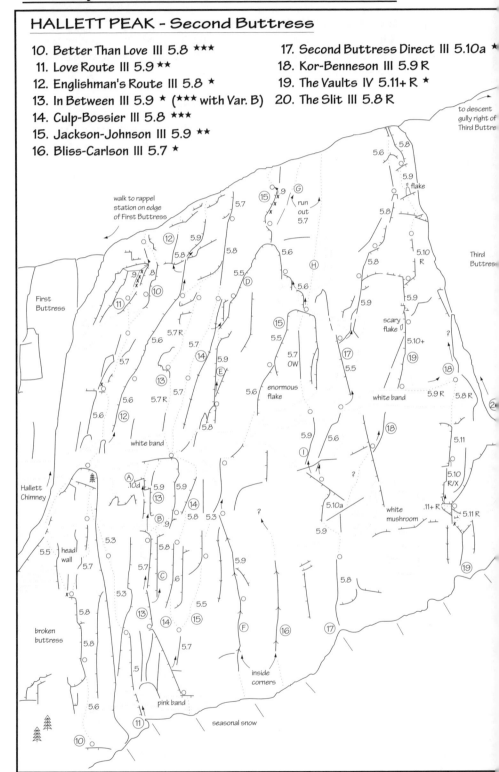

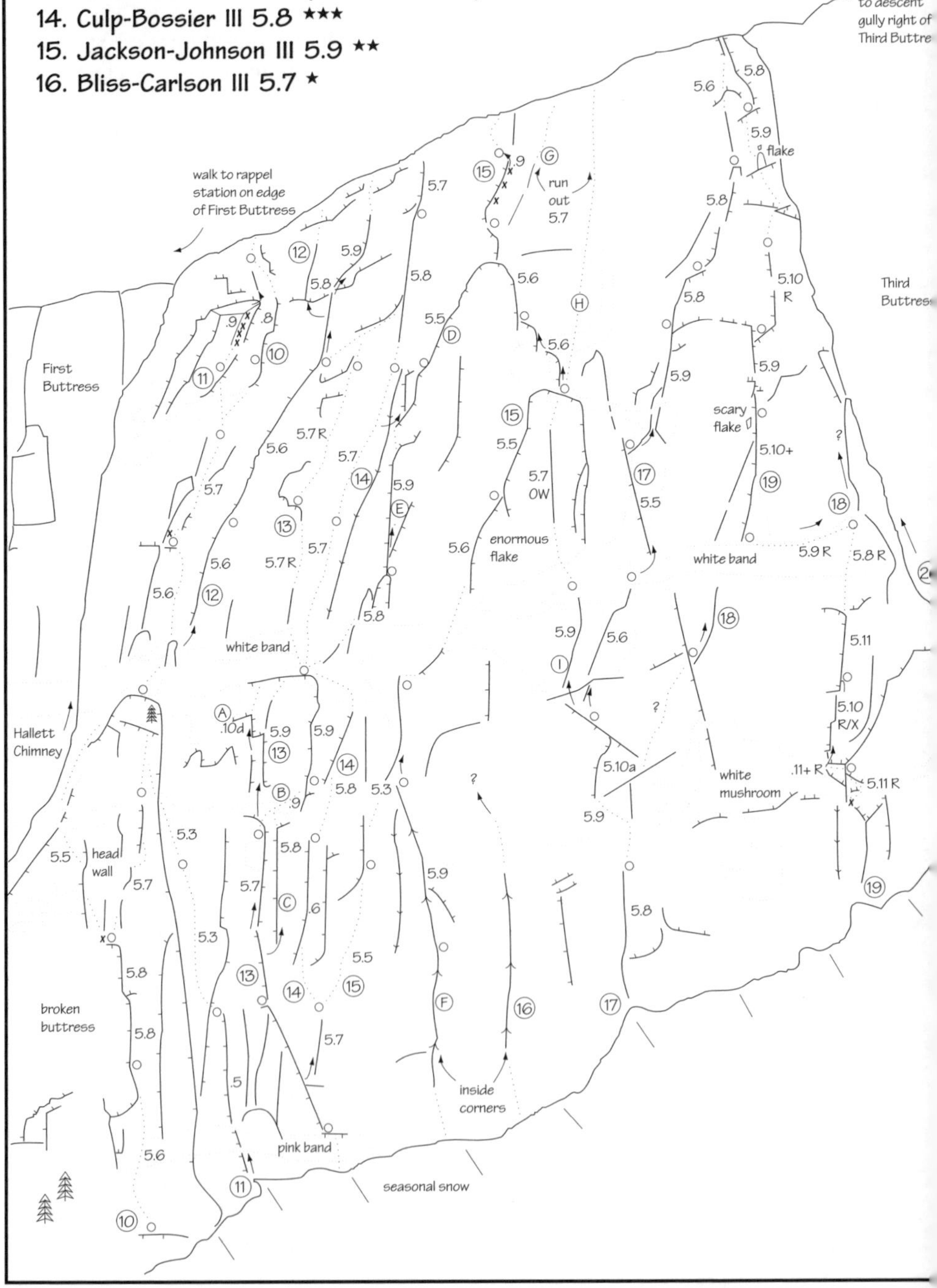

12 Englishman's Route III 5.8 ★
This line ascends the obvious, arching corner right of **Love Route**. Start with its first three pitches, or climb **Better Than Love**. 4 and 5. Follow the arch for two pitches (5.6, 5.7), either climbing it directly or staying just right of it. 6. Go straight up from the end of the arch in a steep crack, then face climb left before reaching the small roofs above. Climb through overlaps into the next crack system and take it to the ridge with a short last pitch. One can also traverse right from the top of the arch to join **In Between**'s finish, or traverse even further to end on **Culp-Bossier** (this is called **Turner Cut-off**, and was first done in 1962 by Jack Turner and Bob Boucher). FA: David Isles and John Wharton, 1958.

The following three lines begin from a good ledge (fixed pin) at the base of a left-leaning dihedral 70 feet right of **Love Route**. Boulder up to the ledge (5.5, ten or twenty feet depending on snow depth) near the right end of a pink band of rock.

13 In Between III 5.9 ★ (★★★ with Variation B)
Also known as **Hesse-Ferguson** (the first ascent team). 1. Lead up the left-leaning, right-facing dihedral for a long pitch, 5.5. 2. Climb into a left-facing dihedral and arrange a belay below a rotten roof. 3. Pop over the roof, go up a left-facing corner, and take on the right side of the much bigger roof above, 5.9. Belay on a big ledge in a white band of rock. 4 and 5. Face climb along sparsely protected rock in between the arch on **Englishman's** and the prow on **Culp-Bossier**, 5.7 R. Belay below a small, left-facing corner. 6. Ascend the corner (5.8), then move right across a smooth slab and join **Culp-Bossier**, or move slightly left and go straight up a right-facing flake (5.9). FA: Mark Hesse and Duncan Ferguson, 1974. There are several options in the vicinity of the crux roof that can be taken. **Variation A**: Move left from the second belay and climb a corner to the big overhang just left of the crux roof. Pull through that (5.10d, FA: Roger Briggs, 1979) to the third belay. **Variation B**: Step right from the second belay onto a clean, rose-colored slab. Traverse up right (fifty feet, dicey 5.9) to the base of a hanging, right-facing corner and belay. Jam and stem the corner, perfect 5.9, and move left to the big ledge. This is perhaps the best pitch on the north face of Hallett, and one of the best protected (lots of medium stoppers). Now join **Culp-Bossier**. **Variation C**: Start up the second pitch, but move right from a grassy ledge into a right-facing dihedral — this is the leftmost of three similar dihedrals; **Culp-Bossier** climbs the next one right. Ascend the left dihedral (5.8), climb through an overhang, and join Variation B. **Another variation:** A direct entry to the perfect right-facing dihedral on Variation B can be done from **Culp-Bossier** (5.11a, poor rock).

14 Culp-Bossier III 5.8 ★★★
Great rock, exceptional position and lasting sun are among the amenities of **Culp-Bossier**. Start on the ledge above the pink band. 1. Go up the leaning dihedral of **In Between** for fifty feet, then balance right to the base of a nice finger crack. Jam the crack to a stance, 5.7. 2. Aim for the middle of three right-facing corners and climb to its top. 3. Traverse up right along a ramp and spring over a little roof, 5.8. Climb along a leaning corner, then head left on easy ground to the right end of a big ledge. 4 and 5. These two leads face climb just left of the prow that runs up the middle of the Second Buttress, with good exposure and perfect rock, 5.7. It's also possible to climb right up the prow, run out 5.8. 6 and 7.The normal finish contin-

ues straight up a steep groove (5.8) and corner system (5.7) for two more pitches. One can also angle up right on an easy, long ramp to join **Jackson-Johnson** below its crux pitch (**Variation D**). FA: Bob Culp and Floyd Bossier, 1961. **Wilson's Variation** (E): Angle right from the third belay to a crack in the big white band (5.8), then climb to the top of a white flake; this is on the right side of the prow. Belay at the base of a steep crack. Climb straight up the crack and over a roof at its top (5.9) to the long ramp (D) that angles right to **Jackson-Johnson**. FA: Tink Wilson and Dan Davis, 1960 or 1961.

15 Jackson-Johnson III 5.9 ★★

One of the longer routes on Hallett, although most of the climbing is moderate. 1. Do the first pitch of **Culp-Bossier**. 2. Go straight up to and over a little roof (5.5) then head right to the base of a leaning corner. 3. Make a long traverse out of the corner to a chimney on the right. 4. Ascend the chimney for a short stretch, then head right again to the left side of an enormous flake. Stretch the rope up the flake as high as possible, 5.6. 5. The flake becomes an easier chimney; go to its top and belay on a spacious ledge. 6 and 7. Two pitches of short right-facing dihedrals (5.6) end at the base of a steep, leaning, right-facing dihedral. 8. Stem up the dihedral (5.9, several old bolts and pitons) and step left to a belay. 9. Wander up loose, square-cut blocks; first left, then back right. FA: Dallas Jackson and Dale Johnson, 1957. **Variation F**: A loose and poorly protected direct start (5.9) ascends the major, right-facing dihedral 150 feet right of the normal start. **Variation G**: The ramp that connects **Culp-Bossier** with this route continues up parallel to the crux pitch (it's not nearly so distinct in its upper half). Follow that to the top of the wall (5.7 with very little pro). **Variation H**: Go more or less straight up the wall from the fifth belay atop the enormous flake for three pitches of sustained and run out 5.7 — good belay stances are scarce.

16 Bliss-Carlson III 5.7 ★

This little known route begins in the next dihedral right of the direct start to **Jackson-Johnson** (**Variation F**). Climb the dihedral and a crack above; belay on a ledge at 120 feet. The next lead is long, face climbing between small corners to the "...second belay on the **Jackson-Johnson** route," (DuMais). Given that the second belay on that route is well to the left, this description seems improbable at best; perhaps the pitch angles hard left and joins **J-J** near its third belay. From here the route appears to go up and left again, bypassing a steep section on the right, and ending on a big ledge beneath the prow of the wall (i.e. somewhere in the vicinity of **Culp-Bossier**). Above the big ledge, the description in DuMais' guide reads just like **Culp-Bossier**. FA: R. Bliss and Dave Carlson, 1972.

17 Second Buttress Direct III 5.10a ★★

Several climbers have experienced difficulty in locating the initial pitches of this route. It's crucial to get this right as a long roof band bars access to the upper wall in most spots. Begin 100 feet left of the big white "mushroom" on the lower right side of the Second Buttress at a vague corner and crack system (two corners up from **Bliss-Carlson**). 1. Climb along the right side of the system, 5.8. 2. Go up a short distance, then move left into a right-facing arch (fixed piton), and climb the small right-facing dihedral above the arch, 5.10a. Belay on top of a big, left-leaning ramp. 3. Climb a right-angling crack to a stance in the long white band, 5.6.

4. Move right on the band to a pronounced right-facing dihedral, and climb that for a pitch (5.5). This is obvious from the ground as it ascends through the lower curve of a huge S-shaped dike (the dike appears as an even larger "3" when the lighting is right). 5. Take a diagonal line right along cracks and flakes, passing through two small overhangs, 5.9. Belay at a stance above the second. 6. Continue up right in the same system to a ledge, 5.8. 7. Another lead of right-trending corners ends on a good ledge, 5.8. 8. Bend left to a notch at the top, 5.6. FA: Layton Kor and Floyd Bossier, 1963. The original line may differ somewhat from the description given here. **Variation I**: Climb up rather than right on pitch three, and belay where possible (perhaps in the white band). Angle left on the next pitch, aiming for the base of the prominent offwidth crack that splits the enormous flake on **Jackson-Johnson**, 5.8 or 9 (?). Jam the offwidth to the top of the flake (5.7), and join **Jackson-Johnson**. FA: Douglas Snively and Billy Westbay.

18 Kor-Benneson III 5.9 R

Start with the first part of **Second Buttress Direct**, traverse up and right to a section of ledges which lead to the right side of the face, then climb straight up for five pitches. FA: Kor and Benneson, 1960s.

19 The Vaults IV 5.11+ R ★

Uphill from the stalk of the white mushroom (see above) are two prominent aretes that form the edges of an open book corner. 1. Climb the corner and move out left to a bolt, then climb up and right on difficult terrain to a recess (5.11 R). Climb around the recess on the right, then angle left to a belay in a roof-capped corner facing left. 2. Traverse left under the roof (5.11+ R) to a shallow groove, and follow this (stepping right around an overhang) to a belay stance on a pillar that is located in a prominent, right-facing dihedral. The last half of this pitch is poorly protected (5.10 R/X); a few KBs and LAs might help to protect this section. 3. Climb the big dihedral (5.11) to a large ledge on the left. Angle up right to a grassy ledge (on top of the big white band) that leads all the way over to **The Slit**. 4. Step down from the belay and traverse the white band left (5.9 R) to a faint right-facing dihedral — a narrow triangle of white rock reaches up into this dihedral. The FA team notes that this point can probably be reached directly from the large ledge on pitch three. 5. Follow the faint dihedral (5.10+) to a stance where a good threaded runner can be placed. This is just up and right of a scary perched flake. 6. Continue up the shallow dihedral system (which turns to left-facing) until an easy ramp leading right is reached. Belay on the ramp. 7. Go to the end of the ramp, then work up compact dihedrals (5.10 R) to a poor belay twenty feet short of a long overhang. 8. Breach the roof at a small break, face climb to a big flake on a ramp, go up its left side, and then move left and up to a bigger ramp. 9. Follow a curving, left-facing dihedral to a chimney and the top. It's possible that this route overlaps the previous two climbs near the top of the wall. Bring lots of RPs and small cams for this run out and intimidating climb. FA: Andy Donson and Terry Murphy, 1999. A bolt hole was found on the first pitch; they plugged in a bolt and forged on. **Variation:** Note that the three initial pitches can be avoided by climbing **The Slit** to the white band, and then traversing left into the line.

20 The Slit III 5.8 R

This is the wet chimney that divides the Second and Third Buttresses. It has been reported as loose, run out and unappealing by some, but the FA party of **The Vaults** found some decent climbing in the lower section.

Third Buttress

This is the western buttress on the north face, featuring good rock and engaging route finding.

21 Northcutt-Carter III 5.7 ★★★

Important, see **Warning** note below! As one of three RMNP routes included in *Fifty Classic Climbs of North America*, the **Northcutt-Carter** sees much action. It was touted as the hardest climb in America after its first ascent (largely due to the lack of communication within the climbing community). However, a pair of California climbers proved this assertion to be well off the mark. Still, it represented a landmark route in Colorado, and paved the way for more difficult climbs in the years to follow. Start near the left end of the Third Buttress, underneath the right side of a large tract of white rock. Clamber up 3rd class rock to the base of two corners. 1. Climb the right corner to a slot, face climb left, and lieback a white flake to a good ledge. 2. Follow a dihedral on the left to face climbing that goes back right and ends at a little ledge. This is level with the top section of the large white patch. Several accidents have occurred here; don't go straight up (see "Another variation" below). 3. Go up a bit, then perform a long, rising traverse left past several cracks and corners, 5.6. Jam a crack to the top of a pillar at the end of the traverse and belay. This pitch is notorious for route finding errors; see variations below. 4. Follow easy cracks (5.5) straight up to a belay alcove below a roof. 5. Climb through the right side of the roof (5.7), jam a good crack, then trend left to a sloping, grassy ledge. 6. Head right to a roof near the end of the pitch, skirt it on the left, and go to another ledge, 5.6. 7. Work left into a chimney, and stretch the rope out to a belay. 8. Finish up the chimney. FA: Ray Northcutt and Harvey Carter, 1956. **Variation J**: The major, right-facing dihedral just left of the pillar at the end of the traverse (pitch 3) provides three pitches of 5.7 before angling back to the sloping ledge at the end of pitch 5. This was the line taken on the first ascent. **Variation K**: A long crack system extends upward midway through the third pitch traverse. This can be followed for two to three pitches, passing several exciting overhangs, before rejoining the regular route, 5.8. FA: Yvon Chouinard and Ken Weeks, 1959. **Another variation** (see **Orange Beyond**): Climb straight up on the second pitch in a steep, roof-capped dihedral, then move up past two more overlaps to the second belay ledge, 5.9. **Yet another:** Go left from the upper portion of the route, and climb steep, lichen-covered rock to the top. FA: Douglas Snively and Diane Russel, with a few aid moves off nuts.

WARNING! In July of 1999, a huge rock fall destroyed the lower two pitches of **Northcutt-Carter**. The resulting scar is visible for miles, and this area of the cliff may be unstable at this writing. Topher Donahue and Mike Pennings did the route in its new state and found 5.10 climbing along the margin of the rock fall (hard to protect). It was part of their "Amble in the Park" in which they climbed **Pervertical Sanctuary** on the Diamond, **North Ridge** on Spearhead, **South Face** on Petit Grepon, **Northcutt-Carter**, and **Spiral Route** (in the dark) on Notchtop, all in 22.5 hours.

22 Orange Beyond III 5.9 ⋆

This route begins with **Northcutt-Carter**, but continues up right to a difficult chimney splitting the left-hand of two prows high on the wall. 1. Climb **Northcutt-Carter** for most of its first pitch, but traverse left to a dihedral facing left, and belay. 2. Follow the dihedral, cross **Northcutt-Carter**, and continue up and right to a good ledge — it's likely this is the line of "Another variation" listed in **Northcutt-Carter**. 3. Follow a right-leaning crack that begins near **Variation K** listed above, and belay on a ledge, 5.7. 4. Continue up the same crack as it turns straight up into a groove, and wander past the left edge of a couple overhangs to an alcove at the base of a right-facing, roof-capped dihedral (a long 5.8 pitch). 5. Climb the dihedral over the left edge of the roof, then traverse right when the going gets tough to a sloping belay on a big flake. 6. Go up to a wide crack, and jam it for fifty feet to a ledge below the final chimney. 7. Climb the chimney, 5.9. FA: Malcolm Daly and Michael Finsterwald, 1976, though it's possible their route shares ground with two variations listed in Fricke's guide, one done by the Spitzer party in the 1960s. These variations leave the **Northcutt-Carter** from the beginning of pitches two and three, and diagonal up and right all the way to the pinnacles above the descent gully. **See WARNING above.**

23 Kor-Van Tongeren III 5.9 ⋆

There are two prows on the upper right side of the Third Buttress, and a long, prominent chimney drops down from the notch between them. **Kor-Van Tongeren** follows the chimney and finishes with a steep crack on the right prow. Two possibilities exist for the initial pitches, and both are devious. 1. Begin near the right end of a thin white dike that originates from the white mushroom on the Second Buttress. Climb up and right to the base of a leaning slash and belay. 2. Climb this slash over the roof (5.8), and jam a leaning crack to a big grassy ramp, or take the stepped, right-facing dihedral left of the slash and gain the lower left end of the grassy ramp. In either case, belay below a trough facing left. 3 and 4. Climb the trough for two pitches to the base of the prominent chimney, 5.8. 5 and 6. Struggle up the chimney for two pitches. The crux comes at the end of the sixth lead with an overhanging crack on the right. 7. Scramble right along an easy ramp to the base of a deep crack in the middle of the right prow. 8. Follow the crack, 5.9. FA: Kor and Butch Van Tongeren, 1962. **Variation L**: Begin 100 feet right of the white dike, and angle up right on a ramp to an optional belay below a steep, dark wall. Go up the wall for forty feet, then head left beneath several square-shaped roofs to a tiny stance on a slab (belay). Continue up left to the upper end of the grassy ramp, and traverse fifty feet left on this to the second belay (at the base of the trough). This was the line of the first ascent; it is not at all obvious. **Variation:** Climb a direct line that parallels the third and fourth pitches thirty feet left, and then move back right into the standard route (5.9+ R **, FA: Steve Morris and John Marrs, 1987).

HALLETT PEAK - Third Buttress

20. The Slit III 5.8 R
21. Northcutt-Carter III 5.7 ★★★
22. Orange Beyond III 5.9 ★
23. Kor-Van Tongeren III 5.9 ★
24. Mayrose-Bucknam III 5.8

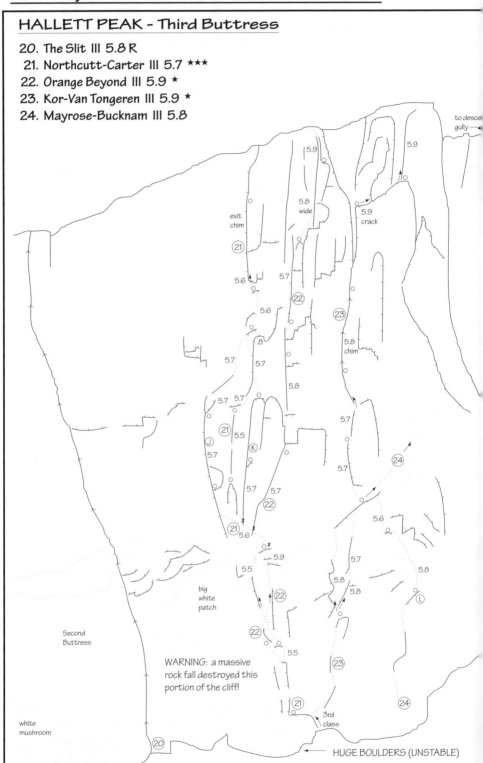

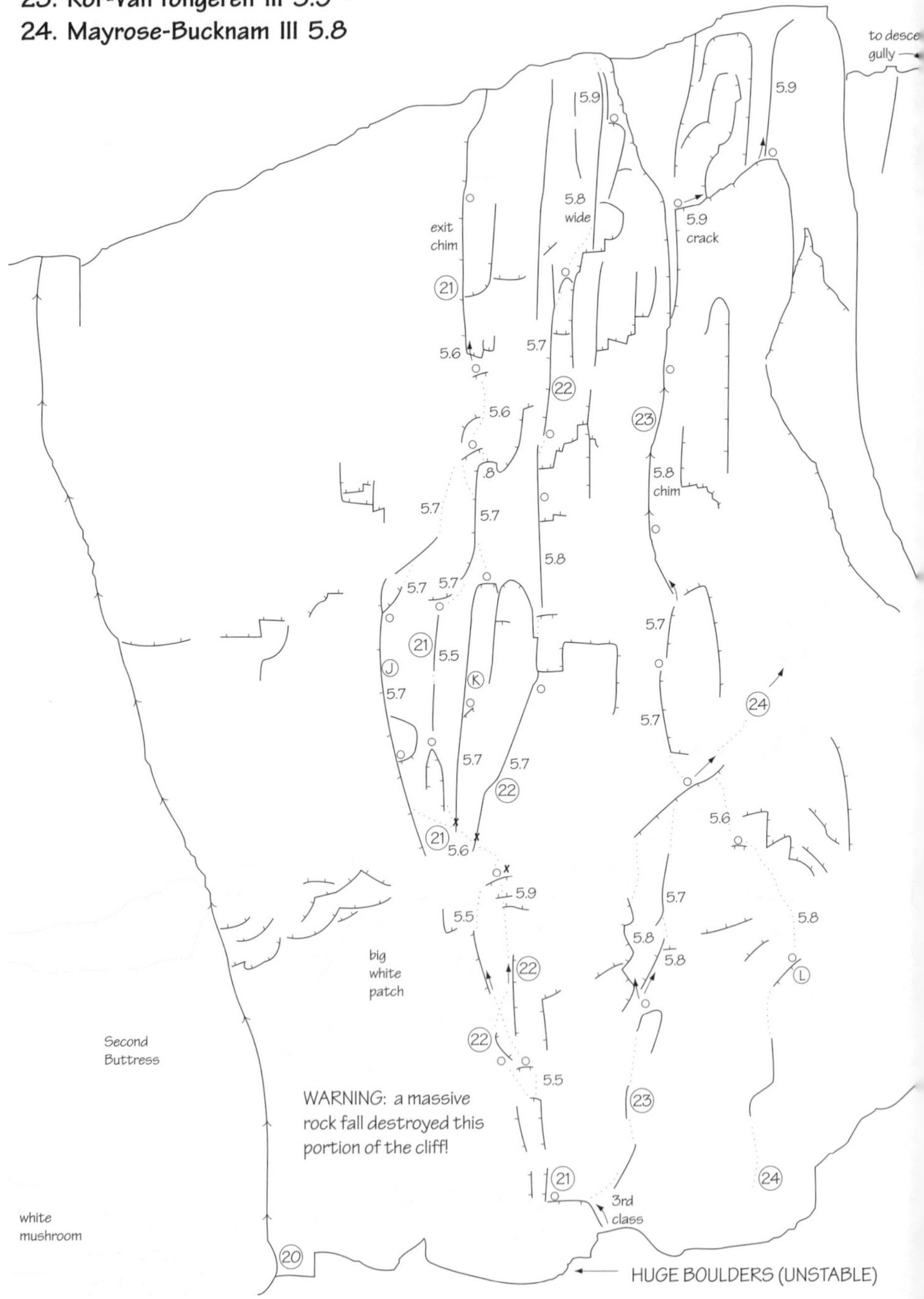

24 Mayrose-Bucknam III 5.8
Begin with the first pitches of **Kor-Van Tongeren** (the original pitches, **Variation L**), then make a long traverse to the right side of the Third Buttress. Climb straight up the edge of the face for a few pitches, avoiding several pinnacles on the upper wall. The last pitch climbs a west-facing shield split by a single crack (5.8). FA: Paul Mayrose and Bob Bucknam, 1961.

25 North Face Girdle Traverse IV 5.9
Reverse the First Buttress descent gully and climb to the white band on the top of the rounded buttress (4th class). Traverse across all three buttresses in the vicinity of the white band, reaching the western descent gully after twelve pitches. FA: Larry Bruce and Mark Hesse.

FLATTOP MOUNTAIN

The south side of Flattop, directly across Tyndall Gorge from the north face of Hallett, is endowed with several interesting spires, ribs and ridges. These features have never garnered much attention, though Dragon's Tail affords some reasonably enjoyable climbing in the mountaineering vein, in addition to a new and difficult rock climb.

Approach: Hike to Emerald Lake from the Bear Lake trailhead (see page 181); the approach from here is obvious (around the north shore of the lake). Routes are described from upper left to lower right.

Tyndall Spire

This is the sharp spire on the upper left side of the group. The standard descent does not return to the base of the routes; carry all gear to the top.

1 South Ridge II 5.7
Follow the south rib of the buttress upon which the upper spire resides, passing several gendarmes and climbing over a few of them, then ascend the southwest corner of the spire. Escape the summit by scrambling north to the main mass of Flattop, and walk north until intersecting the Flattop trail. Walk down that to Bear Lake. FA: William Buckingham and party, probably late 1950s.

2 Southeast Buttress II 5.7
Climb the right side of the buttress mentioned above (4th class), cross a break in the ridge, and continue to the summit shelf. Finish on the south side of the spire. Descend as in **South Ridge**. FA: Richard Rossiter, Linda Walling, and Steve Ross, 1979.

3 East Face II 5.7 A3
The only available information on this route is that it climbs directly up the steep east side of the spire, beginning half way up the gully on the right. Four pitches, some poor rock. FA: Dakers Gowans and J. Johnson (probably 1970s).

D-15 Tower Gully II AI 2 M2
The gully between Tyndall Spire and Dragon's Tail — see ice climbing section.

Dragon's Tail

Dragon's Tail is the big buttress and tower immediately right of Tyndall Spire; it is the main attraction on Flattop.

Descent: The top of the tower, as seen from Emerald Lake, is the southeastern end of a long connecting ridge leading back to Flattop. The descent follows this ridge for several pitches, beginning with a down climb into the notch behind the top. From the notch, one can climb back up to the ridge and negotiate several pinnacles along the way, or stay below the ridge on its east side. The Flattop trail is reached soon after the technical difficulties are over; follow that down to Bear Lake (bring all gear up the wall).

4 West Slab III 5.7

Two major, tree covered ledges traverse the lower-angled apron below the tower. This route begins on the higher ledge (scramble in from **Tower Gully**). Move up easy terrain until a rope is warranted, then climb the left side of the buttress for several leads, aiming for the notch between the summit and a big gendarme on the right. Climb directly to the summit from the notch. FA: Molly Higgins and Harry Kent, 1970s.

FLATTOP MOUNTAIN - Dragon's Tail

7. Dragon Slayer IV 5.11c ★

DRAGON'S TAIL

6. South Ridge III 5.7
7. Dragon Slayer IV 5.11c ★
8. Mosquito Wall II 5.8
D-14. Dragon's Tail Gully II AI2 M2

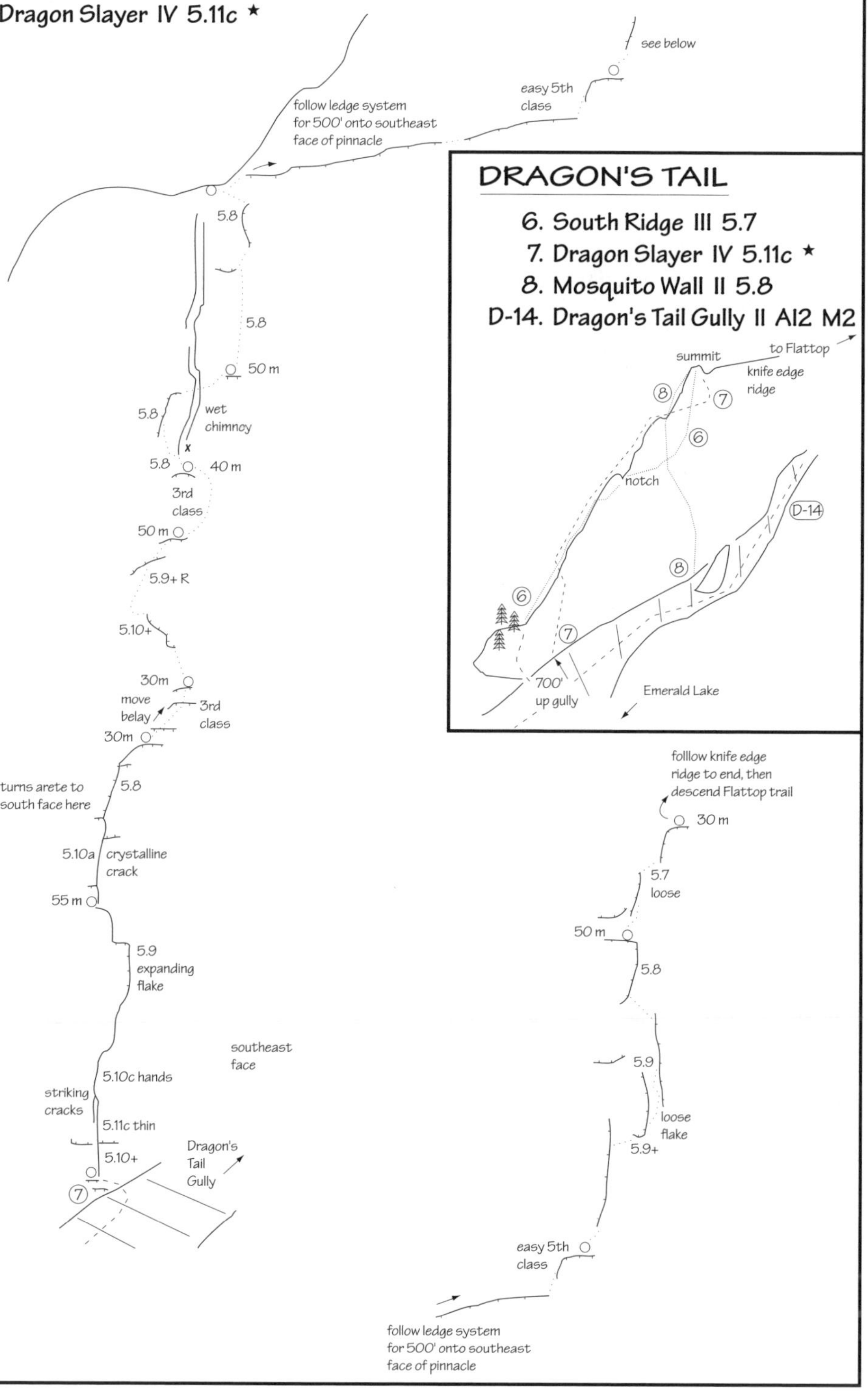

5 Old Route III 5.7

Begin from the middle of the lower tree covered ledge described in **West Slab**, and angle up and right to the south ridge of the buttress; follow that to the top of the big gendarme south of the summit. Traverse to the notch behind it, and join **West Slab**. FA: William Buckingham and Bob Boucher, 1954.

6 South Ridge III 5.7

Gain the right side of the lower tree covered ledge (approach from **Dragon's Tail Gully**), and walk to the right-hand of two grooves. 1. Climb the groove (5.5) for a long lead to a bushy ledge. 2. Step left and ascend the right side of a chimney, then move right on a ramp to the prow of the south ridge. 3. Step around right and climb a short wall, then proceed to a block-filled notch on the ridge. 4. Traverse right for 200 feet along a rising ledge leading onto the southeast face. 5. Go up a short wall to some ledges, and go right on these until below the notch between the summit and big gendarme (a few hundred feet above). 6. An easy pitch leads up right. 7. Continue up right on steeper rock, connecting several corners and flakes, 5.6. 8. Climb a pronounced, left-facing dihedral (visible from below — aim for this) to the top. FA: Richard DuMais and D. Johnston, 1980.

7 Dragon Slayer IV 5.11c ⋆

This route begins about 700 feet up **Dragon's Tail Gully** below a striking pair of steep cracks in the southeast face — this is just uphill from the tree-covered ledge on **South Ridge**. After three difficult pitches, it intersects the previous route, then continues up with an independent line. After five pitches, one can escape to the summit, but the route goes 500 feet right on a ledge system, which leads into the middle of the upper southeast wall. From here it climbs to the ridge behind the summit. Rack up to a #4 Camalot, and bring 60 meter ropes. FA: Doug Byerly and Terry Murphy, 1998.

8 Mosquito Wall III 5.8

This route also begins from the **Dragon's Tail Gully**, uphill from **Dragon Slayer**, and just past a section of low overhangs. Climb broken rock to an obvious crack, face climb just left of it, then enter the crack. Go past a bolt at the end of the crack and belay on a big ledge, 5.8. Move right on the ledge, then follow a dihedral that clears the right end of the overhangs (5.7), or climb off the left end of the ledge, go left, then back right (passing a couple ledges) and move around the right side of a big roof. Both of these options end on the same big ledge. The third and fourth pitches climb short walls interrupted with several ledges, and these end at a chimney. Follow the chimney to the notch between the summit and the big gendarme on the left, and continue via **West Slab**. FA: Paul Mayrose and Bob Bradley, 1964.

D-14 Dragon's Tail Gully II AI 2 M2

This is the couloir on the right side of Dragon's Tail — see ice climbing section.

NOTCHTOP MOUNTAIN

Located one mile north of Hallett Peak and just north of Flattop, Notchtop possesses a grand east face, nearly 1,000 feet in height. The mountain juts out east from the Continental Divide, and a distinctive notch along this ridge lends the name.

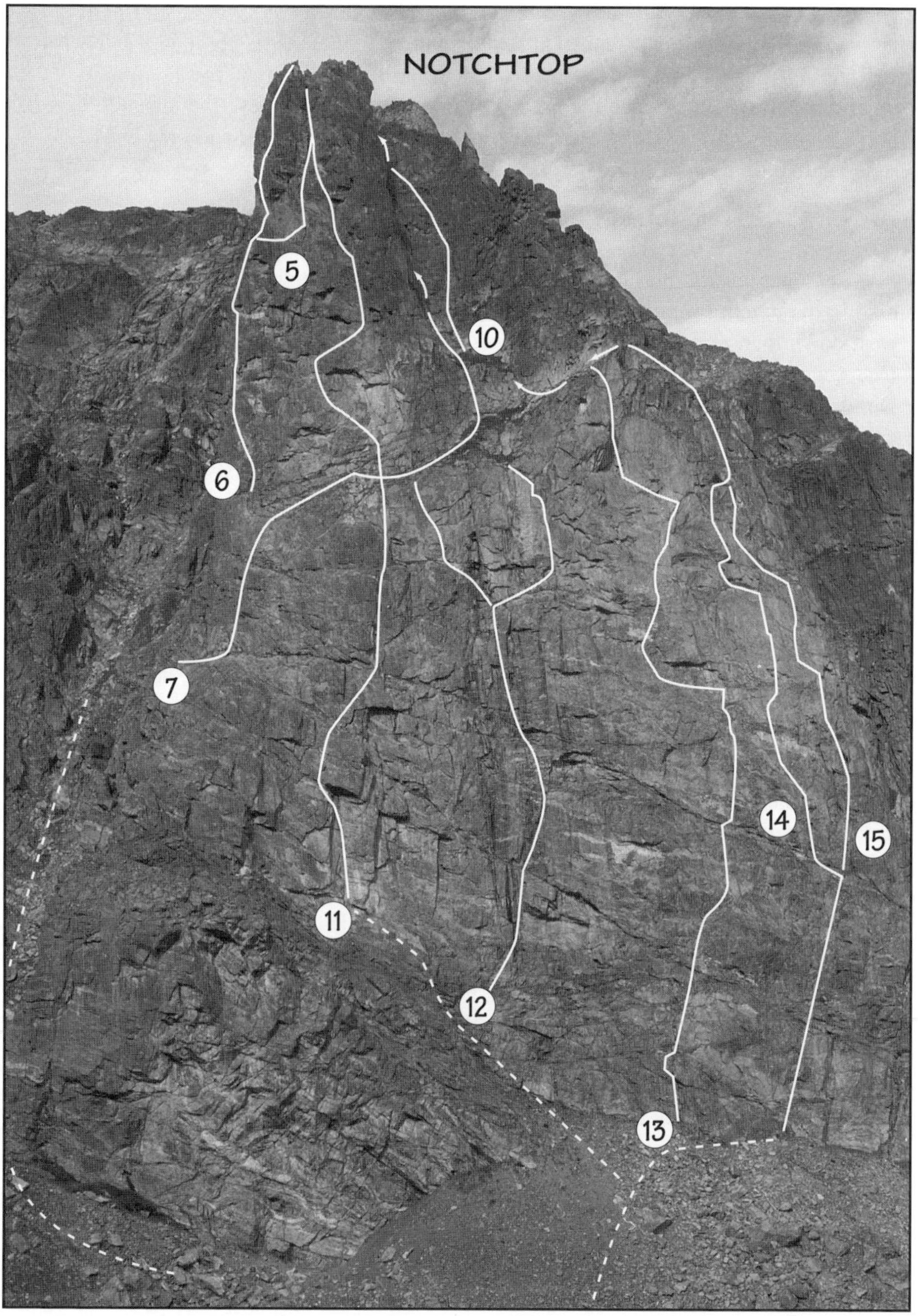
NOTCHTOP
5
6
7
10
11
12
13
14
15

Approach: The approach to Notchtop is a quick three miles, beginning at the Bear Lake parking lot. Hike to Lake Helene (described under Bear Lake Area, see page 181), cross its outlet, and skirt the lake on the northwest side. A faint path leads up to a plateau above Grace Falls, ending at a small, unnamed tarn. Leave the trail shortly after clearing the tree line (before the tarn). Cross a stream and scramble up a short talus field to reach the base. The first ten routes are described from left to right, following the line of **Spiral Route** to the East Meadows, and then left to right again along the east face.

Descent: Descending from Notchtop is a bit problematic, although never harder than fourth class if the correct line is chosen. To descend from the summit block, go west down several short steps and gullies and reach a ledge system that traverses over to the notch. From here, scramble up a ridge, pass a gendarme, and then go west down a short gully. This leads to an exposed ledge system above the west face. Carefully traverse the ledge to its end at a saddle well below the Continental Divide — a few cairns mark the way. A long, easy gully (on the west side), with one or two short rock steps, drops down from the saddle all the way to the base. Consider using a rope. Another option for the descent from the notch uses the bolt anchors on each of the belay stations of the first route listed below.

1 Instant Clarification II 5.9 ★★

Hike up the west gully (the standard line of descent) until reaching a large, grassy terrace near the top, which leads out to the west face. Walk about 200 right on the terrace, and look for a cairn beneath a gray streak on the wall — this point is just right of the fall line from the notch. 1. Follow the gray streak to a bolt, move left into a shallow right-facing dihedral, and climb to its top (5.9, fixed pin). Head up right to a ramp (facing right), and take this to a bolted belay on the right. 2. Step right to a right-facing corner and climb it to a large ledge (5.8). Continue straight up to two bolts. 3. Climb to the top of a short crack, move right, and ascend a short corner. Head back left (5.9), then go up incipient cracks to a bolted belay. 4. Head up left on 3rd class to the notch, or rappel three times from the top of the third pitch (all of the belays have two coldshuts). Bring a double set of TCUs and RPs, and several long runners. FA: Brandon Latham and Chris Kalous, 1999.

2 Raven Song IV 5.11c R ★★

Raven Song begins from the bottom of the descent gully. Start at the toe of the south prow in a right-facing dihedral capped by a roof. 1. Climb to the roof (5.9), then pull through at a crack on the right, 5.10. Belay on a big ledge at 165 feet. 2. Climb through a left-facing corner to another big ledge, 5.7, 165 feet. 3. Take a groove from the left side of the ledge and continue to the bottom of the rising ramp on **Spiral Route** (5.9, optional belay, from which one can join **South Ridge**). Walk 75 feet left to twin cracks on the west face (yellow rock, and left of the next route), and climb the right one to a belay between opposing corners. 4. Climb a right-facing corner for half a pitch. When it switches to a ramp facing left, traverse up left to another right-facing corner; belay at 180 feet (small stance). 5. Zigzag left to a right-leaning dihedral, and take that to a belay below a big overhang with a white patch of rock beneath it, 5.9, 165 feet. 6. Move right to the crack and thin

NOTCHTOP - West Face

1. Instant Clarification II 5.9 ★★
2. Raven Song IV 5.11c R ★

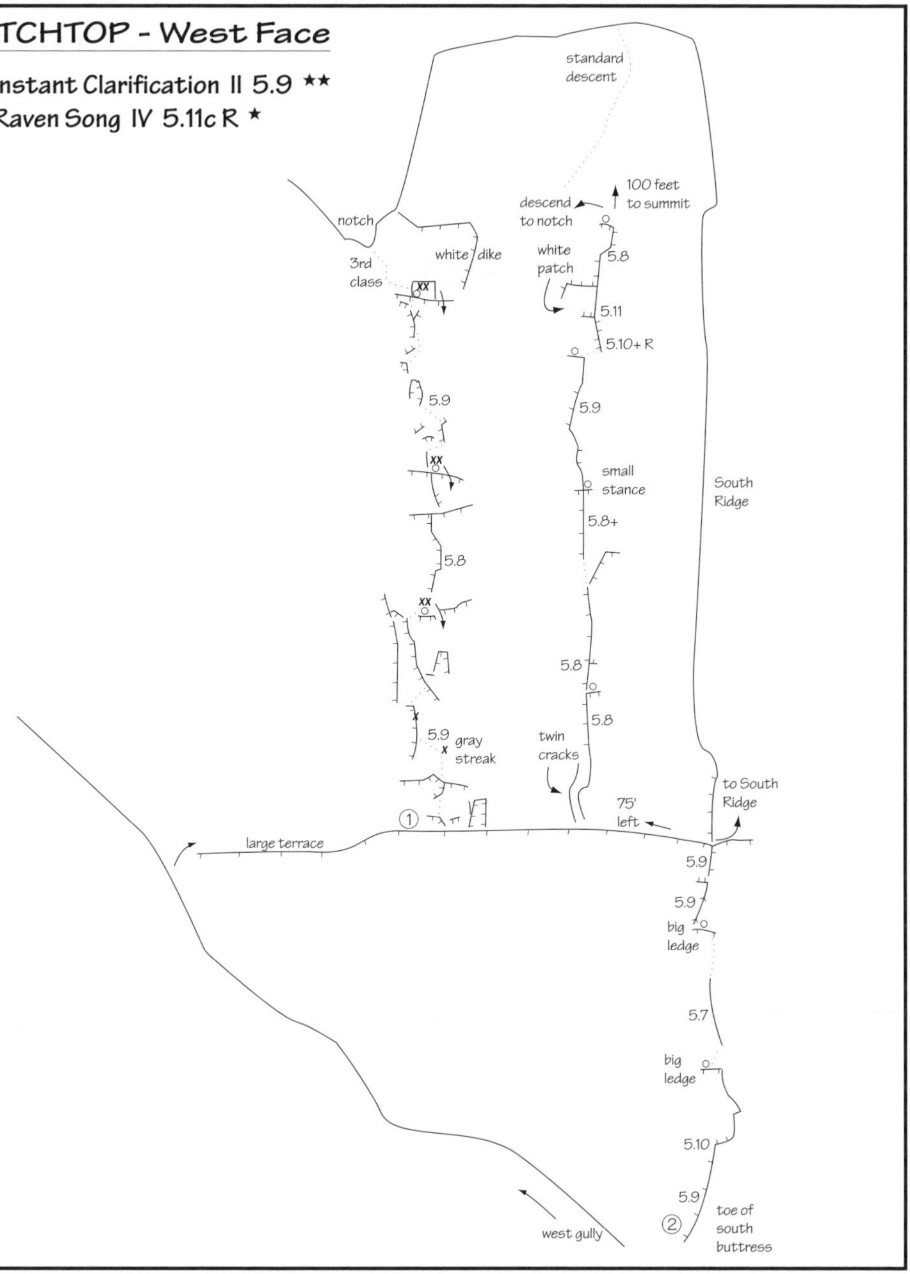

NOTCHTOP - East Face

4. South Ridge West III 5.10a ★★
5. South Ridge III 5.8 ★★★
6. South Ridge East III 5.10d ★★★
7. Spiral Route III 5.4 ★★
8. East Buttress II 5.8+ ★★
10. Mornin' II 5.7
11. Religion III 5.8 R ★
12. Optimissmus III 5.9 ★★
13. White Room III 5.11 R/X ★
14. Topnotch III 5.11c ★★★
15. Pessimissmus III 5.10d ★
16. Northeast Ridge III 5.8

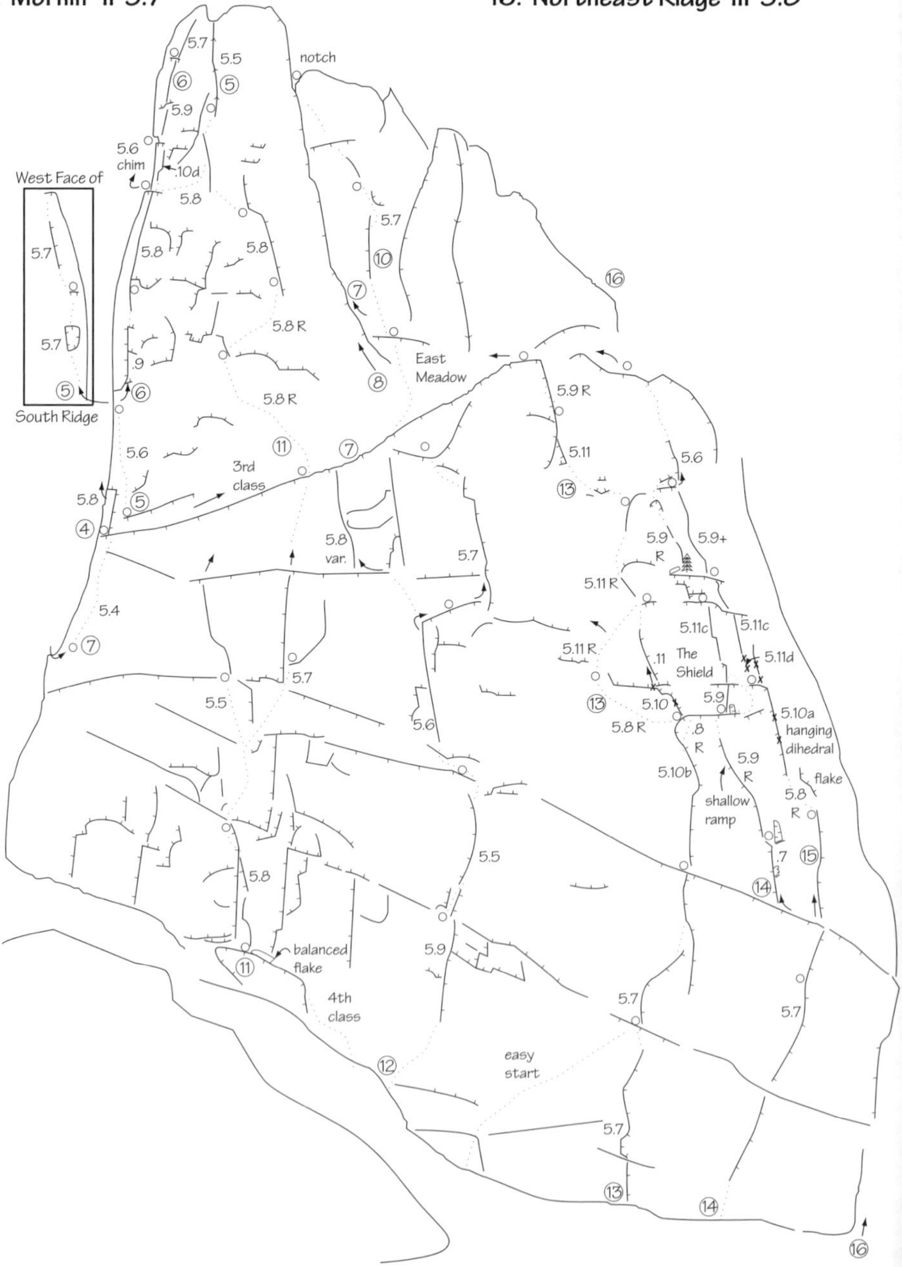

corner line dropping from the right edge of the roof. Work up this line (5.10+ R to strenuous 5.11), and make a funky exit out the right side of the roof. Continue up 5.8 corners to a ledge. 7. An easy pitch up and right leads to the summit block, or one can descend left, over to the notch. Bring 60 meter ropes. FA: Doug Byerly and Terry Murphy, 1998.

3 West Face III 5.8 R

This route begins with the first two leads of **Spiral Route** to the base of the rising ramp, then traverses left onto the west face — a more difficult direct start from the descent gully also leads to this point (the first part of the previous route?). From here, it follows a line of dihedrals just left of the south prow (**South Ridge**) for five pitches, all of them 5.7 or 5.8, with the last pitch being somewhat unprotected. The exact line of ascent is not known, though it probably overlaps the upper part of **South Ridge West**. FA: Bob Culp and Larry Dalke, 1960s.

The west and east faces of Notchtop meet at a superbly formed ridgeline. The original route on this feature traversed back and forth across the ridge; this is described below as **South Ridge**, and it is the easiest way up the prow. It is also possible to climb the ridge entirely on the left or right sides (**South Ridge West** and **East**). All versions begin with **Spiral Route** until the large, grassy ledge is reached (two long pitches). An obvious, inside corner rests at the left end of the ledge, and a higher ledge sits above and right of the corner.

4 South Ridge West III 5.10a ★★

This version pieces together several variations on the left side of the ridge, some of which were probably climbed first with **West Face**. Begin at the roof-capped inside corner at the lower left end of **Spiral Route**'s rising ledge. 1. Climb the corner, but traverse left around to the west face before reaching the roof, 5.8. 2. Take a steep, left-leaning dihedral that draws one away from the prow, 5.10a. 3. Continue up steep corners just left of the third pitch on the original route. 4-6. Go straight up a crack and corner system, joining the last pitch (or more) of **West Face**. It is also easy to join the next two routes after three pitches.

5 South Ridge III 5.8 ★★★

This is the original route up the prow. Begin right of the inside corner (see **South Ridge West**) on the higher of two ledges. 1. Ascend a well featured wall (5.6) to a belay stance on the east face. 2. Step left to the arete and cross over to the west face, arriving at a flake. Climb over the flake (5.7) to a ledge beneath a left-facing corner. 3. Go up the corner and back onto the prow at a good ledge, 5.7. 4. Traverse right below a white step, and cross a 5.8 slab to a crack. Follow this to the base of a big groove. 5. Climb the groove for a full pitch to a small notch in the summit block, 5.5. FA: Chuck Schobinger and Al Auten, 1958. **Variation:** A nicer finish moves left on pitch four to a 5.6 chimney on the west side, and then joins the next route for its last two pitches (5.9).

6 South Ridge East III 5.10d ★★★

This is the best way up the prow. 1. Do the first pitch of **South Ridge**, (5.6). 2. Move up right and climb through an overhang to gain a right-facing dihedral. Climb that and the roof at its top to a small stance (delightful 5.9). 3. Climb a nice 5.8 crack to a good ledge on the prow. 4. Step up right to a tiny crack in perfect white rock, and follow that to an exposed stance on the prow, 5.10d. 5. Lead up right to a bulging hand crack; jam the crack (5.9) to a belay below a dihedral. 6. Finish with the dihedral, 5.7. Bring RPs for the crux pitch. FFA: The fourth pitch was listed as an A1 variation in DuMais' guide; it was climbed free by Bernard and Robert Gillett in 1993. The FA parties of the other pitches are not known. **Variation:** The grade can be kept at 5.9 by moving left on pitch four to a 5.6 chimney on the west side. This leads to the exposed stance on the prow.

7 Spiral Route III 5.4 ★★

This highly enjoyable line winds its way around the south and east walls of Notchtop and goes to the notch. From there, one can continue to the summit by reversing the descent route, or descend directly. Begin in the west gully where a rising ramp system leads to the south buttress. Climb the low-angled buttress (5.4) to a large, grassy ledge that slants up right. Walk along the ledge for several hundred feet and climb into a huge cirque called the East Meadow. The easiest line up to the notch goes left before reaching a steep wall (see **Mornin'**), and ascends short steps to a ramp. Take the ramp up and right (across the north side of the summit block) to easy ledges below the notch. Step onto the west face from the notch, and traverse south on ledges to a 4th class groove that leads to the summit.

The next three routes are variant endings to **Spiral Route** that begin in the East Meadow.

8 East Buttress II 5.8+ ★★

This route climbs the northeast arete of the summit block. Begin near the bottom of the East Meadow at a ramp that slants up left to a prominent right-facing dihedral. 1. Climb the ramp and belay at the dihedral, 5.5. One can also climb straight up to this belay with a difficult right-facing corner (5.10). 2. Follow the dihedral to a belay flake at its top, 5.8+. 3. Follow a thin crack above the belay (5.7), then traverse left on knobs around a corner to a chimney. Take that to a notch belay. 4. Ascend a short headwall (5.7), and lead up a gully to the summit. FA: Richard DuMais and Steve Komito, 1987.

9 Relief Train II 5.7

Scramble up the left side of the East Meadow to the rightmost of several dihedrals; an overhang caps it. Do the dihedral to the overhang, then face climb up left to a ledge with moss and belay. Follow a direct crack and gully line on the next lead. FA: C. Harrel and R. Olson, 1982.

10 Mornin' II 5.7

This route climbs straight up the steep wall above the middle of the East Meadow. Scramble to the highest of several grassy ledges and set a belay below an obvious crack in the center of the wall. Follow the crack to a good belay ledge (5.6), then maneuver up and right across a depression, and go back left around an overhang to easier ground, 5.7. Belay on any of several grassy ledges (**Spiral Route** comes in from the left at this point), or stretch the rope out to the notch. FA: M. Magnuson and S. Schneider, 1983.

11 Religion III 5.8 R ★

The most prominent feature on the lower east face is a set of three parallel, roof-capped dihedrals near the south edge. This route starts on a huge flake (atop of which is a balanced flake) and climbs the left dihedral. Scramble in from the right along a 4th class ramp to get to the top of the flake. 1. Go up the dihedral (5.8), and move left below the overhang to a belay. 2. Trend right along flakes and cracks, threading a line between two inverted L-shaped features, and belay in a right-facing dihedral. 3. Climb the dihedral to the big ledge on **Spiral Route** (5.7). 4. Move the belay up the grassy ledge to the top of a pillar leaning against the wall, and locate two prominent overhangs above. Diagonal up and far left between the overhangs to a grassy ledge below a short dihedral, 5.8 R. 5. Traverse back right over the top of the higher overhang until reaching an overhanging groove. 6. Climb the groove, but escape left near its top to a good ledge. 7 and 8. Move up left to the final groove on **South Ridge** and follow that. Bring some large pieces. FA: Larry Hamilton and Keith Bell, 1973. **Variation 1:** The second and third pitches can also be climbed straight up (staying left of the Ls) on easier territory — this is the original route. **Variation 2:** Keep going hard left from near the tail end of the fourth pitch (5.9 R), all the way to **South Ridge East**, and join that route just below the first overhang on its second pitch.

12 Optimismus III 5.9 ★★

Optimismus leads up black-washed rock right of **Religion**. It is often wet in early season and after long periods of rain. 1. Climb through a chimney along the west end of some overhangs near the right margin of the black streaks, 5.9. 2. Continue up blocky rock in a large recess and move left. 3. Go left across a slab to a short chimney and the dihedral above. Belay on a spacious ledge. 4. Take twin cracks on the right into a left-facing corner, ending on a big, grassy ledge, 5.7. It is also possible to move left into a nice 5.8 hand crack. Finish with **South Ridge** for an excellent tour of Notchtop, or go up into the East Meadow and choose any of routes **7 – 10**. FA: Walter Fricke and Dan Bench, 1970.

13 White Room III 5.11 R/X ★

This is a serious and circuitous line up the middle of the east face. Start beneath the right edge of a long black roof, which is 350 feet up the wall. 1. Climb to a long ledge that stretches across a large portion of the lower face. A much easier start angles in from the left. 2. Do a long moderate pitch, aiming for a leaning, left-facing dihedral below the black roof. 3. Lieback up the corner, and break right after a thin, 5.10b crux. Run out 5.8 finds a good ledge. 4. A long traverse left avoids the roof and ends below a break in the roof band. 5. Climb through the steep headwall above the belay (5.11 R/X) and head back right to the left end of a long ledge. An intermediate belay is possible here, as is an escape left to **Optimismus**. 6. Step down from the ledge and gain a thin, incipient crack (5.11 R), then climb up to a belay. 7 and 8. Go left over a slab and navigate along flakes to a huge right-facing corner, 5.10. Follow that to the East Meadow, 5.11 at first, then 5.9 R. FA: Roger Briggs and Larry Hamilton, 1974. **Variation:** A more direct version of this line (**Black Curtains**) climbs directly through the roof (5.11 R) on pitch four. FA: Jack Roberts, Tim and Larry Coats, 1988. The first three pitches of this route can be used to approach either of the next two.

14 Topnotch III 5.11c ★★★

An orange-colored plaque of rock (the Shield) presents itself up and right of the black roof on **White Room**. The fabulous thin crack in its center marks the crux of **Topnotch**. 1. Climb nondescript rock (5.7) to the base of a prominent, leaning corner system. 2. Leave the corner for a steep right-facing dihedral with a bush. Set up a belay left of a pillar. 3. Climb along a poorly protected ramp (5.9 R) to a large, sloping ledge beneath the Shield — belay at the base of a slot (left of a big block). 4. Climb the slot (weird 5.9) to a ledge below the crux crack (optional belay). The slot can be avoided by traversing right around the block, up a ramp, then back left (easy but mostly unprotected). From the ledge, jam a finger crack that becomes very strenuous (5.11c) past a short jog (small TCUs at the crux), and belay on a good ledge. 5. Step left to a short, roof-capped corner, which is turned on the right. Head for a tree next to a fallen pillar and take the right seam of two to a slab (5.9 R). Weave up to a belay. 6. Walk right to a steep corner, climb to its top (5.6), then scramble up and far left to the East Meadow. Finish on any of routes **7 – 10**. FA: Bret Ruckman, Tim and Larry Coats, 1988.

15 Pessimismus III 5.11d ★

Climb the prominent, leaning corner system mentioned in **Topnotch** for two long pitches. Head left from a belay under a gaping flake to an obvious hanging dihedral facing right, and ascend this (5.10a, two fixed pins and tricky stopper placements) to a belay ledge with one bolt. Scratch past two bolts (crux) to a thin seam (5.11c) and up to a high ledge. A left-angling hand crack (5.9+, and running parallel to **Topnotch**'s fifth pitch) leads to the fifth belay on **Topnotch**. Follow that route to the East Meadow, or go up right to the next route. Bring several RPs and TCUs. FA: Ruckman, Kelly Carrigan, Tim and Larry Coats, 1990.

16 Northeast Ridge III 5.8

A 400 foot pillar sits at the right end of the east face, at the bottom of the northeast ridge of Notchtop. Start with the easy gully on the left side of the pillar; ascend this for several hundred feet. Cross an area of slabs to the left, and then go past the left end of a small roof; continue to a belay at the base of a headwall. Go left, then up the wall, then climb easily to another headwall. Climb the left-hand of two corners to a roof, step right around the corner to a prominent dihedral, and climb to its top, then scramble to a pinnacle on the ridge. Several hundred feet of easier climbing leads to the high point on the ridge (west of the notch). Join the descent route at the short gully leading down to the ledges on the west face. FA: Larry Hamilton and Dakers Gowans, 1974.

LITTLE MATTERHORN

The Little Matterhorn is the name given to the eastern spur of Knobtop Mountain; Knobtop is one peak (or bump) north of Notchtop. Its northeast face looks quite impressive from the north shore of Odessa Lake, but in reality, it is somewhat broken and not as steep as it appears. Only one route is known to exist on this wall.

Approach: There are two ways to approach the face. The shortest begins with a hike to Lake Helene (from Bear Lake). Cross the outlet stream as if going to Notchtop, but leave the path around the lake after 50 yards and head north. With luck, the old trail descending into Odessa Gorge will be located, and this can be followed to a marsh below Grace Falls. From here it's a half mile cross-country amble to the base of the face. Those unfamiliar with the old trail can save some frustration by beginning at the Fern Lake trailhead (see Moraine Park, page

210): Hike 4.2 miles to Odessa Lake, go around its west side, and proceed to the base of the northeast face.

Descent: Work west from the top of the climb along a tricky 4th class ridge — keep going until it looks feasible to descend steep scree gullies to the north or south (either way works, though the southern option is easier).

1 Northeast Face Direct II 5.7
This route is said to climb the middle of the wall for seven pitches (some, no doubt, are short) with a few old fixed pins.

TOURMALINE SPIRE

This is the small spire on the east ridge of Gabletop Mountain (just north of Knobtop), located directly above the north shore of Tourmaline Lake.

Approach and Descent: Hike to Odessa Lake from the Fern lake trailhead (see Moraine Park, page 210), and go around its north side a short distance to reach the inlet stream descending from Tourmaline Lake. Walk along the stream into Tourmaline Gorge, and then scramble up a 4th class gully from the lake to the base of the south ridge of the spire. Descend by reversing **North Side**.

1 South Ridge II 5.8
Climb a dihedral on the south ridge to a cave belay in a chimney (5.6). Climb an arching crack out of the back of the cave, 5.8, then move left and climb up. FA: Jim Detterline and M. Keeley, 1985.

2 North Side I 5.4
Scramble up a gully to the east side of the spire from Tourmaline Lake, then move over to the north side and climb a short chimney. FA: Richard Rossiter, 1979.

HAYDEN SPIRES

Hayden Spires is a group of closely clustered towers situated three miles northwest of Notchtop Mountain. The highest tower of the group is the summit of Hayden Spire itself; climbers have named two others: East Pinnacle is the rightmost of the five towers that can be viewed from Lonesome Lake, and Hayden Lake Pinnacle is the big spire east of Hayden Lake's outlet.

Approach: Hike to the top of Flattop Mountain from Bear Lake, and then follow the Tonahutu Creek trail for a couple miles. Leave the trail and head over Sprague Pass, then walk along the Continental Divide to Sprague Mountain and the ridge leading out to Hayden Spire — drop into the head of Hayden Gorge, down to Lonesome Lake or Hayden Lake, depending on the objective. This is eight miles from the trailhead, and most parties will want to bivy at one of the lakes. On a map, it may look like Forest Canyon followed by Hayden Gorge is a better approach, but this is complete folly — both of these remote canyons are known for dense undergrowth and innumerable downed trees, with no trails. Another option comes in from Milner Pass on Trail Ridge Road, hiking over Mount Ida and along the Continental Divide — this, too, is eight or more miles.

Hayden Spire

1 Standard Route 3rd class
The high point of the Hayden Spire massif is most easily reached from the Continental Divide. Approach from Flattop or Milner Pass and scramble along the southwest ridge to the top. Reverse the route to descend.

2 Northeast Ridge II 5.2
Begin at Lonesome Lake, and scramble to the notch at the bottom of the northeast ridge, then follow that the to the top of Hayden Spire. Descend by reversing the previous route to the Continental Divide.

East Pinnacle

This pinnacle can be climbed from Lonesome Lake or Hayden Lake — from the latter, it appears as the tower farthest east.

Descent: From the summit, traverse west to a gully, climb west up this and go over a ridge to a grassy saddle, then drop down a gully into Hayden Lake.

3 Northeast Chimney II 5.4
Start at Lonesome Lake and go up a scree gully leading to the northeast face. Exit the gully and scramble along increasingly difficult terrain to a fifty foot traverse above exposed slabs. Rope up and climb to an obvious chimney (belay), then stem up this to the top. Reverse the route with a rappel down the chimney (as per the first ascent team) to return to Lonesome Lake, or descend to Hayden Lake as described above. FA: Phil Carr and Bob Wellek, 1960.

4 Dihedral Route I 5.8
The best approach for this route and the next may be from the base of the rappel off of Hayden Lake Pinnacle (see below). Otherwise, one can approach from Hayden Lake by following a gully to the notch behind Hayden Lake Pinnacle — go east from the notch to a prominent dihedral which can be identified by the orange and tan walls that form it. Follow a ramp and crack to reach the dihedral (belay on the left), and then climb the corner to the top. FA: Al Czecholinski and Ken Wade, 1977.

5 Diagonal Route I 5.10
Start forty feet right of **Dihedral Route** and climb a right-leaning, overhanging crack (crux) to the edge of the face (belay). Drop down and left for fifteen feet to a crack, lead over a bulge, and continue with more cracks to the top. FA: Czecholinski and Wade, 1977.

Hayden Lake Pinnacle

This is the tower one-quarter mile north of Hayden Spire's summit, and above Hayden Lake's outlet.

Descent: Go east to a little notch, then rappel (two ropes) to a gully. Climb out of the gully to the right, pop over a ridge, and scramble down a talus chute to Hayden Lake.

6 North Ridge II 5.7

Start northeast of Hayden Lake at a gully that meets grassy ledges leading left around to the base of the pinnacle. Descend left to the north ridge, and begin climbing on its right side. 1. Angle right via short steps and cracks to a big ledge. 2. Move right and piece together several cracks and chimneys to the ridge itself. 3. Continue along the ridge for 100 feet. 4 and 5. Go up a short dihedral to regain the ridge, and follow it to the summit. FA: Czecholinski and Wade, 1977.

7 West Face II 5.8

Approach as per **North Ridge**, but go right to the west face. Begin at a left-facing dihedral (with small overhang), then move left after the overhang via cracks that lead to a big belay flake (a long pitch, 5.8). This is all right of an area of red-colored rock. The second pitch goes easily to the top. FA: Czecholinski and Wade, 1977.

MORAINE PARK

The Big Thompson River begins in Forest Canyon, bubbles into The Pool at the mouth of the canyon, and then flows through picturesque Moraine Park. A long cliff band high above the river stretches from The Pool to the Fern Lake trailhead (on the western edge of Moraine Park), covering almost two miles. Unfortunately, most of the rock is rotten and unappealing, with the exception of Rock of Ages and a few nearby cliffs.

Travel Directions: Drive east on Moraine Avenue (Highway 36) from Estes Park to the National Park entrance booth, then turn left on Bear Lake Road. Turn right after two switchbacks (the first available right turn) and follow signs to the Fern Lake Trailhead at the end of the road, passing Moraine Park Campground, a livery, and the Cub Lake Trailhead along the way. The parking lot is small (arrive before 9:00 a.m. during the summer), and though there are several parking spots along the last mile of the road, even these fill up quickly on the weekends.

The first two routes listed below are located on a cliff band about one half mile from the trailhead. The relationship between the two is uncertain.

1 Red Rover 5.11a
Look for a gully cutting through a long, red wall. Start just left of the gully in a clean crack and fist jam over a bulge (5.10a) to a small belay stance at 70 feet. Make the crux reach to the next crack on the right (loose flake), and follow that, 5.10d. Descend the gully to the east with a short rappel at the bottom. FA: Scott Kimball and Hidetaka Suzuki, 1984.

2 Orange Crush 5.8+
This route climbs "Crack Wall," a 250 foot, dome-shaped face with an obvious orange lichen streak running parallel to a crack. The following description was published in the June, 1987 issue of Climbing magazine. 1. Chimney/dihedral on east side of huge ear of rock jutting from base, 80 feet. 2. Crack 20 feet, undercling right, crack 40 feet. 3. Left-facing dihedral, 5.6, 80 feet. 4. Leave ledge to east, 5.5, 40 feet. Top-roped variation on last pitch: left-angling crack, 5.10a. Descend west. FA: Dan Bradford and Angelo de La Cruz, 1987.

ROCK OF AGES

Rock of Ages is a clean wall of perfect granite that has become the premier area for difficult, traditionally protected leads. Several excellent bolted pitches have also been established.

Approach: Begin with a hike toward the Pool from the trailhead, but stop at Arch Rocks after a long mile. These house-sized rocks offer numerous bouldering problems (Dave Rearick established some of them) and provide a peaceful cool-down from the day's rock climbing. Strike out northwest from a point just east of Arch Rocks across a steep boulder field that gives way to loose talus. A large grotto borders the cliff to the west, and a sizable, detached block rests at the southwest corner of the wall, just right of a large pine.

Descent: Head east along 3rd class slabs, or rappel (two ropes) from a tree just west of **Desolation Angels**.

1 Rope Rider 5.12a **

An obvious thin crack shoots up the prow around the corner from **Original Sin** — look for a fixed pin and RP. Rappel from two pins (70 feet). FA: Topher and Patience Donahue, and Keith Garvey, 2000.

2 Original Sin 5.10c

Climb the large, leaning (right-facing) dihedral on the lower right side of the wall. Rappel from a tree. FA: Alec Sharp and Randy Leavitt, 1981.

3 Center Dihedral 5.10d *

Clamber to the top of the detached block, walk right, and pull through an overhang on jugs (5.10a). Go up a short corner, step right to a thin crack, and belay below the prominent, right-facing dihedral in the center of the wall. Climb the dihedral (crux) on pitch two. Bring a #4 Camalot. FA: Dan Hare and Alec Sharp, 1981.

4 Hats Off 5.12b ***

This wild route features an incredible hand traverse on buckets across an otherwise blank span of rock. Begin with the first pitch of **Days of Heaven**. Start up its second pitch, then continue straight up a thin crack (5.12a). Stretch right to a bucket when the crack turns into a seam, and place a #1 Tricam in a horizontal pocket. Hand traverse right along spectacular holds for 20 arm-blasting feet, ending with a thank-god mantle into an easy corner. Follow the corner to a belay half way up a ramp just shy of the top of the wall. The thin crack holds the technical crux, but the traverse is the real clincher. Bring a small wire and a small cam for the hand traverse. FA: Topher Donahue and Bernard Gillett, 1997.

5 The Lock of Rages 5.12d ***

A direct finish to the previous route. Start across the hand traverse, then shoot up a tiny crack system to the same ramp belay. The crux comes near the top of the crack and is followed by some exciting face climbing. Bring RPs. FA: Topher Donahue and Kennan Harvey, 1997.

6 Rope Gun With Silencer 5.12d ***

This is a desperate thin crack and face route in the middle of the wall. 1. Begin left of the detached block and climb through an overhang at an apex (bolt), place a #1 Friend, and continue past one more bolt to a horizontal crack, 5.12a. Traverse right to the first belay on **Days of Heaven**. 2. Do half of the second pitch, but go straight up before its crux reach, and follow tiny cracks with two fixed pins. Complete the pitch with **Celestial Gate**'s 5.11 finger crack (see below). Rack: RPs to 1.5 inches, with a 2.5 inch piece. FA: Topher Donahue and Jeff Ofsanko, 1999. A more direct version adds **Celestial Gate**'s 5.12a finger crack to the mix, and reverses the crux reach on **Days of Heaven** to gain the upper cracks. It will likely have been redpointed by Topher before this book hits the shelves (5.13a, 200 foot pitch).

7 Days of Heaven 5.10d ***

Three short pitches comprise this magnificent line. 1. Start fifteen feet left of **Center Dihedral** on the left edge of the block. Breach the overhang above an evident horn and jam a flare; step right near its top and climb to a ledge. Bring small TCUs for the belay. 2. Work up twin cracks, then hand traverse left along a flake. Stretch left and commit to a leaning finger crack, 5.10c. Ascend this (strenuous 5.10) to a tremendously exposed stance. 3. Jam a flawless hand crack to a slight bulge, step right, and fight through the thin hands crux. Two sets of Friends from #1.5 - #3 are very comforting on this sustained pitch, the best hand crack in the sub-alpine areas. FA: Sharp, Hare and Pete Brashaw, 1981.

8 Celestial Gate 5.12a ***

The left edge of the main south face holds a beautiful route of thin cracks and face climbing. 1. The original line of ascent begins on the right side of the west face beneath a short, scruffy wall with a pine tree or two. Climb to the crest and turn onto the south face at a flake, cross a smooth slab (5.10a R), and belay at a stance beneath a thin crack. This crack leads into the second pitch on **Days of Heaven**. A better start utilizes the first pitch of **Days of Heaven**, then moves left past a fixed pin to the same belay stance. 2. Jam the finger crack all the way to the second belay on **Days of Heaven**. The bottom portion of the crack is very continuous, 5.12a. 3. Complete the route with difficult face climbing or cool crack climbing — pick your poison. The face finish follows the outrageous arete on the left past 5 bolts (5.11c), and ends at a perfect belay seat on the edge of the face (#1 and #1.5 Friends for the belay). The crack variation begins with the 5.9 section of the third pitch on **Days of Heaven**, then slants left along a strenuous finger crack (5.11b; 0.75 to 1 inch cams). Turn right up an easier hand crack to finish the pitch. FA: Bernard Gillett, Chris Hill and Robert Gillett, 1994. Bernard Gillett, Mike Schlauch, and Topher Donahue added the crack variation on the third pitch in 1997. Bring a thin crack rack for the second pitch.

9 Nameless Demons 5.10a **

Begin on the right (west-facing) wall of the grotto at a left-leaning corner. 1. Climb the corner and exit right with a weird belly crawl, 5.10a. Belay on a ledge below a major left-facing dihedral. 2. Lead up the dihedral, 5.10a. FA: Sharp and Brashaw, 1981.

10 Heavenly Daze 5.12c ***

Six bolts, a fixed nut, and a piton are found on the wall left of **Nameless Demons**. Small wires and cams round out the protection on this excellent face pitch that ends at a bolt and piton anchor (bring a 60 meter rope to lower off). FA: Topher and Patience Donahue, 2000.

11 Desolation Angels 5.11d R *

A conspicuous roof presents itself left of **Heavenly Daze**. Follow a broken ramp left, arriving at the base of a dihedral dropping down from the roof's edge (5.6 R), and belay. Climb the right-facing dihedral up to and over the roof (crux) and finish with a demanding corner. A recent ascent claims the run out section can be protected with small cams. FA: Sharp and John Allen, 1981. **Variation:** Jam the lefthand of two fingertip cracks on the outside face of the ramp (**Tipendicular**, 5.13a ***, FA: Topher Donahue, 2000). Bring extra tiny TCUs. A second pitch climbs run out ground left of the normal second pitch (5.10d R, not recommended).

12 Left Out 5.11d **

Start right of **Baptismal Font** and climb an overhanging black face to the same anchor. FA: Topher and Patience Donahue, and Steve Monk, 2000.

ROCK OF AGES

2. Original Sin 5.10c
3. Center Dihedral 5.10d ★
4. Hats Off 5.12b ★★★
5. The Lock of Rages 5.12d ★★★
6. Rope Gun with Silencer 5.12d ★★★
7. Days of Heaven 5.10d ★★★
8. Celestial Gate 5.12a ★★★
9. Nameless Demons 5.10a ★★
10. Heavenly Daze 5.12c ★★★
11. Desolation Angels 5.11d R ★
12. Left Out 5.11d ★★
13. Baptismal Font 5.11c ★★
14. Greensleeves 5.12b ★★★
15. The Wasp 5.13a ★★★
16. Every Pitch Tells A Story 5.10d R ★
17. Got To Get Out of This Place 5.10d

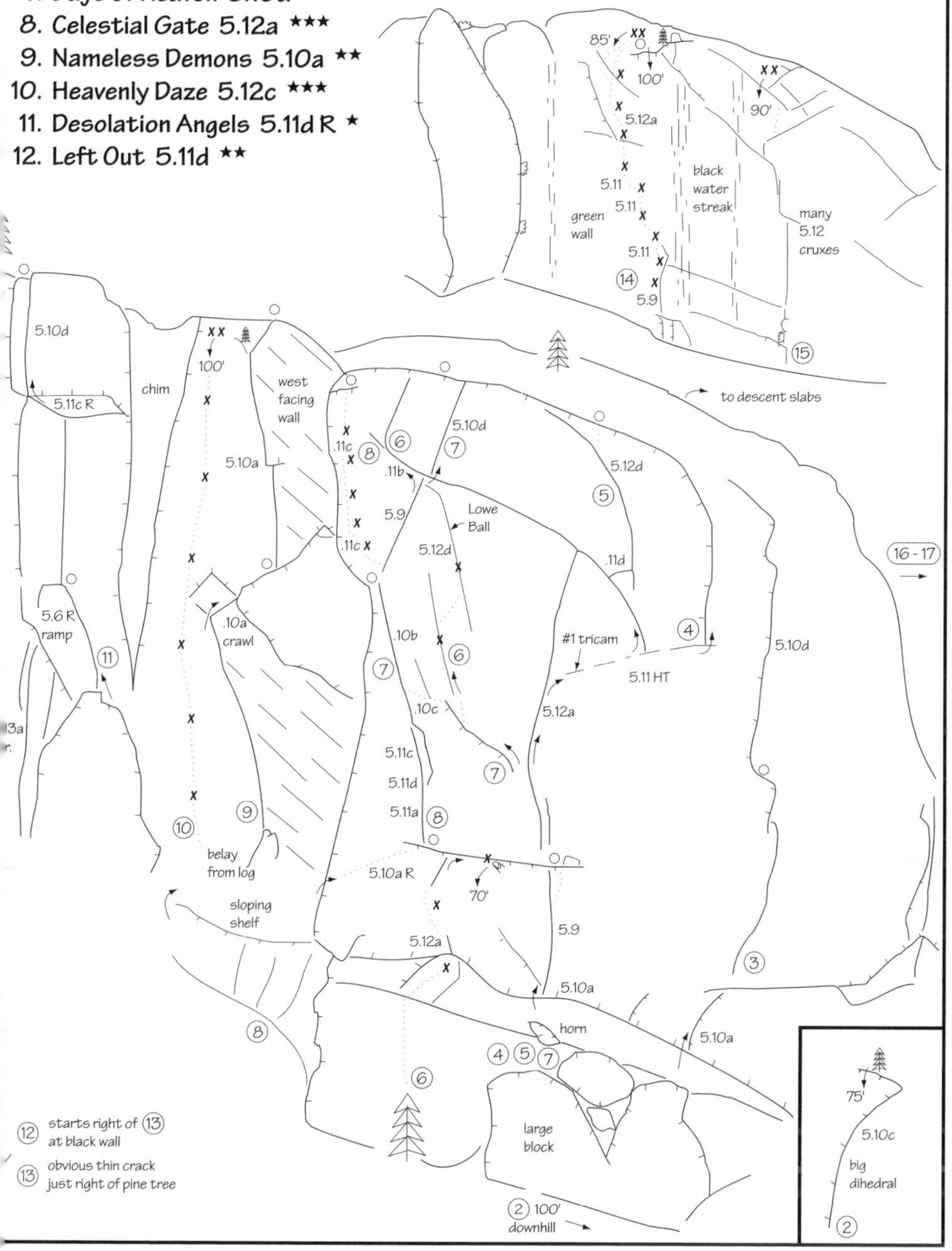

13 Baptismal Font 5.11c ★★

Locate a thin crack through green rock on the short, east-facing wall that borders the left side of the grotto. Start at a spring (may be dry by July or August) just right of a small pine tree and climb past a short stretch of wet rock to a beautiful finger-tip crack. Rappel 45 feet from a bolt and piton. FA: Bernard Gillett and Shawn Preston, 1994.

14 Greensleeves 5.12b ★★★

The smooth wall immediately above Rock of Ages has a bolt route on its left side. Lots of 5.11 with a 5.12a move near the top stack up to create a formidable face climbing challenge. Warm up with a route on Rock of Ages, or reverse its east side descent slabs to arrive at the base. Start with a thin crack just left of a fat, black water streak (wires and TCUs, 5.9), then clip 9 bolts on perfect, green colored rock. Stay with the foot ramp on the left past the last bolt, then traverse right to the anchor, or climb more directly up to it (harder). A 200' rope is useful for lowering off; bring the belayer up and rappel left if a 165' rope is used. FA: Bernard Gillett and Shawn Preston top roped the line in 1994. It was bolted and climbed by Gillett and Sean McMahan in 1997. **Variation:** The black water streak has been top roped (5.13a slab climbing).

15 The Wasp 5.13a ★★★

Climb the thin crack system 25 feet right of **Greensleeves** (one fixed pin). Include three #1.5 Flexible Friends. Rappel 90 feet from a bolt and pin anchor. FA: Topher Donahue, 2000.

16 Every Pitch Tells a Story 5.10d R ★

The sprawling mass of rock right of Rock of Ages has two additional routes. This line ascends to the high point of the mass. Begin to the right of the Rock of Ages' descent slabs at a ramp with bushes that heads right towards the middle of the wall. 1. Go up the ramp (5.10a) and belay at the base of a right-leaning dihedral. 2. Head up the dihedral (crux), then step left to a belay stance. 3. Climb along a right-leaning arch, move left, and head up the imposing wall above (5.10c R). Descend west over the top of the **Greensleeves** wall, scramble down its west side, then join the Rock of Ages descent. FA: Sharp and Allen, 1981.

17 Got To Get Out of This Place 5.10d

This route climbs out the right side of an impressive triangular roof located about 150 yards east of Rock of Ages, right of the previous route. Climb in from the left side and jam a roof crack. FA: Sharp, 1981.

THE LOST WORLD

Several faces of fine granite lie about one-half mile west of Rock of Ages in a broad, talus filled gully — this is the Lost World. Three of the four named features have recorded routes, and it appears as though there is room for more.

Approach: Continue beyond Arch Rocks on the Fern Lake Trail (see approach information for Rock of Ages, page 210) for about five minutes, then head north-west into the woods. The best point of departure is not too difficult to locate: Watch for a rock retaining wall with several logs across the trail shortly after passing through Arch Rocks. Hike past the log section for about 100 yards, look for a ten

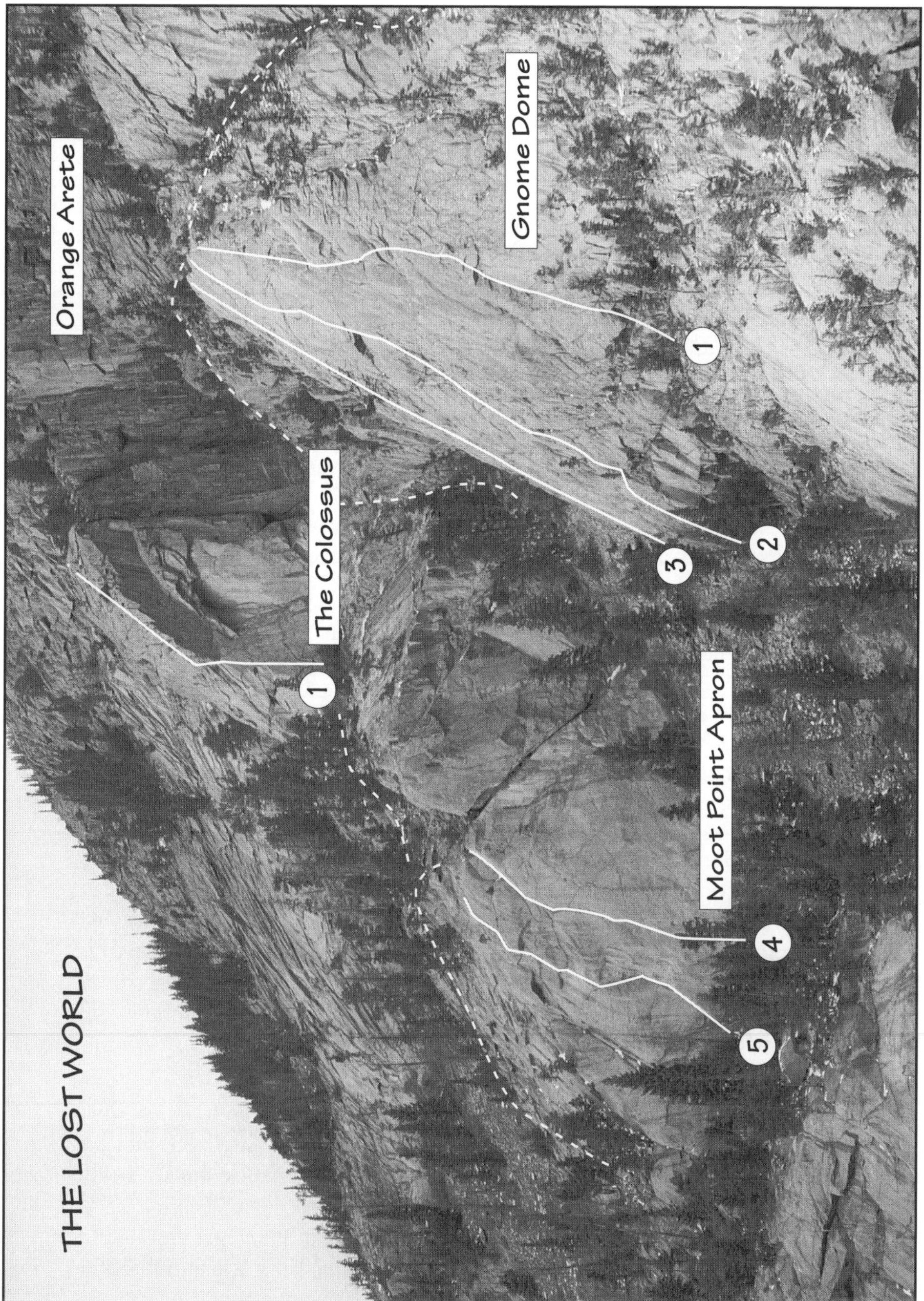
THE LOST WORLD
Orange Arete
Gnome Dome
The Colossus
Moot Point Apron
1
2
3
1
4
5

foot section of retaining wall on the left, go 50 yards beyond this, and then leave the trail on the right. With a bit of luck, a narrow strip of talus with slabs on either side will be found just a minute after leaving the trail. Head to the top of the talus, go north through a short stretch of woods to more talus, and emerge onto a rocky bench. Scramble left (west) on the bench for a few minutes until reaching a lush meadow.

The four cliffs should be apparent from here, fifteen minutes or so to the northwest. The most distinguished wall is The Colossus, a dome of rock missing its right side. Above and right is the Orange Arete, the highest rock of the four. Gnome Dome (to the right) and Moot Point Apron (to the left) are situated on opposite sides of the talus fan emanating from the higher cliffs. Reach these slabs by contouring around the east side of the meadow, then hike up a lightly wooded talus slope.

Gnome Dome

A huge roof cuts low across the southwest side of Gnome Dome; the first route begins to its right. The slab tapers off in angle to the east, and the lower half ends abruptly in a deep chasm.

Descent: There are two choices for the descent; the second is best for parties leaving gear at the base. Head southeast from the top down low angled slabs — follow the trees, plenty of 3rd class. At a point perhaps two thirds of the way down, it is possible to traverse straight east along a tree covered ledge to gain the bottom of the deep chasm; from here an easy gully leads back to the rocky bench described in the approach. The second method traverses a long ledge system toward the Orange Arete (3rd class), then heads down a tight gully beneath The Colossus. A short stretch of 5.4 must be negotiated before reaching the talus fan.

1 Goblins Slab 5.5
Scramble right along a slab/ledge system beneath the huge roof to a large tree growing near the wall (about 150 yards right of the next route). 1. Head up the slab behind the tree aiming for a roof that lies above a short, right-facing corner, but belay just before turning into the corner (5.5). 2. Turn into the corner and pop over the roof (5.5). Continue up past a few overlaps, and belay out left in a small corner above a bush. 3. An easy pitch wanders up and left. FA: Hector Galbraith and Gene Ellis, 1994.

2 Night of the Unicorn 5.8 ★★
Start just left of the huge roof in an obvious groove behind a large tree. 1. Climb the groove (5.4), then head right to a belay tree on a ledge. 2. Angle left along a flake, then step back right and up a thin crack (5.7). Easier rock finds a belay beneath the right side of an obvious roof in the middle of the slab. 3. Climb up to and over the apex in the roof (crux), then angle left along a fine finger crack for a long pitch. 4. Finish with a short and easy pitch. FA: Gene Ellis, Richard Rossiter and Bonnie Von Grebe, 1993. **Variation:** A more difficult version of pitch 3 breaches the roof directly above the belay at a crack (5.10a), then steps back left into the main line.

3 Wandering Star 5.6 ★

A nice hand crack splits the headwall above and left of the obvious roof on **Night of the Unicorn**. Begin about 60 feet left of the previous line, and piece together short cracks and face for two long pitches (somewhat difficult to protect, 5.5). Climb to the base of the hand crack on the third pitch and jam it. FA: Ellis and Galbraith, 1994.

Moot Point Apron

Moot Point Apron sits directly west across the talus fan from Gnome Dome. Descend west via 3rd class slabs.

4 Yosemite Slab 5.10 (?) ★

Look for a dark water streak (with two old bolts) in the middle of the south face; the bolts are visible from the ground. Climb to the streak with a left-facing flake (5.9), pass the bolts (crux), and belay on a ramp leading right. Follow the ramp to finish, then scramble west over the summit to the descent. **Variation:** The blank slab uphill and right with a tree at its top looks like a fine friction test piece for those willing to set up a top rope.

5 Welcome to the Jungle 5.9

Start about 50 feet left of the previous line at a left-facing dihedral. Follow the corner right, surmount a tight bulge (crux), and arc left with the corner to a small belay stance. Go straight up to a roof that is passed on the left (5.8), then angle right to a gully and belay. Scramble west over the summit to the descent slabs. FA: Rossiter, Ellis and Von Grebe, 1993.

The Colossus

A single route has been established on the left side of the east face of the Colossus. Walk west from the summit to descend.

1 Colossus Crack 5.8 R ★★

Follow the leftmost (and largest) of several cracks on the left side of the east face, 5.8. Belay on a sloping shelf just left of the top of the crack (small cams useful). 2. Go straight up, turning onto the south face, then angle left across several right-facing corners (5.8 R). Climb straight up along the right margin of the south face to a short, perfect finger crack, and then continue more easily to a big ledge near the top. 3. Scramble to the summit. FA: Kurt Johnson and Charles Vernon, 1998.

THE MUMMY RANGE

The Mummy Range is the northernmost collection of mountains in RMNP. These summits form the backdrop to Lumpy Ridge, and are responsible for the skin-soaking thunderstorms that so often descend upon that area. Though the range extends beyond park boundaries and includes many summits, locals often use the name to refer to the six most visible peaks of the group: Chapin, Chiquita, Ypsilon, Fairchild, Hagues and Mummy (from south to north as viewed from Estes Park). All of the technical routes on the peaks are approached from the Lawn Lake trailhead (described under Ypsilon Mountain, page 221).

ICEBERG LAKE WALL

This small lava cliff isn't actually in the Mummy Range, though it's nearby, about three miles west of Mount Chapin. Drive up Trail Ridge Road (Highway 34) to a parking area overlooking Iceberg Lake, about one-half mile southeast of the road's high point (12,183 feet). The wall and single route upon it (**Iceberg Lake Wall**, II, 5.6) are quite obvious from here. Descend to the north side of the lake, along a snowfield for most of the season, and head up to the prominent chimney system in the center of the face. Climb rotten rock on the left side of the chimney to a big ledge, 5.0, and belay. Traverse right for thirty feet, across the chimney, and ascend a bulging wall for 80 feet (5.6). The last pitch angles up right on blocky rock to the top of the wall. Walk left back to Trail Ridge Road. FA: Steve Hickman, John Bryant and Dave Johnston, 1962.

MOUNT CHIQUITA

Mount Chiquita is one peak south of Ypsilon Mountain. A single route has been done on the northeast face.

Approach: Hike to Ypsilon Lake (see Ypsilon Mountain below), then follow the inlet stream to Chiquita Lake (take the left fork of the stream mentioned in the approach to Spectacle Lakes).

1 Great White Fright II 5.9 X

This route ascends the northeast face in four pitches, one of which climbs along a long dike of white quartz with a 120 foot run out. Descend the east ridge of the mountain, reaching the approach trail near Chipmunk Lake. FA: Chip Salaun, Randy Joseph and T. Moderson, 1980.

YPSILON MOUNTAIN

The southeast face of Ypsilon Mountain above Spectacle Lakes spans one of the more outstanding cirques in the Park, rivaling even the great east flank of Longs Peak. A magnificent 2,000 foot wall overwhelms the climber as he crests the steep hillside and slabs from Ypsilon Lake and steps into the Spectacle Lakes basin.

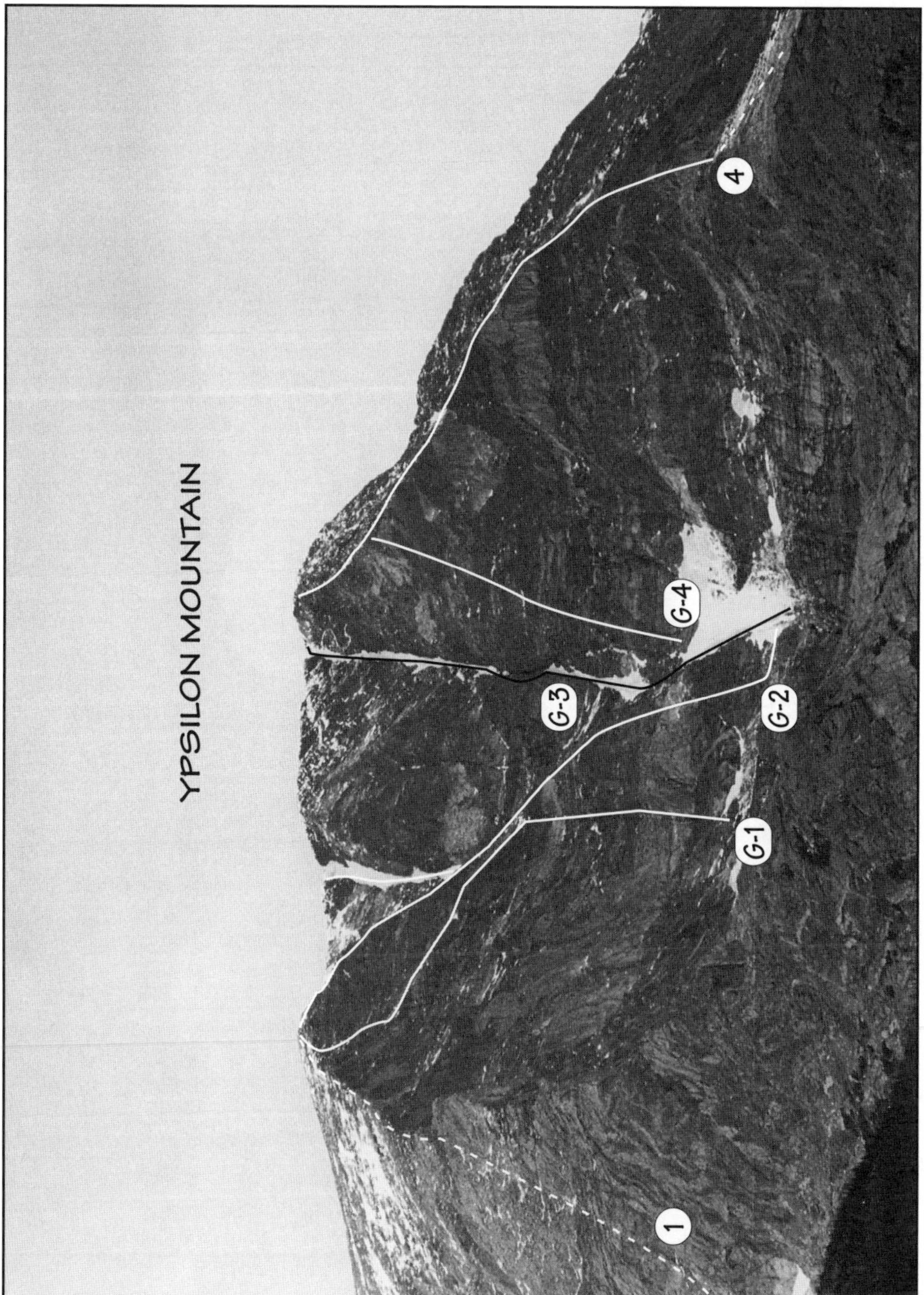
YPSILON MOUNTAIN
4
G-4
G-3
G-2
G-1
1

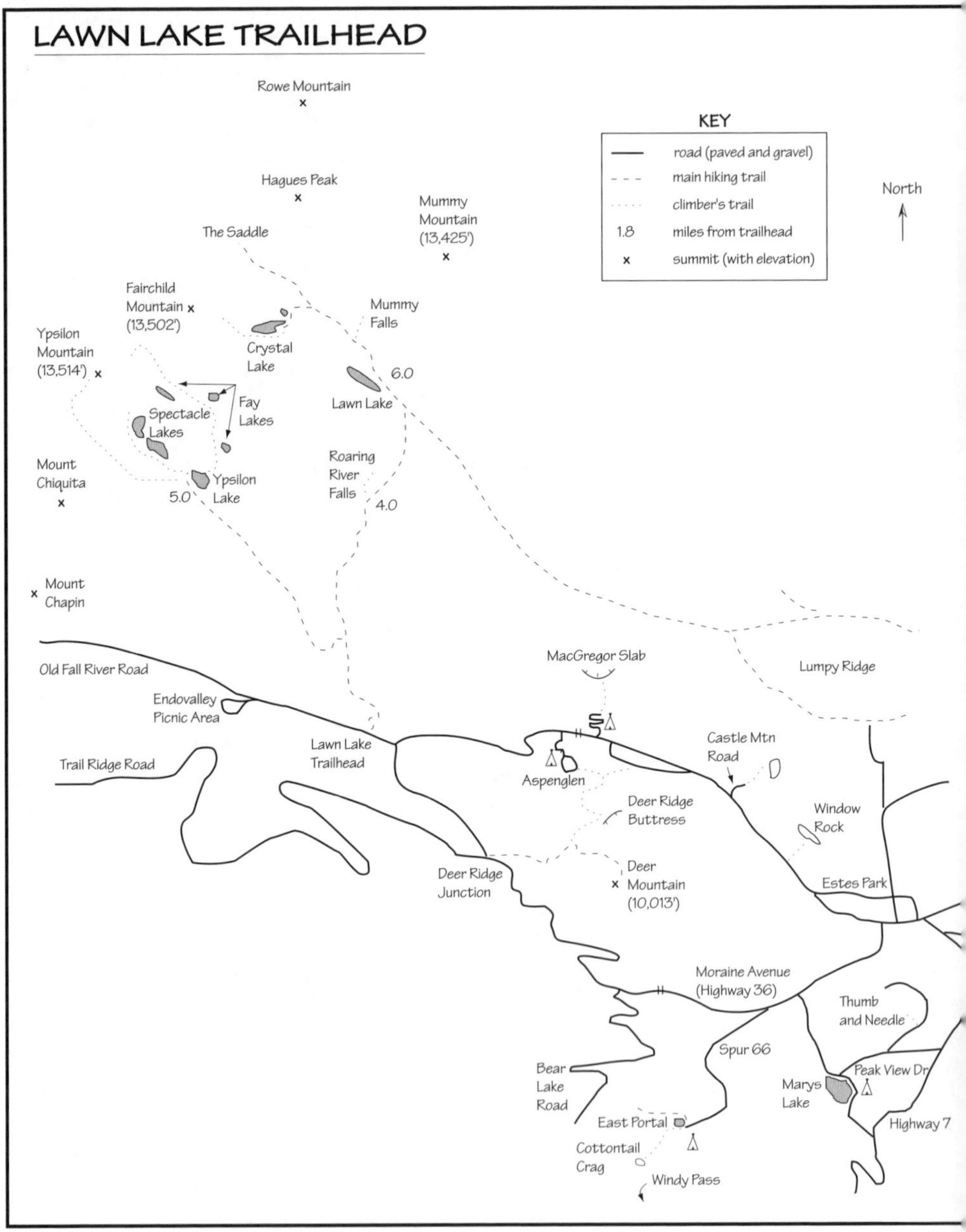
LAWN LAKE TRAILHEAD
KEY
road (paved and gravel)
main hiking trail
climber's trail
1.8
miles from trailhead
summit (with elevation)
North
Rowe Mountain
Hagues Peak
Mummy Mountain (13,425')
The Saddle
Fairchild Mountain (13,502')
Mummy Falls
Ypsilon Mountain (13,514')
Crystal Lake
6.0
Lawn Lake
Fay Lakes
Spectacle Lakes
Roaring River Falls
Mount Chiquita
Ypsilon Lake
5.0
4.0
Mount Chapin
MacGregor Slab
Lumpy Ridge
Old Fall River Road
Endovalley Picnic Area
Lawn Lake Trailhead
Castle Mtn Road
Trail Ridge Road
Aspenglen
Deer Ridge Buttress
Window Rock
Deer Ridge Junction
Deer Mountain (10,013')
Estes Park
Moraine Avenue (Highway 36)
Thumb and Needle
Spur 66
Bear Lake Road
Peak View Dr
Marys Lake
East Portal
Highway 7
Cottontail Crag
Windy Pass

Despite this grand setting, most of the routes here see infrequent traffic as the face offers little in the way of obvious lines, with the exception of the famous **Y Couloir**, and perhaps **Blitzen Ridge**. For challenging winter and alpine climbing, though, Ypsilon is hard to beat.

Identifying Ypsilon is not a problem — its name is stamped on the east face for all to see. Two long snow couloirs form a gigantic Y (the **Y Couloir**), and this is visible for miles. It rests in the middle of the six prominent peaks of the Mummy Range.

Travel Directions: To reach the trailhead, drive west from Estes Park on Highway 34, enter RMNP, and travel about two miles to a right turn that leads to Endovalley and Fall River Road. From here it is a short distance to the Lawn Lake parking lot on the right.

Approach: Hike north for 1.3 miles, then turn left (sign) and cross Roaring River. The right fork leads to Lawn and Crystal Lakes (see Fairchild below) while the left fork climbs out of the river valley onto a long moraine. At about four miles the trail begins to descend, passing Chipmunk Lake, and then continues down to Ypsilon Lake. This is the end of the maintained trail system, and the beginning of the various approaches.

The first seven routes start at Spectacle Lakes, a hard half mile above Ypsilon Lake. Cross the inlet on the west side of Ypsilon Lake on a footbridge, then strike out left on a faint path along the north side of the stream. Stay right at a fork in the path (and stream) and continue up 4th class slabs to reach East Spectacle Lake. The easiest route up the slabs stays with the stream, but the slabs on the left can also be negotiated. Contour around the left (south) side of East Spectacle Lake to reach the west lake.

The approach to **Blitzen Ridge** is included with its route description, and the approach to the snow couloirs on the north side of the mountain is described in the ice climbing section.

Descent: To descend from the summit, head south toward Mount Chiquita into a long gully on the south flank of Ypsilon. The gully usually holds snow all season; one can easily avoid the snow to the west or glissade down it when conditions allow. Turn east at the bottom of the gully and hike along a stream that leads back to Ypsilon Lake. It is possible to traverse across the lower portion of **Donner Ridge** and back to Spectacle Lakes if gear is left there, but it's a hassle. Bring it all to the summit, or leave gear at Ypsilon Lake.

1 Donner Ridge 3rd or 4th class

The left side of the Ypsilon cirque is bordered by Donner Ridge on the south; the route along it, however, avoids the actual ridge for the most part. Begin at East Spectacle Lake (4th class to get here) and scramble south to gain the crest. Hike along the ridge until steep rock bars the way, then move left and stay south of the ridge for several hundred feet until it is possible to regain the crest. The remainder of the ridge is easy 2nd class hiking. **Variation:** An alternate approach (which keeps the grade at 3rd class) begins by reversing the descent route from the summit until it is easy to get onto the ridge.

2 To the Lighthouse IV 5.9

The huge wall left of the Y couloir houses several routes; this is the leftmost of the four. Hike to the back of West Spectacle Lake and scramble up several hundred feet of talus (or snow) left of a slabby area, aiming for a black streaked dihedral below and right of a prominent group of pillars in midface. Climb the dihedral for a couple pitches, then angle left for two more pitches toward the pillars. The next pitch crosses several ledges and ends at the base of a steep crack in a light band of rock. From here, climb to an overhang and belay. Then breach the overhang (crux) and wander up to the base of a white pillar of rock near the top of the face — this is The Lighthouse. Belay a bit higher at the top of a ramp out left. Climb a short crack above the ramp, then continue to the top of the pillar and the end of the route. FA: George Hurley and R. Bliss, 1975.

3 Lighthouse Straits III 5.7

An eight pitch line right of the previous route has been reported. Begin with 200 feet of climbing to a short, right-facing dihedral, then climb through a long roof two pitches higher. Finish along the right side of The Lighthouse. Nothing more specific about this route has been published. FA: George Hurley and R. Bliss, 1975.

G-1 Right Side Chimney III M4 (?)

See the ice climbing section.

G-2 Prancer Ridge III M3/4 (?)

See the ice climbing section.

G-3 Y Couloir II AI 2 or III AI 3 M3

The **Y Couloir** is the most obvious feature on the face of Ypsilon, visible from miles away and the namesake of the peak. A description of the route is found in the ice climbing section.

G-4 Blitzen Face III M4- (?)

See the ice climbing section.

4 Blitzen Ridge III 5th class ★★★

This is the striking ridge that forms the right side of the Ypsilon cirque. It, too, has been the scene of classic winter ascents, though a summer ascent is just as coveted. Hike to the north end of Ypsilon Lake and scramble up a steep, grassy gully onto the ridge. Follow the narrowing ridge to the rope up spot just east of the Four Aces, a series of A-shaped pinnacles on the ridge. Climb directly up the east faces of the first three Aces, down climbing the west sides to the notches in between. An easier way around the first two pinnacles climbs along exposed ledges on their south sides. The final Ace is best passed on its north side with two short pitches, although it can be climbed directly (harder, and followed by a down climb). Ascend the steep headwall beyond the fourth Ace for two leads (5.4), and continue along the easier ridge above to the summit. The difficulty of the route is dependent upon the method in which the Four Aces are negotiated; the easiest way is about 5.4, while the most direct is 5.7. FA: Clint Brooks, Charlie Ehlert, Dave Fedson, James Walker and Phil Ritterbush, 1958. **Variation:** Bypass the four Aces altogether by hiking to Spectacle Lakes. Ascend the easy wall on the north side of the cirque to the notch just west of the fourth Ace.

G-5 Blitzen Ridge Couloir II AI 3

This couloir and the next ascend the secluded northeast side of Ypsilon. See the ice climbing section.

G-6 Northeast Couloir II AI 3

See the ice climbing section.

FAIRCHILD MOUNTAIN

Fairchild is the bulky mountain immediately northeast of Ypsilon. At 13,502 feet, it is the sixth highest peak in RMNP. All of the technical climbing takes place in a secluded horseshoe-shaped cirque on the east side of the mountain, just above Crystal Lake. The upper rim of this cirque is visible from Estes Park.

The north-facing aspect of the horseshoe cirque holds three mixed routes, and the right-hand of these (**Abadoo Scronch**) portions off an 800 foot buttress from the main wall of the mountain. This is Honcho Boncho Buttress, the big attraction for rock climbers. Right of the buttress is a series of shorter ribs, gullies, and walls known collectively as the Lost Buttress.

Approach: The hike to Crystal Lake is long, but pleasant. Begin at the Lawn Lake trailhead (see Ypsilon), and hike for 1.3 miles to a bridge crossing Roaring Fork River. Continue straight up the trail on the east side of the river (the bridge gains the trail into Ypsilon), pass Lawn Lake at 6 miles, and arrive at a signed fork in another mile. Go left to Little Crystal Lake and Crystal Lake, passing both on their south sides, and enter the cirque (the right fork goes to The Saddle, which is the pass between Fairchild and Hagues Peak). Lawn Lake can also be reached from the Twin Owls trailhead at Lumpy Ridge via the Black Canyon trail (joining the Lawn Lake trail about a half mile below the lake), but this adds two miles.

Descent: The descent for the rock climbs begins with a simple walk down the north slope of Fairchild to The Saddle, followed by the trail leading back to Crystal and Lawn Lakes.

G-9 Winterlong IV M4 AI 2

Winterlong climbs the north wall of the cirque (described in the ice climbing section).

G-10 Mirage IV WI 5 M5/6

See ice climbing section.

G-11 Abadoo Scronch III M4 AI 4

This is the obvious snow gully immediately left of the Honcho Boncho Buttress; see ice climbing section.

FAIRCHILD MOUNTAIN
Honcho Boncho Buttress
G-11
1
2
3

FAIRCHILD - Honcho Boncho Buttress

G-11. Abadoo Scronch III M4 AI 4

1. Power Struggle IV 5.11c ★★★
2. Don't You Want to Live With Me? IV 5.11c (A3) ★
3. Honcho Boncho Buttress III 5.7

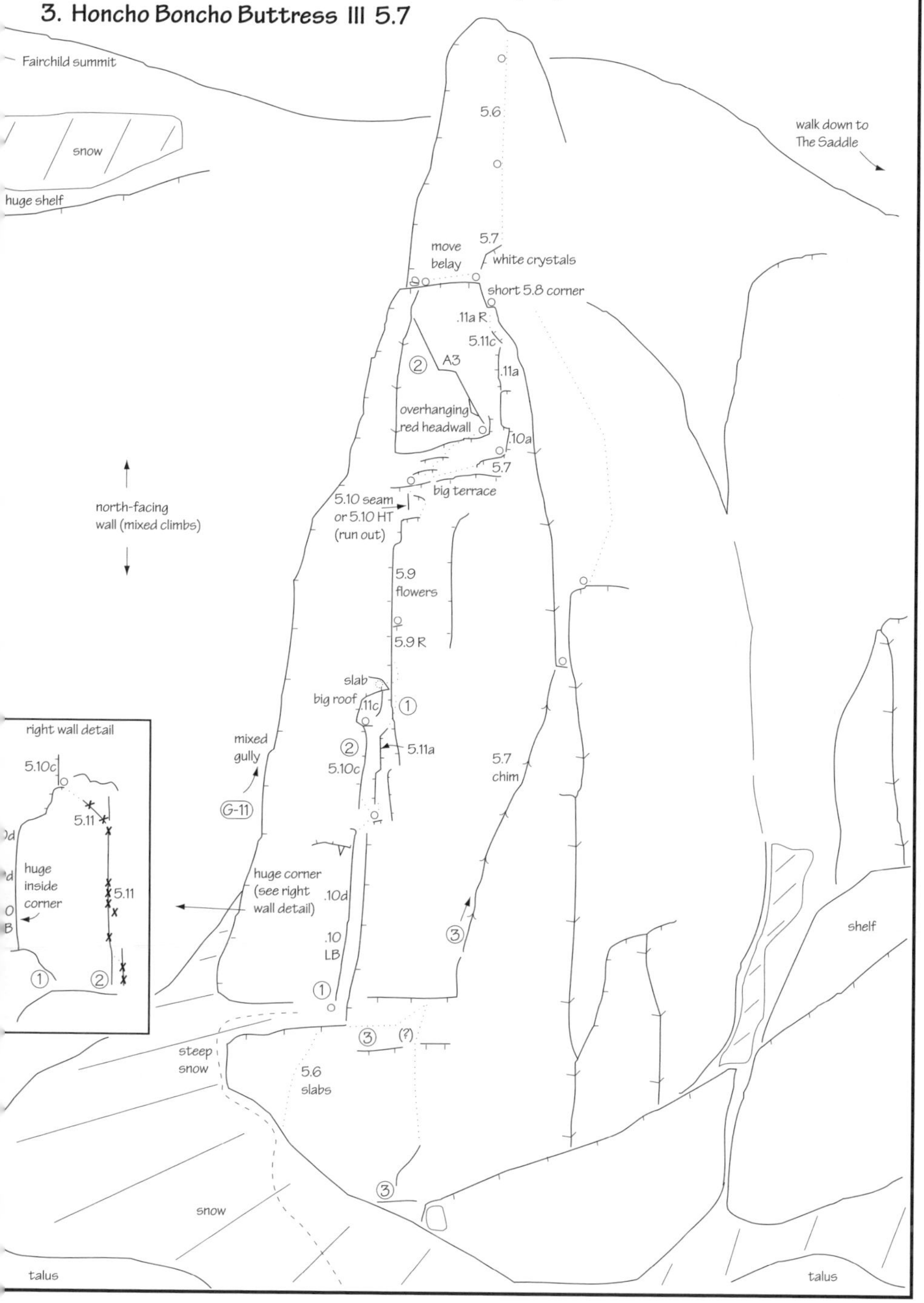

1 Power Struggle IV 5.11c ★★★

This route begins in the massive dihedral on the lower left edge of the Honcho Boncho Buttress, just right of the **Abadoo Scronch** gully. It climbs the southeast-facing aspect of the buttress, and is thus blessed with plentiful sunshine. Begin with a 5.6 approach pitch to the bottom of the huge dihedral, or kick steps up the bottom of **Abadoo Scronch** (40 degree snow) and traverse right into the dihedral. 1. A long pitch climbs the dihedral (solid 5.10d), then steps up and right to a stance at the end of the rope. 2. Climb steep corners on the right to a ledge (5.11a), go right, then follow a right-facing dihedral to a grassy ledge. 3. Continue up the dihedral (5.9+ flowers) to a ledge. Either attack a straight up seam (5.10b, RPs), or move up right to a hand traverse back left. Both of these options are dicey, and both end at the lower left-hand side of an extensive ledge system below a smooth, overhanging headwall. 4. Traverse up and right on the ledges to a stance below a left-facing corner at the right margin of the headwall, 5.7. 5. Link together a series of short dihedrals on the right edge of the southeast face (5.11a), then work up left under a small roof (5.11c fingers), and face climb to a belay ledge (5.11a poor pro). 6. A thirty foot pitch in a left-facing dihedral on the left goes to a good ledge (5.8). 7 and 8. Three hundred feet of moderate climbing up the prow of the buttress ends the technical difficulties. Rack to 3 inches with extra gear from 2-3 inches. FA: Doug Byerly and Terry Murphy, 1992.

2 Don't You Want to Live With Me? IV 5.11c (A3) ★

This line runs parallel to **Power Struggle**, and shares a few of its pitches. The aid pitch can be avoided by climbing the crux on **Power Struggle**. Begin on a big shelf (often snow-covered) at the base of two parallel cracks on the right wall of the huge **Power Struggle** dihedral. 1. Climb the right crack for 30 feet, then switch to the left crack. Continue past a bolt for about 80 feet until a thin crack branches left to a belay in the **Power Struggle** dihedral. There are several fixed pins and wires on this long, sustained pitch (5.11c); a 55 meter rope is handy. 2. **Power Struggle** goes up right from this point to avoid the huge roof above while this route tackles the roof. Climb a short pitch straight up the corner to a big ledge below the roof, 5.10c. 3. Stem up, then muscle out a 25 foot hand crack splitting the roof, 5.11c. Belay over the lip, or traverse 20 feet right to **Power Struggle** and finish its second pitch. 4. Do the third pitch on **Power Struggle**. Move the belay to a short corner on the right side of the highest ledge, just below the smooth, over-hanging headwall. 5. Aid the headwall with a diagonal crack to its upper left arete, and free climb to a belay by boulders. 6. Move the belay up right to a dihedral marked with a cairn and peppered with white crystals. Climb the dihedral, traverse right, then go straight up to a belay, 5.8. 7 and 8. Finish with **Power Struggle**. Bring plenty of thin crack gear for the crux (Lowe Balls helpful), and a small selection of thin pitons (with one RURP and a hook) for the aid pitch. FA: Tom Bohanon and Terry Murphy, 1994.

3 Honcho Boncho Buttress III 5.7

This route climbs a long chimney system in the middle of the buttress; approach from the left with a ledge that leads to the base of the fissure. Climb the chimney (originally done in eight pitches of mostly easy going, with a few short walls and chockstones, 5.7) to some ledges on the northeast side of the buttress. The next five leads angle first right, then back left, linking short walls and slabs. These end on the crest of the buttress. Follow the crest to the northern slope of Fairchild. FA: Pete Robinson and Dave Johnston, 1964.

4 Lost Buttress III 5.7

This route ascends a smaller buttress right of Honcho Boncho Buttress with a wild hand traverse. The exact line of ascent is lost to time. FA: William Buckingham and D. Anderson, 1954. A more recent foray in this area (III 5.6) climbs the wall left of the second gully right of Honcho Boncho Buttress. Hike up the gully (snow) to easy ledges on the left, and step onto the wall. Work up to a wet, wide crack on the left by making huge zigzags (100 feet wide), then traverse right 50 feet on a mossy ledge to a nice hand crack. Jam this for 200 feet (5.6), and scramble along 4th class terrain to the top. FA: Greg Sievers, 1993.

ICE AND ALPINE CLIMBS

The winter weather in Estes Park fluctuates between bitter cold and unseasonably mild, allowing rock climbing periodically but certainly not for any sustained length of time. Thus the preferred mode of ascent becomes ice climbing, generally available from late fall through late spring. RMNP contains the best ice climbing in eastern Colorado, and some of the best alpine climbing in the state.

This chapter outlines most of the ice, snow, and mixed routes located in RMNP, although it is not an exhaustive list. Remember that in describing each climb, it is assumed that the route is fully formed. A phrase like "... the thin sheet of ice on the left is WI 5 ..." makes no sense at all when the thin sheet doesn't exist. The majority of the routes come in every year, but there are a few that form up very infrequently, or only when certain weather patterns persist. Many of the frozen waterfalls stay in good condition all winter long, but the less substantial ice and mixed routes are best climbed in early winter as they tend to deteriorate and even disappear later on. They do, on occasion, reappear in the spring, only to fall down with the next warm day. Most of the alpine couloirs listed here are commonly climbed only in the summer. Early summer ascents are best for some as they melt out later on, but late summer (or early fall) ascents are best for others to avoid avalanche danger and to allow for more challenging conditions.

First ascent information is provided when known; however, several of the alpine routes were first ascended as summer rock climbs. Only in later years were these routes ascended as ice climbs and information is scarce concerning first ascent teams.

Most parties carry a small selection of pitons (in addition to rock gear and ice screws) for the mixed routes in the mountains; the plethora of short pillars in the Park often require only ice screws. Snow stakes or flukes may be helpful on a few of the alpine couloirs, and a two hundred foot rope is useful on the longer routes as its use saves time with fewer belays.

Avalanche danger in RMNP is generally lower than other backcountry areas in Colorado, though it is still a serious threat. Check on current weather and avalanche information before venturing out. The Colorado Avalanche Information Center can be reached at 303-275-5360 from the Denver-Boulder area, and at 970-482-0457 from Fort Collins; these numbers give statewide avalanche information, though only in the winter months. Of course, the avalanche season isn't over with the arrival of summer — wet slides are common, and are extraordinarily dangerous, entombing victims in snow the consistency of cement. On rare occasions, slab avalanches of enormous blocks of ice can cut loose in late summer. In July of 1998, the top layer (eight to ten feet) of the Thatchtop-Powell Icefield slid all the way down to the previous season's snow (a very weak layer from the fall of 1997, coupled with a long hot spell, was the likely cause). Evidence of massive slab avalanches could also be seen on St. Vrain and Arapaho Glaciers in the Indian

Peaks later that summer, from 10 miles away. The chances of surviving a ride with ice blocks the size of a house are zero — the best defense is to climb in the early morning hours.

Routes in this section are arranged by the trailhead used to access them, beginning in Wild Basin to the south and moving to Lawn Lake Trailhead on the north side of RMNP.

RATINGS

Alpine and Water Ice Ratings: Routes that are primarily ice climbs are rated from 1 to 6, with plus (+) and minus (-) signs applied as with rock climbs. Roughly speaking, 1 = low angled ice up to 30 degrees; 2 = good ice up to 60 degrees; 3 = good ice up to 75 degrees, possibly with short vertical sections encountered, 4 = good, steep ice, perhaps with a few rest stances; 5 = steep ice that is typically thin and scary or long and sustained; and 6 = overhanging ice, iced over roofs, telephone poles of ice, etc. This system is further divided into Water Ice and Alpine Ice (WI and AI), but the distinction between the two is somewhat subjective on a few climbs.

Of course, it is more complicated than this. For example, a climb rated WI 4- might consist of 80-degree ice (derived from flowing water) that is solid and thick enough to accept (mostly) bomber ice protection, or perhaps a lower angled but more tenuous flow. A 50-degree gully filled with hard snow (Alpine Ice) might get a rating of AI 2. However, ice is an ever-changing medium and it is important to realize that a simple change in the weather or season can drastically change the condition of a route. Consider the famous **Lambs Slide** on Longs Peak. In early June the snow is often soft enough that one can safely ascend it without crampons; in August it is sufficiently hard that crampons are a must; and in a dry October, the snow has turned to cement-hard black ice. Add to this the extra dimension that rock climbing gives to a route (mixed climbing is often required on the alpine routes), and it becomes obvious that the ratings should be taken with a grain of salt — they give only a general indication of the route's difficulty.

Mixed Ratings: In recent years another rating system has emerged that is useful for routes where mixed climbing is the focus. These routes typically involve dry tooling on rock to connect thin patches of ice, and are indicated with ratings of M1 through M9. While nothing in this book is rated harder than M8, routes as difficult as M9 have been reported in Vail, Colorado, and as this system is open ended, it's likely more difficult climbs will be put up in the future (for example, a recent route in Iceland is supposedly harder than the hardest at Vail — perhaps it's an M10).

It is not clear how to translate traditional rock climbing ratings (such as 5.8) to the newer mixed ratings. Take the classic **Hourglass Couloir** on Arrowhead, which has a traditional rating of 5.6 AI 3. The 5.6 is done with crampons and axes, so it's mixed climbing — but how difficult in terms of the mixed system? And how does the 5.6 on **Hourglass Couloir** compare with the traditional rating of **Hallett Chimney**, which is 5.6 AI 5? In reality, the "5.6" in both instances has almost nothing to do with a 5.6 rock climb on Lumpy Ridge done in summer with rock shoes. Furthermore, a slab and a chimney, both rated 5.6 in the summer, may translate into radically different M-ratings. Climbing in crampons with axes scraping on the rock deserves a different rating scheme, one that does not rely upon the Yosemite Decimal system. There are plenty of routes in the M5 through M9 range that have been published in climbing magazines, and these grades, at least, seem well established. Routes in the M1 through M4 range, however, are nonexistent.

With the goal of a consistent grading system in mind, I talked with mixed climbers in the area to come up with consensus ratings. Following is a list of ratings for several established routes that serve as mileposts in the "M-system" and that help to flesh out the lower grades of M1 through M4. The author would appreciate any additions to this list, or conformations/disagreements on what's been selected (1419 Paramount Pl, Longmont CO 80501; or contact us at: www.earthboundsports.com).

M1 **The Homestretch**, Longs Peak (winter) M1-. **Kiener's**, Longs Peak; M1+

M2 **The Cables**, Longs Peak (in fall); M2-. **Dream Weaver**, Meeker; M2+

M3 **Hourglass Couloir**, Arrowhead; M3. **Lochluster**, Loch Vale Gorge; M3

M4 **Alexander's Chimney**, Longs Peak; M4+. **The Window**, Longs Peak; M4

M5 **Dragon's Breath**, Chasm Lake Area; M5. **Hallett Chimney**, Hallett; M5

M6 **Mixed Emotions**, Loch Vale Gorge; M6-. **Necrophilia**, Thatchtop; M6

M7 **Free Strike Zone**, Loch Vale Gorge; M7+. **Get a File**, Nymph Lk; M7-

M8 **Blade Runner**, Loch Vale Gorge; M8.

M9 **Amphibian** (in Vail); M9. **Fatman and Robin** (in Vail); M9

As with the Water and Alpine Ice ratings, the Mixed grades give only a general indication of the difficulties that may be encountered. Changing conditions can affect consensus ratings by a number grade or more, especially in the lower grades. **The Window**, for example, listed above at M4, can be downright desperate when conditions are bleak. No attempt has been made to put a protection rating on these climbs, though a few are certainly deserving of an R or X rating. Once again, the problem lies in the vagaries of the medium — **The Squid** accepts bomber screws along its entire length when it fills in nicely, but it's an entirely different game when the ice is thin.

One final note: The sport of ice climbing has seen a tremendous increase in the number of participants over the last decade, yet there are only a few easily accessible classic ice climbs in the area. These tend to become crowded, especially on weekends, and conflicts arise when several parties are vying for the same 60 foot chunk of frozen water. Add to this mix the problem of ice climbing near other parties — ice is going to fall on your head if you choose to climb behind another party, while passing a team puts them in the line of fire — and there is real potential for a nasty fight.

Case in point: On January 18th, 1998, the Boulder Camera ran a story about a climber who reprimanded another person for putting his party in danger by climbing nearby. The argument escalated, and one man threatened to kill the other. This led to a bit of wrestling on top of a 100 foot drop (!), and then one guy struck the other with the hammer end of his ice axe, delivering five to seven blows to the ribs, and two shots to the head. (The victim was treated in a hospital for lacerations on the head, which exposed his skull, while the other man was held in jail without bond).

If you decide to visit **All Mixed Up**, **Jaws**, **Hidden Falls**, Loch Vale Gorge, the **Lower Flow** and **Upper Tier** in Big Thompson Canyon, **The Squid**, the climbs around Black Lake, **Alexander's Chimney**, or **Grace Falls**, you WILL encounter other climbers on the weekends, and you may not be able to climb at all.

WILD BASIN

Several short ice climbs have become popular in the southern reaches of RMNP, near North Saint Vrain Creek. Two alpine routes are also available on the bigger peaks.

Travel Directions: Drive south on Highway 7 past the Longs Peak trailhead and turn west into Wild Basin, 12.8 miles from the intersection of Highway 7 and 36. Follow signs toward the Wild Basin Ranger Station and trailhead — the last mile of road leading to the trailhead is closed in the winter. A new entrance station has been installed at Wild Basin; be prepared to pay an entrance fee.

North Saint Vrain Creek

A-1 Hidden Channel WI 2+
This is the nice channel of ice just left of the main line on **Hidden Falls**. Descend east with a steep trail.

A-2 Hidden Falls WI 4-
Located a short distance from the parking lot, **Hidden Falls** is difficult to find unless a telltale path through the snow is present. Hike 0.1 mile past Copeland Falls (0.4 miles from the trailhead), then break left across North Saint Vrain Creek and into the woods. If the approach trail is not evident, hike up the slope on the right (north) until it is possible to see over the trees, then look southwest. **Hidden Falls** drops over a small cliff band one-tenth of a mile from the river, and is clearly visible from this vantage point. The initial portion of the climb (WI 3) ends in an alcove with a rappel station; the upper pillar provides an exciting (WI 4-) finish when it is in. Descend east. This area is very popular; expect company. **Variation:** A thin veil immediately right of the falls usually provides a difficult (M5) top rope problem.

A-3 The Dangler M7- WI 5
Begin in a right-facing corner right of **Hidden Falls**; look for a dagger dropping from an iced-up roof near the top of the wall. Climb the corner to a ledge (belay here to avoid rope drag), and then follow a wide crack to a stem and dangle that

reaches the ice dagger. Most of the route involves dry tooling; indeed, the dagger does not form very often (though the iced over roof is more reliable). FA: Kevin Cooper and Forest Noble, 1998.

A-4 Ouzel Falls WI 2 to 3

A fifty foot column of substantial girth lies three miles from the trailhead, about one-half mile from a trail junction at Calypso Cascades. Several lines of ascent are available, but the lower portion of the climb may be buried in snow.

Isolation Peak

A-5 North Face II AI 3

This is an alpine route on the north side of Isolation Peak. Head south to the base of the north face from Fifth Lake, the uppermost of five lakes on the East Inlet (of Grand Lake). Fifth Lake can be reached either by passing through Boulder Grand Pass from Thunder Lake, or by taking the East Inlet trail from Grand Lake (on the west side of the Park). The first option is preferred as the easiest descent from the peak heads into Wild Basin (and hence your car). Either way, it's a long hike of nine or more miles. The route follows a long couloir just right of center, then angles left on a ramp which intersects the **North Ridge** route about 150 feet below the summit (see High Peaks section, pages 12-14). In the latter part of the summer, the snow on this route melts out, leaving loose rock — climb it in early season. Descend as described in **North Ridge**.

Mount Alice

A-6 Central Gully IV AI 3 M4 A2

Central Gully climbs the most obvious line on the remote northwest face of Mount Alice. Get to the face by hiking to Lion Lake No 1 (seven miles), then continue past Lion Lake No 2 and Snowbank Lake to the pass between Mount Alice and Chiefs Head (consult a map). Go south from the pass down easy slopes to the base of the main couloir on the left side of the face. The seven pitch route follows the couloir for its entire length, encountering chimneys, short cracks and an aid section (about two-thirds of the way up). To descend, go north from the summit along **Hourglass Ridge** (3rd class, see High Peaks section, pages 12, 15-16, 20), which leads directly to the Alice-Chiefs Head saddle.

LONGS PEAK TRAILHEAD

The east face of Longs Peak contains many of the old, classic alpine routes in the park. These routes are long and involved, sometimes requiring a bivouac to complete in the brief winter days. Mount Meeker also holds two long couloirs, and shorter ice climbing attractions exist near Chasm Lake.

Travel Directions: Drive south on Highway 7 from Estes Park, turn right past mile 9, and go one mile to the Longs Peak trailhead.

Approach: With the exception of **The Cables** on the north face, all of the ice climbs on or near Longs Peak are accessed from the Chasm Lake trail. Start on the

Longs Peak trail, the only available option out of the parking lot, and stay left at the first junction, one half mile from the lot (the right trail goes to Eugenia Mine). Go left at 2.4 miles (the right trail goes to Battle Mountain group campsite), and left once again on top of Mills Moraine near a horse rack (the right trail continues through Granite Pass to the Boulderfield and then to the summit — this is the way to **The Cables**). Chasm Lake lies 0.8 mile from the Mills Moraine junction, a short distance beyond a ranger cabin.

Chasm Lake Area

B-1 Dragon's Breath III M5
This four-pitch line follows difficult mixed ground up the slabby wall southeast of Peacock Pool, which is situated 400 feet below the Chasm Lake trail. Drop off the trail toward Columbine Falls (see below), then circle the lake and on up to the base. The belays are all fixed, and although the route is not very steep, it requires delicate moves on thin ice and rock. Usually the first two pitches form up every fall; the last two may not in a bad year. Rappel the route to descend.

B-2 South Side of Lady Washington III M4 to M6
Several lines of thin runnels may be present on the slabby cliffs immediately above the Chasm Lake trail on the south side of Mount Lady Washington, before the next route is reached. The climbs don't last long due to southern exposure, but if conditions are right, they provide difficult mixed terrain up to four pitches. The routes on the left are usually longer, and the middle routes form up most frequently. Bring rock gear.

B-3 Columbine Falls WI 3+/4-
Climb the frozen stream that falls just below the Chasm Lake trail above Peacock Pool. This is about one half mile from the Mills Moraine junction. The bottom portion of the climb may be covered with deep snow, especially later in the winter. One hundred feet left of the falls is a fine flow that goes at WI 3 for a 120 foot pitch.

B-4 Chasm Lake Outlet WI 2/3
Several good lines of lower angled blue ice can be found above the ranger cabin and below the shelf that holds Chasm Lake. These may be obscured by snow later in the season.

Mount Meeker

A few, poorly documented climbs have been completed on the north face of Meeker. **Lober's Ribbon** is among them (5.8 WI 4), but I'm unsure of its location (left of **Dream Weaver**?). See photo page 22 for the following four routes.

B-5 Dream Weaver III AI 3- M2+
This route has gained some notoriety in recent years, especially after it was featured in a climbing magazine article. It can be climbed all year long, but the best conditions are found late spring into early summer, and late fall. Begin immediately left of **Flying Buttress** on Mount Meeker, and climb a narrowing snow gully

for 600 feet. Above this, several constrictions and narrow passages give the route its flavor; these are passed via thin ribbons of ice interspersed with easy to moderate mixed climbing. Finish the route by scrambling up slabs directly to the summit, and descend **The Loft**. An escape is possible at mid height — cross through the notch behind **Flying Buttress** and descend a gully (the beginning of the next route) to the west. Bring a light rack with a few pins.

B-6 Right Chimney III AI 3 M4

The gully on the right side of Flying Buttress is a great option if parties are on **Dream Weaver**. Begin with the easy right couloir for 500 feet. Once above the main Flying Buttress, the route gets interesting, with a few pitches of mixed climbing that go straight up a tight chimney. 1. Follow a 55° mixed gully right of a rock buttress to the base of the tight chimney. 2. Climb the chimney past two difficult bulges to a good belay with rock anchors. 3. An easy section leads into a steeper gully with a 70° curtain at the top of the chimney. Belay on the left. All of these pitches are long and only adequately protected in thin conditions; bring a 200 foot rope. The difficulties ease in the last portion of the route when the gully broadens, climbing several hundred feet to the summit.

B-7 Dark Star III AI 4+ M4

Dark Star follows a hidden slot right of **Right Chimney**. Hike up the couloir (the descent gully for **Flying Buttress** and the start of **Right Chimney**) to the base of the slot; it is located behind a tall rib of rock on the right. Ascend the chimney for four mixed pitches and descend the Ramp below **The Loft** (see next climb). With the right conditions, the right wall of the chimney may also ice up, providing a difficult mixed variation. FA: Duncan Ferguson, Harry Kent and Rich Paige, late 1970s.

B-8 The Loft (or The Apron) WI 3 or 3+

The broad plateau between Longs Peak and Meeker is called the Loft. A short, steep wall below the Loft holds a pitch of ice that can be thin at times; in spring and summer the ice is covered with soft snow or has melted out. Approach from the ranger cabin below Chasm Lake by hiking left of Ships Prow to a low angled snow field which steepens just below the ice — this snowfield, along with the much larger snow pillow above, is known as the Apron (beware of slab avalanches). The left side of the ice wall is WI 3+, while the right side usually goes at WI 3. A prominent ledge system slants left from the base of the ice. This is the Ramp, a 3rd class route to the Loft, and it is a convenient descent for this route and the climbs on Meeker. It begins with a 200 foot traverse left, then goes straight up a snow rib (or easy rock if the snow is gone). The angle eases above the rib, and 300 feet of talus leads to the Loft.

Longs Peak

Most of the following routes are shown on various photos and topos in the High Peaks section (under Longs Peak). Routes on the Lower East Face are also shown on page 237.

B-9 Ships Prow Ice WI 5 M5 (?)
A thin smear or two (rarely substantial) may be found on the right side of Ships Prow above the left shore of Chasm Lake. See photo page 37.

B-10 Flying Dutchman II AI 2 (M2)
This long couloir begins below and left of and is parallel to **Lambs Slide**. It climbs for 1,000 feet until it intersects with **Lambs Slide** a pitch below the north edge of the Loft. A short narrow section near the top provides the crux, which usually consists of forty feet of moderate water ice until it melts out. Expect a brief mixed wall in that case.

B-11 Lambs Slide II AI 2
This famous chute begins left of the Lower East Face on Longs Peak (a few hundred feet above Chasm Lake) and ascends for 1,000 feet to the Loft. It is most often used as an approach for **Kiener's Route** and the mixed routes nearby. Once the Loft is reached, one may descend the Ramp (see **The Loft**), or continue to the summit via **Clark's Arrow** or **Gorrell's Traverse** (see rock climbing section). **Variations:** If the Loft is the goal, the Glacier Rib can be climbed for its entire length (3rd and 4th class) — it is the long band of rock that separates **Flying Dutchman** from **Lambs Slide**. It may also be possible to climb left of Zumie's Thumb on the upper right fork of **Lambs Slide** all the way to the tail end of the Beaver, though a short vertical slot looks difficult (bypass on the left?). **Lambs Slide** is also an excellent expert ski run in spring and early summer (approach via **The Loft** or climb the route), though several skiers have taken long nasty cartwheels in late season attempts. Sharpen your edges!

B-12 Alexander's Chimney III WI 3 M3+ to M5-
Alexander's Chimney ices over in late fall to produce an uncontested RMNP classic. When combined with the **Notch Couloir** or **Eighth Route**, it offers 1,500 feet of alpine climbing in a magnificent setting. Climb **Lambs Slide** for a few hundred feet and do a short stretch of mixed climbing to reach the base of an obvious chimney on the right. A long pitch goes straight up the chimney (often M3 at the bottom), after which there are several options. The original finish (done as a rock climb in the summer) traverses right on a big ledge for 150 to 200 feet to a belay at the last of several large flakes resting on the ledge. Go up for a half pitch (5.5) and then back left to a low angled bowl, which leads up to Broadway. The traditional ice climbing finish keeps going up the chimney beneath a huge chockstone; this is an awesome pitch (M4+) which ends at a piton belay on the left. From here, one can work up and right to rejoin the original line at the bowl, or do a direct finish (M5-) to Broadway. FA: Werner Zimmerman, 1919 (as a rock climb). The ice climbing finish is known as **Trash Patrol** (and was done first as a rock climb, messy 5.7). See topo page 242.

B-13 Smear of Fear IV M6 WI 6-

An amazing line of ice stretches up the Lower East Face right of **Stettner's Ledges**. Normally only three pitches are climbable, and even these can be out of condition. Begin on the right side of a long ledge, which is reached from the left by scrambling up the first part of **Stettner's**. Climb along a leaning, right-facing corner (M5+ or 5.10), and pull over a desperate ice bulge to a belay (WI 6-). In thick conditions, this entire pitch may be climbed directly on ice (60 meters, still very difficult). 200 feet of good ice (WI 4 and 5, with some mixed) leads to a ledge that marks the end of the climb in most years; three fixed rappels go back to the ground. In 1996, the climb was extended to Broadway with more difficult dry tooling on ledges out left (M5+ WI 4). Descend via **Lambs Slide** if going to Broadway. FA: Duncan Ferguson, Jeff Lowe and Malcolm Daly, 1989. **Variations:** The sick smear left of this route is known as **Fear of Smears** (unclimbed?), and a 200 foot stretch of ice 100 feet left of **The Diagonal** sometimes forms up (**Crazy Train**, WI5, FA: Topher Donahue and Kelly Cordes, 2000; marked with "?" on photo page 237).

B-14 Field's Chimney III WI 5 M6+

This infrequently formed route climbs the right side of a fanned out, recessed area right of the Diagonal Wall (and left of **Craig's Crack**, which is a rock climb that may hold ice in the fall). 1. Climb an obvious pitch of WI 4 through a constriction to a belay on the left. 2. Climb up to and over a difficult overhang (M6) to a stance beneath an overlap. 3. Go straight up thin ice and cracks and belay at the base of a ramp angling up and left (M6+). 4. Follow the ramp left to Broadway. Descend from Broadway by rappelling **Crack of Delight** (four rappels from bolt anchors, see rock climbing section, page 53). FA: Jack Roberts and Michael Bearzi, 1996.

B-15 Eighth Route III WI 3 M3

This route ascends the broad gully immediately above **Alexander's Chimney**, which is sometimes used as an approach. One can also reach it by traversing Broadway from **Lambs Slide**. Climb the middle of the gully for two pitches of classic ice (WI 3, see Ships Prow photo in High Peaks section, page 37). Above this, the angle eases for several hundred feet until two big chimneys block the way. The standard finish avoids these by traversing right to a low-angled slab. Go up the slab to a wide crack (belay), and then angle up and right to the ridge. FA: Werner Zimmerman climbed this route in the summer of 1919. Its second and better known ascent came in 1940 by Paul Hauk, Ernie Field, and Warren Gorrell. **Variation 1:** The lower portion of **Joe's Solo**, up the gully (described in the rock climbing section on pages 62 and 64), is occasionally lined with ice. A mixed route (WI 3 M3?) joining upper **Eighth Route** can be had in these conditions. **Variation 2:** At least one of the big chimneys at the top of the route has been climbed for a difficult direct finish (the left may be WI 4 while the right may be Wilford and Sherman's line). Climb the chimney with ice in the back until a constriction forces the leader to move out of the slot and onto the face (crux); continue to the top of the ridge. FA of direct finish: Mark Wilford and John Sherman, 1995. **Variation 3:** Climb left after the first two pitches along a ramp leading to the notch behind Zumie's Thumb (**Thumb Route**, FA: Grant and Jones, 1946, though a marked photo by Warren Gorrell dating from 1936 has this route delineated). Where it goes from there is

B-14
12
?
LOWER EAST FACE
B-17
B-16
B-13
B-15
B-12
B-11

not certain — either rappel south to reach the upper right fork of **Lambs Slide**, or try a line to the ridge of the Beaver (this was marked on Gorrell's photo, but it looks improbable). The easiest descent from the ridge hikes down to **The Loft**. If the summit is the goal, one can climb the Beaver (overlooking the Notch) and rappel 100 feet into the Notch (pick a finish described in that climb).

See Longs Peak overview photo (page 66) for routes **B-16** through **B-19**.

B-16 Notch Couloir II AI 2+ M3-

The obvious couloir on the left side of the Diamond is best climbed in summer or fall, and is usually approached via **Lambs Slide** and Broadway or **Alexander's Chimney**. The crux comes after a jog in the couloir at a short wall. The wall may be covered with good water ice, filled in with snow, or even require some harder mixed climbing. Easier snow with one short rock wall leads to the Notch. There are several methods of escape from the Notch: 1. Drop over to the south side of Longs (4th class), cross over the top of Keplinger's Couloir, and join the Homestretch. 2. Drop out of the Notch as above, but back track along **Clark's Arrow** to **The Loft**. 3. Traverse 30 feet right on the east side of Longs to an obvious weakness, follow that to the southeast ridge (5.5), and then continue to the summit. This is the standard finish (called **Stepladder**) and is quite enjoyable. Another option exits right below the Notch to join the upper section of **Kiener's Route**. Huge avalanches sweep the couloir in the winter and spring if conditions are bad. FA: J. W. Alexander may have soloed the general line of this route in 1922; the next day he repeated the feat with Jack Moomaw, beginning with **Alexander's Chimney**. It is unclear, however, whether these ascents took place in the couloir itself. A published account of the climb by Moomaw mentions "climbing out of the Notch Chimney," and photographs accompanying the tale show Alexander on a rock wall "above Broadway." This supports an ascent nearer to present day **Kiener's Route**, perhaps up the Notch Chimneys, which lie directly above and left of Kiener's Chimney (and which are a favorite route finding error while climbing **Kiener's**). Another (erroneously labeled) picture shows Table Ledge on the Diamond — this photo could only have been taken by traveling well to the right of the couloir (again, on or near present day **Kiener's**). Godfrey and Chelton's book *CLIMB!* gives credit to the seven member party listed in the FA of **Little Notch** (see **SE Ridge Variations** in High Peaks section), presumably garnering information from Warren Gorrell's 1936 marked photograph. It is not known whether any of these ascents chopped steps up the entire length of the couloir.

B-17 Kiener's Route III AI 2 M1+

A popular winter tour of the east face of Longs climbs up **Lambs Slide**, traverses right on Broadway and wanders up broken ground left of the Diamond. This route is described in more detail in the High Peaks chapter as a rock climb (see page 43). Though **Kiener's Route** is easy to moderate in difficulty, it should not be taken lightly in winter — escape is difficult, and a bad storm can make this a serious outing. First Descent of approximate line: Elkanah Lamb, 1871. FA: Walter Kiener, Agnes Vaille and Carl Blaurock, 1924.

B-18 Schobinger's Cracks II M6

Traverse Broadway from **Lambs Slide** past the bottom of **Notch Couloir** and belay at the base of a pronounced chimney, about 200 feet right. **Schobinger's Cracks** follows a narrower chimney on the right for a pitch, steps right to a crack leading to a ledge, and then follows the left-hand of two slots (this is called Eubanks' Chimney; look for a chockstone) to upper **Kiener's Route**. FA: This was first done in 1958 by Chuck Schobinger and John Amato as a rock climb. Will Gadd and Mark Twight did it as a mixed climb in 1996.

B-19 The Window III M4 (?) WI 4+

A giant, exfoliated flake, shaped like a K with a hole at its middle and located on the far left edge of the Diamond, is the namesake of this awesome route. Climb **North Chimney** (a disagreeable affair at best, see High Peaks chapter) and traverse left on Broadway for several hundred feet until directly below the Window. This point is more easily reached from **Lambs Slide**. Angle right toward the Diamond on easy ground to the base of double, right-facing corners, and ascend the left corner to a belay on top of a block (two half pitches, or one long pitch). Step down from the block and move right into the second corner, go up a short distance, then hand traverse right to the right-facing dihedral that forms the base of the K. One can also take the corner and arete above the block to a good ledge (80 feet), then traverse right to the K (4th class). When conditions permit (late spring and early fall), the slab below the Window is lined with exciting ice. Climb to a belay in the Window, then go through the hole and rappel south. Traverse left along a ledge and take the second chimney with a chockstone (this is Eubanks' Chimney) to the upper part of **Kiener's Route**. FA: Bill Eubanks and Brad Van Diver, 1950. **Variation:** A direct start, which may be best for an ice climbing ascent, begins 150 feet right of the normal route in a big, north-facing dihedral. Two pitches (mixed or WI 4+ depending on conditions) gain the base of the K. FA: Dale Johnson and Cary Husted, 1960.

B-20 The Cables AI 2 M2-

The north face of Longs Peak is the normal descent route for Diamond climbers in the summer, but in the winter, it becomes a classic mountaineering route. Hike up to the Boulderfield, then head south to Chasm View at the edge of the Diamond (see Longs Peak Overview topo, page 29). The route starts about 150 feet above Chasm View at a prominent right-facing dihedral. It is easy enough to reach the base in good conditions (3rd class), but in winter or spring it may be prudent to rope up for an approach pitch. The dihedral usually begins to ice over as early as September; by spring it is filled with snow (and is usually easy in these conditions). Climb the corner in one long pitch, passing two huge eyebolts along the way (may be buried in snow). Belay at the second one, or go a bit higher to a more comfortable stance. These eyebolts formerly anchored a $^5/_8$ inch stainless steel cable used for ascending the peak from 1925 until 1973. A second cable was installed immediately above the first belay, and although this pitch is much easier, a rope is still advisable. Scramble left from the first belay, then go back right into a low angled, left-facing corner, and belay from a nice ledge at the top of the corner. From here the difficulties taper off to 2nd and 3rd class climbing. The best route goes left from the second belay along a good ledge for several hundred feet. Climb along a faint rib from a point near the left end of the ledge, then angle left toward the summit, zigzagging as necessary to avoid short walls and slabs. The most common mistake is to continue too far along the good ledge beyond the faint rib — this leads to dangerous slabs, which fall directly to the edge of the Diamond. Reverse the route to descend, rappelling from the eyebolts in the dihedral. FA: Enos Mills, early 20th century, or perhaps Carlyle Lamb (Elkanah's son). The two were neighbors at the foot of the mountain, and worked together to build the first trail up the peak. Paul Nesbit's Longs Peak guide (first published in 1946) lists Mills as the first person to climb the North Face, but no date is given. He made his first ascent of Longs Peak in 1885, and owned the Longs Peak Inn by 1902 (he bought it from the younger Lamb), so it is possible he had climbed the relatively easy north face by this date. Godfrey and Chelton's book claims "about 1912." Mills also made the first winter ascent of Longs in 1903, and was instrumental in lobbying Congress to set aside land for Rocky Mountain National Park, which happened in 1915. Carlyle Lamb first climbed Longs with his family in September of 1879. When the north face received its first descent in 1922, the Estes Park paper wrote an article about the event, and recounted the history of the route: "Years ago Carlyle Lamb scaled this portion of the peak...and Enos Mills says he was able to make the climb, but not the descent." Though it's not clear from the article who made the trip first, Lamb had been living in the area for seven years longer than Mills, so perhaps credit should be given to him.

B-21 Left Dovetail II AI 2 M2-

The snowfield beneath the North Face is known as the Dove as it resembles a diving bird. This route climbs partway up the tail of the Dove to the toe of a low-angled rock buttress. Ascend the buttress toward a small snowpatch (see next route), and stay just left of it for a pitch that leads to a ledge. Traverse the ledge a bit, then up a wall to the summit slopes. FA: Warren Gorrell, Alene Wharton, and Watson, 1935.

B-22 Right Dovetail II AI 2+ M1

Climb the tail of the Dove to a headwall, then up a tight couloir, which leads to a small snowpatch in a bowl. Move onto the buttress left of the patch and climb a pitch of good rock to a ledge, then traverse right on this break all the way to a notch in the **Keyhole Ridge**. Follow that route (see page 89). FA: Melvin Wickens, 1930, though it may have been climbed by William Ervin and Bruns in 1925.

GLACIER GORGE TRAILHEAD

The heart of RMNP ice climbing lies in Glacier Gorge. Despite the tedious approach to most of the climbs, this area is quite popular. The routes are excellent, the views tremendous and the long ski out provides a welcome treat at the end of the day. The first 23 routes are located in Glacier Gorge; the remaining climbs are in Loch Vale (these are the two major valleys accessed by the Glacier Gorge trail system).

Travel Directions: Drive on Bear Lake Road to the Glacier Gorge Junction Trailhead, located inside a hairpin turn about a mile before the end of the road. The parking lot is small and fills up even in winter. Additional parking can be found 0.1

A typical weekend day on All Mixed Up, Glacier Gorge. No fewer than twelve climbers can be seen in this foreshortened photo.

LONGS PEAK - Lower East Face

B-12. Alexander's Chimney III WI 3 M3+ to M5-
B-13. Smear of Fear IV M6 WI 6-
B-15. Eighth Route III WI 3 M3

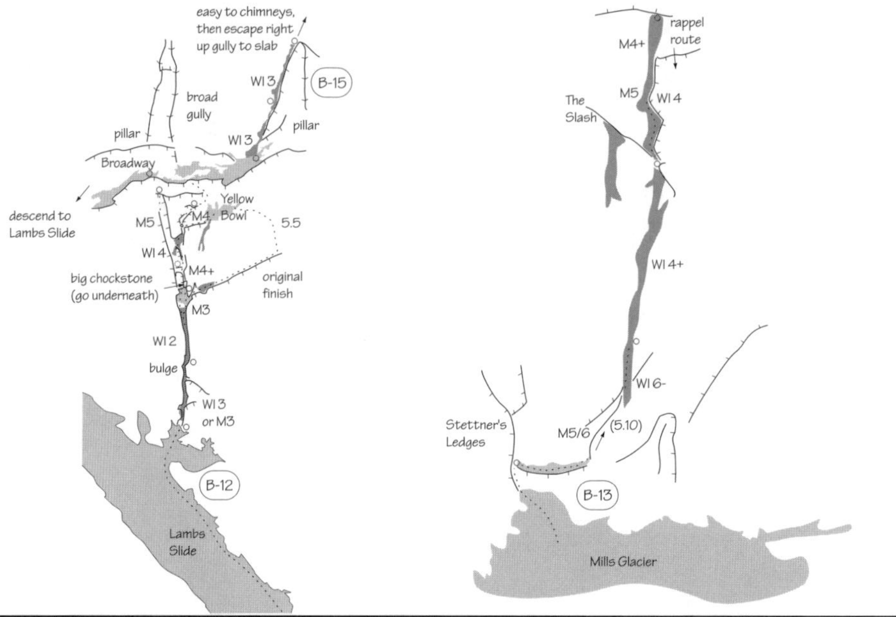

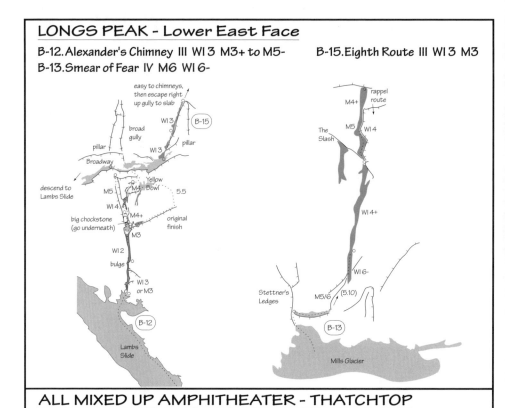

ALL MIXED UP AMPHITHEATER - THATCHTOP

C-2. All Mixed Up WI 4
C-3. Pipe Organ M4 WI 4+
C-4. Dazed and Confused WI 4+

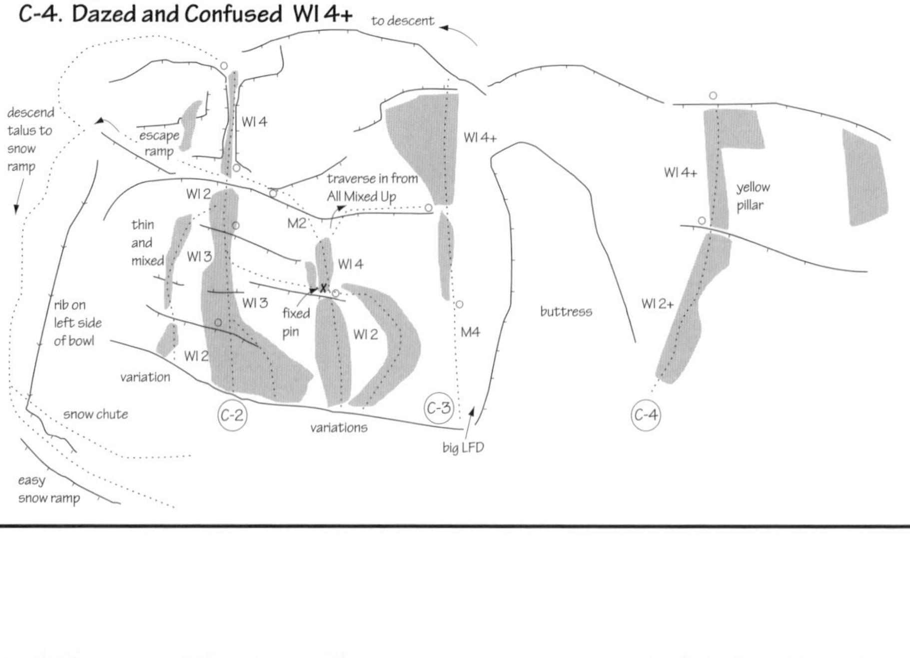

mile down the road or at the Bear Lake Trailhead (at the end of the road, one more mile). A 0.3 mile trail leading southeast from the Emerald Lake trail (which begins at Bear Lake) connects the two lots. Or, use a 0.25-mile trail from the east end of the Bear Lake parking lot — this isn't as well known, and may not be tracked in the winter.

Approach: The main trail heads south out of the lot toward Alberta Falls. It passes the North Longs Peak trail at 1.5 miles, and then hits a junction at 2.0 miles. This junction can be reached more quickly with a short cut that follows an unnamed creek on the north side of Glacier Knobs, and it is almost always tracked in winter. (The short cut can also be followed in summer with an old path that stays above the creek, though the Park Service frowns upon its use for some reason. It was built in 1921 as the standard route to Loch Vale, replacing a trail built by Abner Sprague in 1913, before the Park was born. The present day trail was built in 1927 to include scenic Alberta Falls in the trip to Loch Vale). At the junction, the right fork leads into Loch Vale on the north side of Thatchtop and ends at Sky Pond (4.5 miles), which is situated below the north face of Powell Peak and the east face of Taylor Peak. The left fork leads into Glacier Gorge, passes Mills and Jewel Lakes, and continues to Black Lake at 4.5 miles. A third trail very near to this junction leads to Lake Haiyaha, and then drops into Tyndall Gorge just below Dream Lake; all of these trails are signed.

C-1 Parking Lot Wall WI 3 to M6

A short cliff (100 feet high and visible from the parking lot) lies just west of the trail to Mills Lake about one tenth of a mile from the car. Bits and pieces of ice can be found in several locations; these are usually top roped due to poor protection. A hidden wall right of this (look for a perched boulder) also sports a few top ropes. It is best reached by leaving the trail at a boulder just past the first bridge — hike upstream for 100 yards, then angle left for a few minutes to the wall. These cliffs have also seen some rock climbing action in summer, though nothing of lasting merit has been recorded.

Thatchtop (Glacier Gorge side)

C-2 All Mixed Up III WI 4

This beautiful route goes up an iced over cliff band in the back of a bowl which lies on the northeast side of Thatchtop high above Mills Lake — the bowl also contains the next three lines. **All Mixed Up** can be seen from several spots along Bear Lake Road, though it may look like nothing more than a snow ribbon from this distance. Hike to Mills Lake and wallow up the eastern slope of Thatchtop above the south side (far end) of the lake. Often there is a trail beaten through the snow; expect a workout if the duty of breaking trail falls on your party. Three pitches of lower angled flows (WI 3) lead straight up to a snow ramp belay below the final crux pitch, a steep pillar in a chimney. Belay high on the second lead to avoid getting stranded on the snow ramp (which may have inadequate anchors in heavy snow). Descend the rib forming the south (left as you face the climb) side of the bowl, then take either of two snow chutes back to the base. This route has become extremely popular, and it's not unusual to find more than five parties in the area on the weekends. **Variations:** The lower pitches can be done in several ways: straight up the middle is the standard route; to the left is a smattering of icy slabs intermixed with rock; to the right one will encounter a few short, WI 4 curtains and a bit of mixed ground at the end; and further right a switchback ramp system can be followed. All of these end at the snow ramp, which can be traversed left to avoid the final pitch and the massive traffic jam on busy days. Note that there are at least two unnamed half-pitches of ice near the shores of Mills Lake. One is immediately right of the approach to **All Mixed Up** (WI 2+), and the other on the black wall at the north end of Mills Lake (thin and difficult, and forming only rarely; FA: Douglas Snively and Duncan Ferguson).

C-3 Pipe Organ II M4 WI 4+

The huge left-facing dihedral right of **All Mixed Up** sports a steep pillar and curtain of ice one pitch off the ground. Approach via a couple mixed pitches (on rare occasions ice will go all the way to the ground), or traverse in from the rightmost variation described in **All Mixed Up**. FA: Milan Proska and John Marrs, 1984.

C-4 Dazed and Confused WI 4+

This is a good route on the right side of the bowl that is also known as **Middle Finger of Dr. Wazz**. Look for a yellow pillar/curtain near the top of the face, and climb a long stretch of lower angled ice to reach it. Descend by walking south around the top of **All Mixed Up**, then join its descent. FA: Malcolm Daly and Larry Day, early 1980s, or perhaps John Marrs and Dan Bankard, 1984. **Variation:** Another short curtain lies right of the crux pillar (unclimbed?).

C-5 Overflow WI 3

Hike past Jewel Lake (which is just south of Mills Lake) and look for a 75 foot flow in the trees, low down on the east fact of Thatchtop. FA: Richard Rossiter, Ralph Baldwin and Tim Hogan, 1977.

Arrowhead and McHenrys (Solitude Lake Cirque)

The following four routes begin in the Shelf and Solitude Lakes cirque, which is the hanging valley between Thatchtop and Arrowhead, backed by McHenrys Peak.

C-6 Hourglass Couloir III AI 3 M3

The north face of Arrowhead (the spur originating from McHenrys Peak) holds a superb mixed route of moderate difficulty. The route comes into condition in late spring and usually lasts well into June. Hike (or ski) toward Black Lake, but head right across Glacier Creek (3.75 miles from the trailhead) where Shelf Creek comes in from the west. Climb the steep hill on the north side of Shelf Creek to reach Shelf Lake, then continue to Solitude Lake. Consider bivouacking here as the approach takes several hours and the route consists of eight pitches. Follow the obvious chimney line in the middle of the face straight to the summit, passing several chockstones in the lower chimney and a mixed band at midheight. A splendid, ice-filled slot on the left with seventy degree water ice leads to the upper snowfield. Descend into the Solitude Lake cirque from the summit via third class gullies and ramps (described in the rock climbing section under Arrowhead; see Descent Three).

C-7 Sister Sweetly III M4 AI 4

This route climbs the steep gully about 100 yards right of **Hourglass Couloir** in six pitches. The initial pitch consists of difficult mixed climbing, and is followed by a pitch of AI 4. Continue along easier ground above, then go straight up another section of M4. The final section works up a slab, and then bends left. A 60 meter rope was used on the first ascent, and all six leads are long. FA: Jon Allen and Clay Wadman.

C-8 North Face Direct III M4 AI 4+

This line climbs the north face of McHenrys Peak, beginning at the back of the hanging valley which holds Shelf and Solitude Lakes. Hike beneath the previous two routes, and begin at an ice chimney which leads to the first of three obvious snow bands. The route's ten pitches alternate between mixed climbing and alpine ice as it passes through the snow bands, and finishes on the north ridge right of the actual summit. Descend the next route, or climb over McHenrys' summit and down its southeast ridge to Stone Man Pass. From there, a snowfield leads to the broad plateau above Black Lake. FA: Bill Feiges and Peter Metcalf, 1979.

C-9 McHenrys Notch II AI 2 4th class

The wide couloir at the back end of the Solitude Lake cirque leads directly to a prominent notch on McHenrys' north ridge. Follow the ridge (4th class) to the summit, descend the southeast ridge to Stone Man Pass (3rd class), then drop into the plateau above Black Lake.

Black Lake

Routes **C-10** through **C-16** are situated below and around the shores of Black Lake.

C-10 Reflections WI 3

Several ice climbs form on the cliff bands below Black Lake, east of the final steep slope that leads into the Black Lake basin. The most obvious is a two-pitch route up thin ice on a long slab followed by a tiered section. Short pillars and slabs can be found on either side of this line.

C-11 Scotty M4- WI 4

Named for its similarity to mixed climbs in Scotland, this route climbs a wide, iced over crack/chimney (one long pitch) right of **Reflections**.

C-12 Black Lake Ice WI 2 to 3

The broad slab southeast of the lake (just right of the summer trail to Spearhead) holds a thick sheet of classic blue ice that reliably forms up every winter. Pick any of several lines up the slab (WI 2) and finish with short walls and pillars at the top (up to WI 3). Walk toward Longs Peak and back down to the base.

C-13 West Gully II WI 4

The **West Gully** is the best route in the Black Lake basin. Located in a channel above the west end of the lake, it consists of a low-angled pitch to a steep pillar. Above the crux, two hundred feet of iced-over slabs lead out of the basin onto the plateau below McHenrys Peak. Descend as for **Black Lake Ice** or down ramps and gullies below Arrowhead. This area is subject to slab avalanches. FA: Duncan

Ferguson. **Variation:** A narrow chimney left of **West Gully** holds the southern inlet to Black Lake (coming from Frozen Lake). It appears as though it would be a classic ice climb in late fall — perhaps it fills in with snow and thus has never been reported.

C-14 Stone Man WI 5

This is the left-hand of the two thin pillars right of **West Gully**. Two pitches of thin, brittle ice end on a ramp below Arrowhead. Scramble off right.

C-15 Yellow Tears WI 5

The yellow ice pillar right of **Stone Man** provides an exciting lead. Several thin slabs right of **Yellow Tears** may provide additional attractions.

C-16 Blue Moon WI 5

A forty foot icicle occasionally hangs over a rock band above and right of the previous line.

The last seven routes in Glacier Gorge are situated on the walls surrounding the plateau above Black Lake.

Chiefs Head

C-17 Slant Gully III M2 AI 2

This is the left-leaning gully system above the right side of the Northeast Face of Chiefs Head (see photo page 103). Approach by hiking left of Spearhead, and then climb easy mixed ground (with poor protection) for 300 feet on the far right side of the face. This leads to the slanting gully, which is followed up left for 800 feet to the east ridge of Chiefs Head (AI 2). Walk to the summit, and descend to Stone Man Pass, or descend the snow gully between Pagoda and Chiefs Head. Best conditions are found in late winter and spring.

C-18 Central Rib II M4- (?)

This route climbs the vague arete dropping down from the summit of Chiefs Head to the saddle behind Spearhead. It was reported as 5.7 in the DuMais guide, though it was climbed first in winter. Hike around the right side of Spearhead and scramble up to the saddle at the base of the rib. The first half of the rib is easy going, and ends at a big shelf; an escape right over the top of the Northwest Face of Chiefs Head is possible from here. Otherwise, continue along the arete for several pitches. Bruce Spozi and Ron Matous, 1975.

C-19 April Fools II M6

This route and **May Day** are located about half way between the Northwest Face of Chiefs Head and Stone Man Pass. Look for a stepped, left-facing dihedral with a snow patch above it left of long roof on a smooth wall. Climb the dihedral (M6) to the snow patch and belay. The second pitch ascends steep snow toward a roof, then goes right under the roof to a smear of ice. Continue along a narrow groove for 100 feet to belay on the right. Rappel the route to descend. FA: Eric Winkelman and Michael Bearzi, 1996.

C-20 May Day II M5

Locate a chimney system fifty feet right of the long roof on the smooth wall (see above), and traverse into it from the right along a sloping ledge, M3. The crux pitch follows the left side of the chimney, pulls through a roof at the top, and belays to the right on a long ledge. Go back left on the last pitch to a right-facing dihedral, then follow the chimney. Rappel the route to descend. FA: Bill Myers and Eric Winkelman, 1994.

McHenrys Peak (East Face)

See photo on page 130, and topo on page 131, in the High Peaks section.

C-21 Snow Bench II M3 AI 2

This fun mixed route follows the obvious left-leaning snow ramp in the middle of the east face of McHenrys Peak. A winter ascent involves much snow groveling; do it in late fall or spring. Begin below the summit near the high point of the snowfield that lies below the face. Angle up left on rock to reach the ramp — there are several choices here. Follow the ramp all the way to the notch in the ridgeline and continue to the summit, or descend to Stone Man Pass. FA: Ernie Kuncl and John Deeming, 1965. **Variation:** Go straight up near the top of the ramp into the steeper, right fork couloir (M4?).

C-22 Big Mac Couloir III M4- AI 4-

Climb **Snow Bench** to the ramp, but head straight up where that route angles left. Follow the long couloir left of an evident buttress (mixed) all the way to the summit headwall. Escape right to the 4th class northeast ridge, or aid up the headwall (A1). Descend along the southeast ridge to Stone Man Pass and down to Black Lake. FA: Joe Hladick and Scott Kimball, 1979.

C-23 Right Gully III M4 AI 4+

This route also begins with **Snow Bench**, but it traverses right underneath the large buttress to a gully on its right side. Follow the gully to the top of the buttress (with several ice steps) to an impasse at a headwall (a pitch below the summit headwall). Traverse left on a sloping ledge system to intersect **Big Mac Couloir**. FA: Joe Kaelin and party.

The remaining routes accessed from the Glacier Gorge Trailhead are in Loch Vale, the long valley north of Thatchtop. The first eleven of these are found in a ravine known as Loch Vale Gorge. Loch Vale Gorge is located above Icy Brook, about one-quarter mile below The Loch, on the north side of Thatchtop.

Loch Vale Gorge

Approach: Follow the Glacier Gorge trail for two miles to the junction (or the winter short cut mentioned in the introductory material to Glacier Gorge). Take the right fork toward The Loch for a quarter mile, and leave the trail just before the first switchback — the climbs are visible a short distance to the south, just across Icy Brook. The switchback is, of course, covered with snow in winter, and the winter snowshoe trail usually bypasses it altogether by following Icy Brook, but Loch Vale Gorge is easy to find as it has become very popular and a trail will likely lead up to it. Routes are described from left to right. Many of the climbs in Loch Vale Gorge have multiple names; to avoid confusion, only one was chosen and the others are not listed.

John Gillett hooking across to *Mixed Emotions*, Loch Vale Gorge.

LOCH VALE GORGE

C-24. Mixed Emotions M6- WI4+
C-25. Strike Free Zone M7+ WI 5
C-26. Blade Runner M8 WI 5+
C-27. Gorge Yourself WI 3-
C-28. Low Tide WI 1
C-29. Short Cut WI 3
C-30. Glass Curtain M5+
C-31. Loch Ness Monster WI 4+
C-32. Lochluster M3
C-33. Young Dracula WI 4
C-34. The Delicate Straw WI 5

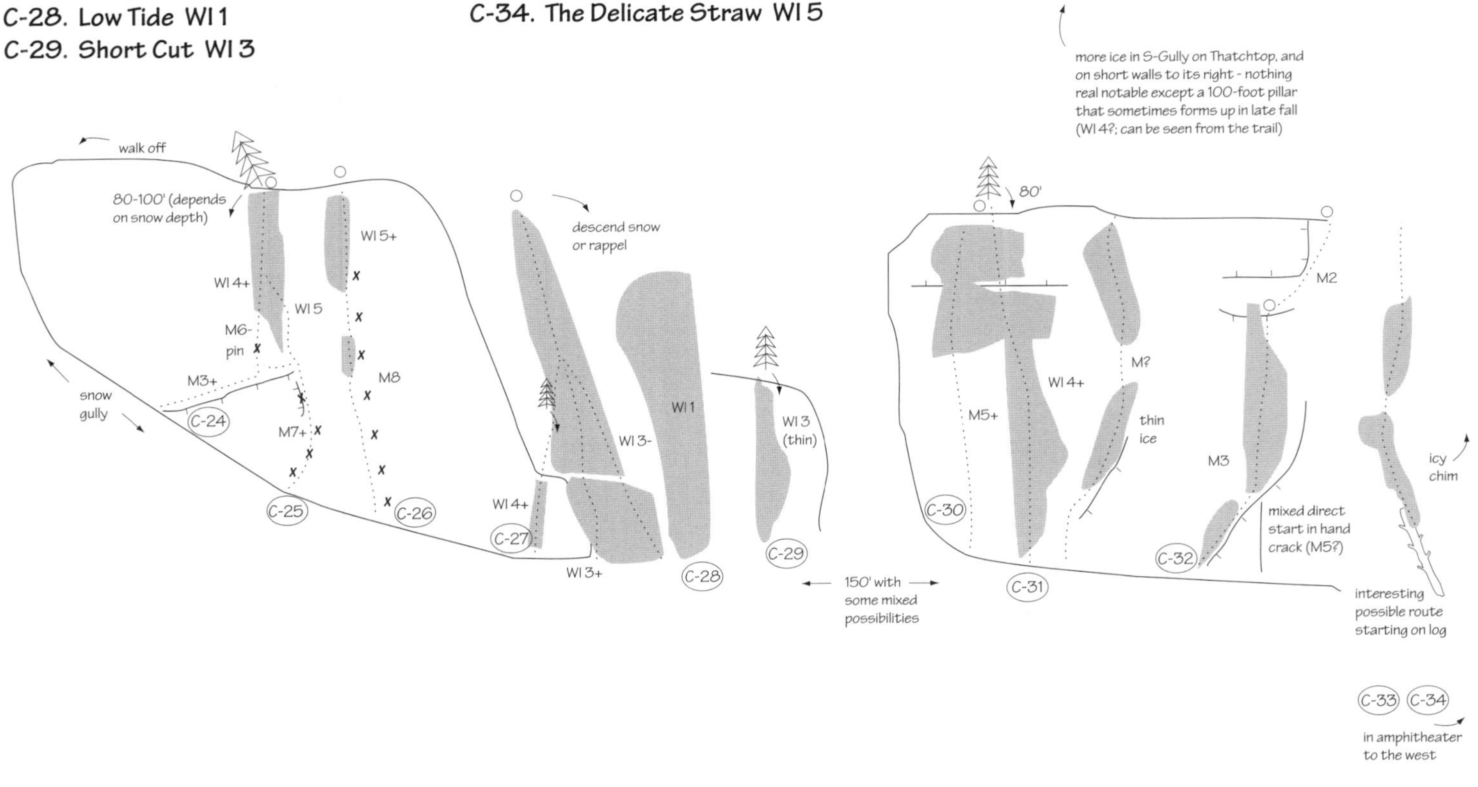

C-24 Mixed Emotions M6- WI 4+

An undercut cliff on the left side of the area hosts three brilliant mixed routes. Look for a forty foot swath of ice that ends abruptly some sixty feet above the ground. Reach the ice by performing a long hand traverse from the left along a horizontal break (light rack including a #4 Friend). Dry tool straight up past a fixed piton, hook the ice, and struggle over a bulge. The angle tips back to comfortable, steep ice (WI 4+ when fully formed) after the bulge. Rappel from a large tree, which leans out over the top of the climb, or walk east to the top of the snow ramp that lies beneath the route. FA: Alex Lowe and Dave Gustafson, 1981.

C-25 Free Strike Zone M7+ WI 5

This is a difficult (and somewhat run out) direct start to the ice on **Mixed Emotions**. Climb thirty feet of overhanging rock past three bolts, one fixed pin, and a few cam placements to a no hands rest. A few more rock moves up and left gains the ice on its right side or join **Mixed Emotions**, less run out. FA: Dave Sheldon, 1996.

C-26 Blade Runner M8

Blade Runner is the most difficult mixed pitch in RMNP to date. It begins with sixty feet of overhanging rock right of the previous route (protected by three bolts and four fixed pins) and finishes with forty feet of poor ice. Descend by rappelling from a tree, or walk down east. FA: Gary Ryan, 1997.

C-27 Gorge Yourself WI 3-

The cliff on which the previous three lines reside ends at a snowy bowl to the right. The left side of this bowl features a pitch of ice that fades into the snow higher up; the length of the climb is dependent upon current snow depth. **Variation:** The climb can be made more difficult with a short, steep section on the left (usually about WI 3+) or a more difficult hanging pillar further left.

C-28 Low Tide WI 1

An easy route up the middle of the bowl often forms up in early season, but gets covered with snow later on.

C-29 Short Cut WI 3

A short pitch to a pine may be present on the right side of the bowl.

C-30 Glass Curtain M5+

Another cliff rises above the creek right of the snowy bowl mentioned above. Its left side harbors a nice pillar of ice and a wide curtain above it. This route climbs difficult mixed terrain to get to the left side of the curtain, and then goes straight up. FA: Jim Detterline, late 1980s.

C-31 Loch Ness Monster WI 4+

This popular line climbs the pillar of ice mentioned in **Glass Curtain**. The approach trail leads directly to its base, and trees on top provide anchors for rappelling (or top roping).

C-32 Lochluster M3

Begin right of **Loch Ness Monster** at an icy ramp which trends right to join up with a flow that leads to a belay alcove. Rappel from slings around a questionable block, or do another short pitch up and right into the trees, then scramble down west.

C-33 Young Dracula WI 4

An amphitheater west of **Lochluster** holds a couple short lines. **Young Dracula** climbs an iced up corner on the left side of the amphitheater for forty feet. FA: Detterline.

C-34 The Delicate Straw WI 5

This route climbs a pencil of ice on the right side of the amphitheater described above. FA: Detterline.

Hike to The Loch to reach routes **C-35** through **C-41**.

Thatchtop (Loch Vale side)

C-35 Deep Freeze III WI 6- M4+

A deep chimney system cuts through the buttresses above and right of Lakeside Wall (which is described in the rock climbing section, page 147). **Deep Freeze** begins one hundred yards left of the next route with two pitches of mixed climbing (M4+) in the lower chimney followed by two easier pitches of WI 3. The final pitch is a spectacular telephone pole of ice leading up to and over a roof, protected by a good crack running alongside it (to determine the condition of the upper

Vanquished Buttress
LOCH VALE
C-42
C-43
C-44
C-45
C-46
Lake of Glass

pillar, walk around the north shore of The Loch until it comes into view). Rappel the route to the top of the second pitch, and then traverse west along a ledge to the top of the rappels on **Necrophilia**, or traverse off east from the top of the route to an easy gully leading back to the base of the wall. Bring rock gear. FA: Alex Lowe and Eric Winkelman, 1982. **Variations:** An alternate start begins with **Necrophilia**, or one can traverse in from the far right over the top of **Necrophilia**. The buttress left of the chimney was taken on the first ascent (5.7 rock), and it may be possible to skirt even this by hiking up the gully just right of Lakeside Wall for several hundred feet to a traverse across a wide sloping shelf (this last option should be scoped out before committing to it).

C-36 Necrophilia WI 5 M6

Several terraced cliff bands wrap around the north face of Thatchtop just above the south shore of The Loch, 2.5 miles from the trailhead. Thin sheets of brittle ice in a left-facing corner usually form two pitches of scary mixed climbing on the lower band. Bring rock gear. Scramble off west, rappel from fixed anchors, or join **Deep Freeze** (if it's in). Best conditions are usually found in late fall; high winds often whittle away the route by mid-winter. FA: Eric Aldrich and Dakers Gowans, 1980s (?).

C-37 Broken Axes III M5 WI 5-

This route begins above and right of **Necrophilia** and follows an iced-over offwidth and chimney system for three or four pitches. Approach by climbing **Necrophilia**, or scramble in from the west. Rappel the route to descend. FA: Mike Bearzi and Jack Roberts, 1996. Duncan Ferguson climbed another route in the area at an earlier date (could be the same line).

C-38 Northwest Face III AI 3 to 4

A long (partially hidden) gully system scores the left side of the northwest face of Thatchtop. Mostly moderate terrain follows the gully line for several pitches, with crux sections found at a few bulging walls. This is right of **Broken Axes**. FA: R. Grange and R. Greenman, 1981.

The Loch Area

C-39 The Crypt WI 4

A steep curtain of good ice forms on a short wall north of The Loch. The left pillar is more difficult (WI 4+), while the center and right options are prone to avalanches from the gully above.

C-40 Freezer Burn WI 4

One quarter mile west of **The Crypt** is another short cliff band with at least two ice pillar routes. **Freezer Burn** takes the right pillar for 80 feet. Rappel from trees or scramble off southwest.

C-41 Cold Storage WI 4

This is the left-hand of the two pillars mentioned above; it is shorter (60 feet) and a bit easier.

The remaining routes in Loch Vale all begin in the vicinity of Sky Pond. Follow the trail past The Loch for a half mile, cross Andrews Creek, and go left at a trail junction (the right trail contours around the north side of Cathedral Wall and ends at Andrews Tarn below Andrews Glacier; it is sometimes used as a descent for the climbs on Taylor Peak). The left trail passes Lake of Glass shortly before reaching Sky Pond. Climbs are described counterclockwise around the Sky Pond basin.

Powell Peak Area

C-42 Vanquished IV WI 5+ M5+

This route climbs the north face of an unnamed, minor summit on the ridge between Thatchtop and Powell Peak, southeast from Sky Pond, and left of the next route. It is very sustained in its difficulty, climbing an iced up dihedral system for five hard pitches; the best conditions usually occur in late spring or fall. Look for a direct line of ice about 75 feet left of a huge right-facing corner that is in the middle of the wall. The first pitch is the crux: climb a verglas slab (WI 5+), make difficult moves past a chockstone (M5), then belay on a ramp. The remainder of the route goes straight up the corner system from here (with pitches of M5, WI 4, WI 5, and WI 4 M5, see topo next page), ending well below the top of the subpeak at an area of lower angled slabs. Descend by traversing right (toward Taylor Peak, 4th class, one rappel), or continue for 500 feet to the top of the buttress. The quickest descent from the top heads down tricky and exposed slabs (4th class) toward Thatchtop, then back down an easier gully to Sky Pond. It is also possible to descend the north fork of the **Thatchtop-Powell Icefield** if conditions allow. FA: Michael Bearzi and Bill Myers, 1991.

C-43 Thatchtop-Powell Icefield II AI 2+

This is the evident, forked snow route located above Sky Pond between the summits of Thatchtop and Powell Peak. The lower portion is straightforward; either side of the upper fork involves steeper snow/ice (AI 2+ to 3), although the left is usually easier. Both options become more difficult in icy fall conditions. The descent from Powell is problematic, involving a long, but easy hike around the summit of Taylor and down Andrews Glacier; a down climb of Taylor Glacier; a 4th class scramble down the buttress left of Taylor Glacier (difficult to find the correct line); or either of the options from the top of the ridge described in **Vanquished**. It may be easiest to descend the route just climbed. In the summer of 1998, a huge fracture cut across the entire icefield (the slab avalanche that followed must have been tremendous), leaving an eight foot overhang. It looked as though an entire season of snow slid down to a poor layer beneath. **Variation:** Branch right from the lower slope into a direct chimney line, which goes to the summit of Powell Peak. Mixed rock and ice (M4) lead up the chimney for several pitches.

C-44 North Gully III AI 3 M4

North Gully cuts up the right side of the north face of Powell Peak, beginning a few hundred yards west of the previous route. After an easy section of low angled snow, the gully tightens to an overhanging impasse. Exit right on the gully wall (M4) until it is possible to traverse back left into the gully, and then continue up. Several options are available for the descent (see the previous two climbs). FA: Dakers Gowans and party, 1975.

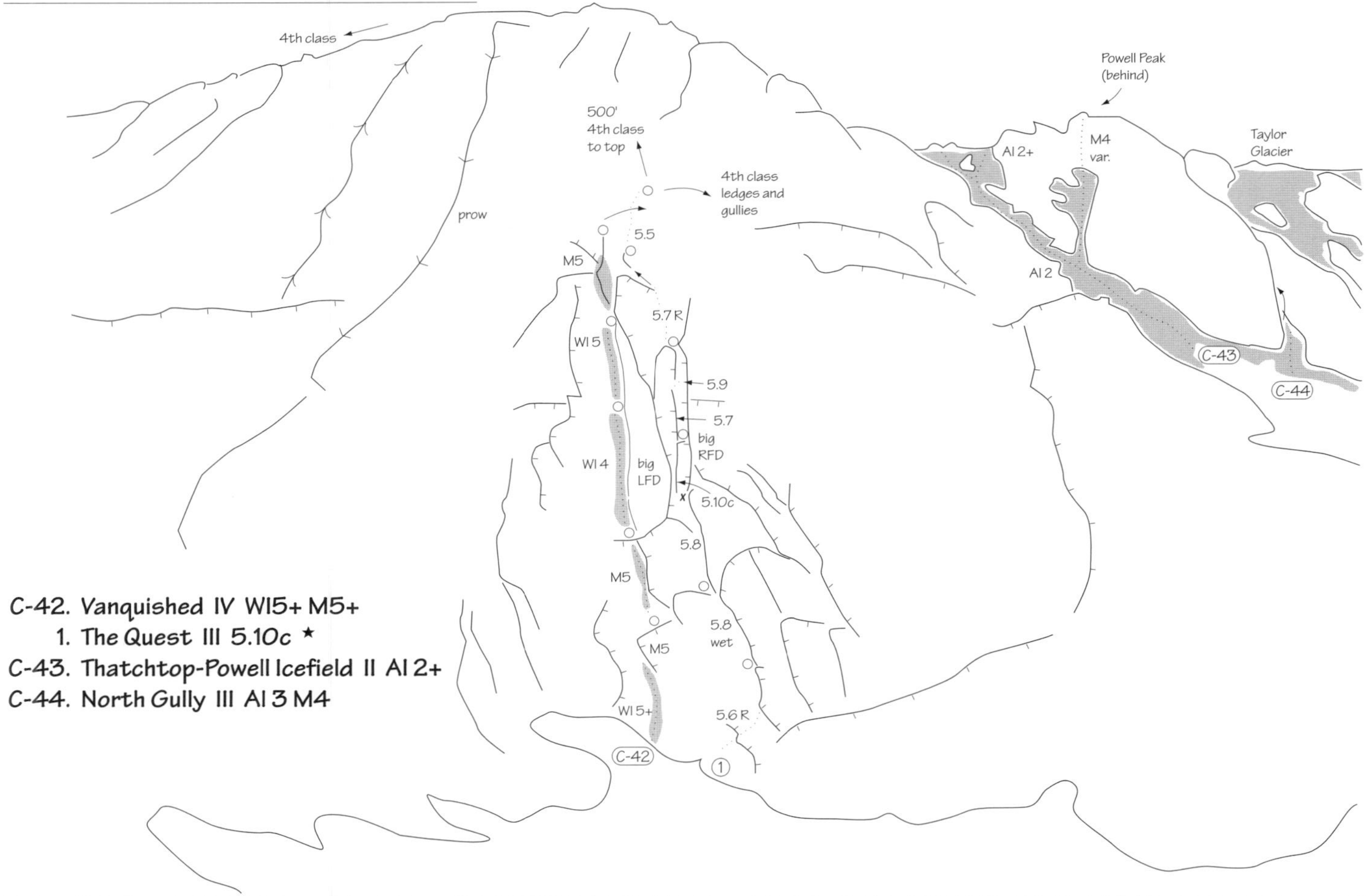

C-42. Vanquished IV WI5+ M5+
1. The Quest III 5.10c ★
C-43. Thatchtop-Powell Icefield II AI 2+
C-44. North Gully III AI 3 M4

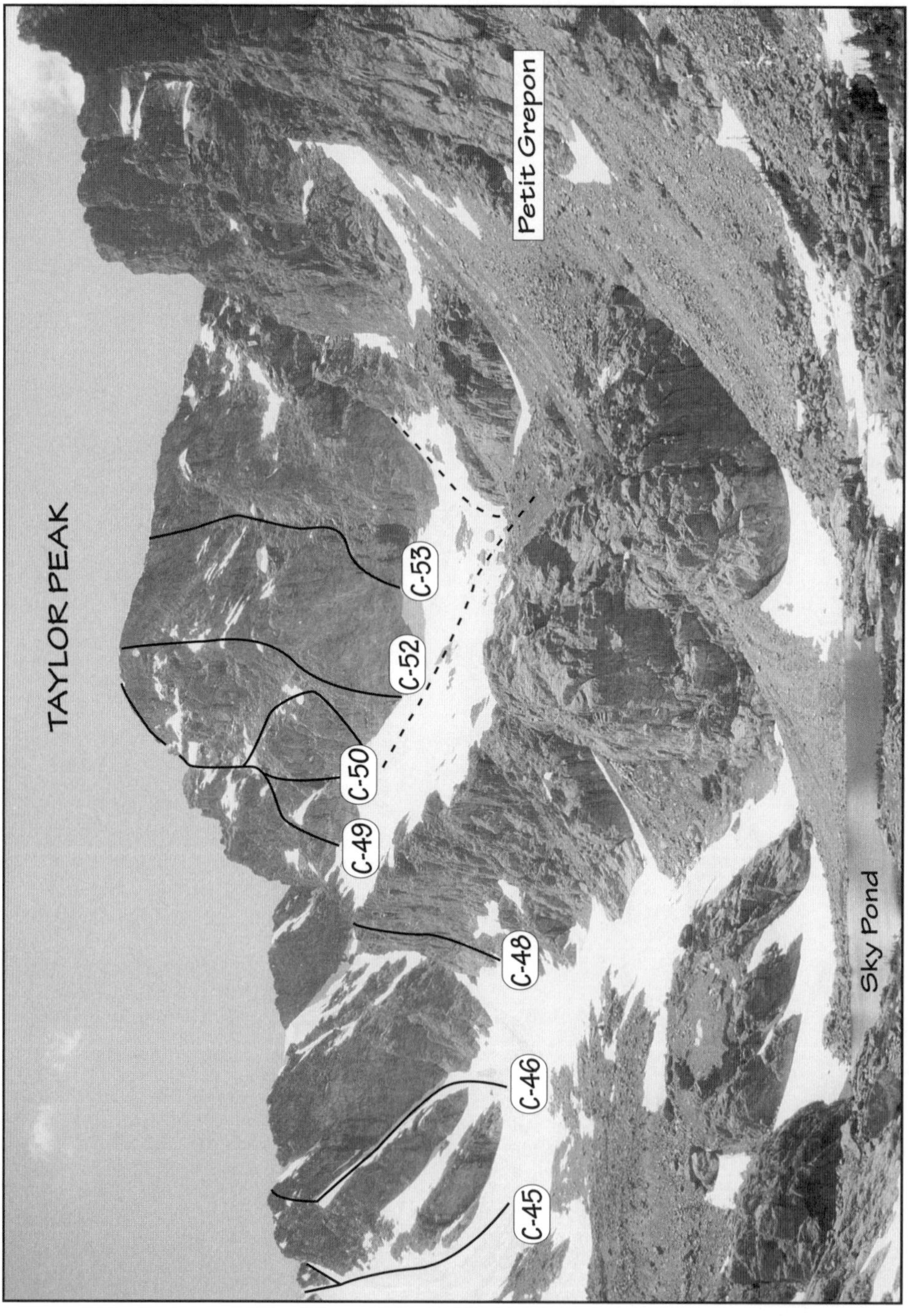
TAYLOR PEAK
Petit Grepon
C-53
C-52
C-50
C-49
C-48
C-46
C-45
Sky Pond

Taylor Peak

C-45 Taylor Glacier II AI 2

Taylor Glacier sits at the very end of Loch Vale, leading to the low point between Powell and Taylor Peaks. Most of the route involves easy snow travel; the difficulty of the last bit to the saddle, where there are a few options, is largely dependent upon the condition (or absence) of the cornice. Experienced skiers descend this route in late spring. Walk off by climbing over the summit of Taylor and down Andrews Glacier.

C-46 Taylor Glacier Buttress II AI 2 M2

A prominent, snow covered ramp slants from right to left on the buttress immediately right of **Taylor Glacier**. Hike past the bottom of the glacier to access the ramp, and follow it for six pitches. The entire route may be filled in with snow, but normally a pitch of mixed climbing is necessary half way up the ramp. Continue to the summit of Taylor, and then descend Andrews Glacier. FA: Michael Covington and B. Hostetler, 1970s.

C-47 New Sensations III M5+

This line is hidden from view for most of the approach, as it climbs a chimney up a south-facing buttress on the left side of Taylor Peak. Hike beyond the start of the previous two routes into the gully between the Taylor Glacier buttress and the main mass of the peak. Locate an obvious chimney system on the right side about 300 feet up the gully, and ascend it for 800 feet. The crux sections are well protected mixed moves over chockstones; the route comes into condition in late spring or fall, if at all. FA: Bearzi and Meyers, 1991.

C-48 South Face II 5.10 WI 5

A long snow ramp on top of a cliff band lies beneath the massive east face of Taylor Peak. This route climbs an ice chimney in the middle of the band and ends on the left end of the snow ramp near the beginning of the next route. Begin with a pitch of 5.10 rock to reach the ice, then follow the chimney to the ramp. Rappel the route, continue with a climb on the upper face, or walk down the ramp. FA: Charlie Fowler and party, 1980s?

The following six routes climb the east face proper of Taylor Peak, and all begin on a snowfield that rests atop a cliff band below the face (the same cliff band described in **South Face**). Arrive at the right end of the snow ramp by hiking around the right side of Sky Pond, up the valley, and through a break in the cliff band. Descend from the summit of Taylor by walking down its northwest slope to Andrews Glacier, or by scrambling down the gully on the north side of the east face (3rd class). A few of these routes were put up in the summer, but the face is broken in general, and lends itself to mixed winter climbing.

C-49 South Ridge II M2 (5.0 in summer)

Start near the left end of the snow ramp and locate a notch in the skyline. The route goes up for a steep pitch, and then slants right on terraced ground to reach the bowl beneath the notch. Head for the notch, then follow the south ridge. FA: Paul Mayrose, 1970.

C-50 Quicksilver III M3+

Begin directly beneath the notch mentioned above (at the high point of the snowfield) and trend left for a pitch to a left-leaning ledge. The ledge system leads into a gully, which is followed straight up to the bowl under the notch. Join **South Ridge** to finish. FA: Harry Kent, Michael Covington, and Casey Swanson, 1974. **Variations:** Two variations are available for the initial pitches. The first (M5) begins just right of the normal start and goes straight up a trough to a large corner in a headwall. Climb right up the headwall, pass a roof, and lead through mixed ground to a belay at a large boulder. Angle left to join **South Ridge**. FA: Rick Strong and John Marrs, 1987. The other variation begins further right and angles up a ramp/gully toward the central buttress, then back left over the top of the headwall and on up to the notch.

C-51 Central Buttress Left III 5.8

The first ascent of this line was done in the summer; it is not known if it has seen a winter ascent. A prominent belay ledge lies one pitch off the snowfield left of the prow on **Central Buttress**. Pick one of several similar, gray dihedrals that lead to the ledge and climb (5.8) to the belay. Follow small dihedrals up for another pitch (5.7), then climb two pitches of 4th class rock to the left side of an outcropping on the buttress. Avoid the bulge on the left and go to a belay at the base of a chimney. Follow this past an overhang, then climb past a ledge to a twenty foot block. Two long pitches (4th class) followed by two short pitches (5.6) end at the very summit. FA: Greg Sievers and Rob Cassidy, 1994.

C-52 Central Buttress IV M4 (or 5.8)

A rock climb from the 1950s, **Central Buttress** is better known as a mixed climb in the winter. The route begins in a difficult chimney that slants up and right to reach the major prow in the middle of the east face, and then follows the prow for a pitch. At this point an escape is possible to the left by going all the way to the notch on **South Ridge**. However, the route continues up the prow for several moderate pitches to the base of a steep headwall, which lies below the summit. The headwall can be climbed directly (5.8 A1) or may be bypassed to the right (?). FA: Fonda and party, 1950.

C-53 East Face Right IV M4 A1

This route climbs the huge bowl between the central prow and a smaller prow to the right. A snow tongue reaches up into the bottom of the bowl; begin on its upper left side. Angle right for several pitches to reach the upper bowl, then trend a bit left on the second half of the route to a final headwall. A bit of aid is employed on the headwall before the summit ridge is reached. Good belay ledges and anchors are scarce on this route. FA: Harry Kent and Joe Hladick, 1970s.

C-54 Far Right Gully III M4

Start at the right end of the snow ramp and head right into the bottom of the descent gully that drops down along the north side of the east face. Look for a deep chimney system on the left wall of the gully. The route climbs the chimney (M4) and easier ground above it to reach the summit ridge. FA: Kent and Hladick, 1970s.

Cathedral Spires and Cathedral Wall

C-55 Left Gully II M2+ AI 2
Climb the snow gully left of Stiletto, the furthest west of the Cathedral Spires. A mixed band at midheight provides the crux.

C-56 Womb with a View III WI 5 M6-
This difficult route climbs the huge chimney on the left side of the #2 Buttress on Cathedral Wall (see photo page 168 in the High Peaks section). Start with three hundred feet of easy ground left of the chimney, then traverse to a belay inside. Three mixed pitches lead to a large cave. Climb the right wall of the cave for thirty feet to access an ice curtain and belay on a small ledge behind the curtain. The first ascent team cut a hole in the ice, then squeezed through to a belay ledge. A final pitch reaches the top of the chimney. Scramble off west. FA: Bearzi and Myers, 1991.

BEAR LAKE TRAILHEAD

The ice climbs of Tyndall Gorge (between Hallett and Flattop) and Odessa Gorge (between Flattop and Notchtop) are easily accessed from the Bear Lake Trailhead, which is at the end of Bear Lake Road. See travel directions under Glacier Gorge in the rock climbing section, pages 93-94.

Approach: To reach Tyndall Gorge, follow the trail to Emerald Lake. This trail heads left before reaching Bear Lake (which is just one hundred yards from the parking lot), and climbs past Nymph Lake at 0.5 mile, Dream Lake at 1.1 miles, and ends at Emerald Lake (1.8 miles). Note that an auxiliary path branches southeast (left and downhill) from the Emerald Lake trail at 0.1 mile; it is used to reach the Glacier Gorge Junction Trailhead.

For climbs in Odessa Gorge, hike west from the parking lot and go around the right side of Bear Lake for one hundred yards to a sign that marks the Flattop trail. Turn right here, then switchback left at a fork in the trail about 0.25 miles further on (the right trail goes to Bierstadt Lake). Another fork appears a short mile from the trailhead; the left branch goes to the summit of Flattop Mountain while the right branch heads into Odessa Gorge. At about three miles, the trail descends briefly to Lake Helene and, after a sharp right turn, descends more rapidly into the gorge toward Odessa Lake. Do not follow the trail at the sharp turn; the point of departure for all climbs in this area (the last eight listed below) is Lake Helene.

Bear Lake

D-1 Bear Lake Ice WI 2+
A little cliff above the northwest side of Bear Lake usually sports a short pitch of ice followed by a snowy trough; it is visible from the east shore of the lake. Several other short bouldering and mixed opportunities usually form up in this area as well.

Nymph Lake

The following five routes are found on an eighty foot cliff west of Nymph Lake, about 25 minutes (0.5 mile) from the trailhead. An easy hike off the cliff to the northeast allows for convenient top rope access and is also the descent, but the sloping shelf above the climbs should be avoided during periods of high avalanche danger — everything right of **The Road Less Traveled** slid in 1998. If the conditions found during the winter of 1997-98 are the norm, most of the routes are thin and somewhat difficult to protect on the lead, and they may be obscured by snow. Routes are described from right to left.

Approach: After reaching the lake, follow the summer trail around its east and north sides (often there is a trail though the snow on the south side of the lake that avoids this loop). The summer trail cuts directly beneath the wall as it climbs to the Nymph Lake overlook.

D-2 The Road Less Traveled M3
A large pine tree grows next to an alcove/overhang on the right side of the wall; its shelter makes for a convenient gearing up spot. This route climbs several ice bulges right of the tree and ends with a sketchy slab. Wade through snow to a belay at a big tree fifteen feet higher. FA: Douglas Snively, Jerry Hill, and Bernard Gillett, 1997.

D-3 Urinalysis WI 5-
This problem is difficult enough to be interesting, but short enough to ignore. Begin just left of the large pine mentioned above, and climb a pole of yellow ice dangling from an overhang to two big pines 30 feet up the wall. Rappel from here, or continue more easily to the top. FA: Gillett, 1998.

D-4 On the Rocks M3+
Two ribbons of thin ice flow down the middle of the wall, about thirty feet left of **Urinalysis**; they may be covered by snow. The left ribbon ends with icicles hanging over a bulge. Begin either ribbon by traversing in from the right along a rock ramp (bring stoppers), and then head for three small trees at the top. FA: Gillett, Jerry Hill and Snively top roped the line in 1997; Gillett and Chris Hill led it in 1998 (a week later). **Variation:** An excellent direct start dry tools through the right side of the bulge past two bolts and a fixed wire (M6/M6+, bring quick draws and short screws).

D-5 Get a File M7-
This thin smear 25 feet left of **On the Rocks** starts with difficult dry tooling and finishes at a rappel tree. The crux at the bottom becomes a bit shorter later in the winter when snow piles up at the base. Bring a couple short screws to supplement a fixed pin and three bolts. One can also continue beyond the tree up a short ice flow and belay at an aspen back from the edge, but the slope above the climb is prone to avalanche. FA: Gillett and Sean McMahan, 1998.

D-6 Icecapade WI 3-
This is the very short flow on the left side of the wall that leads to an obvious snow ramp. Belay at a group of large trees and descend the ramp, or continue up right (easy). FA: Jerry Hill, Gillett, and Snively, 1997.

D-2. The Road Less Traveled M3
D-3. Urinalysis WI 5-
D-4. On The Rocks M3+
D-5. Get a File M7-
D-6. Icecapade WI 3-

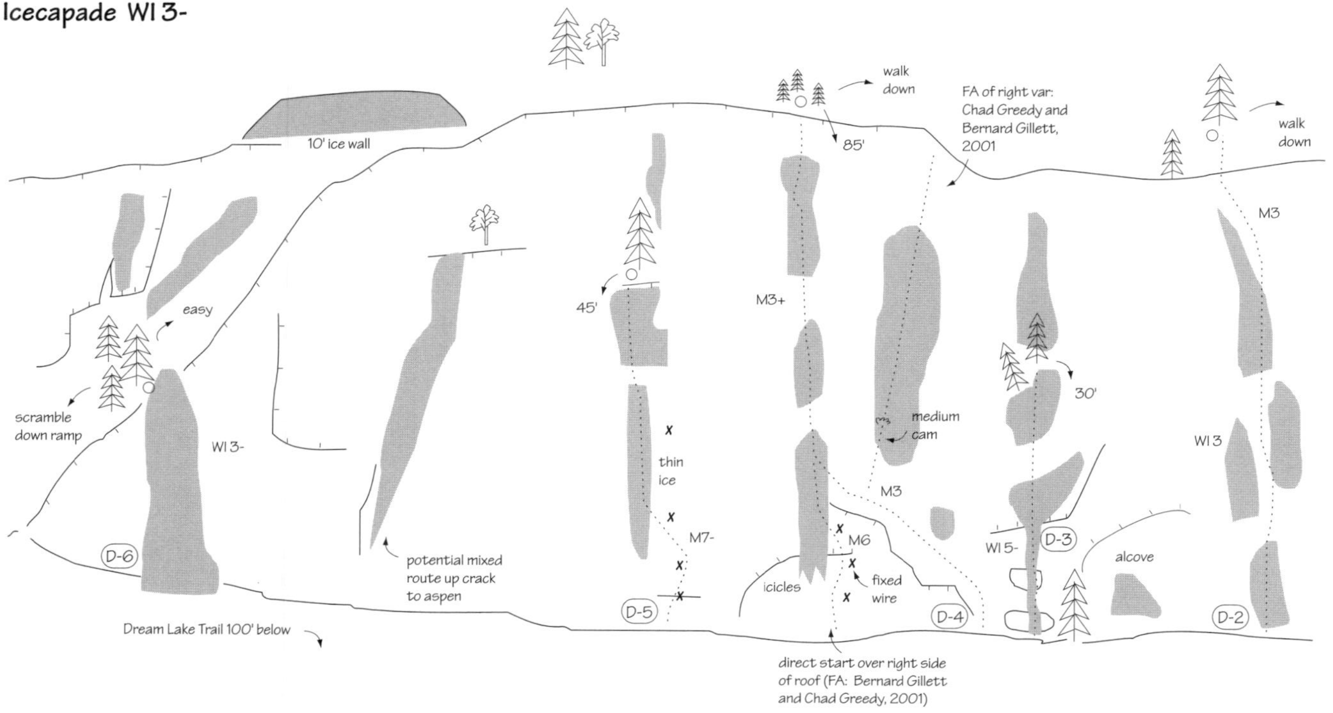

Chaos and Tyndall Creek Drainage

Several small patches of ice form over the cliffs found southwest of Nymph Lake, between Chaos and Tyndall Creeks. Three routes have been established near a curtain of steep ice about a half mile from the lake. The curtain is difficult to locate from the hike through the woods. It is best viewed from the north end of Nymph Lake (stand near a sign — "Restoration Area" — and a wooden bench, and look southwest for the top of a pillar).

Approach: Snowshoe through the woods directly toward the ice (crossing Tyndall Creek) until a low cliff band is reached, go around its left (south) end, and traverse along a shelf atop the cliff until the curtain comes into view. The shelf can also be approached from the north, which is shorter, but more difficult to find the correct path: continue up Tyndall Creek until an area of huge boulders is reached, then go south past the boulders and cross an avalanche prone slope. Aim for a set of trees on top of the lower cliff band (midway up the slope) and turn the corner to find the ice.

Note that several other attractive routes in this area have not been reported as climbed. The low cliff band sports a few thin slabs of ice directly below the shelf with the look of WI 3 (poor pro?). An iced over slab (WI 3?), followed by a hanging veil of ice (WI 4?), is located above the avalanche prone slope.

D-7 The Luge WI 1 or 3

This is the iced over slab (WI 1) on the left side of the shelf that leads to a short, steep section at the top (WI 3). The slab is fairly extensive and several lines of ascent are available. The upper crux can be avoided on the left, and the slab is covered in snow most of the time. Walk around the south end of the slab to descend. FA: Gillett and Snively, 1998.

D-8 Olympic Games M6- WI 5

The pillar of ice that can be seen from Nymph Lake is actually just the right side of a wide curtain spilling from the lip of an overhanging wall. **Olympic Games** features a splendid dry tool traverse to reach the left side of the curtain. Begin at a short pillar of ice emanating from a seam in the wall (just right of **The Luge**), climb to a piton at its top, then hook across plentiful holds past a bolt and two pins. Follow the left side of an overhanging pillar and belay from a tree higher up. Walk down south (same descent as **The Luge**). FA: Bernard Gillett, Doug Snively and John Gillett, 1998.

D-9 Speed Skating WI 5

Speed Skating climbs the short but strenuous pillar that can be seen from Nymph Lake. It is located twenty feet right of **Olympic Games**. Easier ice above the pillar leads to a small tree — rappel from a sling or descend to the south. FA: Gillett and Snively, 1998.

Bernard Gillett making the first ascent of *Olympic Games.*

PHOTO: JOHN GILLETT

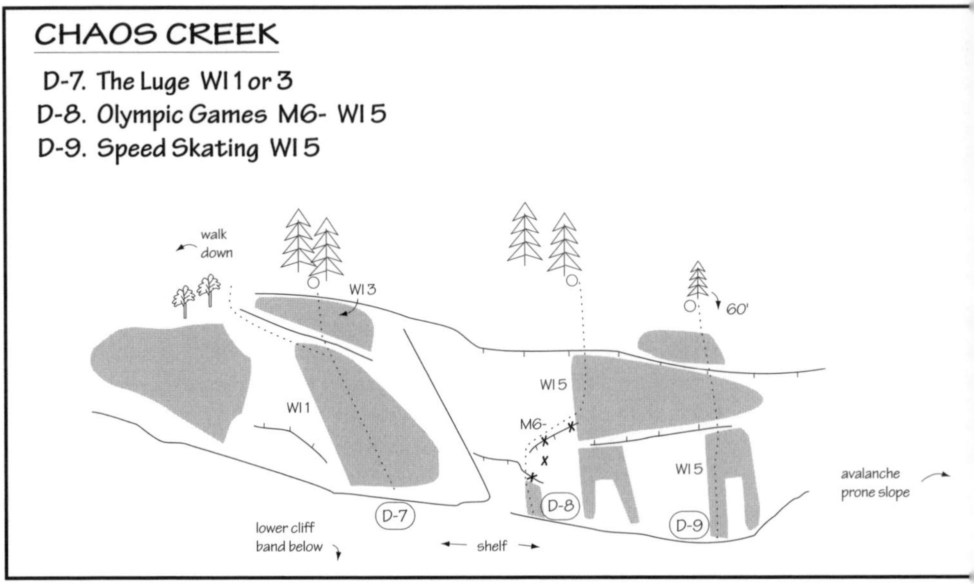

Emerald Lake Area

D-10 Tentacles WI 5 M4

Thin ice sheets sometimes form up 100 feet left of **The Squid**, with several possible lines of ascent. A gully on the left is easiest (M3). The standard line goes up steep rock to the right and is more difficult. All options will likely require mixed climbing.

D-11 The Squid WI 5 (often M6-)

A south-facing cliff presents itself just before Emerald Lake on the hillside north of the trail. **The Squid** takes the obvious, awesome pillar in a large dihedral (140') followed by a short pitch of thin ice. A difficult stretch of mixed climbing in the dihedral (M6-, bring a #4 Friend) is necessary when the route isn't filled in. Best conditions are usually found early in the season (late November through early January) — the main pillar often falls off later on, leaving thin, wind sculpted ice and a difficult roof. FA: Duncan Ferguson and Douglas Snively, 1974.

D-12 Calamari WI 5-

Calamari is the rightmost of the three routes on this wall, and is more difficult (WI 5 M5-) most of the time. Begin about 100 feet right and around the corner from **The Squid**. FA: Alex Lowe, Sandy Stewart and Eric Winkelman, 1982. **Variation:** Another broad curtain forms right of **Calamari**, though it doesn't reach the ground, and it is not known whether it has seen an ascent.

Climbers on the second pitch of *The Squid* near Emerald Lake.

Eric Ming climbing out of *Hallett Chimney* on the First Buttress.

PHOTO: DOUGLAS SNIVELY

Hallett Peak

D-13 Hallett Chimney IV AI 5 M5

A deep chasm separates the First and Second Buttresses on the north face of Hallett Peak (see photo page 182). In the winter it is usually loaded with snow and prone to avalanche, but by springtime it forms a classic mixed route (a wet fall may also produce good climbing). The bottom 1,000 foot long section goes quickly while the middle and upper sections serve up a mean fare of thin runnels. Bring a full rack of rock gear (pitons are handy) and a few screws. Get an early start. See page 184 for descent information. FA: Glendenning party, 1951. As a mixed climb: Brad Johnson and Dick Jackson, 1975. **Variation:** Climb half way up the chimney, then traverse left just below the big white band for two hundred feet or more to the left-hand chimney/dihedral in the left side of the headwall on the First Buttress (i.e. the **Standard Route** described in the rock climbing section, page 186). This was done by Douglas Snively and Eric Ming around 1980 after a big spring storm dumped a load of snow on the face. The route provides excellent alpine climbing in these conditions.

Flattop Mountain (Tyndall Gorge side)

D-14 Dragon's Tail Gully II AI 2 M2

Several prominent pillars on the south side of Flattop grace the skyline when viewed from Emerald Lake. The largest of these is Dragon's Tail; the gully climb of the same name climbs along its right margin to the plateau on Flattop (descend the Flattop trail). Much of the route is of a moderate nature, though a few steep sections with a bit of mixed climbing will be encountered. This route is best climbed in late spring or early summer, but avalanches routinely scour this climb and the next — get an early start. Hike around the north side of Emerald Lake and follow a snowfield (or talus) to the base. See photo page 196. **Variation:** Note that a short wall just west of the lake may hold a pitch of ice (WI 4) directly below a large pine tree.

D-15 Tower Gully II AI 2 M2

The gully on the left side of Dragon's Tail and right of Tyndall Spire (the next rock formation up the gorge) usually melts out by mid summer; late spring is the best time for an ascent. Short sections of easy mixed climbing may be encountered depending on conditions. See photo page 196.

D-16 Tyndall Glacier AI 1 to 2

The large snowfield at the head of Tyndall Gorge is easily ascended on its right side; the left side is steeper. Like **Ptarmigan Glacier** (see below), this is a popular ski descent in the spring. Down climb/glissade the glacier to descend, or hike down Flattop.

Odessa Gorge and Notchtop

D-17 Grace Falls WI 4+

Although only one pitch long, this route is well worth the trip. Ski to Lake Helene and contour along a cumbersome, rocky slope below the lake, aiming toward Notchtop. The falls are obvious after dropping below Lake Helene. The central pillar provides a sustained, steep pitch (WI 4+). **Variations:** The thin sheet of ice left of the main line is WI 5-. The short, easy flow further left is WI 3.

D-18 Hot Doggie WI 6 or M7-

Several smears sometimes form on the steep rock step (called Odessa Wall) below the north face of Notchtop between **Grace Falls** and **Guide's Wall**. **Hot Doggie** is the most obvious of these, and it is near the left side of the wall. A magazine article rated the route M7-, but others have called it WI 6. It's a difficult test piece in any case, with a freestanding, thin pillar to start. Descend via rappel, or walk off up and left. One may also continue with **North Face Route** (see below). FA: Alex Lowe, early 1980s. This route should not be attempted when avalanche danger is high as it lies below **North Face Route**.

D-19 The Hourglass WI 4 or 5

This lies on the right side of Odessa Wall. There is some discrepancy on the rating (probably because it doesn't come in very often, and is quite variable in its condition). Other smears sometimes form up between **Hot Doggie** and **The Hourglass**. Descend as with **Hot Doggie**. This route should not be attempted when avalanche danger is high as it lies below **North Face Route** (see below).

D-20 North Face Route III AI 4 M4

The north face of Notchtop has three documented routes; this is by far the most frequented and classic. It ascends the middle of the huge concave bowl that forms the extensive north wall. Access the bowl with a chimney below the northeast ridge (left of Odessa Wall) and traverse right to a large snowfield. Climb straight up past three iced-over rock bands for several pitches. Note that mixed climbing will be encountered unless an undue amount of snow exists; in this case the route should not be attempted as the face is very prone to avalanche. The best conditions are usually found in late fall. The other routes lie to the left and contain more rock climbing (up to 5.8, FAs by Doug Snively and Michael Covington, and Covington and D. Ketchum). Descend by continuing to the Continental Divide (500 feet of easy scrambling), then hike past the top of **Ptarmigan Glacier** to the Flattop trail. An alternate descent, which leads back to the base of the wall, drops down the west gully of Notchtop. This is the same gully used in the summer for all rock climbs on Notchtop. FA: Tom Hornbein and Bob Frauson, 1952.

D-21 Guide's Wall WI 2

Downhill and right of **Odessa Wall** is an excellent pitch of lower-angled ice. This is about a quarter mile southwest of Grace Falls.

D-22 Notchtop Couloirs II AI 2 to 3

Two long, parallel couloirs lie on the slopes between **Ptarmigan Glacier** and the summit of Notchtop. Hike west from Lake Helene up a small rise to reach a plateau with a tiny tarn; the climbs are visible from here. The line on the right tends to melt out in summer, while the left line remains in good condition into the fall, and is a classic outing of this nature. Winter ascents are dangerous as these gullies are prime avalanche territory. Both end on the Continental Divide about one half mile from the summit of Flattop. Descend the next route, or hike down the Flattop trail.

Flattop Mountain (Odessa Gorge side)

D-23 Ptarmigan Glacier AI 1

This is the low angled and broad snowfield at the very end of Odessa Gorge between Flattop and Notchtop. It is useful as a descent for the nearby gully climbs, and is popular as a ski descent in spring and early summer. Hike west from Lake Helene and head for the saddle.

D-24 Flattop Couloirs II AI 2 to 4-

Three obvious snow gullies drape down the northwest flank of Flattop Mountain, southwest from Lake Helene. The left gully is the longest, and has come to be known as **Fancy Farnan Couloir**. The middle the steepest, and the right couloir contains an interesting pinch midway up, with an optional finish out left on rocky outcroppings. All three are relatively moderate in the summer when the snow is soft, but become more challenging in the fall (the middle is considered the most difficult and may yield up to AI 4- in its steepest sections). As with the Notchtop Couloirs, winter ascents can be dangerous (Brad Farnan and his partner perished in an avalanche here a few years ago). Descend the previous route, or hike down Flattop.

D-25 Flattop Gully II AI 2

A narrow, zigzag gully runs up the side of Flattop left of the previous three lines, with a steep section at the top. FA(?): Topher Donahue, 1999.

BIG THOMPSON ICE

At least one good ice flow forms each winter in Big Thompson Canyon, east of Estes Park. The approach is the shortest available for all of the ice described in this guide; this aspect coupled with the mellow nature of the routes make it a popular beginner's area.

Travel Directions: Drive east out of Estes Park on Highway 34 for about ten miles (7.1 miles from the intersection of Highway 34 and Mall Road). Park on the south side of the road at the Handicapped Fishing Access pullout.

Approach: Cross the Big Thompson River (usually frozen). Hike 100 yards east into a drainage gully (crossing the National Forest boundary line) to reach the base of the ice.

E-1 Lower Flow WI 2

The initial portion of the flow is low-angled and 25 feet long. A steeper, fifty foot pitch lies just above. Belay from a tree after the second tier. Descend west.

E-2 Upper Tier WI 2 to 3

Hike two hundred yards up the creek bed above the **Lower Flow**. The right side is less steep (WI 2) while the middle and left sections yield nearly vertical ice (WI 3).

FERN LAKE TRAILHEAD

The Big Thompson River runs underneath another popular ice climbing area fifteen miles upstream.

Travel Directions: Drive into RMNP (Moraine Avenue/Highway 36 entrance) and turn left on Bear Lake Road. Turn right toward Moraine Park Campground and follow signs to the Fern Lake trailhead. During winter the last half mile of the road is closed; park just before a gate.

Approach: Follow the road to the Fern Lake trailhead. From here, a good trail runs alongside the Big Thompson River, and beneath all of the climbs listed below.

F-1 Silly'cicle M6+

This route is located in a deep and clandestine cleft about twenty minutes uphill from the trail and one drainage down canyon from Windy Gulch Cascades (see below). It is difficult to see what little ice there is from the trail; seek out the cleft instead, and hope for good conditions. The climb itself ascends the wall of the cleft in half a rope length (rappel from a tree), and the first ascent party notes that at least two other attractive (and similarly difficult) mixed climbs could be completed here. FA: Topher and Patience Donahue, and Felicia Ennis, 1998.

F-2 Windy Gulch Cascades WI 2

This is the stream that runs across the trail and into the Big Thompson River about a third of a mile from the (summer) trailhead. The ice in the gulch above the trail is not visible until further along; it consists of very short pillars and flows. Look for several large boulders just off the north side of the trail (site of a recent rock fall); the gulch begins immediately beyond the rock fall.

F-3 Short But ... M7-

The steep wall and chimney left of **Windy Gulch Cascades** occasionally sports several hanging icicles. Scramble up to a belay below this feature, mix it up (pins and some rock gear) past the thin ice, and follow the chimney. Rappel east from slings around a tree, then down climb the bottom portion of **Windy Gulch Cascades**. FA: Topher Donahue and Kevin Cooper, 1997.

F-4 Jaws WI 4 to 5

Hike (or ski) to the trailhead and then follow the trail for a long mile until almost at Arch Rocks. **Jaws** is the obvious wall of ice to the north. Located one quarter mile east of Rock of Ages (see page 210), **Jaws** derives its name from the conspicuous opening on the right side of the wall. The climb is usually led in one very long pitch, although one can belay at the base of the upper pillar. The right side of the wall offers vertical WI 5 columns while the left side often forms an easier (WI 4) double pillar. Rappel 165 feet from a large tree at the top. The southern exposure of this route allows for excellent plastic ice on sunny days, but poses an obvious threat in late season outings or balmy winter weather.

Leading the classic *Jaws* in Moraine Park.

PHOTO: JERRY HILL

LAWN LAKE TRAILHEAD

The Lawn Lake trailhead is the starting point for all climbs in the Mummy Range. See Ypsilon and Fairchild Mountains in the High Peaks section for directions to the trailhead and descriptions of the trail systems (pages 220-221).

Ypsilon Mountain

The first six routes (see photo page 219 for the first four) climb the flanks of Ypsilon Mountain, six or seven miles from the trailhead. A bivouac at Ypsilon Lake is recommended if these routes are attempted during winter.

G-1 Right Side Chimney III M4 (?)
The right side of the great north wall of **Donner Ridge** ends at **Prancer Ridge**. **Right Side Chimney** begins a few hundred feet left of **Prancer Ridge** at an obvious cleft. Follow this for several hundred feet (crux) until a gully out left can be accessed. Turn a roof left at the top of the gully to a small snow patch, and then follow a left-slanting ramp to the top of the face. The lower pitches in the chimney are usually lined with ice and snow from fall to spring. FA: Harry Kent and Rich Paige, 1980.

G-2 Prancer Ridge III M3/4 (?)
This is the ridge that separates the north wall of **Donner Ridge** from the **Y Couloir**. Start up the couloir and pass the first constriction, then angle left to access the ridge. The first ascent was done in winter, and as such, it involves a good deal of mixed climbing. FA: Harry Kent and Joe Hladick, 1980 (?).

G-3 Y Couloir II AI 2 or III AI 3 M3
The classic, branched gully system on the east face of Ypsilon holds two renowned routes. Hike around the south side of Spectacle Lakes and climb the large triangle of snow above the west lake to a thin neck — in summer parts of this neck may have melted out. Continue up moderate snow to the fork of the Y, about 1,000 feet above the lakes. This section is straightforward, though difficult to protect unless snow flukes are included on the rack. The left fork is the easy way out. It, too, may have sections missing in late summer. (An August ascent by the author found a 100 foot stretch melted out some 500 feet from the top. Rather than fording up the resulting stream, the party traversed left onto rock, 5.4, and continued in this manner all the way to the top). The upper portion of the left fork steepens dramatically in the last 100 feet (AI 2+) and ends at a cornice. Escape left on easy rock if the cornice looks grim, or tunnel left underneath it. The right fork presents a formidable challenge half way up as it is usually melted out by mid summer (it may be a wall of ice by late fall, WI 4+). Traverse left onto rock at the break and climb to a ledge that leads back right into the couloir. This section was reported as 4th class in Walter Fricke's 1971 guide; others have found it considerably more difficult (as hard as 5.7). Continue with the couloir above the break with excellent exposure to the summit cornice, AI 3. Avoid the cornice on the left with a ramp, or climb it directly (AI 4) on its right side. Unless suicide is the desired outcome, this route should not be climbed in spring and early summer. Winter conditions vary with snowfall; the safest bet is late summer through fall.

G-4 Blitzen Face III M4- (?)

This line was first done in the winter as a mixed route. Climb the **Y Couloir** for half its length, then veer right up the middle of the buttress that flanks the right fork of the Y. The first portion of the buttress is moderate, while the last two or three leads up to the final portion of **Blitzen Ridge** contain 5.7 climbing. FA: S. Thornberg and Scott Kimball, 1980s (?).

G-5 Blitzen Ridge Couloir II AI 3

Begin with lower section of the next route, then go left into a snow and ice gully for a few hundred feet. Stay right at a fork in the gully and follow that to the last part of **Blitzen Ridge**. FA: Richard Rossiter, 1994.

G-6 Northeast Couloir II AI 3

This fine route climbs the long channel that cuts through the northeast face of Ypsilon. Begin the approach as with **Blitzen Ridge** (see rock climbing section, page 222) up the gully north of Ypsilon Lake to a saddle in the ridge. Contour around to the north side of the ridge and head for upper Fay Lake (the highest of the three Fay Lakes). Go north from the lake, staying right of its inlet, to reach a shelf above the lake. Traverse left along the shelf, over the stream, and head for the obvious couloir. Follow the couloir for 1,500 feet and pass a cornice on its left to reach **Blitzen Ridge**. A final pitch up this finds the summit. The narrowest portion of the couloir melts out by mid summer; the wet section can be bypassed on the left with low fifth class rock. FA: Rob Mardock and Todd Jirsa, 1992.

Lawn Lake Area

G-7 Roaring River Falls WI 3-

Hike about four miles toward Lawn Lake to a set of switchbacks; this is very near to the confluence of a small tributary of Roaring River. Leave the trail to the west and hike up Roaring River until the falls are reached. The climb is mostly low angled and 100 feet long. FA: Jim Detterline, 1997.

G-8 Mummy Falls WI 4+

Mummy Falls lies on the left end of the southwest face of Mummy Mountain. Approach by hiking to Lawn Lake (six miles, gentle terrain after the first mile), and continue around its north shore on the trail to Crystal Lake. Within a half mile, the climb should be visible to the north. Walk up to its base and follow it for one or two pitches; the descent is an easy scramble west, or a rappel from a horn. The best time for an ascent is late fall or early winter as the route may fill in with snow later on.

Fairchild Mountain

G-9 Winterlong IV M4 AI 2

This route climbs the north face of the horseshoe cirque on Fairchild Mountain above Crystal Lake. Hike past Lawn Lake and beneath the previous route, then turn left at a trail junction (the right trail leads to The Saddle) and continue to Crystal Lake (seven miles from the trailhead). Head for the left end of the snowfield at the base of the north face, and traverse left to its high point. Switchback right, and follow a prominent ramp system for several pitches as it rises to the right across the middle of the wall. When it ends, go straight up along a rib on the right side of a big chimney system. This leads to a long snow patch below the summit headwall. Avoid the headwall by traversing left on the snow patch all the way to the ridge above the north face. The summit is just a short distance right up an easy ridge. Tag the summit, reverse the easy ridge, and then continue east along the ridge until reaching the long talus slopes that drop down to Crystal Lake. Descend into Crystal Lake to retrieve gear, or go further east to slopes leading to Lawn Lake. FA: Dan Stone and Rich Paige, 1983.

G-10 Mirage IV WI 5 M5/6

Mirage climbs the wall left of **Abadoo Scronch** to the right side of the hanging snow patch on **Winterlong** in five zigzagging pitches. It may be possible to traverse the snow patch right to gain the easy ridge that leads back to the Saddle; otherwise, traverse all the way left as in **Winterlong**. This climb is seldom in good condition. FA: Duncan Ferguson and Dakers Gowans.

G-11 Abadoo Scronch III M4 AI 4

This route climbs the obvious, deep gully right of **Winterlong** and left of the Honcho Boncho Buttress (see photo page 224). Follow the main gully to the summit ridge (avoid a smaller left branch part way up), passing through several steep sections (four long pitches, with mixed climbing on the first and last). Descend the north ridge of Fairchild to The Saddle (the pass between Fairchild and Hagues Peak), turn east and hike to the trail junction mentioned in **Winterlong**. FA: Jim Gregg and D. Kenyon King, 1964.

COW CREEK TRAILHEAD

Two short waterfalls are accessed from the Cow Creek Trailhead, which is located at Indianhead Ranch (McGraw Ranch on old topographic maps). Both routes form up only after a prolonged cold snap due to the low elevation.

Travel directions: Drive north from Estes Park past Lumpy Ridge on MacGregor Avenue; this turns into Devils Gulch Road at the Lumpy Ridge turn off. Bear left on a dirt road 3.5 miles from the intersection of MacGregor Avenue and the Highway 34 bypass, and follow it to a parking spot just before the ranch. A sign marks the beginning of the trail system.

H-1 Bridal Veil Falls WI 1 to 2

Follow the trail out of the west end of the ranch for two miles, go right at a fork in the trail, and continue for another mile to the falls. The left side is WI 2 while the middle and right options are easier. Another short flow (WI 1) lies above. FA: Jim Detterline, 1998.

H-2 West Creek Falls WI 3

This route climbs fifty feet of ice in a seldom visited area of the park. Head north from the ranch along the North Boundary trail for about a mile, then turn left up West Creek for another mile. The falls are located just within the boundary of RMNP. FA: Detterline, 1997.

Life imitating art: Shawn Preston, celebrating a late season ascent of Yellow Wall on the summit of Longs Peak, imagines himself as an Olympic discus thrower.

SUGGESTED READING

The following books and pamphlets contain interesting historical and geological information on the Estes Park region. Some are long out of print, but most can be found in the Estes Park Library (on Elkhorn Avenue), a quiet refuge on a rainy day.

CLIMB!: Rock Climbing in Colorado, Bob Godfrey and Dudley Chelton, 1977. The definitive work on the history of climbing in Colorado. Mandatory reading for all climbers.

Climbing in North America, Chris Jones, 1976. A thorough history of the progression of rock climbing in the United States and Canada.

Vertigo Games, Glenn Randall, 1983. Stories and pictures of difficult Colorado climbs established during the 1970s and 80s. Several of the featured routes are included in this guide.

Mountaineering in Colorado — The Peaks about Estes Park, Frederick H. Chapin, 1889. This is often considered to be the first climbing guide for the Estes Park region. Its style is a far cry from the guidebooks of today, as it is a collection of stories concerning Chapin's scrambles in the mountains rather than a detailed description of available routes. The Bison Book Company, with new forward and extensive notes, republished it in 1987.

Longs Peak: Its Story and a Climbing Guide. First published in 1946 by Paul Nesbit (updated by his son Norman in 1972, then by Stan Adamson in 1995), this was the first true climbing guide to the Estes Park area. Though it lacks route descriptions, it features several photos showing all of the technical routes completed on Longs Peak through 1972.

Climbers Guide to RMNP, Walter Fricke. This was the first extensive guide to climbing in Estes Park. Published in 1971, much of the information is outdated, but it is a good reference.

The High Peaks, Richard DuMais. The latest edition came out in 1987. It is now out of print, but it is provides thorough coverage of the high mountain routes.

Rocky Mountain National Park Hiking Trails, Kent and Donna Dannen. Many editions, the best hiking guide to RMNP.

Classic Lunch Spots In Rocky Mountain National Park, Philip Gillett. Whimsical hiking guide to RMNP.

Raising the Roof of the Rockies, Gerald M. Richmond. Geological history of RMNP.

RMNP: A History, C. Buchholtz. The story of Rocky Mountain National Park.

Recollections of a Rocky Mountain Ranger, Jack C. Moomaw, 1963. Moomaw was a Longs Peak ranger in the early years of RMNP, and is best known among climbers for his ascent of Alexander's Chimney in 1922.

The Saga of Black Canyon, Glenn Prosser. Detailed history of the MacGregor clan in Estes Park; Lumpy Ridge provides the backdrop to the MacGregor Ranch.

Estes Park: From the Beginning, Dave Hicks. The story of early life in Estes Park.

The Glen Haven Story, Joseph G. Knapp. History of Glen Haven, the small community between Lumpy Ridge and Combat Rock.

High Country Names, Louisa Ward Arps and Elinor Eppich Kingery, 1972. Origins of the names in RMNP and surrounding regions; fascinating reading.

Trails and Trailbuilders of the Rocky Mountain National Park, William C. Ramaley. History of the trail systems in RMNP; good reading for those familiar with the Park. I am uncertain whether the book was ever published (my parents have a copy of the manuscript) — inquire with the Nature Association at the RMNP visitor center.

The Estes Park Library has an audio section that contains several cassette tapes recorded at the Longs Peak Symposium held during the 75th Anniversary celebration of RMNP, in 1990. Persons associated with the history of Longs Peak, including Layton Kor, Dave Rearick and Bob Kamps, delivered many talks and speeches.

INDEX

ROUTE INDEX BY RATING (Free Climbing)